Capitalisms and Capitalism in the Twenty-First Century

Capitalisms and Capitalism in the Twenty-First Century

Edited by
Glenn Morgan and Richard Whitley

OXFORD
UNIVERSITY PRESS

OXFORD
UNIVERSITY PRESS

Great Clarendon Street, Oxford, OX2 6DP,
United Kingdom

Oxford University Press is a department of the University of Oxford.
It furthers the University's objective of excellence in research, scholarship, and education by publishing worldwide. Oxford is a registered trade mark of Oxford University Press in the UK and in certain other countries

First Edition published in 2012
First published in paperback 2014

Published in the United States of America by Oxford University Press
198 Madison Avenue, New York, NY 10016, United States of America

British Library Cataloguing in Publication Data
Data available

ISBN 978–0–19–870878–0

In memory of Marianne Risberg: a fine friend and colleague

Preface

Like many others before it, this book originated in the Standing Working Group (SWG) on Comparative Economic Organization formed within the European Group on Organizational Studies (EGOS) and coordinated by Richard Whitley, Glenn Morgan, Peer Hull Kristensen, Sigrid Quack, and Marie-Laure Djelic. The SWG has met continuously at EGOS since the early 1990s. For the final meeting of the SWG to be held at the 2010 EGOS colloquium meeting in Lisbon, the editors conceived the idea of a book which would build on past achievements but most importantly point to future research topics. In doing so, we sought to draw in others from political science and elsewhere who may not have considered themselves 'EGOSIANs', to use the vernacular common within EGOS, but were nevertheless working in cognate areas. David Musson at Oxford University Press was, as always, an encouraging presence in this process, as were many others who over the years have participated with us in the SWG and other collective projects. We would, of course, like to thank the authors for their efforts in writing and in responding to our comments in timely and constructive ways.

Glenn Morgan
Richard Whitley

Contents

List of Figures

List of Tables

List of Abbreviations

AFP	Administradoras de Fondo de Pension
AFTA	ASEAN Free Trade Area
APEC	Asia-Pacific Economic Cooperation
ASEA	Association of Southeast Asian Nations
AWG	Advocacy Working Group
BRICs	Brazil, Russia, India, and China
CADE	Administrative Council for Economic Defence
CAN	Andean Community
CARICOM	Caribbean Community
CC	Creative Commons
CCi	Creative Commons International
CDO	Collateralized debt obligations
CDS	Credit default swaps
CEE	Central and Eastern Europe
CET	Common external tariff
CISG	United Nations Convention for the International Sale of Goods
CME	Coordinated market economies
CMHN	Consejo Mexicano de Hombres de Negocios
COMESA	Common Market for Eastern and Southern Africa
CSR	Corporate social responsibility
DFG	German Federal Research Ministry
EADS	The European Aeronautic Defence and Space Company
EBL	Enterprise Bankruptcy Law
ECB	European Central Bank
EFTA	European Free Trade Association
EPL	Employment protection legislation
EPZ	Export processing zone
EU	European Union

FDI	Foreign direct investment
FMPDG	Flexible mass production of differentiated goods and services
GATT	General Agreement on Tariffs and Trade
GCC	Global commodity chain
GTZ	Deutsche Gesellschaft für Technische Zusammenarbeit
GVC	Global value chain
HHMI	Howard Hughes Medical Institute
ICN	International Competition Network
ICT	Information and communications technology
IDB	Inter-American Development Bank
ILO	International Labour Organisation
IMF	International Monetary Fund
IPF	Investment Privatisation Fund
IPO	Initial public offering
ISIC	International Standard Industrial Classification
ISO	International Organisation for Standardisation
KOSA	Korean Composite Stock Price Index
KRX	Korean Exchange Statistics
LME	Liberal market economies
LOWESS	Locally weighted scatterplot smoothing
MD	Market design
MGI	McKinsey Global Institute
MOU	Memorandum of understanding
NAFTA	North American Free Trade Agreement
NGO	Non-governmental organisation
NIF	National Investment Fund
NTB	Non-tariff barrier
OECD	Organisation for Economic Cooperation and Development
OEM	Original equipment manufacturers
PBC	People's Bank of China
PE	Political embeddedness
PHARE	Poland and Hungary: Assistance for Restructuring their Economies
RTA	Regional trade agreement
SADC	South African Development Community
SDPC	State Development Planning Commission
SEC	Securities and Exchange Commission

SITC	Standardised trade classification
TLO	Technology Licensing Office
TRIPS	Trade-related aspects of intellectual property rights
TVE	Township and village enterprises
UNcomtrade	United Commodity Trade Statistics Database
UNCTAD	United Nations Conference on Trade and Development
UNIDO	United Nations Industrial Development Organisation
USAID	United States Agency for Economic Development
VoC	Varieties of capitalism
WTO	World Trade Organisation

List of Contributors

Ruth V. Aguilera, University of Illinois at Urbana-Champaign, USA

Jennifer Bair, University of Colorado at Boulder, USA

Steven Casper, Keck Graduate Institute of Applied Life Sciences, Claremont, California, USA

Ben Clift, University of Warwick, UK

Colin Crouch, University of Warwick, UK

Marie-Laure Djelic, ESSEC, Paris, France

Francesco Duina, University of British Columbia, Canada

Volkmar Gessner, University of Bremen, Germany

Michel Goyer, Birmingham Business School, University of Birmingham, UK

Luiz Ricardo Kabbach de Castro, Universitat de les Illes Balears, Spain

Peer Hull Kristensen, Copenhagen Business School, Denmark

Barbara Krug, Rotterdam School of Management, Erasmus University, The Netherlands and Johann Wolfgang Goethe University, Frankfurt am Main, Germany

Jun Ho Lee, University of Illinois at Urbana-Champaign, USA

Matthew C. Mahutga, University of California at Riverside, USA

Glenn Morgan, Cardiff Business School, Cardiff University, UK

Sigrid Quack, University of Duisburg-Essen, Germany and Max Planck Institute for the Study of Societies, Cologne, Germany

Grahame Thompson, Copenhagen Business School, Denmark, and Open University, UK

Andrew Tylecote, The Management School, University of Sheffield, UK

Richard Whitley, Manchester Business School, University of Manchester, UK

Cornelia Woll, Sciences Po, Paris, France

Jihae You, University of Illinois at Urbana-Champaign, USA

Capitalisms and Capitalism in the Twenty-First Century

Introduction

Richard Whitley and Glenn Morgan

The early twenty-first century is witnessing both an increasing internationalization of many markets, firms, and regulatory institutions and a reinforcement of the key role of nation states in managing economic development, financial crises, and market upheavals in many Organization for Economic Cooperation and Development (OECD) and developing economies. On the one hand, the distinctive forms of socio-economic organization that became institutionalized as different kinds of capitalism under the Bretton Woods System (hereafter BWS) of global financial management after WWII may have become less nationally distinct and specific in an era of floating exchange rates, increased cross-national capital mobility, and expanding multinational companies (MNCs). On the other hand, national systems of credit control, property rights, capital–labour relations and other institutions constituting and regulating markets remain important influences on the nature and operation of firms, competition, and innovation (Boyer 2011; Casper, Gessner, Morgan and Goyer, and Whitley in this volume). It is still predominantly at the national level of political organization and territorial control that the key institutions governing economic activities develop sufficiently strong complementarities to establish distinctive kinds of economic organization and competitive competences in leading firms.

It is these combinations of particular ways of organizing competition, innovation, and collective capabilities with particular kinds of dominant political–economic coalitions and institutions governing the constitution and behaviour of economic actors that constitute different types of capitalism. In comparing these types historically and internationally, it is how they become established, reproduced, and changed, together with their consequences for economic outcomes in different industries, that are the primary foci of concern.

While often nationally specific, especially during the heyday of the BWS, the extent to which such types do indeed differ between nation states and are homogenous within them is quite varied and changeable, as the examples of the local production systems in Italy and elsewhere, Danish machinery firms, and contrasting patterns of industrial development in Germany attest (Crouch et al. 2001; 2004; Herrigel 1996; Kristensen 1992; 1996; Whitley 2005).

The breakdown of the BWS, expansion of some forms of transnational governance (Braithwaite and Drahos 2000; Djelic and Sahlin-Andersson 2006; Djelic and Quack in this volume), especially those supporting the internationalization of product and service markets (Duina in this volume), and growing internalization of trade within MNCs have encouraged greater heterogeneity of dominant firm types and competitive strategies within certain national boundaries (Bair and Mahutga, and Whitley in this volume). The weakening of some national institutional complementarities as a result of internationalizing firms learning new competences and influencing established patterns of organization and competition, together with increasing support for cross-national collaboration, have enabled both large and medium-sized firms to experiment in how they develop new products and services with varied business partners (Kristensen et al. 2011; Kristensen and Morgan in this volume).

When considering the development of different forms of capitalism as distinctive socio-economic systems in the twenty-first century, then, the conditions under which they become nationally distinctive and coherent have to be analysed in a more internationalized and multilevelled institutional environment than existed for much of the twentieth century. Previous approaches have sometimes tended to assume either that particular combinations of political and economic institutions would generate specific patterns of firm strategies and competitive advantage within established political boundaries, or alternatively that international competition automatically selects the most efficient form of organization. In this century, we need to take more account of the variety of ways in which rule following involves rule changing, as recently emphasized by Streeck (2011), and how pervasive uncertainty limits rational actions and prevents optimization in exploring how particular kinds of institutions and interests combine to develop and change particular patterns of economic coordination, control, and competition. This increasing variety and changeability of influences and understandings of how the world works are particularly important when examining the circumstances in which these processes result in specific outcomes, such as those generating the financial crises of 2008–9 (Campbell 2011), and involves integrating approaches and frameworks drawn from different academic fields.

Comparative and international political economy with its focus on states and international institutions, for instance, needs to take more account of the strategies and competences of different kinds of firms. Economic geography and the study of regions and localities need to be more integrated with the analysis of multinationals and the organizational coordination, development, and exploitation of innovation. The sociology of institutions and social movements needs to be connected to the analysis of capitalism as a global system and the evolving relations between various forms of capitalism. On top of this, there is a need to break out of narrowly Eurocentric or Atlanticist views of these processes and to take more account of the emerging economies in different parts of the world, both in terms of their role in the wider order but also as specific forms of social, economic, and state organization that require different modes of analysis.

By bringing together contributions from a variety of scholars from political science, sociology, business and management studies, and other fields, this book attempts to further such integration in exploring current developments in the organization of firms, markets, and innovation, and how particular combinations of institutions, interests, and actors are likely to become established and change in the twenty-first century.

The first chapter, by Morgan and Kristensen, develops these points in more detail. It provides an account of how established views of different twentieth-century capitalisms, their institutional underpinnings and effects on firm strategies and structures provide a basis for the study of twenty-first century capitalisms, emphasizing the importance of ambiguity and change of institutions, and the role of actors in reshaping institutional contexts. Secondly, it links this to the increasing variety of forms of coordinating economic activity across national borders. It describes the tensions and limits to two specific forms of international coordination—the first where the large MNC dominates the coordination process, and the second which is characterized by a more open network model of coordination in which small MNCs play a role. These different forms of coordination have contrasting implications for institutional developments. This leads into a discussion on the central role of the state in the current period, and particularly the capabilities of states in terms of moulding institutions to respond to new challenges.

After this, this book is divided into three sections. The first examines how the relations between political authority at different levels of collective organization and economic activities are evolving, and with what effect on the structure of firms and economic organization. The key theme here concerns the changing connections between the political and societal contexts of economic activities and dominant economic rationalities in a much more internationalized world than that discussed by Karl Polanyi in his *The Great Transformation*. Political authority is now, and will probably continue to be, multilayered, with subnational and supranational regional political entities becoming more significant in governing economic activities than in much of the twentieth century, while some economic actors and transactions have become more detached from national institutions and constraints.

This does not, though, imply that supranational market logics have become established that dominate economic activities in isolation from societal contexts, let alone that they are identical with contemporary neo-liberal ideologies. As the financial crises since 2008 have emphasized, the nation state remains the most powerful actor in maintaining business organization; in most OECD countries, it is the state that has the authority and the resources to intervene in order to sustain economic activity. However, neo-liberal ideas are embedded in international institutions such as the World Trade Organization (WTO) and in certain areas in the European Union (EU), so conflicts between authoritative institutions and actors are likely to intensify. This is even more probable when one considers the role of private actors in these processes—both market participants, who seek to ease the development of global markets by establishing shared, private rules, and global social movements which aim to push governments towards stronger internationally binding agreements, for example around climate change.

An important feature of the changing international political–economic order has been the emergence of a range of formal trading blocs such as the EU, North American Free Trade Agreement (NAFTA), Mercosur, and Asia Pacific Economic Cooperation (APEC), which are the focus of the following chapter by Francesco Duina. These trading blocs vary in the extent and nature of economic integration, their political purposes, their level of legitimacy and their creation of common frameworks and policies. Their establishment reflected, however, a general recognition that, even in an open global economy, trade was increasingly intensive at the regional level, multilateralism through international institutions such as the WTO was faltering and difficult to control, and influence could best be exerted by establishing alliances with neighbouring countries. Integration has generally progressed in most of these blocs, but neither evenly nor without challenges to state interests and autonomy, with national sovereignty in some cases being threatened at both the regional and the sub-national levels.

Despite the rise of neo-liberal economics in the late twentieth century that appeared to some to signal the withdrawal of the nation-state from key areas of economic life in the industrialized world, states remain the key source of political legitimacy in the modern world. As Ben Clift and Cornelia Woll emphasize in their 'The Revival of Economic Patriotism', states have to balance their commitment to open markets with an awareness that without coordinated action: a) to encourage the development of business in their home territory (in terms of education and skills, infrastructure, active labour market policies) and, b) to maintain their ability to sustain social pacts and social order (through welfare systems and other mechanisms of redistribution), their legitimacy will be undermined. This has led to the rise of active states and the articulation of various forms of economic nationalism and economic patriotism. The recent financial crises have demonstrated clearly how states remain the actor of last resort when the business system begins to collapse. International efforts at coordination have been dwarfed by the fiscal policies of states to revive their economies. These efforts at revival reveal the underlying differences which remain between states, and how economic policy-making in crisis responds most directly to threats to the national system.

One of the problems of much 'varieties of capitalism' analysis is its concentration on a small number of variables across different environments, and consequent tendency to ignore variations in context and combinations of institutions that lead these variables to behave differently when set in different *ensembles*. On the other hand, this approach does achieve simplicity of focus that can be lost when analysis tries to be overly comprehensive. One way out of this dilemma is to concentrate on only one element of an economy rather than the whole system, but to try to do so comprehensively. In his 'National Varieties of Labour Market Exposure', Colin Crouch focuses on how national variations in labour market governance and social protection affect employment participation and economic growth. In general, he finds that the continuing diversity of national arrangements in Europe, Japan, and the USA helps to explain significant differences in national employment outcomes, and that neo-liberal ones by no means outperform more 'coordinated' institutional environments.

The second section of the book examines more directly the nature of institutional internationalization in the current era. It consists of four chapters analyzing the global financial system, the development of international law, the growing significance of international standards and rules governing economic behaviour, and the connections between cross-border outsourcing and innovation. In Morgan and Goyer's 'Is There a Global Financial System? The Locational Antecedents and Institutionally Bounded Consequences of the Financial Crisis', they show how the financial crisis highlighted the role of different national regulatory systems in structuring the risks that finance could take. Countries remain distinct in terms of how they organize their financial sector, how that is regulated, and how credit and debt (personal, corporate, and state level) are created, managed, and monitored. Wherein, then, might the global nature of the system lie? One answer is in the way in which actions in certain parts (London and New York) can affect all the other parts depending on the degree to which those other parts have become interdependent or have put in fire breaks between their own financial systems and these broader forces.

The expansion of international law and law-like institutions governing contract negotiation and dispute resolution is discussed by Volkmar Gessner in his 'Enabling Global Business Transactions: Relational and Legal Mechanisms'. While contract enforcement is offered by highly diverse institutions created by international agreements or non-state actors like trade associations, the protection of property rights—a basic condition for every economic activity—remains a domain of the nation state. The number of both formal legal and more informal private structures governing international trade increases dramatically every year, opening a new field of professional activity for international law firms, arbitrators, and consultants. While states try to catch up with this professional expert knowledge by enhanced internationalization of courts, of administrative structures, and legal education, firms develop their own governance devices through relational contracts, mergers, and long-term forms of cooperation.

An increasingly important mechanism for dealing with the uncertainties of international trade is the establishment of standards and conventions governing firm behaviour. Marie-Laure Djelic and Sigrid Quack show how different kinds of actors can form transnational communities that construct international standards in particular, yet connected, ways in their 'Transnational Governance through Standard Setting: The Role of Transnational Communities'. Comparing the development of the International Competition Network and the Creative Commons Community, they suggest that both top-down and bottom-up processes of cross-border standard setting demonstrate the need to identify the different forms of collective actors that emerge and develop in the social space 'in between' nation-states, and how repeated interactions within and around standard-setting bodies can lead to the emergence of collective identities that transcend purely national ones.

The expansion of international trade and facilitation of managerial coordination of supply chains across the world have encouraged firms, and their investors, to reduce costs radically by relocating many production processes to developing economies. In his 'Innovation Versus Going South: A Strategic Challenge for Capitalism in the Early 21st Century', Andrew Tylecote argues that the ease of profiting from low wages and other costs in the countries of 'The South' has reduced the willingness of managers and financial institutions to get to grips with the financing, governance, and coordination of innovation during the current technological revolution focused on information and communication technology (ICT). These latter activities have been little understood outside a narrow circle of specialist venture capital firms, and when other organizations have been tempted in en masse (as in the New Economy bubble of 1996–2000) it has ended in tears and losses. The technological ignorance of financial institutions is particularly apparent in the City of London. This is ironic, since the organizations which have shirked the financing of innovation have embraced innovative financing. The reverses they have suffered in the latter may help to force them back to grapple with the former.

The third section of the book considers how firms and markets are evolving in the twenty-first century. It consists of six chapters exploring the changing relationships between owners, managers, and institutions governing capital and labour markets as firms internationalize their operations, and states modify their management of economic development and markets.

In his 'Internationalization and the Institutional Structuring of Economic Organization', Richard Whitley focuses on how the increasing internationalization of trade, firms, and capital markets in the second half of the twentieth century has affected the predominantly nationally based forms of capitalism that developed under the BWS, as well as the nature of MNCs and other modes of cross-border economic coordination in the twenty-first century. Emphasizing the semi-globalized nature of markets (Ghemawat 2003) and the continuing authority of national legal and political systems over firm governance and strategies, he also highlights the limited development of MNCs' transnational organizational capabilities, and the difficulties of combining international organizational integration with significant learning from subsidiaries in diverse institutional environments. However, the growing diversity of firm types and competences within national borders as companies internationalize their operations is restricting the national specificity and homogeneity of business systems.

The processes by which particular national institutions continue to structure key patterns of economic development are explored in detail by Steven Casper in his 'National Research Systems, Career Structures and the Effective Commercialization of Academic Science'. He shows how major differences in the organization of public science systems and professional labour markets in Germany and the USA help to explain contrasting patterns of research commercialization of results in cell biology, and the development of biotechnology more generally. Despite recent attempts by many governments in Europe and elsewhere to restructure national academic systems along lines thought to be more similar to that of the USA, it seems likely that such differences will remain (Whitley et al. 2010).

The role of supply chain internationalization in weakening the authority of national institutional regimes over firm governance and strategies is directly addressed by Jennifer Bair and Matthew Mahutga in their 'Varieties of Offshoring?'. This chapter compares changes in the degree of spatial fragmentation of value chains in the garments, electronics, and vehicle-manufacturing industries to see whether cross-border vertical disintegration is greater in liberal market economies than in more coordinated ones, or reflects more sector-specific logics. While they find some convergence in this within each industry, nationally distinct differences in the ways that such inter-firm contracting is carried out remain.

The internationalization of capital markets and proselytization of the Anglo-American conception of corporate governance in the last few decades of the twentieth century have led to the widespread diffusion of the shareholder value ideology, despite its inherent ambiguity and contradictions. In his 'What is Happening to Corporations and What of their Future?' Grahame Thompson considers the changing relationships between investors and managers in large companies as equity financing declines. He suggests that the 2008–9 financial crises and consequent cutbacks in public expenditure in many OECD countries are likely to involve private firms more in the provision of public services and politically sensitive activities. This may well lead to the limited liability company being regarded more as a distinct collective entity with its own rights and responsibilities, rather than as a purely private organization pursuing shareholders' interests exclusively.

The extent to which corporate ownership and Anglo-American forms of corporate governance have become institutionalized in emerging markets is addressed by Ruth Aguilera, Luiz Ricardo Kabbach de Castro, Jun Ho Lee, and Jihae You in their 'Corporate Governance in Emerging Economies'. On the whole, their study of ownership in Brazil, Chile, South Korea, the Czech Republic, Hungary, and Poland reveals that concentrated ownership remains dominant, and business groups constitute the major form of corporate structure in these countries, as in many other ones. However, the nature of these owners and how control is exercised are nationally specific and continue to reflect path-dependent processes.

Despite the important role of the state in supporting, if not directing, rapid economic development in many East Asian countries in the twentieth century, as well of course in much of Europe and elsewhere, political embeddedness of economic activities is often thought to be antithetical to the establishment of effectively functioning markets. In her 'Political Embeddedness in China: Strengths and Limitations', Barbara Krug examines the contrasting results of Township and Village Enterprises, the reform of public utilities, and the Enterprise Bankruptcy Law in contributing to the creation of sustainable markets in China. She suggests that three conditions were critical to the apparent success of the first, relative to the outcomes of the second and third modes of political embeddedness: strong informal norms that aligned the interests of all involved parties, clear and uncontested decision rights, and equivalence of the territorial boundaries of markets and political processes.

The contributions in this book outline an agenda for the future study of capitalism and capitalisms in the twenty-first century that will be increasingly inter-disciplinary and increasingly diverse in the economies with which it is concerned. Political authority and power at national and international levels is increasingly intertwined with the decisions of firms about location and organization. The impact of state structures and state policy-making on the decisions of firms contributes to institutional change, whilst firms themselves engage in reshaping institutions in unexpected and unanticipated ways. Finally all of these processes occur within the framework of an emerging system of global capitalism that is unstable, subject to crisis, and continually generating new and unexpected outcomes. In an era when much academic research and publication is becoming more narrow and specialist in scope it is important that these larger issues do not slip out of view. The chapters in this book make some contribution to that goal.

References

Boyer, Robert (2011) 'Are There Laws of Motion of Capitalism?' *Socio-Economic Review*, 9: 59–81.

Braithwaite, John and Peter Drahos (2000) *Global Business Regulation*, Cambridge: Cambridge University Press.

Campbell, John L. (2011) 'The US Financial Crisis: Lessons for theories of institutional complementarity', *Socio-Economic Review*, 9: 211–34.

Crouch, Colin, Patrick le Gales, Carlo Trigilia, and Helmut Voelzkow (2001) *Local Production Systems in Europe: Rise or demise?* Oxford: Oxford University Press.

————————(2004) *Changing Governance of Local Economies: Responses of European local production systems*, Oxford: Oxford University Press.

Djelic, Marie-Laure and Kerstin Sahlin-Andersson (eds) (2006) *Transnational Governance: Institutional dynamics of regulation*, Cambridge: Cambridge University Press.

Ghemawat, Pankaj (2003) 'Semiglobalization and International Business Strategy', *Journal of International Business Studies*, 34: 138–52.

Herrigel, Gary (1996) *Industrial Constructions: The sources of German industrial power*, Cambridge: Cambridge University Press.

Kristensen, Peer Hull (1992) 'Strategies against Structure: Institutions and economic organisation in Denmark', pp. 117–36 in R. Whitley (ed.) *European Business Systems*, London: Sage.

——(1996) 'On the Constitution of Economic Actors in Denmark: Interacting skill containers and project coordinators', pp. 118–58 in R. Whitley and P. H. Kristensen (eds) *The Changing European Firm: Limits to convergence*, London: Routledge.

——M. Lotz, and R. Rocha (2011) 'Denmark: Tailoring flexicurity for changing roles in global games', pp. 86–140 in P. H. Kristensen and K. Lilja (eds) *Nordic Capitalisms and Globalization: New forms of economic organization and welfare institutions*, Oxford: Oxford University Press.

Polanyi, K. (2001) *The Great Transformation: The political and economic origins of our time* (2nd Beacon pbk. ed.), Boston, Mass.: Beacon Press.

Streeck, Wolfgang (2011) 'Taking Capitalism Seriously: Towards an institutionalist approach to contemporary political economy', *Socio-Economic Review*, 9: 137–67.

Whitley, Richard (2005) 'How National are Business Systems? The role of states and complementary institutions in standardizing systems of economic coordination and control at the national level', pp. 190–231 in G. Morgan, R. Whitley, and E. Moen (eds) *Changing Capitalisms? Internationalization, institutional change and systems of economic organisation*, Oxford: Oxford University Press.

Whitley, Richard, Jochen Glaeser, and Lars Engwall (eds) (2010) *Reconfiguring Knowledge Production: Changing authority relationships in the sciences and their consequences for intellectual innovation*, Oxford: Oxford University Press.

1

Theoretical Contexts and Conceptual Frames for the Study of Twenty-First Century Capitalisms

Peer Hull Kristensen and Glenn Morgan

Introduction

The study of different forms of capitalism, their institutional underpinnings and effects on firm strategies and structures has become a well-established field. However, there is no doubt that much of this field was shaped by the experiences of the second half of the twentieth century, and in particular the trajectory and development of a relatively small number of industrialized societies with stable and well-established political and economic institutions. Contemplating the world economy from the perspective of the second decade of the twenty-first century provides a very different perspective from that which appeared to authors contemplating the analysis of comparative capitalisms in the late 1980s and 1990s or even during the 2000s. During the years of the Cold War, it was possible to see the world, despite obvious variety and diversity, primarily in terms of two competing forms of economic organization—capitalism and a form of state-organized planning and bureaucracy which claimed the label of socialism. As the Soviet bloc crumbled and capitalism emerged as the dominant form of economic organization, national variety and diversity became more prominent. In Eastern and Central Europe, 'post-socialist pathways' generated a variety of forms of capitalism (Stark and Bruszt 1998). In Northern, Western, and Southern Europe, increased attention to distinctive patterns of firm organization and strategy emphasized the degree of diversity even within a limited geographical area (Crouch and Streeck 1997). In Asia, an increasing number of societies became integrated into the global economy but again showed different institutional characteristics from those in

Europe and North America as well as between themselves (Whitley 1992). There were of course precursors to this form of analysis: sociologists such as Bendix (Bendix 1956), political economists such as Shonfield (Shonfield 1965), industrial relations scholars such as Crouch (Crouch 1993) and Streeck (Streeck 1992), and organizational analysts such as Maurice (Maurice, Sellier, and Silvestre 1986), to name but a few who were publishing through the 1960s, 1970s, and 1980s on national comparative differences.

In this first phase of comparative institutional analysis, there was a focus on describing differences between capitalist societies and explaining these in terms of key institutional configurations, ranging from the parsimonious model of Hall and Soskice (Hall and Soskice 2001) to the more elaborated typologies of authors such as Amable (Amable 2003), Whitley (Whitley 1999), Boyer and Hollingsworth (Hollingsworth and Boyer 1997). In the 2000s, this gave rise to a second phase of analysis clearly distinguishable by a concern with first, the impact of globalization, multinationals, and forms of international regulation and coordination of economic activities; secondly, the issue of institutional change; and thirdly the nature of agency in relation to path dependencies and lock-ins (for a summary of these developments see Morgan 2007: for a comprehensive review of these developments see; Morgan, Campbell, Crouch, Pedersen, and Whitley 2010). These theoretical issues clearly emerged in response to empirical research on different forms of capitalism where increased interconnectedness between economic actors across national boundaries was opening up new possibilities in terms of the organization of firms and in terms of processes of institutional reproduction and renewal. Such developments were not simply responses to markets but were also, at least in part, stimulated by the development and shaping of such markets by powerful international institutions such as the EU, the WTO, and the range of private international standard-setting bodies emerging in particular areas (see the chapters in this book by Duina, Gessner, Djelic and Quack for discussion of these developments).

The reason for this chapter and for this book, more generally, is to argue that we are now moving into a third phase of comparative institutional analysis. The following phenomena are the most obvious aspects of this third phase.

First, the position of the emergent economies and Brazil, Russia, India, and China (the BRICs) is central to the analysis of twenty-first century capitalism and capitalisms. Previous phases of comparative institutional analysis focused primarily on a small group of advanced industrial economies that industrialized along similar time-scales and within a world order where their military dominance of other areas of the globe provided them with access to cheap resources. Indeed, most of these societies were formed into nation states with relatively coherent institutional orders at a similar moment in time where the influence of the Enlightenment and the French and American Revolutions created a political framework based on the rule of law, liberalism, nationalism of varying kinds, individualism, and property rights. At the same time as these nation states were formed, their imperial rivalries and ambitions drove them into many other parts of the world. In these other parts of the world (with very rare exceptions, the most obvious being Japan), they created colonial or quasi-colonial entities which precisely lacked the characteristics of sovereignty and legitimacy that were part of the European nation-state model, and facilitated the building of those nineteenth-century institutional orders. This is not to gainsay the fact that the European nation states almost destroyed themselves in two world wars because of the struggle between liberal and conservative, reactionary forces about the meaning of this model of sovereignty, empire, and power. Nevertheless, a reinvigorated model of the nation state along these lines emerged as the dominant pattern for political authority in world and European politics after 1945 (Milward, Brennan, and Romero 2000).

However the conditions for forming new nation states were now set in a different international context, one at first defined by the Cold War and the effective subjugation of national institution-building in the Eastern bloc to the requirements of Soviet rule. In much of the West, the US played a similar role, even if most of the time it preferred the use of 'soft power' and persuasion to that of coercion. For much of the period up to the late 1980s, therefore, even if formal empires had been dismantled, strong informal empires continued to shape in direct and indirect ways the institutional structures of most of the world. Not surprisingly, therefore, most discussion of forms of capitalism focused on the relatively strong nation states, the powerful economies in Europe, the US, and Japan, and the rest of the world (again with the exception of some Asian countries—the New Asian Tigers) was relatively ignored.

The breakdown of the Soviet bloc and the expansion of foreign direct investment (FDI), overseas portfolio investment and deregulated financial markets, combined with the internal dynamics of these emerging societies, fundamentally changed the picture. Capitalism in the twenty-first century cannot be understood just from the perspective of a limited set of long-established capitalist economies. On the contrary, the most economically dynamic parts of the world are from outside the countries usually considered within the comparative capitalisms literature. Most dramatic of all is the rise of China to a major role in the world economy, but India too, as well as the other BRICs and a further tier of large and emerging economies (such as Mexico, South Africa) are reshaping the flows of production, labour, and capital around the world. The next stage of comparative institutional analysis is going to be centrally concerned with these societies and their position in the global division of labour.

A key aspect of the emergence of these societies concerns the way in which they organize the relationship between the state, civil society, and the economy. Here the compromises which led in the older societies to forms of democratic welfare capitalism and particular patterns of state/civil society association are yet to be achieved. In the main these emerging economies lack comparable developed welfare systems, which provides an enormous source of competitive advantage in terms of brute economies of cost, but in terms of social order and institution building creates high levels of uncertainty. Whilst certain aspects of the European state model may, subject to many conditions, be copied to an extent by these powers as they become richer, for example investment in forms of education and training, other aspects such as collective welfare provision for health, old age, and unemployment may be only minimally imitated if at all. What Polanyi (Polanyi 2001) described in the European context as the dual movement (from market dominance towards the creation of institutions that protect the population from the market and create a more regulated market and a welfare state) may take very different forms in the emerging economies of the twenty-first century (see Krug's chapter in this book).

Secondly, much comparative capitalisms' analysis carried a set of hidden assumptions concerning the nature of the international environment. This was that there were certain rules of exchange and trade that as Ruggie pointed out, enabled countries to pursue their own distinctive model of capitalism (Ruggie 1998). Embedded liberalism, as he described it and as it emerged out of the Bretton Woods rules, combined trade openness with stable internal social settlements that were diverse in their character and their degree of state management. However, the whole system depended on the US, as a guarantor of the rules, as the largest open market, as the provider of the dollar as a global currency.

All of these conditions have been undermined over the last two decades, but particularly in the 2000s. Although it appeared in the immediate aftermath of the Soviet collapse that US dominance was guaranteed, in fact the rising powers of the emerging economies and the collapsing US economy, particularly after 2008, have revealed a growing weakness in the ability of the US to set the framework for the international economy. In certain areas of trade liberalization in the WTO as well as in multilateral meetings such as the Copenhagen summit, the USA is no longer able to get its way. This is more than a political phenomenon. It particularly reflects the growing weakness of the USA, made visible after the financial crash in terms of its dependence during the 2000s on a credit-induced inflationary asset boom, funded by China and other outsiders. This credit boom had temporarily compensated for stagnating real incomes amongst the lower and middle ranks of American society (Hacker and Pierson 2010). Stagnating real incomes further related to the inability of US-based manufacturers to compete against producers from low-income areas such as, most notably, China. The result is an increasing multipolarity in the formation and governance of the international economic system, reflected for example by the extension of the G7 to the G20. The existence of this more uncertain international environment fundamentally changes the context of nationally specific varieties of capitalism. Further it is likely that these changes are more than an interim stage between a declining *pax americana* and a new *pax sinica*, and that the instability will remain endemic for the foreseeable future. What sort of an international order will emerge and how will it shape, constrain, facilitate national institutional structures? Further investigation of this international system is required (see chapters by Djelic and Quack, Duina, Clift and Woll, Morgan and Goyer).

Thirdly, and worth treating as a phenomenon in its own right, is the impact of the financial crisis of 2008 and its continuing aftermath. In the main, comparative capitalisms treated finance from the perspective of its role in funding industry. The whole mode of analysis was couched within the contrast between bank provision of funding and capital market provision and how this impacted on firm structure. Although there were efforts to rethink the role of finance (Boyer 2000), comparative capitalisms was relatively ill equipped to comment on the financial crisis of 2008. The idea that finance had in some contexts become central to patterns of growth as an independent sphere, increasingly at several degrees of remove from production, was identified, but that it could in turn lead to a global crisis was barely foreseen. The crisis revealed the weakness of the US economy and how it had become dependent on borrowing from China for its consumption (see the chapter by Morgan and Goyer). The association of deregulated financial markets with economic growth and the continued supremacy of the US were undermined by the financial crisis. Emergent economies seemed to recover most quickly following the initial collapse of world trade, whilst the US and the UK continue to make very slow progress to recovery. Having a financial sector that drives the economy as a whole has been shown to be a high-risk endeavour, not just in the US and the UK, but also in places like Ireland and Iceland. Even where the financial sector is not so dominant, the fact that financial institutions could move funds around and become enmeshed in networks of contracts that could lead to them potentially owing to their counterparties monies, not just beyond their own capital reserves, but beyond in some cases the capacity of their home nation states to repay, showed the fundamental interconnectedness of economies as well as their potential frailty. Understanding finance in twenty-first century capitalisms is therefore an urgent task (see the chapters by Thompson, Morgan and Goyer, Tylecote, Aguilera et al. in this book).

Fourthly, the vestiges of the Chandlerian and Fordist models of production and organization, dominant in the post-war US and imitated to varying degrees in other countries, continue to decline and mutate, their vast hierarchies of bureaucratic managerial authority, internal labour markets, internal R + D systems, and internalized value chains no longer capable of responding to global competition. In its place, building on and adapting local institutions, more complex ensembles of networks, alliances, and value chains have arisen, organized through new forms of contract and social relationships, based on a variety of forms of work organization ranging from high-skilled team-working and project organization through to more intensive forms of classic labour exploitation in sweatshops, domestic work, and highly disciplined and controlled forms of factory work.

The new world of consumption which is the outcome of these processes has also proliferated and become more differentiated, making simple divisions between manufacturing and service no longer relevant to many phenomena which are combinations of both, whether we think of personal consumption items such as mobile phones and computers, or of the corporate purchase of huge capital investment projects such as airplanes, power stations, etc. Large firms in such a context are loose international coalitions of functionally differentiated units, some of which are owned, some under semi-permanent sub-contracting relationships, some under arm's length contracts, and others temporary project alliances. Global value chains integrated within firms or coordinated by large firms across organizations of different scales, are an increasingly predominant feature. The emphasis given by comparative capitalisms analysis to an understanding of firms as based within one country, or one sector, or one market is no longer viable. What sort of control and coordination is it possible to exercise across such distributed value chains, and how does this relate to locally produced patterns of economic organization (see the chapters by Bair, Casper, and Whitley)?

So if we conceive of twenty-first century capitalism as global, not just in terms of its trading patterns or flows of labour and capital, but also in terms of the range of powerful and significant economic actors and spaces that are now interconnected through finance and through networks of production and innovation, what sort of comparative institutional analysis do we require? In this chapter, we identify a series of interconnected elements in response to such a question, beginning with a discussion of institutions and actors, and moving from this into an analysis of what this means for firms and economic organization. We then shift our analysis to a more macro-level to discuss the relationship of states and political powers to this process. Finally, we return to the implicit distinctions between capitalism, capitalisms, markets, finance, and institutions which are frequently invoked but rarely analysed, in order to frame our overall argument about the emergent third phase of comparative institutional analysis.

1. Institutions, actors, and change: the basic frame

In the first section, we build on and develop recent analyses of the nature of institutions, institutional change, and institutional reproduction. In recent decades, the concept of an 'institution' has offered to policy makers, politicians, and social scientists alike a relief from the dominance of free-market economics, and associated with this the sense that the world consists of a floating volatility of complex interwoven, ongoing processes of human action and interaction at a multiplicity of levels that can barely be described, let alone controlled. By labelling social processes as 'institutions', we have been able to circumscribe complex social processes with an idiom that transforms these phenomena into an 'object' with 'its' own distinctive characteristics so that the isolated mechanisms of the 'object' can now be studied and elaborated. Its strength is exactly that it allows one to 'objectify' such diverse phenomena as a law, an informal code of conduct, rules of a game, regulatory agencies, and organizations such as schools and universities, hospitals and asylums, firms and investment banks that provide services and societal value to citizens. Focusing on social phenomena as institutions gives an indication of something stable, maybe structural, but also creates a focus for interaction about changing 'the institution', an approach to the world increasingly taken up, both by international organizations seeking to 'reform' countries and make them more competitive, and by academics engaged in policy formation (e.g. Rodrik 2007).

In our view, however, this objectification of institutions is increasingly subject to criticism for its lack of understanding of the dynamics involved. By interpreting and objectifying institutions, actors relate to institutions, and by reinterpreting them they change this interaction, the meaning of the institutions, and in consequence thereof, they change the nature of their own agency and their own constitution as actors. Thus the concept of 'institution' can perform a heuristic purpose by providing a static template of self-reproducing social relations, but from a dynamic perspective, more emphasis needs to be placed on the interlinkage between actors and institutions (Campbell 2004, 2010; Crouch 2005; Deeg and Jackson 2007; Jackson 2010). The current situation in institutional theory and academic discussions on the place of institutions can therefore be seen as a phase of transition from a predominant perspective in which institutions determined behaviour (institutions as constraints which can be managed and manipulated by powerful actors in society) to one in which strategic behaviour by actors at multiple levels of the social hierarchy determines the design, use of, and function of institutions (institutions as enablers) within contextual constraints and loose path dependencies and institutional complementarities. What makes which kinds of actors able to do this, and in what circumstances? It is important to note that in our perspective, the category of actor should not be reified. Actors are no more stable and causally effective than institutions, or at least the conditions under which particular kinds of social entities became actors in specific ways need to be researched and explained rather than assumed. We therefore aim to consider how categories of actors evolve and change through their engagement with institutions, and how their potential agency and power actually becomes capable of being exercised is an empirical question for us.

In many societies of today, it can be argued that institutional change is an everyday activity, and it could be that one of the biggest problems nowadays—in politics as well as in social science—is that these changes may often go on unnoticed whilst policy elites construct and seek to effect institutional change through top-down policy reform. Rather than seeing the 'institutional formation' of a country as basically stable, we thus see it as continuously worked on, permanently contested by some quarters or groups of society—and always made new use of as actors redefine themselves towards other actors and place the institutions that they redefine in a new setting of mutual re-enforcement. Streeck and Thelen, and Thelen's subsequent efforts to identify types of slow incremental yet consequential changes in institutions and the role of different types of agents in these processes reflect a similar sense of how actors making small changes to their expectations and behaviours in response to shifting internal and external environments can eventually rebuild from the inside, or build anew from the outside, different institutions (Mahoney and Thelen 2010; Streeck and Thelen 2005; Thelen 2009).

Whilst this is partly an ontological approach to the nature of institutions and actors, we also emphasize that this dynamic approach is particularly relevant in the current era because of the intensity of international competition and flows of technology, capital, and labour across national boundaries, challenging existing patterns. Under these changed conditions, which we see as having co-evolved with globalization, analysts can only discover what counts as institutions, by studying actors and by discovering which institutions they make use of in shaping their action and relations with other actors. Comparing what a formal analysis of the institutional formation should contain and what is actually entering into the practices of actors may reveal very important information, about the changes that go on in a social system. We might learn a lot about which institutions have been de-selected and which retained, and by doing so understand empirically how the system is evolving, how certain institutions are growing and others declining. Dynamic, actor-centred institutionalist thinking forces us so to move from one actor to the larger setting of interacting actors, such as organizational fields or business systems, if we want to understand in a dynamic way social change and institutions' place in this larger picture. Actors are not only creative in changing institutional systems, they are simultaneously also creative in developing new synergies among existing institutions, and therefore creating new complementarities that cannot be detected by formal institutionalist analysis, but only by studying how actors go about making novel use of institutions. Thus, rather than seeing institutions primarily as constraints, they should be seen as transactional focal points in societies that may be turned into resources for action, or for joining novel actions of a multiplicity of actors together in novel ways. They are the constitutive elements that can be taken for granted as objects for being sculptured so they serve changing ends in the strategies of social and economic actors.

When actors constantly change their identities because of processes going on in organizational fields, they might, in consequence of this, alter the institutions so these in turn enable them to take on new roles and make new rules of the game that can integrate transactions among new role-holders. Alternatively, they might exhaust the institutional formation in which they are embedded by undermining old rules of the games, former assemblages of professional identities, and the way they mutually helped define each other as interest groups and classes (see for instance Streeck 2009 on the exhaustion of the institutional foundations of the German post-war model). From this perspective, some national institutional systems become contested formations in which experimental searches for new ways of ordering, of governing, of creating new identities and integrating them in new forms of economic organization take place.

We can anticipate, however, that other societies have less room for these patterns of experimentation because individuals and their potential for creativity is constrained. Some of these constraints, such as a lack of resources or the dominance of a closed ideology, may crush all potential for adaptive change, as may conditions of high uncertainty where return on investments in new processes and institutions may be so risky as to inhibit all but conservative behaviour. Other features revolve around the nature of the state itself, the degree and nature of the control which it is able to exercise over citizens and institutions. Does it constrain the sort of experimentation described, conserving institutions and specifically restraining them from change in order to preserve them against change? In some contexts, such conservatism leads to a cycle of decline, as the society gets left behind wider social, economic, and technological changes. Alternatively, states might allow a space for economic experimentation and change whilst seeking to rigidly preserve other institutions, setting up an increasing tension between different parts of the system, for example as in China between single-party control of the state on the one hand and increasing economic freedom on the other.

Therefore, in the current era, we can see varying speeds of experimental change, various forms of change, and a range of different outcomes from the economic perspective. One can seek out laboratories of experimental search which create a fertile ground for fast-mutating divergent capitalisms. In these contexts, some societies may find new dynamic complementarities that contribute with new elements to create a new architecture of capitalist expansion, whereas others may fail precisely because the changes produce an increasing disjuncture between the institutional formation and the organizational field, limiting the dynamics of both. On the other hand, there are societies where there is little experimental search activity; in some cases, states constrain actors to work within limited frames, whilst in others the weakness of the state means that there is very little certainty and actors behave conservatively depending on groupings and relationships which are beyond the state, such as ethnic groups, extended families, or even just temporary armed gangs. It is also clear that any such developments occur in a highly uncertain environment where unexpected and unanticipated interactions can set off chains of events which throw off course experimental efforts. In particular, the continuing ramifications, not just of the financial crisis itself but how governments, firms, and populations responded to that crisis since 2008, reveal how quickly it is possible for new vulnerabilities to be revealed which can set off their own chains of consequences, for example as in the Eurozone crisis of 2010–11.

Comparative institutional analysis needs to step back and identify the conditions under which these different levels of dynamic relations between economic organizational fields and institutions occur. It must become a movement and a method to map and to understand how different nations constrain or enable in distinctive ways processes of socio-economic development to come about. Instead of being primarily interested in how different capitalisms reproduce themselves in distinctive ways, our interest focuses on how far they are able to mutate and find novel ways to deal with emerging challenges.

2. Competition models and institutional frames

In the previous section, we emphasized the need to build more dynamic models of the relationships between actors and institution across different sorts of context. Such an emphasis comes in particular because of a sense of the changing nature of economic activity in the current era. In this section, we relate this particularly to the nature of firms and global competition in the contemporary period.

Initial analyses of comparative capitalisms were basically theories of sectoral specialization. They identified how particular institutional configurations proved particularly suitable for establishing sectors of activity where firms would have the resources and capabilities to be world leaders. A key distinction was between sectors characterized by incremental change (essentially most manufacturing and engineering sectors) and sectors characterized by radical change (identified with high-technology arenas where new inventions or applications could cause industry upheaval and reconfiguration). In the classic analyses, institutions determined which sorts of sectors evolved in particular societies, since institutions shaped the presence of the appropriate resources which could facilitate either incremental or radical change, for example in terms of the provision of appropriate forms of skill, capital, technology, etc. (Hall and Soskice 2001; Quack, Morgan, and Whitley 2000).

This dualistic model has, however been increasingly challenged. Whitley, for example, identifies a range of 'competition models' which combine the basic radical–incremental distinction with other characteristics, most notably the speed and the scale of innovation and production (Whitley 2010). The most familiar competition models are Fordism, craft production, flexible specialization, and diversified quality production. To these he adds three other competition models. The opportunistic model refers to activities characterized by low skill and low investment in fixed plant or technology, which enables the firm to switch between different markets and products quickly and at low cost; it is a model which firms pursue in producing cheap novelty and seasonal goods, for example toys, tourist goods, cheap clothes. The flexible mass production of differentiated goods and services (FMPDG) competition model focuses on the rapid development and commercialization of new improved goods, based on a combination of existing skills, targeted research and development investments, and high-impact marketing, for example in consumer electronics. The discontinuous innovation competition model focuses on generating and commercializing disruptive technologies that radically change markets; it requires the acquisition and use of new scientific and technological knowledge through networked forms of R + D and through the provision of high-risk investment capital, for example Internet businesses and biotechnology. Whitley argues that each of these competition models depends on particular sorts of labour power, particular sets of knowledge, and particular types of capital. He shows the sorts of institutional features which are conducive to being successful in producing the appropriate elements that can be combined into a particular competition model.

In many ways these competition models depict the competitive positioning among a set of economies during the 1980s and 1990s. Certain institutional features as described by Whitley made it easier to pursue a particular competition model from inside a specific society than from inside another. Had this continued it is possible to imagine that the world would have proceeded as a deepening of such competition models, where each country would have cultivated their institutions to become increasingly better at supporting their own competition model as a way of gaining space in globalization. However, there are good reasons for believing that this model of extended self-reproduction at the national level is declining and that the situation is actually much more unstable, requiring more active adaptation and response to changing conditions.

The first reason for this is that sectors are increasingly populated by firms using, not one, but elements of several different competition models. The co-presence of Fordist and diversified quality production models has long been recognized in the car industry, but this situation of co-presence is now more general across sectors. There are a variety of ways of competing within particular sectors, depending on the segmentation of the market, across 'sub-products', across income, life style and status segments, across geographical spaces. Moreover these segments are not static and hermetically sealed, but can be reconfigured by changes led by companies as well as changes emanating from different economic conditions. This pressurizes firms, not just to improve on their existing processes in relation to known competitors, but also to look to be more innovative to protect against the entry of different types of firms using different competition models. It is therefore becoming increasingly difficult to identify particular sectors with a particular type of competition model (as Hall and Soskice in their original varieties of capitalism approach sought to do). Sectors are more differentiated and segmented in ways that are impermanent and unstable and continually subject to renegotiation through competitive processes, particularly in a world where there are so many more options in terms of location.

Secondly, this relates to the fact that competition models are becoming more inter-connected. A firm operating a flexible specialization system for its consumer products may source some of its basic components from Fordist suppliers, and vice versa—this is not new, as was shown in some discussions of French capitalism in the 1980s. A firm that engages in discontinuous innovation may seek to secure its position by engaging with Fordist production techniques to make its products, as for example Apple has done. A firm cannot therefore confine its perspective to the one competition model with which it is familiar: it must become adept at hybridizing processes across competition models. Indeed as firms become larger and more multinational, they tend to participate in a number of competition models, depending on the sectors and markets in which they operate.

Thirdly, the development of complex global supply chains where final products are assembled out of various components produced in-house or outsourced leads to learning and change as participants in the value chain engage in higher levels of cooperation and exchange of information and knowledge (Herrigel 2010; Herrigel and Zeitlin 2010). Customers are increasingly embedded in this learning process, thus changing the nature of competition from simply relying on a commodity that is transferred across a boundary to being a package of goods and services that is in part relationship based. The complexity of the internal process of production becomes mirrored by the complexity of the external process of selling and realizing value.

Generating stable returns to firms under present market conditions is therefore highly uncertain. This drives actors on to modify, extend, and develop their competition models, and to restructure work and employment relationships, using existing institutional resources but also engaging in forms of institutional change as well as moving across borders to create global value chains or production networks.

This relates to our argument regarding the nature of institutions and actors, in which we see change and experimentalism as a normal part of the functioning of firms in competitive markets. On the one hand, institutions still shape particular forms of resources that enable the development of particular types of competition model. On the other hand, firms are not passive 'takers' of the institutional resources of their home context, but active searchers across national contexts for resources, and active makers and remakers of institutions in different locations. Thus, strange combinations are emerging through the interaction between institutional change, firm-level strategizing, and the new dynamics of global competition. Localities that looked similar barely thirty years ago find themselves moving rapidly in different directions because of these changes. For example, during the 1980s, Prato in Italy and Herning-Ikast in Denmark looked in many ways similar, both characterized by industrial districts of SMEs concentrated within the fashion industry. Today, Prato's firms have to a great extent been taken over by Chinese owners and workers competing within cheaper segments of the market, whilst in Denmark the garment district has off-shored all production, but created a very strong position in design, logistics, and quality control, making Denmark a distinct centre for fashion in Europe.

These patterns of search, experimentation, and recombination are coordinated in various ways (see e.g. the global value chain research tradition; Bair 2009; Gereffi, Humphrey, and Sturgeon 2005; Gereffi and Korzeniewicz 1994). Over the last decades original equipment manufacturers (OEMs) in developed countries have been off-shoring and out-sourcing production to low-wage countries in order to achieve cost-advantages. This has been part of the restructuring, but not the disappearance, of the large firm form of organization. Alongside this has emerged an experimental space occupied by various forms of small, medium, and large- scale firms, linked together in a variety of networks.

Herrigel and colleagues' detailed empirical work on these processes reveals an interesting picture on the nature of this space, and the relationship between the different actors (Herrigel 2010; Herrigel and Wittke 2005; Herrigel and Zeitlin 2010; Whitford 2005). In their analysis of Fordist competition models, suppliers work under arm's length contracting and price is the dominant parameter. Terms are highly specified by the OEM, which uses suppliers for repetitive tasks or as 'buffer'. In such relations, suppliers are not profitable enough to be endogenously innovative. In other competition models, for example Japanese Keiretsu networks, relations are autocratic and captive, and OEMs and suppliers develop complementary forms of specialization. Suppliers are dependent on a single OEM and follow its lead in changing products and processes. Cooperation becomes closer over time, almost as if the supplier was an internal team of the OEM, limiting risks of opportunism and moral hazard. Such collaboration tends to ignore the possibilities outside the pre-established network but provides a stability unavailable in the Fordist model.

Distinctive from both these models is what may be termed normal contract manufacturing—often found in flexible specialization competition models—where the lead firm provides suppliers with design and technical specifications for their tasks and then it is up to suppliers to do the task as fast and cheaply as possible. Modular manufacturing is often connected to this, and standardized interfaces among components make it possible for suppliers to improve within the realm of the module, but mostly to attain high volumes. OEMs are constantly looking for better suppliers while suppliers are searching for additional customers. This creates a possibility for broader learning but risks also that in the next contract round, cooperation collapses because the two parties fear that they have given up too much knowledge. Competition prevails over cooperation and makes it difficult to really invest assets in building up tight collaboration.

Relational contracting has been seen as a way out of this dilemma. As Herrigel (2010: 149) says '... relational contracting is the limit case in the global trend toward vertical disintegration. The relationship differs from the captive supplier relationship in that there is near parity in the power balance between customer and supplier.... (It) differs from the contract manufacturing relationships in that the competence and capacities of both partners are jointly indispensable... (also) for design and development.... (And) collaboration begins as a joint exploration of the possibilities for the definition of a product between customer and supplier. Neither party has a clear idea ex ante of what the precise contours of the final product of the cooperation will be or of its specific articulation or interface with the overall design of the end product.'

For Herrigel and others, the tensions around these relationships lead to the emergence of another pattern of cooperation which, whilst symbiotic with the network organized by the large firm, is distinctive in nature. This is where the small and medium-sized suppliers start to develop their international markets and global production capabilities through organizing amongst themselves in a form of networked innovation system. By going international, suppliers search for other customers, while at the same time having the ability to stabilize relations to previous customers independently of the large MNC. In this way the small firms, many of which have been encouraged into existence by the reorganization of the large firms, begin to become nodal actors in establishing what Herrigel describes as 'sustained contingent collaboration' amongst a wider network of organizations. To stabilize this form of cooperation, the small MNCs need to invent new ways of institutionalizing the relationship. One solution is new forms of contracting that are open ended (concerning outcome) but specify the procedures by which conflicts (over costs and outcomes) are negotiated and handled, and at what levels of the two organizations. Gilson, Sabel and Scott have found such contracts in a variety of forms among OEMs in the US (Gilson, Sabel, and Scott 2009).

In this process, small and medium-sized firms, some of which may become international in their scope, begin to constitute highly viable networks of innovation, which in many ways take over what used to be the dynamic role of large, traditional MNCs. Thus, SMEs that used to supply repetitive components for the large OEMs become much more innovative. Innovation shifts from being dominated by large MNCs to being dispersed among all firm sizes, collaborating mutually in open innovation or networked innovation systems. By following the large MNCs' foreign expansion, innovative SMEs have become small multinationals. For small MNCs to stay alive it is decisive that they become tied into innovative relations with a multiplicity of customers globally and that they can cooperate with other firms. Without the latter their size would limit their ability to do the former.

Kristensen and Lilja have shown how firms in the Nordic countries interacted in searching for these sorts of new roles globally (Kristensen and Lilja 2011). The firms which they studied become small MNCs by supplying products (e.g. speciality tools, hospital equipment) and then developing services to continuously improve a particular business area (e.g. the entire tool-managing system or a hospital's acute section) for a multiplicity of costumers globally. In this process they accumulate comparative knowledge of how to solve problems so they can create a codex of best practices and refine this codex to ever increasing levels. In this way the small MNC is able to move gradually up to servicing the most demanding customers and to identify complementary products that may be useful in performing its tasks, thereby establishing a global network of suppliers that can assist the firm in fulfilling its role. This process may under certain conditions result in the creation of a global value chain, but partners are more equal and depend collectively on the network's capability for innovation. They expand primarily because of the pressure, for instance, on large MNCs to reduce costs and continuously improve. Their major problem then becomes to learn to learn in a coordinated way across countries. The better they learn to solve customer problems in one subsidiary, the better they can master solving customer problems in another, provided that the international organization is able to carry learning from the first (over the home organization) to the second subsidiary and vice versa.

As already indicated, to the degree that small MNCs learn to solve these and related problems they may constitute highly viable networks of innovation, which in many ways takes over what used to be the dynamic role of large MNCs. There is a sense in which two systems of global coordination of economic activities are emerging that are inter-related and inter-dependent but distinctive in their logics. One is centred around the large MNC, whilst the other reflects a different mode of development based on smaller firms, open innovation networks, and the deepening of institutional attachments.

Large MNCs can however no longer be characterized simply as Chandlerian, Fordist firms imposing their strategies and policies on other firms, their employees, and states. Their boundaries are more open: they engage in extensive relationships with other institutional locations through subsidiaries and outsourcing to other firms. They manage these interfaces in a variety of ways depending on the nature of the input and the technology involved, the institutional location, and the sources of profitability and value in the global production chain. These decisions reflect assessments on the sorts of resources forthcoming from different locations, for example low wage costs, plentiful skilled labour, and highly innovative knowledge networks (such as those described by Casper in this book). Thus they may have pockets of highly skilled activities in one part of the value chain and in a particular set of institutional locations that support these skills, and in another part there may be highly Taylorized systems of production.

What are the limits of this sort of model of production coordination present in large MNCs? We would emphasize four sets of limits. The first is one of managerial capacity. There is now substantial evidence that MNCs of the sort described are extremely complex to manage and frequently engender high levels of micro-politics as groups within them struggle for positions (see, for example, the contributions in Almond and Ferner 2006; Collinson and Morgan 2009; Dörrenbächer and Geppert 2011; Geppert and Mayer 2006; Kristensen and Zeitlin 2005; Morgan, Kristensen, and Whitley 2001). The nature of these processes is shaped by institutional contexts and the resources which different actors bring together in order to struggle over the imposition of centralized management policies, information systems, budgeting and accounting systems, as well as over the allocation of capital allowing a subsidiary to grow and expand, or conversely the withdrawal of head office support for particular plants, leading to closure or divestment. Understanding the variety of ways in which MNCs are managed and the limits to success arising from issues of institutional distance and politics is therefore crucial to an appreciation of the vulnerability of the large firm model.

The second limitation for the large firm model is the issue of finance and corporate governance. As Aguilera et al. demonstrate in their contribution in this book, ownership of large firms takes different forms when we switch attention away from either the US/UK model or the various forms of 'patient capital' model which have characterized European systems. Increasingly it appears that all large MNCs have to call to varying degrees on financial markets for funding, but there are large variations in first, the degree of dependence on outsiders for funding, secondly, the influence which outsiders can expect to have on the firm and thirdly, related to this, the nature of the connection between ownership and political power in particular contexts. MNCs that are highly dependent on financial markets and outsiders have to continually assess their processes of internationalization, experimentation, and innovation by reference to the short-term requirements of the financial markets (see Tylecote's chapter). Of course, access to these markets is also useful, giving firms the financial capacity to crush potential small rivals through price wars, takeovers, or acquisition of key intellectual property or managerial ability.

However, firms strongly tied to the financial markets are also most easily affected, not just by factors associated with their own performance, but also by broader swings in bull and bear markets, interest rate changes, and financial fads, fashions, and crises. All of this makes it more difficult to establish steady relationships with either subsidiaries or with suppliers, because as financial conditions change for the MNC, rapid changes are sought in the structure of the company. Thus Kristensen and Zeitlin (2005) describe how top management in the MNC which they studied were continually concerned with managing their position in the financial markets and had little detailed knowledge of the processes or qualities of their subsidiaries, relying instead on accounting, production, and manpower metrics.

Where firms can insulate themselves from this, either through corporate structures that maintain insider control or through close relationships with the state and political actors (as most obviously in the case of Russia and China, but also to a lesser degree in France and other countries), then their relative freedom of manoeuvre is greater. Their approach can, if appropriate, be longer term. So finance is particularly a limiting factor for those MNCs in places like the US and the UK but probably less so (at least at this stage in their development) for MNCs growing out of the BRIC and emerging economies.

The third limiting factor has already been mentioned and that is the degree of embeddedness of the MNC in the politics of the home country and the host country. Clift and Woll in their chapter in this book discuss the first of these phenomena in terms of the emergence of the concept of 'economic patriotism', that is that the state provides support for firms in developing their competitiveness in ways which remain within the rules of current trade regimes. The support of a home government for its MNCs is important, both in terms of negotiating international rules in bilateral treaties and wider regional trade agreements (see Duina's chapter), and in terms of shaping the institutional resources in ways which support and strengthen particular competitive advantages. In turn this impacts on how incoming MNCs are treated, for example in terms of formal rules on the degree of foreign ownership allowed, or informal rules regarding access to key institutional resources. Thus, MNCs are not simply free to establish their networks wherever they want: in some contexts there are forms of adaptation which are required or prohibitions on certain sorts of activities. Alternatively the MNC may seek to reshape the rules of the market in order to expand access (Morgan 2009).

The fourth limiting factor in terms of the ability of the large MNC to coordinate and control its network of resources is the strategizing of the firms in its supply chain. Herrigel's model of different types of relationship suggests that supplier firms may become locked in and relatively powerless in supply chains, or they can struggle to develop their own distinctive resources and use them to increase their autonomy from large firms. The more they establish their relative independence yet remain essential to the large MNC, the more collaborative and relational the linkages between the supplier and the supplied OEM are likely to become.

Thus, whilst there are many reasons for acknowledging that the large MNC currently predominates in the organization of the global economy, there are limits to that dominance. These limits also suggest that there are possibilities for the development of small and medium-sized enterprises working collaboratively and internationally in certain forms of market. In general, such firms have fewer problems of management coordination, their financial requirements are lower, and their flexibility of response to market changes is generally quicker and higher. Much of the discussion on networks, particularly in high-technology industries has focused on how small firms facilitate rapid innovation by providing high incentives to participants to engage in intensive high-risk operations (Casper 2007, 2010: also the chapter by Casper in this book; Kenney 2000).

On the other hand, it is immediately obvious that in many crucial ways the SME model of the multinational is highly vulnerable, but in different ways from the large MNC. First, it generally has to be highly innovative, and for this reason it tends to be closely dependent on its home institutional structure where the state is active in supporting innovation and change at the level of sectors, firms, skill sets, and individuals. Its connection with the home institutional context is therefore likely to be stronger than the large MNC which is increasingly able to move across different contexts. The large MNC has little incentive to invest in building up its own institutional structure because of the extent of its internationalization which effectively loosens its attachment to its origins. It takes advantage of different institutional resources but is not likely to be central in developing them—and indeed in some cases can be highly exploitative of the investment of others in institutional development. Indeed the large MNC may destroy institutional resources, for example by taking over local firms and then later closing them when market conditions change, thus weakening the ability of the local context to develop and change.

The small MNC on the other hand is likely to be very dependent on the ability of its home institutional context to continue to provide it with the resources that allow it to compete in global markets. It has every incentive to work with the state and other local actors to reform and improve institutions.

Secondly, the small MNC is more vulnerable because it does not in itself have the resources to explore and develop global markets. In this respect it is dependent on its position in global production chains to pull it through into wider markets, either through linkages with big MNCs or through building open innovation networks that offer access into these broader contexts.

To summarize this section, therefore, our argument is that the previous emphasis in comparative capitalisms research on sector specialization and associated firm level specialization in certain processes of production facilitated by the institutional context has been undermined by the development of off-shoring, outsourcing, and the geographical relocation of products and services. We need to examine more how firms experimentally construct and participate in global value chains that combine different production methods and competition models. In particular, it is important to note that such value chains and networks vary both in their degree of closure and in their degree of hierarchical coordination. Large MNCs continually try to control the chain and its participants at the same time as they seek to ensure competition in terms of price, quality, and innovation amongst suppliers. They combine different competition models and seek out institutional locations that provide the best combination of resources for certain links in the value chain. They are opportunistic towards institutions, are likely to avoid significant investment in building institutional capacities, and can in some cases by their actions in relocating and shifting production actually destroy institutional resources. Large MNCs suffer from weaknesses because of the complexity of their organizational structure and the resulting stresses on managerial capabilities; they also face issues of managing their financial models which can have varying impacts depending on the degree to which ownership is shielded from outside pressures. Because of their size they also face political issues; these can be favourable, that is they become supported by their home state, but they can also be problematic because other states may retaliate if a firm is seen as in some ways an arm of a foreign government.

Smaller firms seek to extend their autonomy and control of their own destiny by avoiding being captured by one large MNC and instead cooperating in their own networks or seeking for business with other large MNCs. They tend to be more deeply embedded in particular institutional contexts, and thus committed to building in these contexts. Under particular circumstances, their size can facilitate flexibility and innovativeness but in other senses it creates vulnerabilities.

Our view of firms in twenty-first century capitalism, therefore, is of a broad shift away from Chandlerian hierarchies towards more intensive and extensive forms of experimentation in terms of firm structures and competition models. The ability to reach new resources and to create value chains that combine both different modes of organization and different firms, subsidiaries, and locations creates an intensity of competition on a global scale. This depends in part on using and developing institutions, but we see here a series of complex cross-currents in which large MNCs and networks of SME multinationals, although intertwined in many ways, are starting to pursue different strategies towards institutions, in terms of their degree of embeddedness in particular contexts and their degree of involvement in changing institutions. These issues, however, necessitate a more focused analysis of how states relate to firms and economic development to which we turn in the next section.

3. States, societies, and institutional change

In this chapter, we have frequently invoked the concept of the state and the idea of politics as a way of understanding institutions and economic organization. In this section, we want to follow this through in more detail because the environment of twenty-first century capitalisms enables us to see more clearly the diversity of forms of interaction between these phenomena. Our starting point follows on from the previous discussions and concerns how institutions evolve and change, and the role which the state plays in this process. In the Polanyian perspective, it is impossible to understand the evolution of institutions outside of the idea of the 'double movement' between market forces and forces of social protection. This is certainly an important part of our perspective and we return to it in discussion, but as a social form the European state predates market society and the Weberian perspective on the state in terms of legitimacy should not be reduced to an ideological veneer.

If we start from the European nation-states, it is possible to interpret developments from a perspective in which the power and authority of the state is gradually infused with the idea that the state has a legitimate role to play in the lives of its citizens. The state is not co-terminous with those lives; it does not dominate but it facilitates and makes possible the actions of citizens. In terms of the discussions in the 1980s, the state is not a 'capstone' state, that is, a bureaucratic structure which sits on 'top' of society and extracts surplus from it, but rather a power generator (Hall 1986, 1994; Mann 1986, 1993). By creating institutions and citizens that share identities and are linked through particular practices, the state makes it possible to do things in ways which had previously not been possible. In Hirschmann's terms, the 'passions' of the feudal and absolutist warfare states with their hierarchies dominated by militarized aristocracies are replaced by the 'interests' of the urban bourgeoisie in wealth, economic growth, and the victory of 'doux commerce' (Fourcade and Healy 2007; Hirschman 1977, 1982).

Of course, this does not mean that vested interests will not try to limit the emergence of new ideas, suggested political reforms, innovative new products, the emergence of new entrepreneurial groupings, new associations of individuals, new publics, etc. but it does suggest that as these freedoms were established, rival groupings within society evolved ways of engaging with each other in ways which were not simply zero-sum distributional conflicts but were also ways of increasing and improving performance and outcomes.

Under certain conditions, related to the balance of forces between different classes and groups in a society, these internal transformations in the constitutional order create spaces for deliberation among rivalling actors, making it possible for them to mutually civilize each other, transform opposed interests into integrative synergies, and find novel ways of collaboration. In this way, a production-apparatus for the dynamic search and construction of institutional complementarities can come into place. Lock-in, path dependency, and the vicious cycle of redistributional politics is complemented to varying degrees by a dynamic of consensual institutional change and economic restructuring.

From this perspective, therefore, the competitive position of a country might well in the short run be dependent on a stable state equilibrium with strong complementarities between existing institutions, but in the longer run it will rather be the country's ability to modify, recombine, and change its institutions to form new, more dynamic complementarities as situations change that determines its capability to maintain its competitiveness. And here the constitutional ordering of the politics of a society may become much more important than we have noticed so far. We can distinguish a number of different examples of these processes.

For example, it is of interest to note that authors are increasingly showing how forms of political representation shape and structure politics and the capacities of the state. Of particular interest has been the degree to which different interest groups or political coalitions take into consideration their adversaries and rivals (Cusack, Iversen, and Soskice 2010; Iversen and Soskice 2006; Iversen and Stephens 2008). Politics will have very different logics for integrating different interests under a majoritarian electoral system than in one with proportional representation, where frequent minority governments have to compromise with a complex opposition. At lower levels of the polity there might be huge differences between, on the one hand, pluralist systems where professional groups are competing under shifting majoritarian governments for social space, and on the other hand, neo-corporatist structures of proportional electoral systems in which actors have to come to terms with and mutually agree on making sense of political reforms that have come out of muddy political compromises around minority governments. If the constitution furthermore secures localities—municipalities, counties, etc—autonomy and taxation rights, whatever agreements have been negotiated nationally need to be reaffirmed and adapted at local levels through processes of open deliberation. It is clear that in certain contexts this can go so far as to create a stalemate, for example as seems to have happened in Belgium where differences between language groups have become so embedded in rights and privileges that the national state seems increasingly incapable of functioning in a coherent way.

Majoritarian electoral representation may result in punctuated equilibria in which power swings dramatically between different interests, reducing possibilities for collaboration and negotiation and increasing the use of coercive top-down mechanisms to reproduce or change institutions. Thus, in both the US and the UK, the victories of the Right in the late 1970s and early 1980s enabled an imposition of certain neo-liberal institutional changes with consequent changes in the patterns of employment, inequality, and power, even in the face of substantial opposition. Mobilizing to reform institutions in this context tends to occur in punctuated cycles, where the possibility of incorporating rival groups is limited and electoral politics undermines continuity and consensual negotiation in processes of change and adaptation.

In Nordic countries, on the other hand, with proportional electoral systems and the absence of a strong Christian Democratic party, the whole society is set up for a myriad of deliberations and negotiations at a multiplicity of levels. Political reforms generally take into consideration much broader sections of social groupings, which is why reforms are less clear. This has a number of effects. First, it has the consequence that there is no authoritative interpretation of what an institution actually means; institutional ambiguity is, so to speak, written into the very existence of institutions. Secondly, hardly at any level will it be possible to change an institution without taking into consideration the roles, interests, and prospects of others. In this way, deliberation almost by definition becomes a search for finding mutually benefitting complementarities by which identities and interests of participants may be changed in a mutual processes of re-construction. Such figurations therefore have a tendency to function in an inclusive way, but in different ways across sectors and localities of society. Iversen and Stephens (2008) suggest that in countries with proportional electoral systems and a strong Christian Democratic party, there are similarities to the Scandinavian model but also some differences, in that the main focus is on disagreements amongst those who are already included in the coalition while ignoring the interests of groupings outside the coalition (see also the work of Esping-Andersen 1996; Esping-Andersen 1999; also the chapter by Crouch in this volume). Jobs, access to training, regulation of rules and roles, etc. happens for those that are included in the coalition and new, emergent groups, publics, and interests may have a very difficult set of barriers to overcome if they want to make changes in the institutional architecture of a country. These three types of regimes therefore structure the process of experimentation and change differently.

This analysis reveals how different institutional legacies shape the capacity of actors to experiment and institutions to evolve, even in societies with similar levels of economic development and state structures. A crucial aspect of this process in the current era concerns the way in which the welfare state becomes knitted to production to broaden and deepen competitive advantages. Sabel et al. 2010 have expressed the challenge of current changes in labour markets to welfare states in this way:

> The welfare state is in transition.... Underlying the relatively recent but widespread realisation of the requirement for life-long learning for diverse kinds of students, and the increasing emphasis in policy discussion on skill development in 'active' labour market policies for different groups at risk of exclusion, is the recognition that to safeguard social solidarity, a welfare state must today provide effective enabling or capacitating services, tailored to particular needs, to equip individuals and families to mitigate risks against which they cannot be reliably insured. The shift away from insurance and towards skill-based risk mitigation, moreover, can increase the productivity of the economy as well as its capacity for innovation: the increased availability of skills makes firms more flexible, allowing them to undertake novel projects that would have previously overtaxed their ability to respond to unfamiliar situations.... To the extent that increases in individual skill levels reshape the labour market and the reshaped labour market influences the organisation and strategy of firms the shift towards a welfare state based on capacitating services of each can contribute to the prosperity of all (Sabel, Saxenian, Miettinen, Kristensen, and Hautamäki 2010)

Hardly any country can be said to have built such a welfare state but it is relatively easy to perceive that efforts at the creation of active labour market policies in Denmark and the other Scandinavian societies suggest a move towards them, in contrast for example to welfare state reform in the UK which remains driven more by cost considerations. For example, there is no doubt that there is a strong circle of self-re-enforcement (or complementarity) between the evolution of highly decentralized learning organizations in industry and the high level of public social service provision in the Nordic countries. Social services have made it much more possible for blue-collar workers to take part in an unpredictable working life, where content, location and speed of job assignments often change. Social services in a way have elevated the average worker to take part in an increasingly difficult working life that again has made it possible for industry and the public sector to organize in novel ways (Kristensen and Lilja 2011). But as industry advances along the path sketched above, the need for enabling services becomes both more and more advanced and dependent on the single individual employee, and therefore such a path of industrial strategy is only possible if the public sector is able to constantly innovate and continuously improve these services, both in terms of their level of advancement and in terms of tailoring them for individual needs. To create an innovative public sector that is able to move with private industry is one of the foremost challenges that confront the Nordic countries, but it is a path along which these states seem set. Comparative studies of the welfare state in advanced economies such as those being conducted by Crouch (see his chapter in this book) show that there remain very distinctive forms of welfare states in Europe, North America, and Australasia, and they respond in particular ways to the current changes, redistributing risks across genders, across generational groups, across localities, and across nations in new more complex ways.

In the context of twenty-first century capitalisms as a whole, however, debates about the link between the welfare state and the economic system are of limited interest. These European ideas of the state as legitimate, as neutral to some degree, as acting as a social protector, and as evolving to being a power container capable of facilitating the development of its citizens are not necessarily appropriate in other contexts. Perhaps the closest to these models are in Central and, to a degree, Eastern Europe. The struggles for independent statehood in Eastern and Central Europe took different paths in terms of the role of old elites versus the emergence of new groups ((Stark and Bruszt 1998; Szelenyi and Wilks 2010); similarly the degree to which the Soviet bloc states had destroyed previously existing forms of civil society clearly differed, for example the role of the Catholic Church and trade unionism in Poland. The sorts of institutions which had survived in civil society under dictatorial and undemocratic regimes varied and responded differently as these states were replaced or opened up by the existing elites. Some of these states had strong legitimacy in the immediate aftermath of the decline of the Soviet system but had to sustain this in the face of policy pressures to follow free markets and thus dismantle institutions without replacing them with anything other than foreign investment, mainly from the large MNCs described earlier. As a result they became fragile and dependent on overseas investors, for whom the investment was often temporary and not fixed. Resulting boom and bust periods led to the rise of new forms of politics often centred round nationalism and conservatism, where the use of the state to develop institutions that could support industrial development was financially impossible and ideologically ruled out. Further into Eastern Europe, where the old elite hung on to power in many ways, foreign investment was more scarce, state support for industries was retained to a degree, whilst potentially profitable opportunities in raw materials were controlled through the state and its tightly connected business elites.

At the other extreme, we can identify contexts where state capacities of any sort are either non-existent, for example in 'failed' states, or states that are so lacking in resources or legitimacy that they cannot effectively negotiate with or influence either civil society or the economy except through force of arms and occasional bursts of violence (Hall 2010). In other circumstances, civil society may be strongly organized through ethnic or religious identities that marginalize outsiders; where these groups are able to capture the state, they make it weak as an independent force for defending the rule of law, property rights, and democracy. Instead the state comes to serve the interests of the dominant groups in civil society, and others seek to protect themselves from the state. Division and conflict is built into the state and civil society, requiring coercion and control to sustain institutional compromises. Efforts to change institutions become forms of rebellion and subjected to harsh punishment. There is a lock-in effect that makes the development of experimental change processes unlikely. Instead, such societies are likely in the current period to see the build-up of internal pressure (from marginalized groups for some sort of inclusion) and of external pressure (as the inability to modernize through engaging the population worsens the terms of trade and pushes the society backwards in terms of economic development, though this pressure can be resisted where plentiful raw material resources generate a steady stream of wealth and income for those at the top of the society as in parts of Africa and the Middle East).

Finally, one can identify those societies where the state has become the dominant force in a society and it is state action which is necessary to initiate institutional change and reform, but where the legitimacy of the European state has not become embedded. In these contexts, therefore, state action is almost invariably along the lines of the 'capstone' model, where actions from the top can have drastic effects on citizens but cannot in general shape civil society through a process of mutual constitution. Instead, the state incorporates certain sections of the civil society through patronage, through providing support, through favouritism, whilst other sections remain outside. Institutions in the sense of regularized patterns of interaction may emerge or spring up separate from state sponsorship, creating tensions between different parts of the society. Resulting differences in rates of economic growth exacerbate local and regional inequalities and lead to outbreaks of sporadic violence and rebellion and occasionally more institutionalized demands for local autonomy. Such states may have advantages. They may be able to institute plans for reform and change rapidly, though these may run into resistance in civil society and peter out. This depends in part on the degree to which the capstone state has found ways to control citizens and force them into forms of obedience. The Arab Spring of 2011 and its aftermath reveal the nature and complexity of these inter-twined struggles over democratic legitimacy, control of the state, and processes of economic development capable of overcoming extremes of wealth and inequality.

The variety of state–civil society–economy relations which exist has therefore substantially broadened since 1989. In particular, in terms of developing economic organization, this is no longer a competition solely between democratic welfare states which share similar problems in terms of maintaining the expectations of their citizens for a decent life whilst competing intensively in a global market. Most of the rest of the world has never had anything like the European welfare state; many states have never been used to the idea of democratic mandates. These 'new' states start from different positions, and the challenges which they face in contexts of crisis and uncertainty are huge.

Countries like Brazil, South Africa, and India, for example, are moving forward economically but with a huge population of urban and rural poor, existing in complex interdependencies with the new rich. Maintaining stability, particularly in the urban areas, appears continually problematic as it does to a degree in parts of China, particularly inland, where the decline of state-owned enterprises is not compensated for yet by the rise of private firms. Nevertheless these states are rapidly building their capacities for development through investing in education and skills, infrastructure, and technology. Thus twenty-first century capitalism will involve more intense competition between different forms of capitalism where shaping institutions to support firms and particular business models will be a central task for states but a task which they will approach with very different sets of resources and capabilities. This in turn has a further consequence for firms exploring and experimenting with new forms of global organization since they face very different environments with very different degrees of stability and institutional capabilities.

Finally, it is worth making explicit our view that whatever convergence or homogenizing tendencies exist in the current context, there are also very powerful forces that are keeping things different across different institutional contexts. Firms themselves sustain these differences because they often seek to strengthen distinctive local resources. Populations remain primarily oriented to their state to provide the framework for welfare, economic growth, and legitimacy. State actors themselves seek to emphasize their distinctiveness. This concern with difference goes alongside the development of metrics to measure how and to what extent countries and firms perform on an increasingly wide set of indicators. Comparative benchmarking is perhaps one of the most significant means for governance in the world economy of the future (Pedersen 2010; Sabel and Zeitlin 2010; Zeitlin, Pochet, and Magnusson 2005). In many cases it is by these comparative metrics that nations and firms learn about their positioning in the global economic system, the problems they encounter, and the solutions which might be available. Central in this movement has of course been the financial system, which has institutionalized new codes of accounting and financial reporting, ways of measuring how well firms are benchmarking and how to define best practices. But a similar movement has also happened among firms along with their move towards outsourcing and open innovation. Certification—of quality, environmental effects, occupational health and safety, corporate social responsibility—all make it much easier for potential partners to assess the risks of new relationships. Together with these more and more widespread certifications, firms engage voluntarily in competitions about who makes the best product-designs, who has created the best work-place, who constitutes the most socially responsible or most sustainable corporation, etc. (see also Thompson in this volume). In many ways such benchmarking and competitions help firms to cast doubt on their existing practices and constitute independent triggers for searching for novel ways to advance and develop. In a way, the metrics constitute the horizon for what development is all about. But metrics are about difference, measuring and learning from difference. In this sense, we expect to see a twenty-first century characterized by increasingly complex and diverse firm structures linked across multiple institutional settings where states try, in the different ways available to them, to maintain their institutional distinctiveness.

Conclusions: capitalism, capitalisms, markets, and institutions

The argument of this chapter is that we are entering a third phase of comparative institutionalist analysis. This third phase is likely to be characterized by, first, greater emphasis on the initiatives of actors to reshape their firms and institutions, secondly, greater concentration on the internationalization of economic activity and the variety of ways in which this is achieved and, thirdly, greater concentration on how different forms of state establish conditions for institutional change and experimentation.

If we were to summarize this position, then we hold to the importance of national capitalisms; there are plural forms of capitalism which continue to reflect institutional legacies and path dependencies. However, we also hold to the idea of capitalism in the singular in a number of ways. First, the actions of firms are interconnected by their participation in a global system of capitalism where firms compete across borders by organizing international chains of production, innovation, and value distribution. Secondly, and related to this, is the idea that capitalism has created a global marketplace; this is not to say that in each and every context, firms from anywhere in the world compete on an equal basis. That is clearly not the case so long as national governments still play a major role in setting rules about markets. Nevertheless, there is increasing interconnectedness, not just between firms but between markets. Thirdly, it is possible to identify at the level of an ideal type the characteristics of capitalism as an economic system.

In his recent work, Streeck has emphasized this point of 'taking capitalism seriously' (Streeck 2010, 2011). In his view there are certain characteristics which can be identified with capitalism as an ideal type of economic system, and provide a drive and direction to the process of capitalist competition. This is important for a number of reasons. First, as in classic Marxist texts, it pushes us to recognize the limits to experimentation in the terms which have been discussed in this chapter. Secondly, Streeck is quite explicit in his view that capitalism involves a drive towards increased commodification and marketization of social life and the emptying out in the process of moral limits and moral rules. Here he connects back to Polanyi and the argument that as marketization grows, so society seeks to find ways to protect itself against the consequences of that process. Thus the 'dual movement' becomes a central dynamic.

It is clear that there is a temptation to displace the idea of capitalism as Streeck is seeking to revive it by the idea of institutions. Thus, one side of Polanyi's dual movement, the side of institutions, becomes the centre of attention and what may be described as the 'dark side' of capitalism seems to have been domesticated and detoxified. As the events of the last few years should have shown, this would be a big mistake. Institutions have not controlled capitalism: the dominance of neo-liberalism made sure of that, but it tried to justify this in terms of bringing greater efficiency to markets. What it did not do was to reduce the tendency of capitalism to create crises which occurred with increasing regularity from the 1980s up to the biggest one of all in 2008, the consequences of which look as if they will be working themselves out for some years yet.

It is relatively obvious that central to these processes has been the changing role of finance in twenty-first century capitalisms. Early discussions of comparative institutional analysis saw the financial sector as the 'handmaiden' of productive industry, supplying funds and money transmission services to firms in order to enable them to develop on various terms their strategies. The shift which occurred over the last twenty years towards what Boyer termed 'a finance driven regime of accumulation' or what others have described as the 'financialization of the economy' was treated in part as an outcome of existing processes inside liberal market economy forms of capitalism; in so far as it affected other economies, this was conceived primarily in terms of the rise of shareholder value and pressures on existing systems of corporate governance and firm strategy and structure arising therefrom, and the capacity of particular firms and societies to resist or adapt to these pressures.

However, the impact of finance on large firms and productive industry more generally remains profound because of how it facilitates the sorts of restructurings described earlier; however, it does this through the connection to the financial markets where the logics of action have shifted dramatically towards the making of gains from spreads, fees, and speculations on transactions and market movements rather than from lending services provided to non-financial entities. It was the scale of this transaction-based model and the fragile interdependencies which were created that caused the financial crisis. This process of financialization has settled deeply into the structure of firms, the structure of the banking system, and the structure of personal life (through pensions, house prices, credit cards, etc.). It is integrally connected to the phenomena of risk and uncertainty where calculations about credit and debt for governments, firms, and individuals are made. Finance shows us more clearly than anywhere that capitalism red in tooth and claw is still alive and kicking.

In conclusion, we believe it is necessary to recognize both the existence of national capitalisms and capitalism as an ideal type. It is also necessary to see that institutions are part of Polanyi's dual movement, fragile in relation to the impact of crises of capitalism, but fungible in relation to experimentalism. As other authors have noted there is a world of possibilities, but navigating through them to positive outcomes for actors and societies is hugely complex. However, we hold the view that this can be done within our broad schema, which is about creating a new field for comparative economic sociology and political economy. Only by making complex processual analysis of the historical evolution of certain patterns where new institutional and organizational mutations become visible and where dynamic complementarities are detected and analyzed might it be possible to make proper sense of the pragmatic lessons that the world is accumulating. However, the diversity of firms and states in the current era of global competition with a highly financialized core will make this problematic and uncertain. It is in this tension between actors, institutions, firms, competition, and state that the study of capitalism and capitalisms in the twenty-first century needs to be firmly located. The chapters in this book suggest some of the different ways in which that task can be done.

References

Almond, P. and A. Ferner (2006) *American Multinationals in Europe: Managing employment relations across national borders*, Oxford: Oxford University Press.

Amable, B. (2003) *The Diversity of Modern Capitalism*, Oxford: Oxford University Press.

Bair, J. (ed.) (2009) *Frontiers of Commodity Chain Research*, Stanford, Calif.: Stanford University Press.

Bendix, R. (1956) *Work and Authority in Industry: Ideologies of management in the course of industrialization*, New York; London: Wiley; Chapman and Hall.

Boyer, R. (2000) 'Is a Finance-Led Growth Regime a Viable Alternative to Fordism? A preliminary analysis', *Economy and Society*, 29(1): 111–45.

Campbell, J. L. (2004) *Institutional Change and Globalization*, Princeton NJ: Princeton University Press.

——(2010) 'Institututional Reproduction and Change', pp. 87–116 in G. Morgan, J. L. Campbell, C. Crouch, O. K. Pedersen, and R. Whitley (eds) *The Oxford Handbook of Comparative Institutional Analysis*, Oxford: Oxford University Press.

Casper, S. (2007) *Creating Silicon Valley in Europe: Public policy towards new technology industries*, Oxford: Oxford University Press.

——(2010) 'The Comparative Institutional Analysis of Innovation: From Industrial Policy to Knowledge Economy', pp. 335–62 in G. Morgan, J. L. Campbell, C. Crouch, O. K. Pedersen, and R. Whitley (eds) *The Oxford Handbook of Comparative Institutional Analysis*, Oxford: Oxford University Press.

Collinson, S. and G. Morgan (2009) *The Multinational Firm*, Chichester, West Sussex, England; Hoboken, NJ: Wiley.

Crouch, C. (1993) *Industrial Relations and European State Traditions*, Oxford: Clarendon Press.

——(2005) *Capitalist Diversity and Change: Recombinant governance and institutional entrepreneurs*, Oxford: Oxford University Press.

——and Streeck, W. (1997) *Political Economy of Modern Capitalism: Mapping convergence and diversity*, London: Sage.

Cusack, T., T. Iversen, and D. Soskice (2010) Coevolution of Capitalism and Political Representation: The choice of electoral systems, *American Political Science Review* 104(2): 393–403.

Deeg, R. and G. Jackson (2007) 'Towards a More Dynamic Theory of Capitalist Variety', *Socio Economic Review*, 5(1): 149–80.

Dörrenbächer, C. and M. Geppert (2011) *Politics and Power in the Multinational Corporation: The role of institutions, interests and identities*, Cambridge: Cambridge University Press.

Esping-Andersen, G. (1996) *The Three Worlds of Welfare Capitalism*, Cambridge: Polity Press.

——(1999) *Social Foundations of Postindustrial Economies*, Oxford; New York: Oxford University Press.

Fourcade, M. and K. Healy (2007) 'Moral Views of Market Society', *Annual Review of Sociology*, 33: 285–311.

Geppert, M. and M. Mayer (2006) *Global, National and Local Practices in Multinational Companies*, New York: Palgrave Macmillan.

Gereffi, G., J. Humphrey and T. Sturgeon (2005) 'The Governance of Global Value Chains', *Review of International Political Economy*, 12(1): 78–104.

Gereffi, G. A. and M. Korzeniewicz (1994) *Commodity Chains and Global Capitalism*, Westport, Conn: Praeger.

Gilson, R. J., C. F. Sabel, and R. E. Scott (2009) 'Contracting for Innovation: Vertical disintegration and interfirm collaboration', *Columbia Law Review*, 109: 431–52.

Hacker, J. S. and P. Pierson (2010) *Winner-Take-All Politics: How Washington made the rich richer—and turned its back on the middle class*, New York: Simon & Schuster.

Hall, J. (2010) 'State Failure', pp. 587–600 in G. Morgan, J. L. Campbell, C. Crouch, O. K. Pedersen, and R. Whitley (eds) *The Oxford Handbook of Comparative Institutional Analysis*, Oxford: Oxford University Press.

Hall, J. A. (1986) *Powers and Liberties: The causes and consequences of the rise of the West*, Harmondsworth: Penguin in association with Blackwell.

——(1994) *The State: Critical concepts*, London: Routledge.

Hall, P. A. and D. Soskice (2001) *Varieties of Capitalism: The institutional foundations of comparative advantage*, Oxford: Oxford University Press.

Herrigel, G. (2010) *Manufacturing Possibilities. Creative action and industrial recomposition in the United States, Germany and Japan*, Oxford: Oxford University Press.

——and V. Wittke (2005) Varieties of Vertical Disintegration: The global trend towards heterogeneous supply relations and the reproduction of difference in US and German manufacturing, pp. 312–51 in G. Morgan, R. Whitley, and E. Moen (eds) *Changing Capitalisms? Internationalization, institutional change and systems of economic organization*, Oxford: Oxford University Press.

——and J. Zeitlin (2010) 'Inter-Firm Relations in Global Manufacturing: Disintegrated Production and its Globalization', pp. 527–61 in G. Morgan, J. L. Campbell, C. Crouch, O. K. Pedersen, and R. Whitley (eds) *The Oxford Handbook of Comparative Institutional Analysis*, Oxford: Oxford University Press.

Hirschman, A. O. (1977) *The Passion and the Interests*, Princeton NJ: Princeton University Press.

——(1982) 'Rival Interpretations of the Market: Civilizing, destructive or feeble?' *Journal of Economic Literature*, 20: 1463–84.

Hollingsworth, J. R. and R. Boyer (1997) *Contemporary Capitalism: The embeddedness of institutions*, Cambridge: Cambridge University Press.

Iversen, T. and D. Soskice (2006) 'Electoral Institutions and the Politics of Coalitions: Why some democracies redistribute more than others', *American Political Science Review*, 100(2): 165–81.

——and J. D. Stephens (2008) 'Partisan Politics, the Welfare State, and Three Worlds of Human Capital Formation', *Comparative Political Studies*, 41(4–5): 600–37.

Jackson, G. (2010) 'Actors and Institutions', pp. 63–86 in G. Morgan, J. L. Campbell, C. Crouch, O. K. Pedersen, and R. Whitley (eds) *The Oxford Handbook of Comparative Institutional Analysis*, Oxford: Oxford University Press.

Kenney, M. (2000) *Understanding Silicon Valley: The anatomy of an entrepreneurial region.* Stanford, Calif.; [Great Britain]: Stanford University Press.

Kristensen, P. H. and K. Lilja (2011) *Nordic Capitalisms and Globalization: New forms of economic organization and welfare institutions*, Oxford: Oxford University Press.

——and J. Zeitlin (2005) *Local Players in Global Games: The strategic constitution of a multinational corporation*, Oxford: Oxford University Press.

Mahoney, J. and K. Thelen (eds) (2010) *Explaining Institutional Change: Ambiguity, agency and power*, Cambridge: Cambridge University Press.

Mann, M. (1986) *The Sources of Social Power*,Vol. 1, Cambridge: Cambridge University Press.

——(1993) *The Sources of Social Power*, Vol. 2, Cambridge: Cambridge University Press.

Maurice, M., F. Sellier, and J.-J. Silvestre (1986) *The Social Foundations of Industrial Power: A comparison of France and Germany*, Cambridge, Mass.: MIT Press.

Milward, A. S., G. Brennan, and F. Romero (2000) *The European Rescue of the Nation-State* (2nd ed.), London: Routledge.

Morgan, G. (2007) 'National Business Systems Research: Progress and prospects', *Scandinavian Journal of Management*, 23(2): 127–45.

——(2009) 'Globalization, Multinationals and Institutional Diversity', *Economy and Society*, 38(4): 580–605.

——J. L. Campbell, C. Crouch, O. K. Pedersen, and R. Whitley (2010) *The Oxford Handbook of Comparative Institutional Analysis*, Oxford: Oxford University Press.

——P. H. Kristensen, and R. Whitley (2001) *The Multinational Firm: Organizing across institutional and national divides*, Oxford: Oxford University Press.

Pedersen, O. K. (2010) 'Institutional Competitiveness: How nations came to compete', pp. 625–57 in G. Morgan, J. L. Campbell, C. Crouch, O. K. Pedersen, and R. Whitley (eds) *The Oxford Handbook of Comparative Institutional Analysis*, Oxford: Oxford University Press.

Polanyi, K. (2001) *The Great Transformation: The political and economic origins of our time* (2nd Beacon pbk. ed.), Boston, Mass.: Beacon Press.

Quack, S., G. Morgan, and R. Whitley (2000) *National Capitalisms, Global Competition, and Economic Performance*, Amsterdam/Philadelphia: John Benjamins Publishing Company.

Rodrik, D. (2007) *One Economics, Many Recipes: Globalization, institutions, and economic growth*, Princeton, N.J.; Woodstock: Princeton University Press.

Ruggie, J. G. (1998) *Constructing the World Polity: Essays on international institutionalization*, London; New York: Routledge.

Sabel, C. F., A. Saxenian, R. Miettinen, P. H. Kristensen, and J. Hautamäki (2010) *Individualized Service Provision as the Key to the New Welfare State: Lessons from special education in Finland*, Helsinki: SITRA.

——and J. Zeitlin (2010) *Experimentalist Governance in the European Union: Towards a new architecture*, Oxford: Oxford University Press.

Shonfield, A. (1965) *Modern Capitalism: The changing balance of public and private power*, London: Oxford University Press.

Stark, D. and L. Bruszt (1998) *Postsocialist Pathways: Transforming politics and property in East Central Europe*, Cambridge England; New York: Cambridge University Press.

Streeck, W. (1992) *Social Institutions and Economic Performance: Studies of industrial relations in advanced capitalist economies*, London: Sage.

——(2009) *Re-Forming Capitalism: Institutional change in the German political economy*, Oxford: Oxford University Press.

——(2010) 'Institutions in History: Bringing capitalism back in', pp. 659–86 in G. Morgan, J. L. Campbell, C. Crouch, O. K. Pedersen, and R. Whitley (eds) *The Oxford Handbook of Comparative Institutional Analysis*, Oxford: Oxford University Press.

——(2011) 'Taking Capitalism Seriously: Towards an institutionalist approach to contemporary political economy', *Socio-Economic Review*, 9(1): 137–67.

——and K. A. Thelen (2005) *Beyond Continuity: Institutional change in advanced political economies*, Oxford: Oxford University Press.

Szelenyi, I. and K. Wilks (2010) 'Institutional Transformation in European Post-Communist Regimes', pp. 565–86 in G. Morgan, J. L. Campbell, C. Crouch, O. K. Pedersen, and R. Whitley (eds) *The Oxford Handbookf of Comparative Institutional Analysis*, Oxford: Oxford University Press.

Thelen, K. (2009) 'Institutional Change in Advanced Political Economies', *British Journal of Industrial Relations*, 47: 471–98.

Whitford, J. (2005) *The New Old Economy: Networks, institutions, and the organizational transformation of American manufacturing*, Oxford: Oxford University Press.

Whitley, R. (1992) *Business Systems in East Asia: Firms, markets and societies*, London: Sage.

——(1999) *Divergent Capitalisms: The social structuring and change of business systems*, Oxford: Oxford University Press.

——(2010) 'Changing Competition Models in Market Economies', pp. 363–97 in G. Morgan, J. L. Campbell, C. Crouch, O. K. Pedersen, and R. Whitley (eds) *The Oxford Handbook of Comparative Institutional Analysis*, Oxford: Oxford University Press.

Zeitlin, J., P. Pochet, and L. Magnusson (2005) *The Open Method of Co-ordination in Action: The European employment and social inclusion strategies*, Bruxelles; Oxford: P.I.E.-Peter Lang.

Section 1

Political Authority and the Nation State in Twenty-First Century Capitalism

2

Trading Blocs in the Twenty-First Century

Complexity and Consequences

Francesco Duina

Introduction

Trading blocs such as the EU, NAFTA, Mercosur, and APEC have become an important feature of the changing international political-economic order. Without question, most have similar basic objectives: above all, the liberalization of trade. Yet, they also *differ* on several important dimensions, ranging from their specific economic objectives to their levels of legitimacy. These differences reflect, in part, the plethora of *factors driving integration,* from 'rational' ones—such as national responses to faltering multilateralism—to more sociological ones—such as taken-for-granted assumptions about what modern legitimate governments should pursue. Unsurprisingly, given all this, integration has at once progressed at a different *pace* in different blocs and generated significant *challenges* for the member states.

All this suggests that trading blocs are complex projects that defy simple description or generalizations. I explore this complexity in Sections I–IV of this chapter. In Section V, I reflect on its multifaceted implications for the regional expansion of economic actors and the rise of the international economy.

1. Dimensions of difference

Trading blocs occur whenever two or more nations agree to liberalize trade across their borders via the removal of a combination of tariff and non-tariff barriers (NTBs).[1] According to the WTO, nearly 200 blocs were in force at the start of 2010.[2] If blocs currently being negotiated, signed but not yet in force, and those in the proposal stages are taken into account, the figure exceeds 400. With the exception of perhaps fewer than fifteen countries (for instance, Madagascar and San Marino), every nation on earth belongs to one or more trading blocs. Some countries, such as Switzerland, participate in over twenty. Others, such as the United States and Japan, belong to approximately ten. The majority participate in five or fewer. The result is an intricate pattern of relationships that is quite difficult to capture in any simple graphic or diagrammatic depiction (Bhagwati 2008: 63). The sudden growth in the number of these blocs—most came into existence in the 1990s and 2000s—has made matters even more difficult to track. In Asia, for instance, there was a single bloc in 1995 and a stunning sixty-one by 2010 (Wignaraja and Lazaro 2010: 8).

Trading blocs have generated important new regional realities. Any discussion of capitalism in the twenty-first century should therefore examine these blocs. The first step for doing so is to grasp and make sense of their variety: while they are all manifestations of a desire to liberalize trade among nations, major differences set them apart. Four dimensions of difference are especially important: economic objectives, frameworks and policies for the attainment of those objectives, political purposes, and levels of legitimacy.

Economic objectives

The most obvious difference concerns the stated economic objectives. All blocs aim at trade liberalization, but the extent to which liberalization should be pursued varies dramatically. Recall that goods, capital, services, and labour are the essential components of any economy. Given this, we can distinguish among four basic types of blocs, ordered from the least to the most wide-reaching: free trade areas, customs unions, common markets, and economic and monetary unions.

In the lightest and most common cases of integration—free trade areas—member states agree to liberalize trade primarily for goods. Selected services and capital are also often included—as is the case for NAFTA, the ASEAN Free Trade Area (AFTA) along with the relevant side agreements, and the European Free Trade Association (EFTA). To be in line with WTO regulation, free trade

[1] Some blocs are agreements between already-constituted blocs (Mercosur–EU, for instance) or between one or more nations and a bloc (ASEAN–Australia–New Zealand, for instance). For the sake of simplicity, throughout this chapter I refer to blocs as agreements among nations. All of the empirical examples I consider, moreover, involve blocs with more than two member states—for these tend to be the most important.

[2] For up-to-date figures, see the WTO's database on regional trading agreements: http://rtais.wto.org/UI/PublicAllRTAList.aspx

areas (much like other blocs) must comply with General Agreement on Tariffs and Trade (GATT) Article XXIV, which asks that the reduction of tariffs should cover 'substantially all trade' and that member states not adopt protectionist measures towards third parties that are on the whole more restrictive than those in place prior to the bloc's formation. The term 'substantially' leaves open the possibility of significant exceptions. Many experts agree that it implies a reduction of at least 85 per cent of existing tariffs among the member states, but this is disputed (Wignaraja and Lazaro 2010: 14). Thus, partly as a result of this, we observe considerable variation across blocs in terms of the percentage of goods actually moving freely across national borders, though textiles and agriculture continue to be among the most protected sectors in most blocs (Suominen 2009: 38). We also observe varying compliance with the requirement that member states not increase their overall protectionist stances vis-à-vis third parties, with free trade areas showing lesser protectionist tendencies than customs unions or common markets.

Customs unions are similar to free trade areas but introduce common external tariffs (CETs) and possibly other trade policies vis-à-vis non-member countries. The logic behind CETs is to prevent producers in any one member state from having access to cheaper materials than producers in any other member state—something that would jeopardize internal trade much like a tariff barrier among the member states. CETs also give the member states a coordinated way of protecting themselves against foreign competitors and markets, though in principle only when in compliance with GATT Article XXIV. A good example of a customs union is the Southern African Customs Union. There also exist blocs, such as the East African Community, which, on their way to becoming common markets or more, become customs unions as an official stepping stone.

Common markets take aim at all four key elements of an economy—goods, capital, services, and labour—and rely as well on CETs. Given their ambitious coverage, they are fairly rare. At the same time, some of the most important trading blocs in the world—that is, Mercosur, the Andean Community (CAN), and the EU—are common markets. Economic and monetary unions encompass all the elements of common markets plus the adoption of a single currency and coordination in key macroeconomic policy areas. A portion of the EU—the eurozone—and the West African Economic and Monetary Union offer examples.

Frameworks and policies

There is no simple formula for the pursuit of economic integration. Given two blocs with identical objectives, those charged with translating vision into reality have at their disposal a variety of instruments. We observe important overlaps but also variations in those instruments across blocs.

In virtually all blocs, officials rely on the reduction or outright elimination of tariffs on goods. The most critical differences here concern the schedule for that reduction. GATT Article XXIV specifies only that the tariff reduction 'plan or schedule for its [a bloc's] formation is within a reasonable length of time'. Thus, in some blocs the reduction is in theory immediate (i.e. Singapore–Australia). In others, it should occur within five years (i.e. South Korea–United States). In yet others, the period can extend to a decade or more (i.e. NAFTA). Interestingly, Asian blocs are generally rather aggressive with their timing (Suominen 2009). Moreover, within a given bloc, different schedules are likely to apply to different industrial sectors.

NTBs include quotas, subsidies, fiscal incentives, and other instruments designed to protect from foreign competition or simply help in financial terms particular sectors of the economy. As tariffs decline, NTBs acquire increased significance (Helble, Shepherd, and Wilson 2009). Moreover, NTBs are key for the liberalization of trade in services, capital, and labour. Blocs differ greatly in the sorts of NTBs that they tackle—and these differences are not simply correlated with the stated objectives of blocs (establishing a free trade area, for instance, instead of a common market). We also note, again, certain geographical patterns whereby, for example, blocs in the Americas are more likely to focus on NTBs than those in Asia (Suominen 2009: 44).

Another type of NTBs are regulatory differences across member states in important areas such as the environment, workers' rights, product safety and quality, and antitrust. These differences can translate into cost asymmetries that can undermine trade. Regulatory harmonization can be a daunting task. In some blocs, officials have embraced it (for instance, the EU and Mercosur), but in others they have opted to rely on the principle of mutual recognition (as with EFTA and NAFTA). In yet other instances (AFTA, for example), officials have adopted a mixed approach (Duina 2006a).

These instrumental differences are accompanied by variation in another area: the organizational architecture of blocs. Some official body or combination of actors has to produce laws or agreements on tariffs and NTBs. Compliance must be monitored. Conflicting claims inevitably arise and must be addressed. What have countries agreed upon as the appropriate organizational structures for managing these tasks? As Table 2.1 indicates with reference to ten representative blocs, officials have chosen primarily between intergovernmental and supranational institutions (Hancock 2009). In the former case, delegation of authority is given to representatives of the member states—whose mission remains the advancement of their countries' interests. Bargaining takes place with national interests in mind. In the latter case, individuals from the member states are charged with safeguarding and advancing the

Table 2.1. The organizational architecture of blocs

		Supranational Institutions		
		None	One	Two or More
# of Permanent Institutions	Three or More	*No example exists*	CARICOM, SADC	EU, CAN, Mercosur
	Two or Less	NAFTA, EFTA, AFTA, APEC	COMESA	*No example exists*

bloc's interests and objectives. As Table 2.1 also shows, member states have made different choices about the appropriate number of institutions charged with advancing integration.

As is well known, the EU sports an impressive supranational architecture and numerous institutions. But CAN, with its three supranational bodies (a court of justice, parliament, and commission) is not very different, at least on paper (Alter and Helfer 2010). With its many institutions (including a new parliament and a court of justice), Mercosur belongs to the same group. By contrast, blocs like NAFTA, EFTA, AFTA, and APEC are intergovernmental (Capling and Nossal 2009; Narine 2004). They are also reliant on very few institutions to manage their affairs. Other blocs lie in between these two ends of the spectrum. These include the South African Development Community (SADC), the Caribbean Community (CARICOM), and the Common Market for Eastern and Southern Africa (COMESA), all of which have one supranational body (a court of justice). They differ in terms of number of institutions, with COMESA having the fewest.

Political purposes

The primary goal of virtually all trading blocs is economic. Yet, when one examines the foundational treaties or later agreements, explicit references to political objectives often appear, as is the case for instance with SADC, where security, peace, and the pursuit of 'common political values' are recognized as primary objectives (Article 5 of SADC Treaty). Sometimes trading blocs are formed in the context of pre-existing political agreements, as has happened in ASEAN with the adoption of AFTA in 1992. In those cases, the full purpose of a trading bloc can only be understood in reference to those agreements. Additionally, in all cases, blocs have unofficial political purposes that cannot, or need not, be put into formal writing. Thus, any given bloc is likely to have multiple, complex, and sometimes evolving sets of political objectives. Easy categorizations are therefore impossible, though it is probably the case that deeper forms of economic integration often come with more ambitious political aspirations. We proceed below by discussing some of the most salient political purposes and the blocs where they are most readily observable.

We can distinguish between internal and external political purposes. One of the most common *internal* purposes is the coordination of government policies in sensitive areas such as migration, terrorism, labour markets, and industrial development. Coordination can include data collection and sharing, joint identification and articulation of problems, and cooperation on devising solutions. Aware that real benefits can result from these sorts of initiatives, member states at times pursue economic integration with the hope that it will lead to coordination in other areas later on. The EU and Mercosur are cases in point (Jelin 1999). In other instances, policy coordination emerges as a new goal, as happened for instance among members of APEC in 2001 in the area of security with their adoption of the APEC Leaders Statement on Counter-Terrorism and subsequent initiatives (Despeignes 2004).

But more basic political objectives are sometimes on the minds of member state leaders. In Africa and Asia, stable and democratic countries have often worried about the possibility of government breakdowns or dictatorships in neighbouring countries. In South America, Paraguay comes to mind. Poorer, much smaller, and with a higher likelihood to revert back to dictatorships than its neighbours, Paraguay was invited to join Mercosur partly as a way to give Argentina and Brazil influence over its political system (Hakim 1996). Similar arguments have been made for NAFTA in the case of Mexico (McConnell and MacPherson 1994: 170). Lastly, the rapid eastward enlargement of the EU after the collapse of the Soviet Union was seen by many as a way of 'locking in' the newly freed but still potentially volatile countries.

Related to these fears is yet another political objective: the prevention of wars among the member states. Historically, countries with very interdependent economies have been less likely to go to war with each other than countries with less in common. The founding of the EU reflected European fears that Germany might one day cause trouble again in the continent (Milward 1992).

Some of the weightiest political considerations, however, have to do with *external* political purposes. Countries—especially poorer or smaller ones—view integration as a valuable pooling of resources to face external geopolitical threats. Caribbean countries established CARICOM in the 1970s with the expressed objective of coordinating their foreign policies in a Cold War context where, individually, they counted for little. In Asia, countries have pursued economic integration to strengthen their position vis-à-vis other blocs or powerful countries (McConnell and MacPherson 1994: 167; Switky 2000).

Legitimacy

Legitimacy is in the eye of the beholder. When it comes to blocs, two very different types of beholders exist: citizens and actors (organizations, political parties, associations, etc.) inside a bloc, and those outside (other nation states, other blocs, international organizations, etc.). Even allowing for this, it is fair to suggest that some blocs enjoy overall more legitimacy than others—with the variation being a function, among other things, of the objectives, history, institutional efficiency, compliance rates, and recent success of those blocs.

NAFTA, the EU, Mercosur, and APEC are perhaps among the most legitimate blocs, though of course they face plenty of criticisms as well.[3] Average public support for those agreements (the EU and NAFTA in particular) is relatively high,[4] while, at the international level, officials from other governments and blocs take those blocs seriously and seek to maintain good relations with them. CAN, CARICOM, and AFTA probably enjoy less, but nonetheless a real, amount of legitimacy both internally and externally. By contrast, some blocs, such as COMESA and several others in Africa, lack any significant amount of legitimacy (Mistry 2000; West & Central Africa Monitor 2005).

2. Drivers of integration

What has prompted countries all over the globe to establish regional trading blocs? From a substantive angle, we can distinguish between variables active at the global and regional levels (Farrell 2005: 2). Some analysts view blocs as responses to failure by the WTO and multilateralism more generally to further the causes of free trade or as defensive moves against the threats of an emerging global economy and global instability (Sbragia 2008; Bhagwati 2008). Other analysts, by contrast, point to dynamics within regions—typically the interests of local business and political actors, and economic complementarities (Mattli 1999). Such distinction may not be very useful since global and regional-level variables always interact with each other. A more incisive approach may prove more fruitful.

Scholars of various intellectual orientations—rational choice theory, realists, neo-institutionalists, constructivists, and others—have articulated various accounts of what drives regional integration. By and large, we can group them

[3] In NAFTA, for instance, the Zapatista movement in Mexico was launched precisely on the day NAFTA was enacted as a way to protest the agreement. The EU, in turn, is routinely criticized for its 'democratic deficit'.

[4] For data on public support of NAFTA, see Bennett's discussion of what percentages of Americans (58 per cent) and Canadians (66 per cent) perceive NAFTA to be beneficial (2004: 1298), though these numbers have shifted over time (Hall and Nelson 2004).

into two camps. In the first (what we may call the *rationalist* camp), we find those inclined to view national governments and their leaders as calculating actors seeking to maximize the self-interest of their countries or, often more specifically, powerful constituents therein. Consider the words of Andrew Moravcsik in his seminal inter governmentalist analysis of the EU: 'on not a single major issue', Moravcsik wrote in reference to all major agreements in the history of the EU, 'did governments take a position openly opposed by a major peak industrial, financial, or agricultural interest group' (1998: 475–76). On the contrary, those agreements lie on the 'Pareto-frontier', a zone where all decisions 'improve welfare' for the actors involved (1998: 25). A number of prominent international relations scholars have put forth similar claims (Mansfield and Milner 1997; Milner 1997: 77; Haggard 1997: 21, 31), with numerous investigations of single blocs, especially in Latin America (Kaltenthaler and Mora 2002: 90, 92; Sánchez 2004: 31) and North America (Cameron and Tomlin 2000; Mena 2006), offering empirical support.

In the second camp (the *sociological* one), the focus is on dominant models and emulation, unforeseen consequences, cognitive shortcuts, spillover effects, and more. In the EU case, arguments abound about path dependency (Pierson 1996; Ackrill and Kay 2006; Sverdrup 2002; Holzinger and Knill 2002), bureaucratic overreach (Heisenberg and Richmond 2002: 204; Alter 1998: 131), and reinforcing loops between EU institutions and their environments (Sandholtz and Stone Sweet 1998; Bulmer 1998: 373). Evidence on other blocs is also growing (Mayer 1998; Laursen 2003; Dreiling 2001; Malamud 2005). COMESA and CAN, for instance, exhibit institutional characteristics (courts of justice, for instance) which reflect a desire to look legitimate (by emulating the EU) rather than practical or functional considerations (Duina 2010). In Asia, where blocs developed rather late compared to other regions, observers point to the 'domino effect' as a cause for integration (Suominen 2009: 31). In the case of NAFTA, increased—though neither demanded nor expected—coordination, networks, and policy adjustments in the member states have developed as a result of further economic integration (Aspinwall 2009).

The debate will surely continue. For now the conclusion we can draw is quite clear: no simple, single formulation can really account for the past or predict the future of blocs. This, of course, has important implications for both the international economy and business actors, as we shall see later in this chapter.

3. Pace of integration

Any rigorous discussion of the pace of integration in various blocs must take into account the fact that the term 'pace' refers to at least three distinct concepts. Our assessment of any given bloc will be quite different depending on which concept we use.

First, pace can refer to the extent to which formal measures to promote integration have been implemented in practice. Given certain (and surely different across blocs) tariff-reduction schedules and other liberalizing initiatives, for instance, have these been followed on time and applied to all relevant goods? Tariff reduction in NAFTA and CARICOM, for instance, has been overall timely, but the removal of NTBs has proven less punctual (Hall and Nelson 2004; O'Brien and Morano-Foadi 2009). In blocs where regulatory harmonization is required (the EU and Mercosur for example), we see that some countries (i.e. Denmark) have complied quite well with the law and others not (i.e. Greece). This suggests that the pace of integration has been uneven within single blocs. To this, we can add that progress varies across industrial sectors in a given bloc.

A second measure of 'pace' refers to increases over time in the internal movement of goods, capital, services, and labour that have taken place since integration. We are interested here in the practical realization of the ultimate objectives of blocs. Recent analyses show that the huge increase in (well-implemented) trade deals in Asia, such as AFTA, seems to have done little to intra-Asian trade (*Economist* 2009). It would be odd to suggest that the pace of integration there has been impressive. On the other hand, intra-regional trade of goods and investments in NAFTA increased by 300 per cent between 1994 and 2004 (Pastor 2004: 127). Similar observations apply to the EU, of course, but also Mercosur and, to a lesser extent, some of the blocs in Africa, such as SADC and the Economic Community of West African States (Chacha 2008).

Thirdly, and equally importantly, 'pace' can refer to what we may call the addition of further objectives to the original plans for integration. In a free trade area, for instance, member states pleased with progress up to date may opt to pursue a CET. Or industry sectors previously excluded from trade may be taken up for liberalization, as has happened in AFTA. Expansion beyond the original objectives seems to have occurred in the EU, APEC (with its new focus on security), and Mercosur (with its small step towards social security by way of establishing in 2006 the Structural Convergence Fund). It has not happened, by contrast, in NAFTA, though we should note that there private actors, politicians, and government officials have worked in transnational committees, forums, and other formats to seek 'policy coordination' in areas not covered by NAFTA—efforts aimed at the creation of what observers call 'NAFTA-Plus'. The Principles of Cooperation of May 2000 on bankruptcy proceedings for transnational companies is one example (Duina 2006b: 11–12).

These three definitions of 'pace' are not mutually exclusive, of course, and any investigation of the impact of integration on the international economy and economic actors should take into consideration all of them. Any given

Table 2.2. Pace of integration in five blocs*

Bloc	Implementation of agreed-upon integration measures	Increases in intra-regional trade	Expansion beyond original objectives
EU	0	0	+
NAFTA	+	+	–
AFTA	0	–	0
APEC	0	0	0
CAN	0	+	+

* –→ Poor; 0 → Average; + → Impressive

bloc, moreover, can be evaluated in light of all three definitions, as Table 2.2, with its tentative assessment of five representative blocs, suggests.

4. Challenges to nation state integrity

Despite predictions to the contrary, nation states remain the most salient form of political organization in the world. At the same time, the spread of trading blocs has generated real challenges to nation states—even when these blocs have been set up in fully intergovernmental fashion, with limited legal activity and economic objectives, and no explicit political objectives. Unsurprisingly, given all the differences that set blocs apart, no simple overarching formulation of these challenges can be advanced. Instead, three important propositions can be put forth, all, as we shall see later, with implications for economic actors and the international economy.

Legislative autonomy

Blocs have challenged the ability of nation states to control the content and direction of domestic law. The most obvious instances concern blocs where voting processes or judicial proceedings at the regional level can negate the preferences of any given member state (despite the fact that the resulting regional law must be complied with at the national level and is thus of consequence for national law). This happens in the EU because of qualified majority voting in the Council of Ministers, and in blocs with a supranational court of justice (CAN, Mercosur, and the EU, for instance) or other supranational institutions with the power to revise or expand upon, in unforeseen ways, existing regional law.

More subtly, in virtually all blocs integration has been advanced primarily by the executive branches of national governments. Legislative branches have in many cases only ratified key agreements. In the case of major treaties, this is consistent with constitutional provisions and does not amount to a usurpation of the power of legislatures. But in the case where secondary laws are being produced regularly (i.e. CAN, the EU, and COMESA), executive representatives do acquire unusual powers vis-à-vis their legislative counterparts.

There is a third dynamic at work in most blocs: the unintended and unforeseen consequences of regional policies and laws. One of the clearest examples is the expansion of regional law into issue areas not identified nor targeted as relevant to integration—the 'spillover effect' described by neofunctionalists. Other examples are practices and decisions which unexpectedly follow from existing agreements and decisions. This is what happened in NAFTA as a result of chapter 11 (which gives foreign investors at times more power than domestic actors to challenge judicial decisions and laws) (Duina and Buxbaum 2008), and in the EU in the realm of social policy (Leibfried and Pierson 1995).

Transnationalization of politics

Politics in nation states has traditionally been primarily a domestic affair. Business, trade unions, special interest groups, and social movements have historically focused on national-level issues: industrial regulation, fiscal policy, social welfare, etc. Moreover, their membership bases have been domestic. Regional integration has altered matters on both fronts: both the objects of political contention and the actors pursuing them are increasingly regional. New transnational political spaces have opened up, with potentially major implications for economic actors and the rise of a global economy.

Examples abound. In October of 1996, union leaders from the four Mercosur member states established the Coordinadora de Centrales Sindicales del Cono Sur: a 'unified movement of power' fighting against the 'neoliberal' mission of Mercosur (Calloni 1996; La Jornada 1996). The Coordinadora has, since its founding, actively voiced its members' positions on a variety of fronts related to South American integration. In the EU, women's movements have joined to form several powerful transnational groups to represent their collective interests regionally. These include the European Women's Lobby, the European Women Lawyers Association, and the European Federation of Women Working in the Home (founded in 1990, 2000, and 1983 respectively) (Duina 2006c).

In NAFTA, in turn, research indicates that 'NAFTA has encouraged the founding of tri-national labor alliances to confront common employers as well as less formal linkages around specific problems and broad-based lobbying and mobilization coalitions' (MacDonald 2003). Businesses, in turn, have mobilized together across borders to push for policy convergence in areas not officially targeted by the NAFTA agreements—with policies on transnational bankruptcy proceedings being a good example (Duina 2006b).

Secessionist movements

As the history of the EU suggests (Nielsen and Salk 1998), trading blocs represent 'opportunity structures' (e.g. valuable openings) for the assertion of separatist or autonomous movements. Those movements have leveraged blocs to refine their image and visions for the future, and ultimately bolster their destabilizing claims against their nation states. We need only recall here the Zapatista uprising, which was launched on the very day that NAFTA came into effect, or the considerable leveraging of the Parti Quebecois in Canada and the Scottish National Party of NAFTA and the EU respectively to bolster their credentials as cosmopolitan, open-minded parties looking to free their people away from oppressive nation states. Other examples include the Lega Nord in Italy—for whom the EU represents yet another form of oppression that would justify isolation for Northern Italy from the rest of the country or anything bigger than that—and the Convergència i Unió's embrace of the EU as modern and more in line with Catalonia than Spain.

These tensions and problems assume a very local and specific character, of course. What matters for our purposes, however, is that their occurrence can have very serious implications for economic actors and the evolution of the global economy, as we will see in the coming pages.

5. Significance for economic actors and the international economy

Trading blocs are everywhere. While multilateralism has faltered, blocs continue to grow in numbers and, many, in strength as well. There are good reasons to believe that the twenty-first century will continue to see regionalization, and not globalization, progress the most, despite the efforts of the WTO and other organizations pushing for multilateralism. We have seen that blocs appear to be rather simple projects: efforts to liberalize trade among their member states. Yet we have also learned that they are, in fact, rather complex entities. What implications, then, do these blocs have for economic actors and the international economy as a whole?

In the case of economic actors, the most obvious implication is the creation of incentives for regionalization: for the establishment of transnational structures within the geographical areas covered by those blocs. As firms, for instance, find it easier to sell and produce within a given bloc, they have reasons to develop branches, administrative offices, and factories throughout a bloc's member states (Rugman 2005). As labour issues become increasingly the subject of regional-level legislation, trade unions and other affected groups find it advantageous to establish transnational agendas, membership bases, and structures, as we have already seen in the case of NAFTA, the EU, and Mercosur. Interest groups—such as consumer groups or professional associations—follow a similar path. This tendency to expand regionally—structurally but also, as a result, in terms of programmes and agendas—has already been documented empirically, even if with important caveats (Feils and Rahman 2008; Wei, Andreosso-O'Callaghan, and von Wuntsch 2007; Kim 2007).

A second obvious implication for economic actors is increased cross-national movement and transactions within the newly created regions. If barriers to capital movement are removed, for instance, investors' appetite for stocks, bonds, assets, and real estate within a given bloc typically intensifies. In NAFTA, direct investment from the US to Mexico grew between 1994 and 2002 by nearly 250 per cent—far more than investments to the EU or the rest of the world (*Economist* 2004). On the whole, research indicates that intra-regional foreign direct investment (FDI) levels have increased because of integration in the EU, NAFTA, Mercosur, and AFTA (Kreinin and Plummer 2008). Supply chains, in turn, are stretched beyond national borders, labour mobility can at times increase as professional workers especially are more inclined to search for employment in the participating member states, and firms target customers on a more regional, rather than national, level. Valuable data and information, as well, is exchanged with increasing frequency across borders among business partners, vendors, and even competitors.[5]

For the global economy, the most obvious implication of the rise of trading blocs concerns their contribution towards the making of a single, international marketplace. Here, however, the evidence has been contradictory. According to some researchers, blocs represent stepping stones or learning 'laboratories' bound to prepare countries for participation in the global economy (Summers 1991; Gordon 2003: 112; Cable 1994: 12). But other observers have disagreed, arguing that blocs are protectionist and trade 'diverting' projects which at best slow down the rise of the international economy or at worst make it impossible (Bhagwati 2008; Frankel 1997: 214). Arguments put forth by the latter group have found support in works showing that most trade and FDI happens in very specific regions of the world—most notably Europe, North America, and East Asia (Hirst, Thompson, and Bromley 2009; Rugman and Verbeke 2004).

Yet, we must take the complexity of trading blocs into account when reflecting on these matters. Surely, not all blocs will have the same impact on either economic actors or the rise of a global economy. In the case of economic actors, for instance, consider the fact that a 2007–2008 Asian

[5] For representative studies, see Coeurdacier, De Santis, and Aviat (2009), Dumont (2005), and Sciglimpaglia and Saghafi (2004).

Development Bank survey of exporters in Japan, South Korea, Singapore, and Thailand found that only 22 per cent reported taking advantage of the blocs in which they operate (*Economist* 2009). This contradicts the idea that all blocs encourage firms, interest groups, and others to expand their operations across member states (as reasons for their choices, firm leaders listed confusion about overlapping trade agreements and costs of compliance with overly complex regulations). Or consider recent research on CAN indicating that integration has actually led to lower FDI movement in the region (Paez 2008). Regionalization does not happen everywhere, then. Our preceding discussion of complexity suggests, therefore, that much can be gained by considering one key question: *how is each dimension of complexity likely to shape—mediate, limit, magnify, etc.—the regionalization of economic actors and the rise of a global economy*? We can only begin to address the most important dynamics here. Table 2.3 lists each dimension and its impact on the expansion of economic actors and the rise of the global economy.

We turn to economic actors first.

Table 2.3. Economic implications of differentiated integration

Dimensions of Complexity	Expansion of Economic Actors More Likely...	Relevance for the Global Economy
Economic Objectives	...in targeted industry sectors	Blocs can promote protectionism in given sectors; CET can be either a barrier or facilitating factor
Frameworks & Policies	...when regulatory harmonization also takes place	Blocs under pressure to comply with WTO frameworks
Political Purposes	...among interest groups especially if bloc espouses political objectives	Blocs now represent, bargain, and set objectives for themselves at the WTO and other multilateral forums
Legitimacy	...if legitimacy is high	Struggling blocs may help multilateralism; successful blocs may undermine it
Rational vs. Non-Rational Drivers	...when overall pressures for integration are predictable	'Stickiness' of existing agreements, if unwanted or unplanned, can hinder multilateralism
Pace of Integration	...if pace is rapid	Impact a function of overall influence (positive or negative) of blocs on global economy
Legislative Autonomy of Nation States	...if law-making becomes an increasingly regional affair	As regional law and institutions become the object of attention at the WTO and other multilateral forums, nation states matter less
Transnationalization of Politics	...when loci of contention are transnational	If politics becomes regionalized, then WTO and other multilateral forums lose relevance
Secessionist Movements	...if secessionist movements do not pursue protectionism	Positive for global economy if movements embrace multilateralism instead of regional integration

Economic actors

How does each dimension of complexity affect economic actors in trading blocs? When it comes to *economic objectives*, recall that in most blocs some sectors of the economy are exempt from trade liberalization. Liberalization in other sectors is instead being pursued aggressively. If so, within a bloc, we are likely to see the selective expansion of economic actors. Some actors—those in sectors undergoing liberalization—pursue expansion; others—those in protected sectors—do not. This applies to firms but also to interest groups, trade unions, and other actors. Recent research on firms in the dairy industry and on women's groups in the EU, Mercosur, and NAFTA supports this (Duina 2006a). Exceptions exist, of course. For instance, some actors may forge transnational ties with others precisely to pressure bloc officials to liberalize their sector. But in most cases such activities will probably amount to network building and not actual structural expansions.

Second, as to *frameworks and policies*, we saw that officials use a variety of tools to pursue trade liberalization. Each option has implications: all things being equal, regulatory harmonization and other more sophisticated tools for trade liberalization offer strong incentives for transnational expansion, though of course a number of other factors determine firms' decision to expand abroad:[6] harmonization, after all, lowers production compliance costs while making products from one country more easily accepted in another. Reliance on tariff reduction, by contrast, only generates relatively light incentives for expansion. The same can be said for labour movement, especially professionals: harmonization of training and qualification requirements does much to promote cross-border migration.

Third, *political purposes*, in particular those with consequences for the economy, can stimulate the expansion of economic actors, especially interest groups. Consider, for instance, blocs that aim at the coordination of policies in areas such as foreign immigration, unemployment, or defence. A variety of stakeholders—such as labour unions and high technology firms—would have reasons to establish cross-national networks, objectives, offices, and more. They will also have incentives to form alliances with their counterparts in other member states, which can possibly lead to more permanent arrangements (such as mergers) later. When war prevention figures among the priorities of a bloc, this (provided it is pursued in practice) will generate more stability and thus, as the literature on FDI and political stability shows (Kolstad and Villanger 2008), more reasons for actors to reach beyond their national borders.

[6] Research on determinants of FDI is extensive and stresses factors such as regulatory quality, national growth rates, and market size. See, for instance, Torrisi et al. (2008).

But, of course, all of the above considerations are more likely to hold if there is widespread agreement that the bloc in question is *legitimate*. They are also likely to hold if the various stakeholders perceive that the forces pushing integration forward are not uncontrollable or unpredictable but in fact follow a transparent logic (*rational versus non-rational drivers*), and that integration is indeed taking place at a good or at least reasonable *pace*, however defined.

What about the integrity of the member states? Loss of *legislative autonomy* by itself may have little direct impact on actors' structural organization. However, if it is a reflection of the increasing importance of the regional level as the locus of legislative activity, it is bound to encourage actors affected by the relevant laws to expand. Like-minded stakeholders from across the member states are bound to join forces and lobby bloc officials. Thus, actors will surely have reasons to expand if *political activity has become transnationalized*. Interest groups such as industry associations will establish a presence in whatever sites is necessary, and develop regional-level agendas and membership bases (Doh 1999; Greenwood 2003).

Lastly, the strengthening of *secessionist movements* in trading blocs generally creates disincentives for firms to expand, since these movements generally create uncertainty (political, regulatory, and economic). If firms have reasons to believe that a section of a country is moving towards autonomy or even independence, they may actually decide to move away from that region. The experience of Quebec in the 1990s, when many Anglophone firms threatened to pull out from the province, supports this point (Symonds 1996). And, interestingly, for those that have relocated from Quebec, stock market investors rewarded them with increased valuations (Tirtiroglu, Bhabra, and Lel 2004).

International economy

A major strand of research suggests that regional blocs present—via protectionism and trade diversion—major threats to the international economy. If accurate, could this observation apply to all blocs? Differences in *economic objectives* among blocs will actually determine to a good extent whether protectionism and trade diversion materialize, or whether the opposite may in fact happen. The erection of CETs in common markets is a particularly salient matter, but so are a bloc's position vis-à-vis subsidies, quotas, rules of origin, and fiscal incentives. Any claim about the positive or negative impact of blocs for the international economy must take such differences into account. Extensive and oftentimes contradictory research on all of these variables already exists, of course,[7] but not in the context of a comprehensive, comparative discussion of blocs.

[7] See, for instance, Krueger (1999).

Objectives are achieved through *frameworks and policies*. These have enormous implications for the WTO and other multilateral negotiation forums. Complex regulatory environments at the regional level (i.e. the EU, CAN, or Mercosur) but also simpler ones (such as NAFTA) must be compatible with WTO frameworks if agreements are to be reached at the global level. Thus, once again, we must examine closely those frameworks and policies. And, in so doing, we must also recognize that in some cases they empower bloc officials to represent the collectivity of their member states in international negotiations (the cases of the EU and AFTA come to mind), while in other cases this does not happen (Narlikar 2003: 159). When it comes to *political purposes*, therefore, we see that some blocs have formed precisely with the objective of having more power at the WTO negotiating tables, while others have not (Odell 2006).

But, of course, little of the above could be said if blocs lacked *legitimacy*. Blocs with little legitimacy are unlikely to really matter at the WTO or elsewhere, regardless of formal mandates or agreements. At the same time, blocs whose origins and evolutions appear to have followed less than *rational* courses present challenges of their own. Institutions are sticky, and blocs whose objectives and structure have emerged out of isomorphic, path-dependent, mimetic, or other dynamics often prove more difficult to change than those driven by primarily 'rational' forces, as evidence from the EU shows (Sandholtz and Stone Sweet 1998). Moreover, the evolution of those blocs may prove difficult to control. This, too, may generate challenges to the rise of a global economy.

When it comes to the *pace of integration*, we must first consider a bloc's overall impact on the global economy. If countries in a bloc prove, despite GATT's requirements, more protectionist towards third parties than before integration, fast pace only makes matters worse for the WTO and multilateralism. But if the pace is slow, it may undermine the project as a whole and motivate member state representatives to seek alternative (bilateral or multilateral) paths. On the other hand, if a given bloc is indeed functioning as a stepping stone for further inclusion in the global economy, then fast pace is certainly positive for multilateralism, while a slower pace may push member states to leave the bloc and seek alternative arrangements which may, or may not, be beneficial for multilateralism. Determining, with accuracy, whether a bloc is beneficial or harmful for the global economy is not a simple task, but finding examples of countries actually making claims to that effect and then threatening to leave out of frustration with progress is easier. In Mercosur, both Paraguay and Uruguay have repeatedly voiced dissatisfaction at the protectionist tendencies of Brazil and the resulting lack of interest, for Mercosur as a whole, in negotiating trade agreements with other countries—and the

United States especially (*Economist* 2005, pp. 36–7; MercoPress 2001; BBC Monitoring 2002).

Finally, we discussed the various ways in which blocs can challenge the integrity of nation states. National *legislative autonomy* and the *transnationalization of politics* are relevant for the global economy in quite similar ways: if indeed law and politics are regionalizing, then the WTO and other multilateral forums must increasingly turn to blocs for the pursuit of their visions. Moreover, such a regionalization is likely to lead to a diversion of political resources and capital away from multilateral venues, with negative implication for how quickly global agreements can be reached. As Bhagwati put it, 'lobbying support and political energies can readily be diverted to preferential trading arrangements such as FTAs [free trade agreements]... That deprives the multilateral system of the support it needs to survive, let alone be conducive to further liberalization' (Bhagwati 1993: 162). As to *secessionist movements*, the critical variable is their stance towards openness and multilateralism. When blocs invigorate these movements, the position of these movements towards the global economy certainly assumes greater importance.

References

Ackrill, Robert and Adrian Kay (2006) 'Historical-Institutionalist Perspectives on the Development of the EU Budget System', *Journal of European Public Policy*, 13(1): 113–33.

Alter, Karen J. (1998) 'Who Are the Masters of the Treaty? European Governments and the European Court of Justice', *International Organization*, 52(1): 125–52.

—— and Laurence Helfer (2010) 'Nature or Nurture: Lawmaking in the European Court of Justice and the Andean Tribunal of Justice', forthcoming in *International Organization*, 64(4).

Aspinwall, Mark (2009) 'NAFTA-ization: Regionalization and domestic political adjustment in the North American Economic Area', *Journal of Common Market Studies*, 47(1): 1–24.

BBC Monitoring (International Reports) (2002) 'Uruguay's Batlle Tells Brazil's Cardoso Uruguay Seeks Alternatives to Mercosur', 3 April.

Bennett, Scott (2004) 'American and Canadian Assessments of NAFTA: Opinion on continental policy and its drivers', *American Behavioral Scientist*, 47(10): 1285–318.

Bhagwati, Jagdish (1993) 'Beyond NAFTA: Clinton's trading choices', *Foreign Policy*, 91 (Summer): 155–62.

—— (2008) *Termites in the Trading System: How preferential agreements undermine free trade*, New York: Oxford University Press.

Bulmer, Simon J. (1998) 'New Institutionalism and the Governance of the Single European Market', *Journal of European Public Policy*, 5(3): 365–86.

Cable, Vincent (1994) 'Overview', pp.1–16 in *Trade Blocs? The Future of Regional Integration*, ed. Vincent Cable and David Henderson, London: Royal Institute of International Affairs.

Calloni, Stella (1996) 'Centrales Sindicales del Mercosur Rechazan las Politicas Neoliberales', *La Jornada*, October 10.

Cameron, Maxwell and Brian Tomlin (2000) *The Making of NAFTA: How the deal was done*, Ithaca, NY: Cornell University Press.

Capling, Ann and Kim Richard Nossal (2009) 'The Contradictions of Regionalism in North America', *Review of International Studies*, 35: 147–67.

Carranza, Mario E. (2004) 'Mercosur and the End Game of the FTAA Negotiations: Challenges and prospects after the Argentine crisis', *Third World Quarterly*, 25(2): 319–37.

Chacha, Mwita (2008) 'Regional Integration and Trade: Overlapping membership and the challenges of regionalism in Africa', Paper presented at International Studies Association Conference, San Francisco, CA.

Coeurdacier, Nicolas, Roberto A. De Santis, and Antonin Aviat (2009) 'Cross-Border Mergers and Acquisitions and European Integration', *Economic Policy*, 57: 55–106.

Despeignes, Peronet (2004) 'U.S. Wants APEC Agenda to Include Security Issues', *USA Today*, October 20.

Doh, Jonathan P. (1999) 'Regional Market Integration and Decentralization in Europe and North America: Implications for business-government relations and corporate public affairs', *Business & Society*, 38: 474–507.

Dreiling, Michael (2001) *Solidarity and Contention: The politics of security and sustainability in the NAFTA conflict*, New York: Garland Publishing.

Duina, Francesco (2006a) *The Social Construction of Free Trade: The EU, NAFTA, and Mercosur*, Princeton: Princeton University Press.

—— (2006b) 'Between Efficiency and Sovereignty: Transnational actors, the European Union, and the regulation of bankruptcy', *Comparative European Politics*, 4(1): 1–22.

—— (2006c) 'Varieties of Regional Integration: The European Union, NAFTA and Mercosur', *Journal of European Integration*, 28(3): 245–75.

—— (2010) 'Frames, Scripts, and the Making of Regional Trade Agreements', pp. 93–113 in Mark Blyth, Craig Parsons, and Rawi Abdelal (eds) *Constructing the International Economy*, Ithaca, NY: Cornell University Press.

—— and Jason Buxbaum (2008) 'Regional Trade Agreements and the Pursuit of State Interests: Institutional perspectives from NAFTA and Mercosur', *Economy and Society*, 37(2): 193–223.

Dumont, Jean-Christophe (2005) 'International Labour Mobility, Free Trade and Regional Integration: A comparison of the European Union and NAFTA', pp. 594–621 in Richard G. Harris and Thomas Lemieux (eds) *Social and Labour Market Aspects of North American Linkages*, Alberta: University of Calgary Press.

Economist (2004) 'Free Trade on Trial', 3 January.

—— (2005) 'Improbable Allies: Paraguay and the US', 1 October.

Economist (2009) 'The Noodle Bowl', 5 September.

Farrell, Mary (2005) 'The Global Politics of Regionalism: An introduction', pp. 1–17 in Mary Farrell, Björn Hettne, and Luk Van Langenhove (eds) *Global Politics of Regionalism: Theory and practice*, Ann Arbor, MI: Pluto Press.

Feils, Dorothee J. and Manzur Rahman (2008) 'Regional Economic Integration and Foreign Direct Investment: The case of NAFTA', *Management International Review (MIR)*, 48(2): 147–63.

Frankel, Jeffrey A. (1997) *Regional Trading Blocs in the World Economic System*, Washington, DC: Institute for International Economics.

Gordon, Bernard K. (2003) 'A High-Risk Trade Policy', *Foreign Affairs*, 82(4): 105–18.

Greenwood, Justin (2003) *Interest Representation in the European Union*, Houndmills, Basingstoke, Hampshire and New York: Palgrave Macmillan.

Haggard, Stephen (1997) 'Regionalism in Asia and the Americas', pp. 20–49 in Edward D. Mansfield and Helen V. Milner (eds) *The Political Economy of Regionalism*, New York: Columbia University Press.

Hakim, Peter (1996) 'Good News from Paraguay: A coup d'état falls flat', *Christian Science Monitor*, 88(129): 19.

Hall, Keith H. and Douglas R. Nelson (2004) 'The Peculiar Political Economy of NAFTA: Complexity, uncertainty and footloose policy preferences', pp. 91–109 in Arvind Panagariya and Devashish Mitra (eds) *The Political Economy of Trade, Aid and Foreign Investment Policies: Essays in honor of Ed Tower*, Amsterdam: Elsevier.

Hancock, Kathleen J. (2009) *Regional Integration: Choosing plutocracy*, New York: Palgrave Macmillan.

Heisenberg, Dorothee and Amy Richmond (2002) 'Supranational Institution-Building in the European Union: A comparison of the European Court of Justice and the European Central Bank', *Journal of European Policy*, 9(2): 201–18.

Helble, Matthias, Ben Shepherd, and John S. Wilson (2009) 'Transparency and Regional Integration in the Asia Pacific', *World Economy*, 32(3): 479–508.

Hirst, Paul, Grahame Thompson, and Simon Bromley (2009) *Globalization in Question*, Cambridge, UK: Polity Press.

Holzinger, Katharina and Christophe Knill (2002) 'Path Dependencies in European Integration: A constructive response to German foreign Minister Joschka Fischer', *Public Administration*, 80(1): 125–52.

Jelin, Elizaneth (1999) 'Dialogues, Understandings and Misunderstandings: Social movements in Mercosur', *International Social Science Journal*, 51(159): 37–48.

Kaltenthaler, Karl and Frank O. Mora (2002) 'Explaining Latin American Integration: The case of Mercosur', *Review of International Political Economy*, 9(1): 72–97.

Kim, Young-Han (2007) 'Impacts of Regional Economic Integration on Industrial Relocation through FDI in East Asia', *Journal of Policy Modeling*, 29(1): 165–80.

Kolstad, Ivar and Espen Villanger (2008) 'Determinants of Foreign Direct Investment in Services', *European Journal of Political Economy*, 24(2): 518–33.

Kreinin, Mordechai E. and Michael G. Plummer (2008) 'Effects of Regional Integration on FDI: An empirical approach', *Journal of Asian Economics*, 19(5–6): 447–54.

Krueger, Anne O. (1999) 'Are Preferential Trading Arrangements Trade Liberalizing or Protectionist?' *Journal of Economic Perspectives,* 13(4) : 105–24.

La Jornada (1996) 'Reprimene en Brasil a Sindicalistas de Cuatro Paises que Protestaron en la Cumbre del Mercosur,' *La Jornada,* 18 December.

Laursen, Finn (ed.) (2003) *Comparative Regional Integration: Theoretical perspectives,* Aldershot: Ashgate Publishing.

Leibfried, Stephan and Paul Pierson (eds) (1995) *European Social Policy: Between fragmentation and integration,* Washington, DC: Brookings Institution Press.

McConnell, James and Alan MacPherson (1994) 'The North American Free Trade Area: An overview of issues and perspectives', pp. 163–87 in *Continental Trading Blocs: The growth of regionalism in the world economy,* ed. Richard Gibb and Michalak Wieslaw, West Sussex: John Wiley & Sons Ltd.

MacDonald, Ian Thomas (2003) 'NAFTA and the Emergence of Continental Labor Cooperation', *The American Review of Canadian Studies,* 33(2): 173–96.

Malamud, Andrés (2005) 'Mercosur Turns 15: Between Rising Rhetoric and Declining Achievement', *Cambridge Review of International Affairs,* 18(3): 421–36.

Mansfield, Edward D. and Helen V. Milner (eds) (1997) *The Political Economy of Regionalism,* New York: Columbia University Press.

Mattli, Walter (1999) *The Logic of Regional Integration: Europe and beyond,* Cambridge: Cambridge University Press.

Mayer, Frederick (1998) *Interpreting NAFTA: The science and the art of political analysis,* New York: Columbia University Press.

Mena, Antonio Ortez (2006) 'Getting the "No": Defending against demands in NAFTA energy negotiations', pp. 177–218 in John S. Odell (ed.) *Negotiating Trade: Developing countries in the WTO and NATFA,* Cambridge: Cambridge University Press.

MercoPress (2001) 'Uruguay Targets USA', 3 April.

Milner, Helen V. (1997) 'Industries, Governments, and the Creation of Regional Trading Blocs', pp. 77–106 in Edward D. Mansfield and Helen V. Milner (eds) *The Political Economy of Regionalism,* New York: Columbia University Press.

Milward, Alan (1992) *The European Rescue of the Nation-State,* London: Routledge.

Mistry, Percy S. (2000) 'Africa's Record of Regional Co-operation and Integration', *African Affairs,* 99: 553–73.

Moravcsik, Andrew (1998) *The Choice for Europe: Social purpose and state power from Messina to Maastricht,* Ithaca, NY: Cornell University Press.

Narine, Shaun (2004) 'State Sovereignty, Political Legitimacy and Regional Institutionalism in the Asia-Pacific', *The Pacific Review,* 17(3): 423–50.

Narlikar, Amrita (2003) *International Trade and Developing Countries: Bargaining coalitions in the GATT & WTO,* New York: Routledge.

Nielsen, François and Jane Salk (1998) 'The Ecology of Collective Action and Regional Representation in the European Union', *European Sociological Review,* 14(3): 231–54.

O'Brien, Derek and Sonia Morano-Foadi (2009) 'The Caribbean Court of Justice and Legal Integration within CARICOM: Some lessons from the European Community', *Law & Practice of International Courts & Tribunals,* 8(3): 399–429.

Odell, John S. (ed.) (2006) *Negotiating Trade: Developing countries in the WTO and NATFA*, Cambridge: Cambridge University Press.

Paez, Laura (2008) 'Regional Trade Agreements and Foreign Direct Investment: Impact of existing RTAs on FDI and Trade flows in the Andean Community and implications of a hemispheric RTA in the Americas', *Aussenwirtschaft*, 63(3): 231–61.

Pastor, Robert A. (2004) 'North America's Second Decade', *Foreign Affairs*, 83(1): 124–35.

Pierson, Paul (1996) 'The Path to European Integration,' *Comparative Political Studies*, 29 (2): 123–64.

Rugman, Alan (2005) *The Regional Multinationals: MNEs and 'global' strategic management*, Cambridge: Cambridge University Press.

——and Alain Verbeke (2004) 'A Perspective on Regional and Global Strategies of Multinational Enterprises', *Journal of International Business Studies*, 35(1): 3–18.

Sánchez, Rafael (2004) 'Rebuilding the Central American Bloc in the 1990s: An integovernmentalist approach to integration', pp. 31–52 in Finn Laursen (ed.) *Comparative Regional Integration: Theoretical perspectives*, Aldershot: Ashgate Publishing.

Sandholtz, Wayne, and Alec Stone Sweet (eds) (1998) *European Integration and Supranational Governance*, Oxford: Oxford University Press.

Sbragia, Alberta (2008) 'Comparative Regionalism: What might it be?' *Journal of Common Market Studies*, 46: 29–49.

Sciglimpaglia, Don and Massoud Saghafi (2004) Marketing Consequences of European Internal Market Unification: An executive perspective', *Journal of Euromarketing*, 14(1/2): 35–57.

Summers, Larry (1991) 'Regionalism and the World Trading System', pp. 11–21 in *Policy Implications of Trade and Currency Zones* (ed.) Larry Summers, Kansas City: Federal Reserve Bank of Kansas City.

Suominen, Kati (2009) 'The Changing Anatomy of Regional Trade Agreements in East Asia', *Journal of East Asian Studies*, 9(1): 29–56.

Sverdrup, Ulf (2002) 'An Institutional Perspective on Treaty Reform: Contextualizing the Amsterdam and Nice Treaties', *Journal of European Public Policy*, 9(1): 120–40.

Switky, Bob (2000) 'The Importance of Trading Blocs: Theoretical foundations', pp. 13–53 in *The Political Importance of Regional Trading Blocs* (ed.) Bart Kerremans and Bob Switky, Aldershot: Ashgate Publishing Ltd.

Symonds, William C. (1996) 'Business in Quebec Is Voting with Its Feet', *BusinessWeek*, February 5.

Tirtiroglu, Dogan, Harjeet S. Bhabra, and Ugur Lel (2004) 'Political Uncertainty and Asset Valuation: Evidence from business relocations in Canada', *Journal of Banking & Finance*, 28(9): 2237–58.

Torrisi, C. Richard et al. (2008) 'FDI in Central Europe: Determinants and policy implications', *Journal of International Finance & Economics*, 8(4): 136–47.

Wei, Xiaojun, Bernadette Andreosso-O'Callaghan, and Michael von Wuntsch (2007) 'German Investment in Ireland and in the Central and East European Countries', *Intereconomics/Review of European Economic Policy*, 42(3): 156–66.

West & Central Africa Monitor (2005) 'COMESA Customs Union By 2008?' *West & Central Africa Monitor*, 6(7): 4–5.

Wignaraja, Ganeshan and Dorothea Lazaro (2010) *North-South vs South-South Asian FTAs: Trends, Compatibilities, and Ways Forward*, Brugge: United Nations University (UNU-CRIS Working Paper Series 2010/3).

3

The Revival of Economic Patriotism

Ben Clift and Cornelia Woll

1. Introduction

Twenty-first century capitalism is marked by a paradox: whilst we continue to see an internationalization of markets and finance, and also of corresponding laws and regulation, political organization remains primarily national, to a significant degree local and regional, but only very haltingly global. Nation states retain a crucial role in managing economic development, as the current financial crisis has testified. The knowledge creation and production systems that make up the global economy are locally embedded and governed. At the regional level, supra-national organizations like the European Union have an important role in framing and shaping capitalist development in Europe. Markets may stretch beyond these boundaries, but the central organizations for their political governance remain at the national, the local, and sometimes the regional level.

As long as politics divides along these lines, economic governance of globalizing markets will display fundamental contradictions between economic and political boundaries. This is surprising to some observers, who criticize the decidedly particularistic responses to global economic problems. In the late twentieth century, the rise of neo-liberal economics appeared to signal the withdrawal of the nation-state from key areas of economic life in the industrialized world. A decade later, even the most liberal market economies have resorted to national tool kits to prop up their economies and banks, to a point where the US media warned against 'socialism' taking over America, and the United Kingdom was criticized as looking dangerously similar to France. Some analysts have lamented the revival of economic nationalism; others have employed a term popularized in France: economic patriotism. Indeed, a lot of political initiatives look comparable across countries. Former French Prime

Minister De Villepin, who coined the term 'economic patriotism',[1] intervened to try and prevent foreign hostile takeover, President Nicolas Sarkozy attempted to make state aid contingent upon commitments not to delocalize car plants to the Czech Republic and beyond, President Barack Obama has legislated a buy American clause, and Gordon Brown declared 'British jobs for British workers'.[2] To be sure, the financial crisis holds many lessons, but one of the most evident ones is the continued importance of government intervention, even in the most open and interconnected economies.

This chapter begins where these critiques end and asks: are we indeed witnessing the revival of economic patriotism? If so, what does this mean? Is it pathological and linked to the economic downturn or the fact that governments are captured by special industrial interests seeking protection? Investigating the presumed revival of economic patriotism in the 2000s, we oppose popular media and detractors of the phenomenon. To begin with, economic nationalism or economic patriotism should not be confused with mercantilist, protectionist policies. Although they may take such forms, a careful study of their history and use simply points to economic choices that are specifically geared to protect the interests of the homeland. In some cases, this might be best achieved through liberalization, as we will discuss later.

Moreover, economic patriotism should not be understood as a crisis response only. Rather, it is endemic to liberal internationalized capitalism, and results from the tension between transnational markets and territorially bound political organization highlighted above (see also Duina in this volume). Borrowing a felicitous term from Colin Crouch, we have discussed this as the 'paradox of globalized neo-liberal democracy' elsewhere (Clift and Woll 2012).[3] In contemporary capitalism, politicians continue to be held accountable for economic activity which they can no longer, or which they can only partially, control. Economic patriotism lays bare these tensions and helps to analyze political responses as a condition of twenty-first century capitalism. It provides a prism to investigate how actors attempt to resolve or reconcile the contradictions of economic governance by negotiating compromises between abstract notions of economic prosperity and territorially bound political obligations.

Studying contemporary capitalism through this prism, we make two arguments. First, we oppose analysts who warn against an increase in economic

[1] Dominique de Villepin relied on a concept presented in Carayon (2006). See Christophe Jakubyszyn, 'Dominique de Villepin en appelle au patriotisme économique', *Le Monde*, 29 July 2005.

[2] In his Labour Party Conference speech in September 2007.

[3] We would like to thank Colin Crouch for a very helpful discussion of these points during the first Warwick/Sciences Po Economic Patriotism workshop, held at the University of Warwick in February 2008.

intervention and those who suggest that liberal market economies have been characterized by hands-off approach, by underlining that governments have always actively intervened to shape markets and support their economies. Second, we show that the politics of economic intervention are nonetheless different today than they were several decades ago. At the discursive level, politicians now affirm that they can and will intervene in markets, a rhetoric that became taboo in liberal market economies during the 1990s. Moreover, to cope with the increasingly complex overlap of economic and political boundaries, political responses today no longer rely exclusively on the nation state, but can also shift economic governance to protect national production to the regional or local level. This explains why we chose to speak of economic patriotism rather than economic nationalism, which implies an exclusive focus on the nation state.

The chapter is divided into four parts. The next section discusses the genealogy of the concept and its uses among politicians, social partners, consumers, or activists. In the second section, we define the notion with reference to related debates about economic nationalism and political intervention more generally. We then discuss the persistence of economic intervention over time in the third section, before turning to the novel characteristic of economic patriotism in recent years in a final section.

2. The genealogy of economic patriotism

In order to specify what is new, and what is not, within economic patriotism, it is necessary to situate the phenomenon within a broader historical lineage of political economic thought and practice. There is a rich seam of writings which touch upon and evoke the themes of economic patriotism. Friedrich List (1841) most famously highlighted the role of the state in economic governance and the importance of territorial reference points (see Clift and Woll 2012). More broadly, many of the characteristics of modern-day economic patriotism were evoked by the German Historical Schools. Both the 'older' current, led by Wilhelm Roscher, and the 'younger' version, led by Gustav von Schmoller, analyze the economy as profoundly shaped by state–market relations which reflect political power relationships, and highlight the connection between territoriality and economic policy (see e.g. Tribe 2003: 218–25). Within the older German Historical School of political economy, Roscher noted a crucial role of 'state economy' within politics (Roscher 1843: 2; see Tribe 2003: 219–20). Max Weber, part of the younger German Historical school (Hodgson 2001: 117–28), discusses citizenship as 'economic in character' (Weber 1981: 315), and elsewhere distinguishes between outward and inward-looking patriotism (see Beetham 1974: 142). Weber's ([1895] 1994) inaugural lecture entitled 'The Nation State and Economic Policy'[4] offers an analysis which highlights the main issues of economic patriotism today. We concur with these classic authors that economic governance is marked by territoriality, which implies that it inevitably gets bound up with the specific historical conditions of these boundaries. This draws our attention to the evolution of particular political economic spaces.

Such a historicized approach is at odds with the portrayal of a global 'self-regulating' market, assumed to be naturally occurring by many neo-classical economists and advocates of neo-liberal governance. In their time, the German Historical School rejected the marginalist and neo-classical approach to economics as a natural science. Liberal economists of the nineteenth century saw economic phenomena as natural forces. This pervaded Adam Smith's classical liberal approach, which irked—to different degrees—List (1841), Roscher (1843: 2) and Bruno Hildebrand (1848: 29–34).[5] The German Historical School rejected the posited regularities and natural laws of economics, arguing for contingent, historically specific approaches to economic law and economic policy.

Von Schmoller was perhaps the pre-eminent scholar of the younger German Historical School. His advocacy of protective legislative measures to assist small enterprises, and more generally his insistence on the role of the state chimes with our conception of state–market relations. Schmoller's inaugural lecture spoke of 'an historical and ethical view of the state and society', and this 'ethical evaluation of the state' (Tribe 2003: 223–4) contains elements—moral obligation to one's compatriots—that inform economic patriotism. We argue that such a moral or ethical dimension of governmental activism is reflected in the contemporary recourse to patriotism as a legitimating strategy for economic actions.

The conceptual framework proposed by List, Roscher, Hildebrand, von Schmoller, and Weber fits well for the analysis of economic patriotism. With their focus on political intervention and citizenship, their analysis of economic governance even included, in List's case, the possibility of a 'federal' or 'Hanseatic patriotism', which he detected within the cities of the Hanseatic League (1856: 99; 1885: 17). The key difference with current forms of such supra-national economic patriotism is the much denser current set of political, legal, and regulatory infrastructures and institutions. In the EU in particular, politicians and economic actors can therefore rely more actively on these transnational reference points, which makes the phenomenon all the more

[4] The original German version 'Der Nationalstaat und die Volkswirtschaft' is available online: http://de.wikisource.org/wiki/Der_Nationalstaat_und_die_Volkswirtschaftspolitik.

[5] The marginalists subsequently formalized these assumptive foundations, sparking off the *Methodenstreit* with Carl Menger and Gustav von Schmoller as key protagonists (see Hodgson 2001; Gamble 1995).

common. The multi-layered regulation of international markets, which has developed since the middle of the twentieth century (see Djelic and Sahlin-Andersson 2006; Djelic and Quack 2010 and in this volume), offers new battlegrounds for economic patriotic activism and intervention as new forms of regulation emerge on product and process standards, labour standards, food safety, and sustainable development. In each sphere, possibilities arise to direct market outcomes so as to favour insider firms, workers, or consumers. The multiple economic patriotic policy instruments in support of national or regional economic actors are today more disjointed and uneven, but they are no less prevalent than within post-war capitalism (Shonfield 1969).

The contours of economic governance have changed dramatically, not least because political elites have had to circumvent liberal international trade rules and competition authorities. With the rise of supranational agreements aimed at curbing protectionist policies (see Duina in this volume), in particular the World Trade Organization or the competition policy of the EU, governments have had to innovate to reinvent their modus operandi of economic interventionism, for example by reinventing urban policy to serve competitiveness objectives (see Crouch and Le Galès forthcoming). National level politicians have developed new justifications and legitimation strategies for their increasingly innovative efforts to protect and advance the economic interests of their home territory.

Initially, these efforts to find new legitimacy for economic intervention appeared to be a labelling exercise, which one often observes in politics. To avoid being called an economic nationalist, Dominique de Villepin, at the time French prime minister, chose to use the term 'patriotisme économique' in 2005. The context was a desire to warn off Pepsico from a hostile takeover of Danone, considered cherished industrial patrimony—'strategic yoghurt policy' as it was termed at the time. Economic choices, according to the logic of this discourse, should be linked with concerns for one's homeland. Although foreign observers were quick to mock the new concept as a fig leaf for protectionism, the political rhetoric of economic patriotism, and the practice of self-affirmed economic intervention, have become a more visible feature of the political economy of twenty-first century capitalism, especially since the advent of the financial crisis.

For some consumer movements, economic patriotism became a rallying cry to support local production and fight the consumption of foreign products or services. In the course of industrial conflicts, social partners have invoked economic patriotism to fight against relocation of companies (Fetzer forthcoming). At the supra-national level, policy elites within the European Union have defended and advanced European economic patriotic claims that Europe can and shall become 'the most dynamic and competitive knowledge-based economy in the world capable of sustainable economic growth with more and better jobs and greater social cohesion', (see Rosamond 2002, forthcoming; Annesley 2007, Clift 2009b: 207–10; Daly 2006). Despite the presumed liberal nature of European integration, policy elites are quick to use Europe to defend their interests against outsiders such as the United States or China, in a manner that can be both liberalizing towards the inside of the EU and protectionist towards the outside. Developments within European agriculture and food standards (Grant forthcoming) and defence (Hoeffler forthcoming), for example, indicate the complex blend of liberalization and partial market shaping intervention at play within the multifaceted pursuit of EU economic patriotism.

Definition

How then should we define 'economic patriotism' as an analytical concept to preserve the heuristic qualities evoked in political economic analysis since the nineteenth century, but to distinguish it from the explicitly vague and ambiguous use politicians have made of it in the twenty-first century? As Pickel (2005: 2) rightly points out, there are several options for dealing with 'loaded' concepts in the social sciences. Ignoring a phenomenon or abandoning its key concepts as 'hopelessly contaminated' are often unsatisfying. After all, the term 'economic liberalism' is no less loaded, but this has not impeded its critical analysis as a political phenomenon. In the following we will spell out the difference between the normative goals carried by the term 'economic patriotism' and the function economic patriotism has in socio-economic governance.

In a previous article, we have defined economic patriotism as 'economic choices which seek to discriminate in favour of particular social groups, firms, or sectors understood by the decision-makers as insiders because of their territorial status. [. . . . It] entails a form of economic partiality: a desire to shape market outcomes to privilege the position of certain actors' (Clift and Woll 2012). Economic patriotism implies that the interests of the homeland should weigh more heavily than individual interests in the economic choices of consumers, producers, workers, or politicians. In other words, patriotism suggests, normatively speaking, that a person has a moral duty to fellow members of a community that is greater than its obligations to non-members. Economic patriotism—as we understand the term—is more than just a fashionable fig leaf for protectionism. In particular, our deployment of the concept signals two qualities of the phenomenon: the diversity of its policy content, which can range from protectionism to strategic market opening—and the multiplicity of territorial units it can refer to—local, national, and regional.

There are clearly some similarities between economic patriotism and the economic nationalism formulated most notably by Friedrich List. Economic patriotism, just like economic nationalism, needs to be defined by its territorial references and its underlying conceptions of political economic space, as a recent literature has highlighted (e.g. Levi-Faur 1997; Abdelal 2001; Helleiner and Pickel 2005). Neither economic nationalism nor economic patriotism entail a specific or restricted set of policy prescriptions (such as, for example, tariff barriers). Both merely require that economic choices—be they liberal or protectionist—serve the interest of a given territorial unit. Politicians may choose *liberal* economic policies as a selective strategy to further territorial political economic interest, as has been underlined by economic nationalism scholarship (see Helleiner 2002; D'Costa 2009). Thus, equating protectionism or neo-mercantilism with economic patriotism obscures the importance and the multiple facets of the phenomenon in current political debates. In the next section we will map out the variety and range of political interventions in the economy which our conception of economic patriotism encompasses.

The key difference between economic patriotism and economic nationalism is that unlike economic *nation*alism, economic patriotism is agnostic about the precise shape or nature of the unit claimed as *patrie*. It can incorporate local patriotism, such as the defence of regional autonomy through an agreement on labels of protected origins in the World Trade Organization, and supranational patriotism, which is exemplified by the 'fortress Europe' debate. Thus economic patriotism allows us to study a transfer of economic objectives from the national to a supranational level, such as the EU. Abdelal has pointed out that economic nationalism is 'an expression of a constructed social identity' (2005: 22). Economic patriotism recognizes that equally important and significant processes of social identity construction take place and have political economic impacts, at levels other than the national.

Economic choices in favour of territorial insiders can take a variety of forms. As critics like to highlight, they can be equivalent to outright protectionism and barriers to trade, either for an entire market, or by discriminating against foreign producers. We refer to such forms as defensive economic patriotism. Other types of intervention use market integration and support open markets, but only in ways which procure a comparative advantage to home producers. This liberal economic patriotism can take the form of support for home producers in world markets, liberalization according to the standards that apply to home markets, or strategic liberalization of sectors where home firms are particularly competitive. In essence, we extend our analysis to all cases where politicians privilege the defence of national, supranational, or regional interests over abstract notions of market opening, for example in defence of economic prosperity more generally.

Table 3.1. Continuum of political strategies

Type		Liberal economic patriotism		Defensive economic patriotism	
Policy	Unconditional liberalization	Selective, strategic liberalization	Market integration according to home standards	Regulation targeting foreign standards	Protectionism
Motive	Market opening	⟵	⟶		Defence of territorial interests

Admittedly, the defence of territorial interests is very common in economic policy-making, and we would therefore like to underline which political choices are *not* economic patriotism. One limit to the applicability of the concept of economic patriotism is implied in our starting continuum based on the tension between territorial interest and market opening. Although we have identified liberal versions of economic patriotism, we recognize that some liberal policies are motivated solely by economic ambitions and disregard the differential effects the policy might have on a given territory. We refer to such liberal policies as 'unconditional liberalization' in Table 3.1.

But there are also limits to economic patriotism that do not reflect an ideological commitment to market opening and nonetheless disregard territorial effects. The literature on risk regulation and sustainable development has underlined that policy choices require balancing economic objectives against social and environmental objectives. In the course of these negotiations, one can imagine many new regulatory regimes that are not unconditionally liberal, but that prioritize health objectives, social standards, or environmental goals without favouring any one of the existing regimes and without targeting territorial insiders specifically. Put differently, when the defence of territorial interests is not the ultimate factor in the political decision, it would be of little analytical value to speak of economic patriotism.

3. Continuity in economic intervention

Many would agree that the defence of territorial interests is not really a new phenomenon. Why then do observers and public media warn against the rise or return of economic patriotism in recent years?[6] And what is novel about current economic patriotism? Answering these questions requires addressing a common myth about economic governance first: the idea that authorities in

[6] In February 2009, the *Economist* titled its cover 'The Return of Economic Nationalism', depicting a hand coming out of graveyard soil.

liberal market economies do not intervene to direct market outcomes. Once we have argued that economic intervention is indeed common across countries and that governments have continuously steered their economies even during the years where many authors spoke about the 'retreat of the state', we will turn to what we consider the novel aspects of present-day economic patriotism.

Our analysis of economic patriotism entails a conception of state–market relations that sees markets as always embedded in a societal and political context, and thus as continuously and inevitably shaped by political intervention of active states. Such a proposition is not very shocking in light of the financial crisis. Today, it is clear that governments intervene not just to facilitate market exchange: they also actively contribute to shaping and making markets, and they provide substantial aid in times of crisis. A conspicuous feature of capitalism throughout its history, including in the twentieth and twenty-first centuries, has been the pervasiveness and persistence of state intervention. This is as true in 'liberal' or laissez faire systems as it is in organized or institutional economies. Polanyi famously underlined that free markets were the product of deliberate state action, while restrictions on free markets started in a spontaneous way: 'Laissez faire was planned, planning was not' (Polanyi 2001 [1944]: 147). As Vogel (1995) demonstrated, freer markets require extensive rules and regulation.

Therefore, our account of economic intervention entails a more encompassing vision of state action and activism than the governmental defence of institutional comparative advantage suggested, sotto voce, in Hall and Soskice (2001). Governments do not simply diagnose where they have strengths and then go out to defend them, they also try to build these strengths and create new 'national interests'. This has been recognized by all observers of international trade negotiations. Since governments can create comparative advantages, negotiate market shares, and facilitate the sale of national products, international debates almost inevitably address the role of government action in the domestic economic. As Zysman (1983: 15) pointed out almost thirty years ago, very rarely do trade talks simply seek to codify the rules of trade, leaving the market to settle outcomes.

Recognizing this pervasive domestic activism runs counter to some of the neat dichotomies common in current scholarship. In particular, it has been customary in the literature to confine the term 'market-making' to neo-liberal market economies (e.g. Levy 1999: 291–2), deeming that other kinds of state–market relationships deserve different characterizations. Supposedly, market-making liberal state intervention is about securing the free play of market forces (through anti-trust, competition law, merger regulation, and so on). For example, in seeking to map out the contours of state regulatory and intervening practices within contemporary European capitalism, Quaglia draws a distinction between approaches to financial market regulation in Europe. The 'southern European' group (including France) seeks 'market shaping' regulation. The 'northern European' group (led by the UK) seeks 'market-making' (light touch) regulation. In this view Anglo-Saxon 'market-making' reformism seeks to establish free and fair competition, whilst *dirigiste* 'market-shaping' reformism has a whiff of neo-mercantilism about it, seeking to skew or structure markets to secure the best outcomes for its firms (Quaglia 2010, 2011).

However, such a dichotomy is problematic. When one analyzes economic patriotism, a distinction between the market-making liberal state interested in policing the market through competition policy and a market-shaping post-*dirigiste* state is unhelpful. There are a number of reasons for rejecting such a categorical approach. First, as Polanyi pointed out, *all* markets, irrespective of how freely competitive they may be, are 'made'. The pure free or self-regulating market, in the twenty-first as in the nineteenth century, is a myth (Crouch 2005; Levy 2006; Vogel 1995). Polanyi's *Great Transformation* demonstrated how "regulation and markets, in effect, grew up together" ([1944] 2001: 71) in a complex symbiotic relationship. The nineteenth century 'liberal state' which he described was in many ways the architect and author of the misnamed 'self-regulating' market, and central to the processes of regulation without which it could not have existed (2001: 146–7). Free market capitalism, even of a liberal or neoliberal kind, requires extensive and continuous state intervention. The political economy of the state always involves the combination and recombination of public and private within the economy, in the context of a mutual co-constitution of state and market. From a Polanyian perspective, 'no market economy separated from the political sphere is possible' (Polanyi [1944] 2001: 205; Krippner and Alvarez 2007) because of the state's inescapable role in setting the rules and framework for market activity. State intervention is necessary for the governance of, indeed the existence of, markets. Deregulation, of course, involves not simply removing restrictions but active *re*regulation: the new regulatory frameworks differ between countries, regions, and sectors in ways that are designed to promote particular outcomes.

Secondly, market-making involves a wider variety of interventions and regulations than just competition policy. This is why Polanyi noted that 'the road to the free market was opened and kept open by an enormous increase in continuous, centrally organized and controlled interventionism' (2001: 146). The making of markets is by no means restricted to competition policy, where the term is most often deployed. Making markets involves much more than simply regulating competition. It entails, amongst other things, constituting what firms are, and what rights the various actors within firms are entitled to, as well as regulating production through product and process standards, and regulating trade (Fligstein 2001). Once we begin to consider these broader and more varied aspects of market-making, it becomes clear that market-making is a differentiated set of processes and activities. This more thoroughgoing consideration of market-making evokes similar themes to those explored by Chang in discussing the Developmental State. He notes that 'the boundary between the economic and the political is not something "naturally" given but something that can vary across time and place' (Chang 1999: 197). Thus all "free" markets are deeply politically conditioned, and free markets differ across time and space: for example, changing norms relating to slavery and child labour have changed the nature of "free" labour markets. The ubiquity of market-making regulation (over wages, pollution, health and safety and so forth) means that "virtually no price... is free from politics" (Chang 1999: 197). This highlights the pervasiveness of political regulation and market-making intervention.

Market-making is thus not a one-dimensional phenomenon, and it is not exclusively the prerogative of ordo-liberal Germany or neo-liberal Britain. All nation states engage in market-making interventionism, but the kinds of markets they make can differ somewhat, due largely to different political-economic traditions. Market-making practices are profoundly shaped by historical institutional and ideational legacies, such as state traditions of political economy. Therefore market-making can have, for example, ordo-liberal, neo-liberal and post-*dirigiste* variants in Germany, Britain, and France respectively. Analysing twenty-first century capitalism in terms of economic patriotism throws into relief these multi-faceted interventions in all their variety and complexity.

Put differently, studying the nature of economic intervention across countries defies the neat classifications into liberal market economies and organized market economies that constrain free competition. Rather, the phenomenon of economic patriotism, which is common across countries, highlights that all governments seek to accommodate free markets whilst struggling to find an optimal mix of open markets and political control over economic activity. The pervasiveness of the phenomenon is linked to the underlying contradictions between economic and political boundaries. For all governments, the question is therefore not whether to constrain markets or build a liberal market economy, but *what kind* of economic liberalism to espouse.

4. The novelty of current economic patriotism

Despite our insistence on the transversal nature of this problem, we do not share the assumptions of convergence theories (see Bennett 1990), or even more problematic, 'end of history' arguments, such as the one formulated by

Fukuyama (1992), who believed that liberalism has resolved all fundamental contradictions in human life. From our perspective, these theories require qualification because they do violence to the empirical political economic realities and complexities of modern capitalism. We seek to show that many contradictions endure. Given the paradox of neo-liberal democracy, governments are not free to make markets as they please, but rather have to operate both within parameters of international and supra-national rules which may enshrine models of political economy that are not to their taste. They do so within the constraints of domestic, local, or regional politics, which can hold decision-makers accountable to a variety of constituencies.

This tension between domestic politics and an increasingly dense layer of transnational jurisdictions leads to a transformation of economic intervention. Much has been written about the particularistic interests governments pursue when intervening in the economy. But the last decade has also shown that governments are caught in a more general conundrum: they need to defend the interests of their constituents in markets that they only partially control. As the layers of transnational jurisprudential and regulatory regimes became denser, new rules superseded prior national level regulation. In some instances, in particular in relation to traditional industrial policy, these new international laws, rules, and norms contradicted and proscribed pre-existing national practice. Policy elites found their traditional means to defend territorial economic interests outlawed by the liberal international market regimes they themselves had constructed and enmeshed their economies into. This multi-layered fabric of political authority necessary to frame and maintain market activity, operating at sub-national, national, and supranational regional levels, continues to be a feature of twenty-first century capitalism. These international rules and laws are becoming increasingly significant in governing economic activities. As a result, these tensions and contradictions weighed heavier upon economic policy-makers, hemming in their room to manoeuvre, especially in Europe where the overlapping economic governance regimes and their rules are most developed.

In response, governments have become increasingly self-confident in affirming parochial interests in international economic activities. But unlike the mercantilism that characterized international negotiations in the past, the national stakes of states and firms are now presented in a much more multifaceted manner (Fioretos 2011). In particular, we observe today a transformation of instruments and strategic shifts in the location of economic governance. Let us discuss both of these in turn before making a final comment on the novel forms of political rhetoric.

First of all, governments no longer play a central role as planners or economic producers. Comprehensively shielding entire sectors from competition is becoming increasingly delicate, and direct state aid or subsidies need to be justified externally and become therefore relegated to crisis situations. To counteract this loss of influence, governments resort to regulatory battles to safeguard national production advantages. Moreover, they can seek to bury intervention in what seem to be technical details. For these reasons, we now observe an intense debate about the 'hidden protectionism' inherent in regulatory policy-making (Vogel 1995; Jordana and Levi-Faur 2004). Indeed, the majority of negotiations in international economic integration today concern not fully-fledged liberalization or outright protectionism, but effects of domestic regulation for the free movement of capital, labour, goods, or services (Drezner 2007; Farrell and Newman 2011).

The importance of transnational regulation in contemporary capitalism has been fairly widely analysed. Braithwaite and Drahos (2000) in their exhaustive study of business regulation find significant similarities between national regimes, attributing this in part to the emergence of an international epistemic community of business regulators leading to some convergence in global regimes of regulation. A more recent literature offers a less teleological interpretation of 'transnationalization' and the increasing scope and breadth of regulatory and governance activities of all kinds, wherein 'the proliferation of regulatory activities, actors, networks or constellations leads to an explosion of rules and to the profound re-ordering of our world' (Djelic and Sahlin-Andersson 2006: 1). In this view, regulation is 'a complex compound of activities bridging the global and the local and taking place at the same time within, between and across national boundaries' (Djelic and Sahlin-Andersson 2006: 3). This means that 'regulatory boundaries do not necessarily coincide with national boundaries', with states actively embedded in and constrained by a transnational regulatory order which remains 'very much in the making' (Djelic and Sahlin-Andersson 2006: 2; Djelic and Quack 2010 and in this volume).

From our perspective, we argue there are often economic patriotic drivers behind new regulatory initiatives and activism. Some regulation enshrines traditional product or process standards, thus favouring insiders already acquainted with the system, for example licensing procedures or professional qualifications. A virulent debate has ensued about the necessity of maintaining specific standards. However, conflicts are resolved only on a case-by-case basis where a diverse set of regulatory instances determine which standards truly serve legitimate social values (e.g. risk management or environmental protection), and which are simple protectionism clothed in convoluted political rhetoric. In trade policy, the defence of national interests has thus moved from tariffs to regulatory standards. This implies that governments can simultaneously move to open up markets that were previously closed to international competition, but still enshrine standards that give their home producers a slight advantage in such global markets. It would for example make little sense to speak of the General Agreement on the Trade of Services as a protectionist agreement, and yet we will be sure to find national interests buried in the details of the sectoral agreements that constitute the GATS.

Similarly to the transformation of trade policy, governments had to find ways to deal with the deregulation of financial markets and the opening up of corporate finance to foreign investors. To avoid losing control over firms that could be bought by foreign investors at their will, national control had to play out through takeover regulation and corporate governance reforms. Thus the remaking of markets for corporate control can infuse them with economic partiality protecting insiders. The apparently technical issue of takeover regulation becomes highly politicized as it becomes a crucial means for governments to attempt to protect their corporate and industrial 'patrimony' (Clift 2009a). Facilitating outward foreign direct investment whilst simultaneously preventing foreign 'raiders' from acquiring key strategic assets and firms becomes the name of the game. This explains, in the context of the EU Takeover Directive, the German negotiating position and their desire to retain certain takeover defences. With Ford eyeing up Volkswagen at the time, the German government sought to prevent more hostile takeovers of its national champions, as had happened with Vodaphone-Mannesmann in 1999 (Knudsen 2005: 510–11).

As in trade policy and financial markets, governments concentrate on regulation in a variety of sectors to maintain control in markets which they have simultaneously sought to liberalize. The defence of constituency interests does not simply lead to protectionism, it can also entail forms of liberalization that are advantageous to homeland stakeholders, support for home country producers abroad, or the integration of markets at the regional level that is most beneficial to the states' citizens.

A second novelty of economic patriotism is the way in which governments can seize the multiple spaces of economic governance to shape new policy solutions in order to protect their constituents' interests. Particularly in Europe, policy-makers can shift economic governance to the European level and often do so, when their domestic interests stand to gain from further integration. Contrary to a common perception that liberalization runs counter to the protection of special interests, such EU-wide liberalization can actually favour special interests by protecting them against actors outside of the regional unit. This is often cited as the motivation for the Common Agricultural Policy, which helps to preserve French farmers' interests in world markets. Similarly, just as *dirigiste* France is said to have supported liberal European integration to strengthen its role on the world stage, the United States might have endorsed international trade agreements not to promote global welfare, but to establish a world-wide economic pre-eminence in the newly liberalized sectors.

Such supranational economic patriotism can aim to preserve comparative advantages that already exist, which the debate about defensive regionalism and 'fortress Europe' has highlighted. But we also observe supranational economic patriotism that seeks to create new comparative advantages, for example by creating 'European champions', In France, where the support for national champions has a long tradition, politicians nowadays call for support for French and European champions in one single phrase. The industrial cooperation in defence policy or aeronautics, most notably through the European Aeronautic Defence and Space Company (EADS), for example, is clearly motivated by the desire of its participating countries to join forces and stand up against American competitors. When national patriotism has become ineffective, because markets are too large for one country to control the future of its firms effectively, regional agreements provide an alternative that is increasingly feasible, due to the considerable institutional structure already in place in Europe. Today, we can see, for example, national governments within the EU pushing for local territorial discrimination through geographical indications such as Parma Ham to be recognized at the WTO. Both the regulatory venues and the transformation of economic space is thus a novel characteristic of economic patriotism that we have only observed in the last two or three decades.

A final noteworthy aspect is not the kind of political action economic patriotism triggers, but the way in which it is employed in political rhetoric. In fact, after a decade of an apparent neo-liberal consensus that followed the end of the Cold War, the years since 2000 have been marked by a rise in economic patriotism discourse, which had been quite taboo earlier on. Policymakers, even those of impeccable liberal credentials, have become increasingly assertive in staking claims for the defence of territorial insiders within their policy discourse. Reflecting this change, newspapers identify economic intervention increasingly as economic nationalism or economic patriotism strategies. Especially in Europe, the use of such terms was rather uncommon in the 1990s, but gained increasing importance in the 2000s.

Figure 3.1 shows that 2006 marked the peak of articles on the topic, in France especially because the newly invented term 'economic patriotism' gained political currency, but results are not much different in other European countries. One should note, however, that although the increase in usage is comparable in German publications, it is much lower in absolute numbers, which may indicate that an explicitly nationalist discourse is weak in German economic policy and still somewhat taboo, as Medrano (2003) has shown in his analysis of attitudes towards European integration. In the US, by contrast, comments on economic nationalism frequently appear in newspapers, especially in times of economic crisis.

The global financial crisis beginning in 2008 has provided a fertile environment in which these economically partial policy instincts can find increasingly

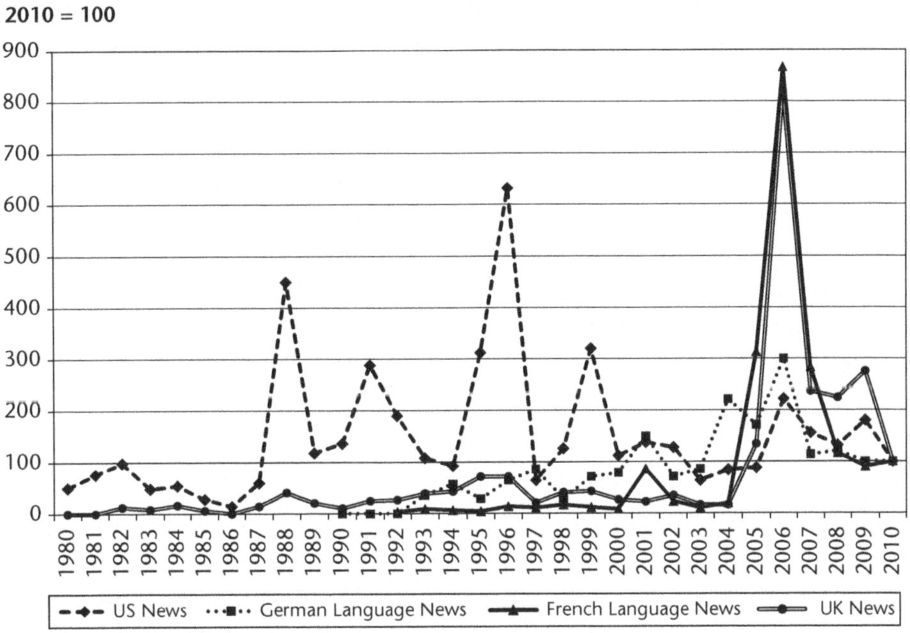

Figure 3.1. Economic nationalism and patriotism in the press

Source: Lexis-Nexis database

Note: Search terms 'economic nationalism' or 'Economic patriotism' or equivalent in French and German. The absolute article count in each series has been scaled to converge in 2010 to allow comparing the evolutions over time.

self-confident expression. And yet, the emergence and arrival of this terminology within the political lexicon of policy elites *before* the downturn illustrates that this is not just a crisis phenomenon. The global financial crisis put a magnifying glass on the inherent tension that exists between liberal integrated international markets and the pursuit of territorial political economic interests. The contradictions between internationalizing liberal market integration and spatially limited political mandates have simply become more visibly reflected in political action and discourse since the Great Recession began.

5. Conclusion

Analysts have warned against the revival of economic nationalism or economic patriotism in response to the financial crisis. We have tried to argue that such diagnoses depend on two fallacies. To begin with, they ignore the persistence of national purpose and economic intervention over time and are build on a myth of self-regulating global markets that supposedly functioned prior to the 'revival' of economic patriotism. Moreover, they do not see that economic patriotism is linked to a profound contradiction of neo-liberal democracies that arises from the mismatch of political and economic boundaries. As a response to this contradiction, economic patriotism is indeed endemic to twenty-first century capitalism, although it manifests itself to different degress within affluent and developing economies.

We do agree, however, that something is qualitatively different about economic patriotism, which is also why we propose to use this recent terminology rather than 'economic nationalism', First, state activism is less central than in the post-war period and governments need to reinvent economic intervention to gain control over national stakes through technical regulation. Second, economic governance can be shifted between different levels of political authority, and governments (and other economic actors) use these possibilities strategically to defend the interests of their homeland producers and stakeholders. Economic intervention that was previously confined to national boundaries can now take the form of supranational economic patriotism, for example, in particular in the EU. These changes increasingly blur the line between policy action aimed at liberalizing economic activity and that aimed at protecting insiders. Economic patriotism is thus not necessarily protectionist, if the interests of home market producers can be best supported through strategic market opening.

The ambiguity of the nature of economic intervention, combined with the pressure politicians face from their constituents who are unwilling to accept that their governments no longer control the central elements of economic activities, has led to a new self-assertiveness of politicians and decision-makers. Both Nicolas Sarkozy and Barack Obama have become unabashed in their readiness to defend their firms or workers, even against the strict rules of the WTO, NAFTA, or the EU. Both at the level of rhetoric and in terms of policy instruments, economic intervention thus adapted to the constraints of overlapping political and economic jurisdictions. Economic patriotism, as defined and deployed here, brings into sharp focus these changed conditions of multi-level economic governance which characterizes twenty-first century capitalism.

References

Abdelal, Rawi (2001) *National Purpose in the World Economy*, Ithaca, NY: Cornell University Press.

—— (2005) 'Nationalism and International Political Economy in Eurasia', pp. 21–43 in Eric Helleiner and Andreas Pickel (eds) *Economic Nationalism in a Globalizing World*, Ithaca, N.Y.: Cornell University Press.

Annesley, C. (2007) 'Lisbon and Social Europe: Towards a European "adult worker model" welfare system', *Journal of European Social Policy*, 17(3): 195–205.

Beetham, David (1974) *Max Weber and the Theory of Modern Politics*, London: Allen & Unwin.

Bennett, Colin J. (1990) 'Review Article: What is policy convergence and what causes it?' *British Journal of Political Science*, 21(2): 215–33.

Braithwaite, John and Peter Drahos (2000) *Global Business Regulation*, Cambridge: Cambridge University Press.

Carayon, Bernard (2006) *Patriotisme èconomique: de la guerre à la paix èconomique*, Monaco: Editions du Rochia.

Chang, Ha-Joon (1999) 'The Economic Theory of the Developmental State', pp. 182–99, in Meredith Woo-Cumings (ed), *The Developmental State*, Ithaca, NY: Cornell University Press, pp. 182–99.

Clift, Ben (2009a) 'Second Time as Farce? The EU Takeover Directive, the clash of capitalisms and the hamstrung harmonisation of European (and French) corporate governance', *The Journal of Common Market Studies*, 47(1): 55–79.

—— (2009b) 'National and European Social Models: Contesting European welfare futures', pp. 195–216 in Andrew Gamble and David Lane (eds) *The European Union And World Politics: Consensus and division*, Basingstoke: Palgrave.

—— and Cornelia Woll (2012) 'Economic Patriotism and the Reinvention of Political Control in Liberalising Markets', *Journal of European Public Policy*, 19(3).

Crouch, Colin (2005) *Capitalist Diversity and Change*, Oxford: Oxford University Press.

—— and Patrick, Le Galès (forthcoming) 'Competitive Cities: Urban development as the reinvention of industrial policy? *Journal of European Public Policy*.

Daly, M. (2006) 'EU Social Policy after Lisbon', *Journal of Common Market Studies*, 44(3): 461–81.

D'Costa, Anthony P. (2009) 'Economic Nationalism in Motion: Steel, auto, and software industries in India', *Review of International Political Economy*, 16(4): 620–48.

Djelic, Marie-Laure and Kerstin, Sahlin-Andersson (2006) 'Introduction: A world of governance: The rise of transnational regulation', pp. 1–28 in Djelic and Sahlin-Andersson (eds) *Transnational Governance*, Cambridge. Cambridge University Press.

—— and Sigrid Quack, (eds) (2010) *'Transnational Communities'*, Cambridge: Cambridge University Press.

Drezner, Daniel W. (2007) *All Politics Is Global: Explaining international regulatory regimes*, Princeton, N.J.: Princeton University Press.

Farrell, Henry and Abraham, Newman (2011) 'The Domestic Institutional Determinants of International Market Regulation', *Review of International Political Economy*, 18(4): 609–38.

Fetzer, Thomas (forthcoming) 'From Nationalism to European patriotism? Trade unions and the European works council at General Motors', *Journal of European Public Policy*.

Fioretos, Orfeo (2011) *Creative Reconstructions: Multilateralism and European varieties of capitalism after 1950*, Ithaca, NY: Cornell University Press.

Fligstein, Neil (2001) *The Architecture of Markets: An economic sociology of twenty-first-century capitalist societies*, Princeton, N.J.: Princeton University Press.

Fukuyama, Francis (1992) *The End of History and the Last Man*, New York: Free Press.

Gamble, Andrew (1995) 'The New Political Economy', *Political Studies*, 43(3): 516–30.

Grant, Wyn (forthcoming) 'Economic Patriotism in European Agriculture', *Journal of European Public Policy*.

Hall, Peter and David, Soskice (eds) (2001) *Varieties of Capitalism: Institutional foundations of comparative advantage*, Cambridge: Cambridge University Press.

Helleiner, Eric (2002) "Economic Nationalism as a Challenge to Economic Liberalism? Lesson from the nineteenth century", *International Studies Quarterly*, 46(3): 307–29.

—— and Andreas Pickel (eds) (2005) *Economic Nationalism in a Globalizing World*, Ithaca, N.Y.: Cornell University Press.

Hodgson, Geoff (2001) *How Economics Forgot History: The problem of historical specificity in social science*, London: Routledge.

Hoeffler, Catherine (forthcoming) 'Industrial Policy Motives Behind European Defence Cooperation', *Journal of European Public Policy*.

Hildebrand, Bruno (1848) *Economics of the Present and the Future*, Frankfurt/Main.

Jakubyszyn, C. (2005) 'Dominique de Villepin en appelle au patriotisme économique', *Le Monde*, 29 July.

Jordana, Jacint and David, Levi-Faur (eds) (2004) *The Politics of Regulation: Institutions and regulatory reforms for the age of governance*, Cheltenham: Edward Elgar Publishing.

Knudsen, J. (2005) 'Is the Single European Market an Illusion? Obstacles to reform of EU takeover regulation', *European Law Journal*, 11(4): 507–24.

Krippner, G. and A. Alvarez (2007) 'Embeddedness and the Intellectual Projects of Economic Sociology', *Annual Review of Sociology*, 33: 219–40.

Lassman, P. and R. Speirs (1994) *Weber: Political Writings (Cambridge Texts in the History of Political Thought)*, Cambridge: Cambridge University Press.

Levy, Jonah (1999) *Toqueville's Revenge: State, society and economy in contemporary France*, Cambridge: Harvard University Press.

—— (2006) 'The State after Statism: From market direction to market support, pp. 4367–394 in J., Levy (ed.) *The State After Statism*, Cambridge: Harvard University Press.

Levi-Faur, David (1997) 'Friedrich List and the Political Economy of the Nation-State', *Review of International Political Economy*, 4(1): 154–78.

List, Friedrich ([1841] 1974) *National System of Political Economy*, New York: Garland Publisher.

Medrano, Juan Diez (2003) *Framing Europe: Attitudes to European Integration in Germany, Spain, and the United Kingdom*, Princeton, NJ: Princeton University Press.

Pickel, Andreas (2005) 'False Oppositions: Reconceptualizing economic nationalism in a globalizing world', pp. 1–17 in Eric Helleiner, and Andreas Pickel (eds) *Economic Nationalism in a Globalizing World*, Ithaca, NY: Cornell University Press.

Polanyi, Karl (2001 [1944]) *The Great Transformation*, Boston, Mass: Beacon Press.

Quaglia, Lucia (2010) 'Completing the Single Market in Financial Services: The politics of competing advocacy coalitions', *Journal of European Public Policy*, 17(7): 1007–22.

—— (2011) 'The "Old" and "New" Political Economy of Hedge Funds Regulation in the European Union', *West European Politics* 34(4): 665–82.

Rosamond, B. (2002) 'Imagining the European Economy: Competitiveness and the social construction of "Europe" as an economic space,' *New Political Economy*, 7(2): 157–77.

—— (forthcoming) 'Supranational Governance as Economic Patriotism? The European Union, legitimacy and the reconstruction of state space', *Journal of European Public Policy*.

Roscher, W. (1843) *Outline of Lectures on Political Economy According to the Historical Method*, Gőttingen: Dieterich.

Shonfield, A. (1969) *Modern Capitalism*, Oxford: Oxford University Press.

Tribe, K. (2003) 'Historical Schools of Economics: German and English', pp. 215–30 in Samuels, Biddle and Davis (eds) *A Companion to the History of Economic Thought*, Oxford: Wiley.

Vogel, S. (1995) *Freer Markets, More Rules*, Ithaca, N.Y.: Cornell University Press.

Weber, Max (1981) *General Economic History*, New Brunswick, NJ: Transaction Books.

—— ([1895] 1994) 'The Nation State and Economic Policy (inaugural lecture)', pp. 1–28 in Lassman and Speirs (eds) *Weber: Political Writings* (Cambridge Texts in the History of Political Thought), Cambridge: Cambridge University Press.

Zysman, John (1983) *Governments, Markets, and Growth: Financial systems and the politics of industrial change*, Ithaca, N.Y.: Cornell University Press.

4

National Varieties of Labour Market Exposure*

Colin Crouch

Introduction

Although they have eventually branched out to embrace most aspects of the economy, theories of capitalist diversity have usually originated in studies of the labour market and social policy. These are also the fields in which this strand of research has had its greatest success in influencing public policy, with the OECD, European Commission and many individual governments having come to accept over the years that there are different institutional patterns among advanced capitalist economies. For a long time this institutionalism tended to be highly neo-liberal, with institutions that protected labour and provided generous social policy being seen as unequivocally associated with economic stagnation, and only economies with labour and social regimes that stayed 'close to market' being able to provide dynamism (OECD 1994; World Bank annual, since 2006).

This approach favoured dualistic analyses that grouped national economies into those under liberal market regimes and those where various impediments to free markets were seen to be in place, with little interest in variations among the forms taken by these impediments. The fact that the liberal market grouping is almost entirely coterminous with Anglophone countries inheriting the English system of common law imparted further tidiness to this category, with the heterogeneity of the large residuum of continental Europe and Japan being left unexplored under a general label like 'co-ordinated' (Hall and Soskice 2001). More recently there has been some moderation of this dualism, as both academic research and the straightforward economic record have made clear the strong

* This chapter was prepared during 2010, before the publication of some new data, especially in the characteristics of industrial relations systems and more recent unemployment statistics.

performance of the Nordic economies, paradoxically those in which certain kinds of labour rights and social policy have been the most strongly developed (Amable 2003; Boyer 2004; Boyer and Freyssenet 2000; Kristensen and Lilja 2011). This has reinforced the reputation of Esping-Andersen's work, dating back to 1990 (four years before the OECD *Jobs Study* and well before the debate over diversity in capitalist economic systems), which had identified three types of welfare state: liberal (Anglophone), social democratic (Nordic) and conservative/corporatist (the residuum of continental Europe). The fact that his typology was initially based solely on the type of income replacement represented in social insurance policies makes its wider relevance particularly remarkable.

Meanwhile, other work has identified further groupings, again focused primarily on social policy regimes. Restricting attention to Europe, both the south-west and the former state socialist economies have been seen to require separate attention and break down the 'continental' residuum. A useful synthetic account of various attempts at a wider classification drawing on these additional sources has been made by the European Commission (2009), which presents the typology shown in Table 4.1. Since this is based primarily on issues important to industrial relations, it is particularly relevant to the topic of this chapter. Although, as one might expect from a Commission document, it uses purely geographical labels, it also contains some ideas about institutional structure, as indicated by its placing of France in the South and Slovenia in the Centre West, and its hesitation over Finland and Hungary. I have therefore added an additional column to the table to indicate the main institutional ideas underlying the classification. The Commission's framework is limited to EU member states, plus the additional members of

Table 4.1. Allocation of countries to social policy regimes (European Commission) [column 2 added by current author]

Social policy regime		Country
EU 'geographical' approach	Institutional approach	
North	Social democratic	Denmark, Finland [possibly Centre West], Norway, Sweden
Centre West	Conservative, 'Bismarckian' welfare state	Austria, Belgium, Germany, Netherlands, Slovenia, Switzerland
South	Similar to Centre West, but with strong welfare role for family	France, Greece, Italy, Portugal, Spain
West	Liberal market economies	Ireland, UK
Centre East	Former state socialist economies	Bulgaria, Czech Republic, Estonia, Hungary [possibly South], Latvia, Lithuania, Poland, Romania, Slovakia

Source: European Commission

the European Economic Area, Norway and Switzerland. In the present chapter we use this basis, removing from it countries with populations of under a million, and adding (where data are available) Japan and the USA. The USA has been allocated to the European 'West', this group being institutionally defined in terms of liberal markets. Japan is sometimes aligned with what the Commission calls the 'Centre West' group, but it will here be kept in a category of its own.

National arrangements, whether of capitalism in general or a specific institutional field like the labour market do not remain frozen in time. They adjust in a mass of little responses by firms and policy-makers to a changing trading and technological environment—minor movements that can accumulate to make major system change, as Streeck and Thelen (2005; Thelen 2003) have demonstrated. Also, policy-makers have been exposed to academic arguments concerning the differential performance of different kinds of economic institution. For several years this has meant exposure to the claims that a liberalization, or more crudely an Americanization, of labour markets and social policy would be necessary if national economies, particularly in Europe, were to regain competitiveness within a new global economy. More recently the policy debate has become more subtle, as first academic observers and then policy-makers have discovered various policy compromises that might combine the flexibility associated with market-sensitive arrangements with the security both sought by work forces and necessary to maintain domestic demand, and without which moves to freer markets might be opposed. Starting with certain policy developments taking place in Denmark and, rather differently, the Netherlands, these combinations have been dubbed 'flexicurity.' As such they have been advocated as strongly across member states of the European Union as simple liberalization had been a few years previously (European Commission 2010). In keeping with the Open Method of Coordination approach to policy-making in these fields within the EU, countries have been left to find their own mixes of flexibility and security, enhancing the diversity of policies to be observed but also diluting the meaning of the concept of flexicurity until it means almost any combination of regulation and deregulation.

In a separate development, international organizations have come under pressure to revise the extreme view of the negative effects of protective labour legislation that had been advocated by them as part of the 'Washington Consensus' since the 1990s. A major instance has been the annual report, *Doing Business,* produced by the World Bank since 2002. This provides indicators of the ease of setting up firms and doing business in most countries of the world. Labour standards were one component of the index, countries being ranked highly if they had no restrictions on, for example, the use of labour, no minimum wage, no protection of workers against dismissal; and lowly if they had strong protective measures on these dimensions. Achieving a high score on the Bank's labour indicators required being in breach of many of the conventions of the International Labour Organization, another major global body. In 2007 the Bank changed its scoring system so that it was impossible for a country to have a high score unless it complied with ILO standards on a number of issues, such as labour contract termination provisions, weekend working, holidays with pay, and night work. In successive years it made similar changes relating to further ILO conventions, until in the 2010 report it announced that until further notice data on labour standards would no longer be used to construct the 'doing business' rankings.

A further new development since most typologies and classifications of economic institutions and policies were produced has been the financial crisis of 2008, which struck particularly at many of the assumptions of the liberal or Anglophone model, not immediately in the labour and social field, but in the more central institutions of its highly liberalized financial markets. The 'impatience' of these markets, identified by Hall and Soskice and their colleagues (2001) as fundamental to the success of these economies, was rapidly seen in a different light.

It is therefore a useful time to reappraise the links that might exist between different elements of labour and social policy institutions, both with each other and with various indicators of economic performance. Our aim is threefold: (1) to test the utility of the dominant approaches to a typology of labour market regimes; (2) to discover if it is possible to construct a revised typology; (3) to relate the findings to certain indicators of economic performance.

A framework of analysis for labour market regimes

The simplest starting point for such a project remains the neoliberal preference for a contrast between the characteristics of a pure market economy and one in which markets are limited by non-market institutions, without differentiating within the two. Analysis must then take the further step of trying to find a basis for identifying any wider diversity. Table 4.2 presents the extreme positions on such a scale across three key elements of labour and social policy institutions. The general principle is to set at one pole the conditions in which labour is exposed fully to the market, and at the other those in which it is protected from such exposure.

First is the industrial relations system, trade unions being one of the main means by which employees have tried to erect protection against the market, unions in liberal societies (as opposed to liberal economies) using collective bargaining as their central instrument for providing this protection. In an ideal neoliberal economy there are no trade unions; but there is a paradox here in that neoliberalism has to accept the general liberal principle of freedom of association. In a neoliberal world, therefore, unions can exist provided they

Table 4.2. Key labour and social policy institutions, extremes of market-exposure continuum

Labour institutions	*Market-exposed*	*Market-protected*
Industrial relations: bargaining coverage	No collective bargaining	Extensive coverage of work force
Industrial relations: bargaining coordination	None	Extensive
Employment forms	Varied; high level of self-employment	Predominance of standard employment
Employment conditions	Unregulated	Strong employment protection laws
Social protection: overall provision	Low	High
Social protection: support for unemployed	Low	High

can have no effect on wages and conditions. This means that in such an economy there should be no institutions for organized industrial relations; that is, no arrangements for collective bargaining. If bargaining does exist, then the smaller the proportion of the work force involved, the better. Also, it should be as close to market as possible; that is, highly fragmented, uncoordinated, preferably limited to individual firms with no cross-firm linkage. These desiderata can be captured through two characteristics: to be compatible with the neo-liberal paradigm, collective bargaining should cover as small a proportion of the work force as possible; and should lack coordination. The perfect neo-liberal economy would have zero scores on both these variables; the extreme opposite position would see 100 per cent bargaining coverage and coordination. But there are also important intermediate positions. There is the possibility of a high value on one of the two variables and a low one on the other: strongly coordinated but weakly spread bargaining, or extensive but weakly coordinated. These differences may have important implications for how labour markets behave, as an extensive literature has studied (much of this is summarized, and considerable new data provided, in Traxler, Brandl, and Glassner 2008). Broadly and paradoxically, high coordination with high coverage is often seen to produce outcomes that conform more with market forces than low coordination with high coverage—because bargainers coordinating across a market economy have a capacity to take strategic action in relation to potentially negative outcomes of their activity. Different again will be bargaining with partial coverage of a work force; this can be associated with arrangements that protect labour-market 'insiders' at the expense of others (Rueda 2005).

Second are practices and measures, which, even in the absence of collective bargaining, can protect work forces from immediate market exposure. These can result from employer behaviour and from government action.

Considering first the former, we must note how what became the normal work form of the twentieth century economy, employment on an ongoing, indefinite contract by a firm or other employing organization, is not fully compatible with complete exposure to the market, as workers are to some extent protected from its rigours from the time that they accept terms of employment at one employer to the time that they change jobs. In recognition of this, the OECD, in its assessments of the degree of fluidity in national labour markets, measures the length of time that employees remain in a post, low levels of job tenure being an indicator of well-functioning labour markets. There is a flaw in this measure, in that low tenure can also indicate poor job matching and economic instability. An alternative approach is to measure levels of self-employment, the purest form of market for labour. This employment form has certainly been encouraged as part of the neoliberal agenda, as the self-employed have no barrier of organizational protection at all. Here, alone among our indicators, a *high* score constitutes high conformity with the neoliberal model.

Government action to protect workers from the market consists mainly in employment protection legislation (EPL) of various kinds. In recent years the OECD, seeking to measure conformity to the free-market ideal, has developed an EPL indicator. This assesses the strength of a number of legally mandated employee rights to protection against individual and collective dismissal, as well as protections for temporary workers (i.e. those on fixed-term contracts) and then aggregates them. There has been considerable criticism of the validity of this indicator. Like the collective bargaining coverage indicator, it takes no account of the self-employed. Here we are dealing with this by setting self-employment as a separate indicator of market pressure on the labour market. Second, questions can be asked about the aggregation procedure; that criticism remains valid in relation to our use of it here.

These two employment protection variables (self-employment and EPL) can operate independently of each other, as they have quite different sources and purposes. In constructing their employment conditions, firms are concerned with their own needs for labour stability, not for employees' needs; stability for workers' lives is a by-product of these arrangements, and subject to employers' decision-making. Of course, this decision-making may be bounded by collective bargaining and by law, but we are dealing with that in other parts of the model. In general, we should expect very different kinds of labour market protection from these two forms.

A third and final area for examination concerns the size of government spending on social protection, as this can be seen as protecting workers and their dependants from the effects of the labour market on their standard of living. Where there is low social spending, market forces impact more sharply on standard of living, which may be expected to make workers more responsive to those forces in their labour market behaviour. This can be seen as operating generally, but with particular impact on unemployment compensation, as this can be considered to raise the reservation wage, keeping wages artificially high and reducing the market's incentives to work. The first datum (general social spending) is easily captured by OECD estimates of spending on social provisions expressed as a percentage of GDP. The OECD has also constructed an index of unemployment generosity that captures both size of payments and the length of time for which support is available. This is expressed as a percentage of the average wage represented by the sum of various unemployment benefits five years after unemployment starts.

Together these variables enable us to access three key components of exposure to and protection from the labour market: the industrial relations system, conditions of employment, and labour-related social expenditure. Other, less direct, areas could be added, and some attention will be paid to this later. But these three are probably the most important. The specific indicators chosen for each are also of major importance, though others might have been chosen. For example, the membership strength of trade unions and the role of different industries in collective bargaining could be added to the study of collective bargaining. The study of employment forms could have taken account of temporary work and the shadow economy. The study of social protection could pay attention to other forms of social spending, such as active labour market policy. To add these and others would, however, make an already complex analysis even more so, so a judgement has had to be made as to relative importance, a richer account being postponed for a more detailed study. Whether the selection made has been the most salient will be a matter for debate and criticism.

Table 4.3 presents relevant data for the selected elements for different countries. The figures are for the most recent year available, which is normally 2008, or in some cases 2007. Table 4.3 also provides, in columns of Roman numerals following each of the variables, an indication of where countries fall, relatively, on the various continua. These values are based on relations to the mean values and standard deviations for the variables concerned, as explained in detail in the note to the table. Addition of further countries or subtractions from the existing list would of course change positions on these lists, which are based on means of the group concerned. This simple methodology is appropriate for the purposes of the chapter, which are to investigate the characteristics of an identified group of nation states, with particular interest in those coming close to the poles of the continua identified in Table 4.2.

This part of the discussion is designed to identify diversity and, if they are present, patterns of diversity. In a later section, we shall see if it is possible to align certain socio-economic outcomes with these differences:

Table 4.3. Protection from and exposure to labour market, *c*.2008

Country	COO		COV		SEM		EPL		PRO		URL	
Austria	0.77	I	0.99	I	13.8	III	1.93	IV	27.3	I	62	III
Belgium	0.49	II	0.96	I	14.2	III	2.18	III	26.6	II	65	II
Bulgaria	0.40	IV	0.25	VI	n.a.		n.a.		14.6	VI	42	V
Czech R	0.38	IV	0.44	IV	16.2	IV	1.96	IV	18.1	V	55	III
Denmark	0.44	III	0.82	II	8.8	II	1.50	V	28.9	I	75	I
Estonia	0.30	IV	0.22	VI	7.7	I	2.10	II	14.9	VI	35	VI
Finland	0.39	IV	0.90	I	12.8	III	1.96	IV	25.5	II	70	II
France	0.27	VI	0.95	I	9.0	II	3.05	I	29.3	I	61	III
Germany	0.50	II	0.63	III	11.7	II	2.13	III	26.7	II	62	III
Greece	0.40	IV	0.85	II	35.1	VI	2.73	I	25.1	II	23	VI
Hungary	0.25	VI	0.33	V	12.3	III	1.65	V	22.3	III	51	IV
Ireland	0.45	III	n.a.		17.3	IV	1.11	VI	20.9	IV	75	I
Italy	0.39	IV	0.80	II	25.7	VI	1.89	IV	26.5	II	9	VI
Latvia	0.42	III	0.20	VI	n.a.		n.a.		12.4	VI	39	V
Lithuania	0.31	V	0.12	VI	n.a.		n.a.		15.7	VI	48	IV
Netherlands	0.59	I	0.82	II	13.2	II	1.95	IV	26.9	II	73	I
Norway	0.40	IV	0.72	III	7.8	I	2.69	I	21.9	IV	73	I
Poland	0.24	VI	0.35	V	22.9	VI	1.90	IV	18.2	V	48	IV
Portugal	0.56	I	0.62	III	24.1	VI	3.15	I	23.2	III	61	III
Romania	0.28	VI	n.a.		n.a.		n.a.		14.1	VI	26	VI
Slovakia	0.51	II	0.35	V	13.8	III	1.44	V	15.5	VI	39	V
Slovenia	0.38	IV	1.00	I	14.1	III	2.51	II	21.0	IV	67	II
Spain	0.46	III	0.80	II	17.7	IV	2.98	I	22.2	III	48	IV
Sweden	0.53	I	0.92	I	10.4	II	1.87	IV	28.8	I	67	II
Switzerland	0.39	IV	0.48	IV	11.1	II	1.14	VI	24.8	II	73	I
UK	0.31	V	0.35	V	13.4	III	0.75	VI	22.7	III	61	III
Japan	0.22	VI	0.16	VI	13.0	III	1.43	V	n.a.		n.a.	
USA	0.29	V	0.14	VI	7.0	I	0.21	VI	n.a.		32	VI

Sources: *COO and COV: European Commission 2008; SEM and EPL: OECD; PRO and; URL: Eurostat. Figures for COV deflated to take account of self-employed.*; COO: index of collective bargaining co-ordination; COV: index of collective bargaining coverage; SEM: percentage of gainfully employed persons in self-employment; EPL: index of employment protection legislation; PRO: percentage of GDP spent on social protection; URL: unemployment pay replacement level; I: more than one standard deviation above mean; II: between 0.5 and one standard deviation above mean; III: between mean and 0.5 standard deviation above mean; IV: between 0.5 standard deviation below mean and mean; V: between one and 0.5 standard deviation below mean; VI: more than one standard deviation below mean

- The proportion of the population of working age in employment (the basic measure of the capacity of an economy to provide economic activity);
- The proportion of young not engaged in education, training, or employment—the so-called NEET population (a measure of the extent to which labour markets institutions protect existing insiders against newcomers);
- A number of indicators of innovation, interpreted in terms of different forms of patent notification.

First it is necessary to review the findings on the market exposure variables.

Industrial relations

Figure 4.1 presents the positions of different countries on the two variables. They are clearly related; the graph has an upward slope, with an R^2 of 0.2893, though there are several examples of positions strongly inconsistent with this. To simplify discussion, we concentrate on those countries that come closest to the extreme positions, using the columns of Roman numerals in Table 4.3. Five countries had values of more than a full or half a standard deviation above the mean on both variables (categories I and II), indicating that they occupy strong positions away from the neoliberal pole. These are Austria, Sweden, Netherlands, Belgium; in terms of Table 4.1, three 'Centre West' (or as it is often described in more institutional terminology, 'conservative Bismarckian') and one 'Northern' or 'social democratic'. Also coming at least above the mean on both values (category III) were Portugal, Germany, Spain, and Denmark—a further Centre West and North case, but also two Southern. Six had values of a full or half a standard deviation below the mean, indicating strong conformity with the neoliberal model (categories V and VI): Japan, the USA, Lithuania, UK, Hungary, Poland; i.e. two 'Western' or 'liberal,' three 'Centre East' or ex-state socialist, and Japan. Two others had values at least below the mean on both variables (category IV): Bulgaria and Estonia, both further Centre East cases. Few cases occupied the 'contrary' positions of high coverage but low coordination (France) or the opposite (Slovakia). For two countries—Ireland and Romania—we have data only for coordination. Ireland occupied an above average position, and therefore differed considerably from its partners in the West group, the UK and USA. Romania, on the other hand, with a score below the mean plus one standard deviation on coordination, looks likely to conform to the pattern of most Centre East countries.

It is possible to challenge the rankings of some countries. Traxler and Brandl (2009), and Traxler, Brandl, and Glassner (2008) have shown how pattern bargaining, where wages across many sectors are strongly determined by

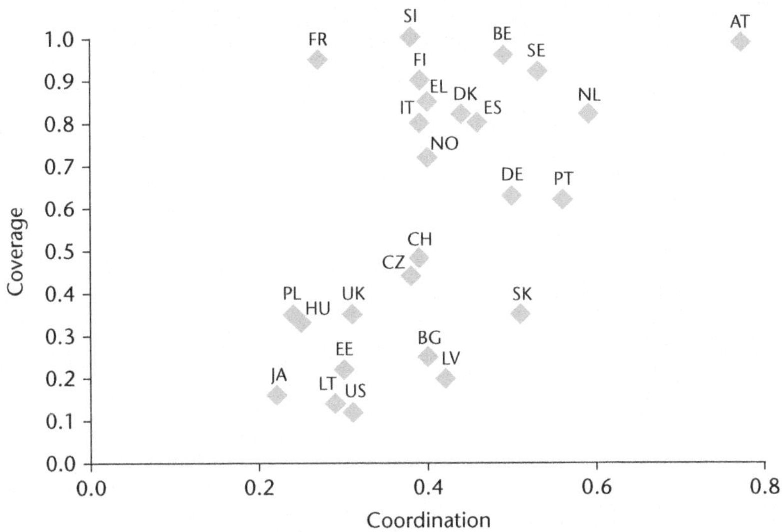

Figure 4.1. Collective bargaining coverage and coordination

Source: Author's calculations based on Visser 2010
Coverage = % of employees covered by wage bargaining
Coordination = Summary measure of centralization and coordination of wage bargaining
Abbreviations: AT Austria; BE Belgium; BG Bulgaria; CH Switzerland; CZ Czech Republic; DE Germany; DK Denmark; EE Estonia; EL Greece; ES Spain; FI Finland; FR France; HU Hungary; IT Italy; JA Japan; LT Lithuania; LV Latvia; NL Netherlands; NO Norway; PL Poland; PT Portugal; SE Sweden; SI Slovenia; SK Slovakia; UK United Kingdom; US United States

bargaining in a dominant export-oriented industry can offer more effective coordination than straightforward organizational coordination. The cases where they identify this occurring are Austria, Germany, Sweden, and Japan. Austria is already the most coordinated, and Sweden fairly strongly so; Japan is rather low-coordinated. One might be justified in adding Germany to the core group on the industrial relations variables (a further Centre West case), but only if there were space to explore this variable thoroughly.

Collective bargaining coverage data apply only to the proportion of the workforce in dependent employment. That is appropriate for most industrial relations research purposes, but here we are interested in how whole labour markets stand on a continuum. Extensive coverage of employees by bargaining might say little about the importance of industrial relations institutions if a large proportion of the workforce is self-employed. This is a separate issue from the role of self-employment as a factor exposing workers to the market (to be discussed below) irrespective of whether employees are covered by collective bargaining. Appropriately corrected data are shown in Table 4.4. Unfortunately we lack relevant data for Bulgaria, Latvia, and Lithuania, but for

Table 4.4. Figures for collective bargaining coverage corrected for proportion of workforce in self-employment

Country	COV	
Austria	0.85	I
Belgium	0.82	I
Bulgaria	0.25	VI
Czech R	0.37	V
Denmark	0.75	II
Estonia	0.20	VI
Finland	0.78	II
France	0.86	I
Germany	0.56	III
Greece	0.55	III
Hungary	0.29	VI
Ireland	n.a.	
Italy	0.59	III
Latvia	0.20	VI
Lithuania	0.12	VI
Netherlands	0.71	II
Norway	0.66	II
Poland	0.27	VI
Portugal	0.47	IV
Romania	n.a.	
Slovakia	0.30	V
Slovenia	0.86	I
Spain	0.66	III
Sweden	0.82	I
Switzerland	0.43	IV
UK	0.30	V
Japan	0.14	VI
USA	0.13	VI

the remaining countries we can note the following changes: the Czech Republic, Finland, Greece, Hungary, Italy, Poland, Portugal, and Spain all drop one category in relation to the standard deviation, pulling them away from the non-neoliberal pole. Norway moves one category in the opposite direction. The effects that this has on our plotting of 'extreme' cases is to remove Portugal and Spain from the circle of cases with relatively high non-conformity with the neoliberal pole, and to bring the Czech Republic into the main neoliberal grouping. Figure 4.2 revises the coverage data displayed in Figure 4.1. In later discussion these revised rankings will be used when referring to this variable.

Overall these statistics enable us to conclude that some, but by no means all, Centre West and North countries conform to the model of coordinated economies in at least their industrial relations, with no systematic differences among the two sub-types; and that most West and Centre East cases come close to the neoliberal pole. This is as anticipated in much existing literature.

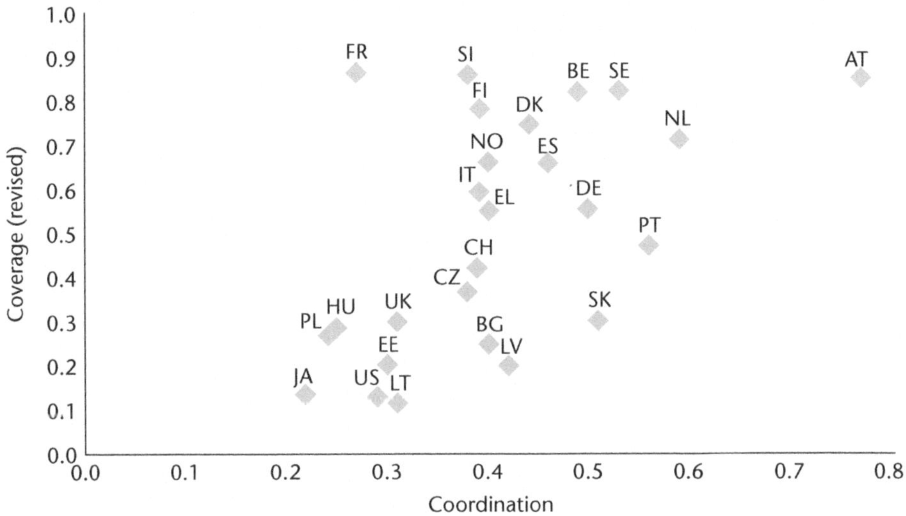

Figure 4.2. Collective bargaining coverage (revised to take account of self-employment) and coordination

Source and abbreviation: as for Figure 4.1
Coverage = % of all workers (employees and self-employed) covered by wage bargaining
Coordination as for Figure 4.1

Employment forms and conditions

Figure 4.3 presents the positions of different countries on the employment variables. Again, the graph has an upward slope, but this time this is surprising, as, if free-market trends are positively associated, high values of self-employment should be associated with low EPL levels. But the R^2 is low at 0.1128. Again we concentrate on those countries that come closest to the extreme positions, using the data in Table 4.3. Only three countries had positions close to the non-neoliberal pole, with values of more than 0.5 above the mean for EPL and below it for self-employment: the very heterogeneous group: Norway, France, Estonia. Germany and Slovenia come at least these sides of the mean on both values. No countries at all are found in the opposing category—high values of self-employment and low values of EPL—that would indicate extreme exposure to the market, though Italy, Poland, and the Czech Republic are close to this position.

There is clearly no association at all between these two labour market exposure indicators of neo-liberalism, and no consistent patterns among groups of countries. The USA, Denmark, and Switzerland are found in the extreme box of lowest self-employment and low EPL. Towards the opposite corner from that, with high EPL and high self-employment, come two South

Figure 4.3. Employment protection law index and self-employment
Source: Author's calculations based on OECD statistics
Abbreviations: as for Figure 4.1, plus IE Ireland
Employment protection law = score on OECD index of strength of employment protection legislative measures, combined index for permanent and temporary workers
Self-employment = % of persons in paid employment who are self-employed

countries, Greece, and Portugal. There is a pattern on the EPL indicator alone, with the lowest positions being occupied by West countries (Ireland and the UK in addition to the USA), and Switzerland. All members of the South group except Italy are found with the highest EPL levels. But none of the other groups had distinctive positions, so this is primarily a 'neoliberal versus southern Europe' contrast. On the other hand, the highest levels of self-employment are found in some South countries (Greece and Portugal, to some extent also Italy and Spain), while the West countries have rather, or in the US case extremely, low levels of self-employment. Self-employed workers are not covered by employment legislation, so the EPL indicator gives a misleading impression of the strength of protection in South countries. This combination of characteristics may indicate strong contrasts between insiders and outsiders in this kind of economy.

Social protection

Data on the social protection variables are presented in Figure 4.4. As we might expect, there is a positive association, but not a close one, between the two indicators (R^2 = 0.2051). Following our usual procedure, we can identify

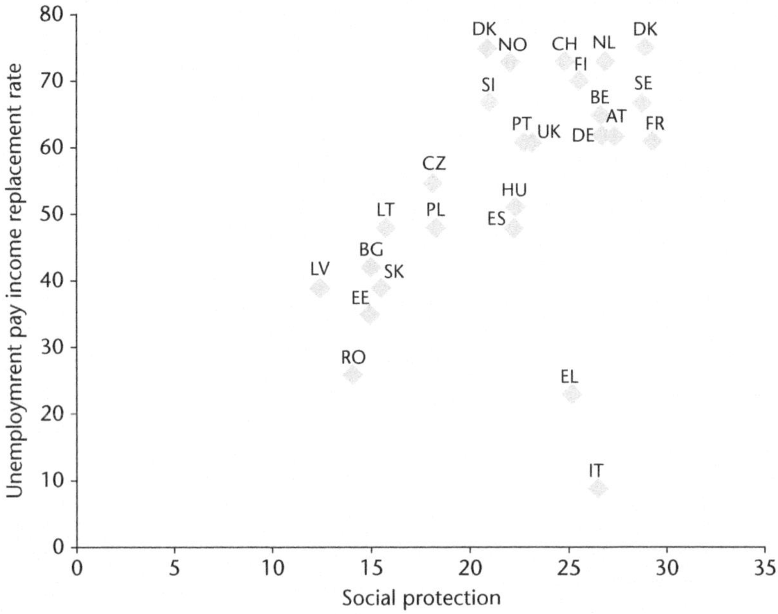

Figure 4.4. Unemployment pay income replacement rate and social protection expenditure

Source: Author's calculations based on Eurostat statistics
Abbreviations: as for Figure 4.3, plus RO Romania
Unemployment pay income replacement rate = Eurostat calculations of proportion of a standardized worker's income received in unemployment compensation after five years without work
Social protection: general government spending on social protection as 5 of GDP

Denmark, Sweden, Netherlands, Switzerland, Finland, and Belgium as occupying the positions furthest away from the neoliberal ideal. This is most of the North group and some Centre West. Austria, France and Germany are not far away from these positions. The neoliberal extreme is occupied by the majority of Centre East countries. We do not have data for overall social protection spending collected on the same basis for Japan and the USA, but we can be fairly certain that in the US case it is low by European standards, and we do have data for the USA on unemployment replacement pay, showing exceptionally low levels. It probably therefore joins the Centre East group at the neoliberal pole as it did for the industrial relations variables. However, the other two West cases, Ireland and the UK, do not occupy neoliberal positions. One contrary extreme position, of high social spending but low unemployment replacement, is occupied by two South countries, Greece and Italy; the opposite extreme of generous unemployment replacement in the context of generally low spending is an empty box.

Summary

Table 4.5 displays these findings in a way that enables us to identify whether the idea of 'families' of nation states is significant in accounting for differences among countries. No strong differences appear between the North and Centre West groups; there are also similarities linking the West (particularly the USA) to the Centre East, and (to the extent that we have the data) Japan. The European South stands rather alone.

Table 4.5. Nation-state 'family' positions on labour market exposure

'Family'	Variable	Strongly neoliberal positions (V, VI)	Indistinct positions (III, IV)	Strongly non-neoliberal positions (I, II)
North	Bargaining coordination		DK, FI, NO	SE
	Bargaining coverage			DK, FI, NO, SE
	Self-employment		FI	DK, NO, SE
	EPL	DK	FI, SE	NO
	Social provision		NO	DK, FI, SE
	Unemployment generosity			DK, FI, NO, SE
Centre West	Bargaining coordination		CH, SI	AT, BE, DE, NL
	Bargaining coverage		DE, CH	AT, BE, NL, SI
	Self-employment		AT, BE, SI	DE, NL, CH
	EPL	CH	AT, BE, DE, NL	SI
	Social provision		SI	AT, BE, DE, NL, CH
	Unemployment generosity		AT, DE	BE, NL, CH, SI
South	Bargaining coordination	FR	EL, IT, ES	PT
	Bargaining coverage		EL, IT, PT, ES	FR
	Self-employment	EL, IT, PT	ES	FR
	EPL		IT	FR, EL, PT, ES
	Social provision		PT, ES	FR, EL, IT
	Unemployment generosity	EL, IT	FR, PT, ES	
West (+ USA)	Bargaining coordination	UK, US	IE	
	Bargaining coverage	UK, US		
	Self-employment		IE, UK	US
	EPL	IE, UK, US		
	Social provision		IE, UK	
	Unemployment generosity	US	UK	IE

Centre East	Bargaining coordination	HU, LT, PL, RO	BG, CZ, EE, LV, SK	SK
	Bargaining coverage	BG, CZ, EE, HU, LV, LT, PL, SK		
	Self-employment	PL	CZ, HU, SK	EE
	EPL	HU, SK	CZ, PL	EE
	Social protection	BG, CZ, EE, LV, LT, PL, RO, SK	HU	
	Unemployment generosity	BG, EE, LV, RO, SK	CZ, HU, LT, PL	
Japan	Bargaining coordination	JP		
	Bargaining coverage	JP		
	Self-employment		JP	
	EPL	JP		

Both the North and the Centre West countries cluster towards the non-neoliberal positions on several variables, and there are only two instances of strongly neoliberal positions among them: Denmark and Switzerland, both on the EPL variable. This is of course one limb of the noted Danish flexicurity model, the other being the very high unemployment pay replacement rate. Switzerland also shares this latter characteristic. The only other country in the whole list to match low EPL with high unemployment pay replacement is Ireland. The strict Danish model has therefore not been widely imitated, though Belgium and the Netherlands both combine only average EPL with high unemployment pay. Strong collective bargaining coverage and social protection (on both indicators) constitute the main non-neoliberal characteristics of these countries; their employment forms (self-employment and EPL) are not clustered at either pole, and strong collective bargaining coordination no longer characterizes many of them (as it did in earlier decades). Slovenia, perhaps controversially added to the Centre West group in the European Commission report, does not in fact appear as an outlier to that group at all.

Most countries in the South group occupy middling positions on most variables, though several have high EPL but also high self-employment, and high social protection levels but not high unemployment pay replacement levels. There is however considerable variety around this position, and France (allocated to South rather than Centre West by the Commission report) appears as particularly deviant. These countries are almost the mirror image of the North and Centre-West group, concentrating their neoliberal and non-neoliberal positions on opposed points. While a good deal of research has followed Esping-Andersen in seeing a division within western Europe between the Nordic countries and the 'continental' group as a whole, these data suggest instead a more stereotypical contrast between north and south.

The West group partly conforms to the neoliberal stereotype found by much research, but it is only the USA that conforms strongly, and then only if one disregards the self-employment variable. The USA presents a strong example of what we might call corporate neoliberalism rather than market neoliberalism, as its workforce is exceptionally concentrated in large employing organizations with only a small, fully exposed, self-employed group. The low level of self-employment in the USA might be partly explained by a greater tendency of owners of small US enterprises to register as companies than those elsewhere, but the great majority of self-employed persons are not entrepreneurs but 'workers on their own account' who are unlikely to register as firms anywhere. Ireland and the UK concentrate their neoliberalism on industrial relations and EPL variables. However, we do not have data on Ireland's bargaining coverage, and it shares Denmark's and Switzerland's distinctive flexicurity combination. It possibly belongs more with the North and Centre West group.

In some respects the USA has more affinities with the Centre East countries than with the British Isles pair, as these countries share its mainly neoliberal profile. We lack important data for Japan, but it too seems to follow a broadly neoliberal profile on the variables being considered here, if not in other aspects of its economic organization.

Labour market exposure and economic performance

The political debate over neoliberal labour market reform has concentrated on the consequences of labour market protection for economic performance. Orthodox economists and international organizations (the EU, the IMF, the OECD, and the World Bank) maintained, at least until recently, that only strong neoliberal labour markets will be associated with a capacity to produce high levels of employment and economic innovation. More recent research has led to an acknowledgement by some of these authorities that the Nordic economies might present an alternative model of success, despite containing some strong non-neoliberal components in their labour markets. We shall explore this issue here by relating our more nuanced findings on labour market exposure and protection to key indicators on these variables. Data for some key indicators of employment and innovation performance are presented in Table 4.6. As before, the methodology is used of identifying particularly strong and weak performances in terms of positions above and below standard deviations from the mean.

The most direct relationships with labour market variables should be with employment levels. We here look at the overall participation rate, and also an indicator that should capture any evidence of labour regimes that privilege insiders. This is the statistic for the so-called 'NEET' phenomenon: the

Table 4.6. Indicators of employment and innovation

Country	EMP		NEET		EUP		HTP		USP	
Austria	71.6	B	11.0	C	195	B	29	C	69.5	B
Belgium	61.6	E	15.4	D	144	C	23	C	53.8	C
Bulgaria	62.6	D	n.a.		4	E	0	E	0.5	E
Czech R	65.4	D	11.0	C	16	E	1	E	2.8	E
Denmark	75.7	A	8.2	A	236	A	46	C	71.6	B
Estonia	63.5	E	15.3	D	16	E	6	E	0.7	E
Finland	66.7	C	13.3	C	306	A	126	A	118.8	A
France	64.2	D	15.1	D	149	C	32	C	53.5	C
Germany	70.9	B	15.2	D	312	A	44	B	127.9	A
Greece	61.2	E	17.7	E	11	E	2	E	1.3	E
Hungary	55.4	F	16.9	E	19	E	3	E	5.3	E
Ireland	61.8	E	12.1		77	D	16	D	38.5	D
Italy	57.5	F	22.6	F	87	D	8	D	29.8	D
Latvia	60.9	F	n.a.		6	E	0	E	2.5	E
Lithuania	60.1	F	n.a.		6	E	1	E	1.8	E
Netherlands	77.0	A	6.9	A	244	A	56	A	82.4	B
Norway	76.4	A	8.8	A	117	C	20	D	45.3	C
Poland	59.3	E	18.3	F	4	E	1	E	0.5	E
Portugal	66.3	C	15.2	D	7	E	1	E	1.4	E
Romania	58.6	F	n.a.		1	E	0	E	0.1	E
Slovakia	60.2	D	19.9	F	8	E	1	E	1.3	E
Slovenia	67.5	C	10.4	B	50	E	4	E	11.9	E
Spain	59.8	D	17.2	E	31	E	4	E	7.2	E
Sweden	72.2	A	13.1	C	285	A	63	A	132.2	A
Switzerland	79.2	A	10.4	B	426	A	45	B	174.9	A
UK	69.9	B	18.1	F	121	C	26	C	51.9	C
Japan	n.a.		7.6	A	n.a.		n.a.	V	n.a.	
USA	70.9	B	16.2	E	n.a.		n.a.	VI	n.a.	

Sources: EMP, NEET: OECD; EUP, HTP, USP: Eurostat; EMP: percentage of population aged 15–65 in gainful employment, 2009; NEET: percentage of population aged 20–24 not in employment, education or training, 2009; EUP: number of patents applied for at the EU Patent Office, 2003; HTP: number of high-tech patents applied for at the EU Patent Office, 2003; USP: number of patents applied for at the US Patent Office, 2000; A: more than one standard deviation above mean (for NEET: below mean); B: between 0.5 and one standard deviation above mean (for NEET: below mean); C: between mean and 0.5 standard deviation above mean (for NEET: below mean); D: between 0.5 standard deviation below mean and mean (for NEET: below mean);E: between one and 0.5 standard deviation below mean (for NEET: below mean); F: more than one standard deviation below mean (for NEET: below mean)

proportion of young people aged between 20 and 24 who are not in employment, education, or training.

For indicators of innovation there are two separate sources, both dealing with patents. There are objections to using patent data, as it is argued that there are different national practices in having recourse to patenting. In particular, small firms may be unlikely to use it, which might underestimate the degree of innovation in a country with large numbers of small enterprises; Italy is probably the main example. However, it is difficult to find an alternative datum that would give any help at all.

First, Eurostat collected data on EU member states on patents applied for at the European Patent Office per million population; a general statistic is given, but since there has been discussion in the literature of a distinction between incremental and radically innovative innovations, we also examine the statistic for high-tech patents. This might not be equivalent to radical innovation, but it will identify innovation in new sectors. Since most existing research considers only the US and not the EU patent office, we also consider statistics given by Eurostat for patents deposited there. Unfortunately the source has no data more recent than 2000, and does not give separate figures for high-tech patents. It is also unfortunate that this patent data is available only for European countries and not for Japan or the USA. These statistics are presented, with those on the employment variables, in Table 4.6, where the same methodology has been applied as above to identify cases close to either extreme levels in terms of standard deviations around the mean. Here Roman letters rather than numerals are used to display the categories, as these are no longer on a scale of neoliberalism but on a ranking from high to low.

Second, the OECD has collected for its member states more recent (2005) combined data on patent registrations at the EU, US, and Japanese patent offices; this does include Japan and the USA, though we lose several central European states. Because patent activity has some bias towards manufacturing, the OECD also collected data from the same countries for the international registration of trademarks, which is more likely to cover many services activities. Data from these lists is given in Table 4.7, again using the standard deviation methodology. Switzerland has an extraordinarily high performance on trademarks, which distorts the standard deviation analysis. A further column therefore gives country rankings without Switzerland.

Employment and labour market regimes

The central neoliberal labour market hypothesis would be confirmed if the countries with the most strongly non-neoliberal labour market institutions had the lowest employment participation levels and the highest levels of NEET. The hypothesis maintains that such institutions prevent employment growth. If there *is* relatively high employment in countries with strong labour market protection, the neo-liberal hypothesis would predict that this will involve protecting existing job holders, or insiders, at the expense of those without work. Insider-protecting regimes should be expected to have high levels of NEET, as it will be less skilled young people who will be kept out of jobs by their older contemporaries already in posts.

Table 4.6 shows that in 2009 the labour markets affording the highest levels of employment were, in descending order:

Table 4.7. Indicators of innovation

Country	IPA		ITM		ITM (-CH)
Austria	48.2	C	54.7	C	B
Belgium	39.6	C	37.6	D	D
Czech R	1.7	E	7.8	E	F
Denmark	57.7	B	78.5	B	A
Finland	62.0	B	42.3	D	C
France	40.0	C	43.9	D	C
Germany	76.0	A	58.0	C	B
Greece	1.2	E	6.4	E	F
Hungary	4.3	E	5.9	E	F
Ireland	17.2	E	80.7	B	A
Italy	13.2	E	36.4	D	D
Netherlands	63.6	B	68.8	C	A
Norway	27.1	D	44.4	D	C
Poland	0.5	E	2.8	E	F
Portugal	1.1	E	16.0	E	E
Slovakia	0.8	E	4.3	E	F
Spain	5.0	E	23.3	D	E
Sweden	87.8	A	73.7	C	A
Switzerland	119.7	A	291.2	A	
UK	27.9	D	64.4	C	B
Japan	112.7	A	24.2	D	E
USA	53.5	B	61.7	C	B

Sources: OECD IPA: number of patents registered at EU, US, and Japan Patent Offices, 2005; ITM: number of international trademarks registered, 2003; ITM (-CH): ITM rankings less Switzerland; A: more than one standard deviation above mean;B: between 0.5 and one standard deviation above meanC: between mean and 0.5 standard deviation above mean;D: between 0.5 standard deviation below mean and mean; E: between one and 0.5 standard deviation below mean; F: more than one standard deviation below mean

A: Switzerland, Netherlands, Norway, Denmark, Sweden
B: Austria, Germany, UK, USA

The worst performing were:

E: Estonia, Ireland, Belgium, Greece, Latvia, Slovakia, Lithuania, Spain, Poland
F: Romania, Italy, Hungary.

Comparison of this list with Table 4.3 shows that, with the exception of the UK, USA, and the neoliberal positions of Denmark and Switzerland on the EPL variable alone, the high performers all have, contrary to the neoliberal hypothesis, strong levels of general labour market protection. This refutes the simple neoliberal hypothesis, but is consistent with other findings that the Nordic economies have found an alternative route to a high employment economy to the so-called Anglo-American one. Previous research on varieties of capitalism—though not that on industrial relations systems alone—has however overlooked the strong performance of all Centre West countries with the exception of Belgium and Slovenia; but Slovenia has the best employment performance of all previously state-socialist economies.

We can go further than this and make an important differentiation among our labour market exposure indicators. With the exception of Norway, none of these countries deploys strong EPL among its labour-protective institutions. It is across the other indicators that they maintain strong protection—including, in most cases, like the USA, low proportions in self-employment. Switzerland is a slight exception, not featuring strong collective bargaining institutions.

A surprising finding for neo-institutionalists is that two high-performing countries on employment—Denmark and Norway—have strong collective bargaining coverage without much coordination. Elsewhere, this combination is associated, as we would expect, with indifferent employment performances: Finland, Slovenia, and with exceptionally high coverage and low coordination, France. The most puzzling country however is Belgium, with a distinctly poor employment record despite having a profile otherwise the same as the high-performing cases.

With the exception of Belgium and Ireland, the poor-performing countries in the above employment list come exclusively from the South and Centre East families. Again, against the expectations of the neoliberal hypothesis, they mainly have weak levels of labour market protection. Again, however, this finding can be nuanced. Setting aside the anomalous cases of Belgium and Ireland, which seem to share no characteristics with the Centre East group, we find several countries close to the neoliberal model for industrial relations institutions and social protection cover, but few with strong neoliberal positions on EPL. However, if we examine those members of the Centre East group that had modest rather than poor employment performances, nothing seems to distinguish them from the others. The model is less useful for considering weak employment records than strong ones.

Statistics for the NEET population present some similar patterns to the overall employment situation, but also some important differences:

A: Netherlands, Japan, Norway, Denmark
B: Slovenia and Switzerland
E: USA, Spain, Hungary, Greece
F: UK, Poland, Slovakia, Italy.

No data are available for Bulgaria, Latvia, Lithuania, or Romania.

Some countries with strong overall employment performances are proving less successful at providing for the younger generation; Slovenia on the other hand is succeeding particularly well. Otherwise the high-performing list is similar to that for overall employment. Much the same is true for the poor performers, with the striking addition of the UK and USA—the two countries which, according to neoliberal theory should be the least likely of all to have labour market outsiders.

Innovation

Links between employment regimes and innovative capacity are far less direct than with employment levels, but neoliberal theorists usually anticipate that what they regard as labour-market rigidities impede innovation, because of problems of implementing them where employees have entrenched rights.

The three different Eurostat measures of patent-led innovation all tell a similar story. Strong or very strong positions on all are taken by Finland, Germany, Netherlands, Sweden, Switzerland, and on two by Austria and Denmark. This is the same as the list of strong performers on employment, with the absence of Norway and the UK. This is therefore identical to the list of North and Centre West countries, less Belgium, Norway, and Slovenia. The list of poor or very poor performers is identical to the list of South and Centre East countries, with the exception of stronger performances by France (in any case a paradoxical member of the South group) and by Italy. This too is substantially the same as the list of employment poor performers. It may be too much to have expected Central East countries, including here Slovenia, yet to have established highly innovative firms: so much of their economic activity depends on branch plants of enterprises whose research capacity is be located elsewhere. But the southern European countries clearly have major problems in innovation. Whether this has anything to do with their labour market institutions is difficult to determine. The only strong conclusion that we can draw from this examination of data is the negative one that they provide no basis for an argument that only neoliberal institutions are likely to be sympathetic to an innovation-based economy. At least those combinations of institutions to be found among the majority of Nordic and Centre West European countries seem to be compatible with high levels of patent activity, including high-tech patents, where there was no evidence of superior performance in Ireland and the UK over Centre West countries.

The differently based OECD data on combined EU, US, and Japan-registered patents tells a similar story. The very highest performers were Germany, Sweden, Switzerland, Japan, Denmark, Finland, Ireland, Netherlands, and the USA, We can now confirm that Japan and, to a lesser extent, the USA are strongly innovative economies; otherwise it is a familiar European group. Without exception the South and Centre East countries are weak, as is Ireland. A slightly different pattern emerges from the international trademark data, showing that innovation does vary by sector for different countries. In particular, two West countries—the UK and especially Ireland—improve their performance; that of Japan declines. However, only Italy manages to leave the poor or very poor performance of the South and Centre East.

Conclusions

The data considered here enable us to make the following claims:

The classification of at least European countries that has developed in recent literature and which was summarized in the European Commission's *Industrial Relations in 2009* report is broadly useful in examining diversity in labour-market institutions. For this particular research, however, the division between the North and Centre West group has not been so important. Without deeper inquiry it is not possible to tell whether this indicates some convergence between the two or just a lack of salience of any differences for the topics chosen for analysis here. There are also strong similarities between the South and Centre East groups, though with important differences. In general, southern countries tend to expose workers to the market through self-employment, Centre East countries through weak protective institutions. Finally, the small West group, with the USA added, conformed broadly to a neoliberal stereotype, but with important divergences within the group.

The neoliberal hypothesis that strong protective labour market institutions in general weaken the capacity of economies to create employment and support innovation is refuted. Some strong protective institutions—coordinated and extensive collective bargaining; and generous social protection expenditure, especially in supporting unemployed workers—may even play a positive rather than a negative role. A low level of self-employment is also associated with strong performance, but high levels of EPL are not. This is in line with the flexicurity thesis that 'successful' protective labour regimes are likely to embody trade-offs between elements of protection from, and those of exposure to, the market. This is seen most clearly in the Danish and Swiss cases, where weak EPL is exchanged for strong unemployment support, but other trade-offs are also at work. It has long been noted that coordination of collective bargaining and probably pattern bargaining (beyond our analytical scope here) are important in offsetting the inflationary or job-destroying potentialities of extensive but uncoordinated bargaining. A part is also being played in the trade-off process by certain forms of social protection. It is likely that some combinations have positive effects for employment; others—perhaps by creating outsiders—negative. This too merits further exploration.

Belgium, France, and Ireland are the three most difficult countries to classify. The first shares characteristics with the rest of the North and Centre West combined group, but without their association with indicators of success. Ireland has a mix of characteristics from a number of models. France is a case all on its own, requiring separate analysis.

Neoliberalism itself emerges from this study with a very mixed record. The USA appears as a strong employment performer, though, like the UK, with currently a very poor NEET record. The overall profile of the USA is unique among the countries considered here, with extreme neoliberal rankings on all indicators except self-employment, where its institutional (or corporate) position was equally extreme in the other direction. The unique size and power of that country within the world makes it unsurprising that it should be a distinctive case. All that is perhaps surprising is that such an unusual place should have become propagated as a paradigm that other nation states ought to imitate and indeed would be capable of doing so. After only twenty years of post-communist history it is still probably too early to assess whether the problems of Centre East Europe result from the burden of the Soviet past or that of an attempted US future.

More broadly, while more recent typologies of forms of capitalism do not emerge very strongly from this study, two earlier approaches suggest themselves as relevant to further research: Polanyian institutionalism and Wallerstein's centre-periphery analysis.

Polanyi's work (1944) has figured prominently in many recent critical approaches to capitalism, because of the continuing value of his insights concerning the complex and contradictory relationship of capitalist entrepreneurialism and other social institutions. As Streeck (2011), following a long tradition of sociological observers of capitalism, has recently described the process, capitalism both needs and destroys a series of institutions on which it depends. If this is the case, we should not expect to find a simple association between economically successful capitalisms of a 'pure' kind, and relatively unsuccessful ones with various institutional impediments to that purity. That much has been generally conceded in the increasingly widespread acknowledgement of the success of the Nordic economies, often reckoned to be fairly extreme examples of heavily institutionalized capitalism, precisely in policy areas that contradict the pure model: strong labour movements and generous welfare states.

But there are institutions and institutions. Economies in which there is a strong dependence on the institution of the family to supplement weak welfare states (a characteristic shared by many South and Centre East European countries) do not seem at present to be associated with success. The data discussed above does not permit us to draw conclusions about which institutions might be complementary to capitalist ones and which impede them: we have just a few clues to guide more intensive research. Already complex, such research also needs to take full account of the Polanyian and Streeckian concept of the way in which capitalism, in reaching out for ever more profit maximization, starts to destroy the very institutions that sustains it. Given that various manifestations of capitalism are constantly changing in both their institutional configurations and their level of success, it becomes a thoroughly difficult research task to discover whether a set of institutions being destroyed at time T_0 did not support economic developments at time T_{-1} which do not start to bear fruit until time T_{+1}.

These complexities help explain why the existing typologies of capitalism have not fared particularly well in the above account, except where they are uselessly defined in terms of the dependent variable. But these typologies all assume that individual examples of capitalist economies are instances of units of a similar kind, with internal institutional mixes that are variations of similar ingredients. An assumption that this is so is methodologically essential to work that uses quantitative data to test associations between variables across cases. But, as Wallerstein (1974, 1980, 1989) and his colleagues pointed out, national economies are not separate units, but are bound together in a system of relationships with each other in which they occupy distinctly different positions. Wallerstein defined those relationships primarily in terms of centre and periphery. Staying just within Europe, as we have largely done in this discussion, we see suggestive evidence in support of that concept. This explains better the similarities in poor economic performance, despite very different institutions, between the South and the Centre East. So much research in comparative capitalism in recent years has been devoted to seeking major policy lessons from whether the USA slightly out-performs Germany or vice versa that we have rather ignored the gaps that exist between either of these and, say, Spain or Poland. The combinations of similarities and differences between the southern and central eastern regions of Europe provide fascinating material for further research.

In doing that work we need to combine the Polanyian and Wallersteinian approaches in two ways. First, to a considerable extent different positions in the centre-periphery polarity can be seen as different institutional configurations: the network externalities enjoyed by central countries in general and the USA in particular constitute extra-market institutional advantages in global economic competition. Second, it is likely that different institutions are likely to gather around different positions on the polarity—as hinted above with reference to the role of family in periphery countries. This suggests major and probably irresolvable difficulties for attempts to distinguish cause, effect, and association; but it may contribute to better understanding, and discourage all simplistic attempts at relating different institutional formations to different levels of economic success.

References

Amable, B. (2003) *The Diversity of Modern Capitalism*, Oxford: Oxford University Press.

Boyer, R. (2004) 'New Growth Regimes, but Still Institutional Diversity', *Socio-Economic Review*, 2(1): 1–32.

—— and Freyssenet, M. (2000) *Les modèles productifs*, Paris: La Découverte.

Esping-Andersen, G. (1990) *The Three Worlds of Welfare Capitalism*, Cambridge: Polity Press.

European Commission (2009) *Industrial Relations in Europe*, Luxemburg: Official Publication Office of the European Communities.

—— (2010) *Europe 2020: A strategy for smart, sustainable and inclusive growth*, Luxemburg: Official Publication Office of the European Communities.

Hall, P. A. and D. Soskice (eds) (2001) Varieties of Capitalism, Oxford: Oxford University Press.

Kristensen, P. H. and K. Lilja (eds) (2011) Nordic Capitalisms and Globalization, Oxford: Oxford University Press.

OECD (1994) *The Jobs Study*, Paris: OECD.

Polanyi, K. (1944) *The Great Transformation: The political and economic origins of our time*, Boston, MA: Beacon Press.

Rueda, D. (2005) 'Insider-Outside Politics in Industrialized Democracies: The challenge to Social Democratic parties', *American Political Science Review*, 99(1): 61–74.

Streeck, W. (2011) 'Taking Capitalism Seriously: Towards an institutionalist approach to contemporary political economy', *Socio-Economic Review*, 9(1): 137–67.

—— and K. Thelen (2005) 'Institutional Changes in Advanced Political Economies', pp. 1–39 in W. Streeck and K. Thelen (eds) *Beyond Continuity: Institutional change in advanced political economies*, Oxford: Oxford University Press.

Thelen, K. (2003) 'How Institutions Evolve: Insights from comparative-historical analysis', pp. 208–40 in J. Mahoney and D. Rueschemeyer (eds) *Comparative Historical Analysis in the Social Sciences*, New York: Cambridge University Press.

Traxler, F. and B. Brandl (2009) 'Towards Europeanization of Wage Policy: Germany and the Nordic countries', *European Union Politics*, 10(2): 177–201.

—— —— and V. Glassner (2008) 'Pattern Bargaining: An investigation into its reasons, causes and evidence', *British Journal of Industrial Relations*, 46: 33–58.

Wallerstein, I. M. (1974, 1980, 1989) *The Modern World System* (three volumes), New York: Academic Press.

World Bank (annual) *Doing Business*, Washington DC: World Bank.

Section 2
The International Context of Economic Organization

5

Is there a Global Financial System?

The Locational Antecedents and Institutionally Bounded Consequences of the Financial Crisis

Glenn Morgan and Michel Goyer[1]

Introduction

Is there a global financial system? This may seem a strange question to ask in the light of the financial crisis which enveloped the world from 2007. The speed with which economies contracted particularly after the Lehman collapse in September 2008 certainly showed the interconnectedness of finance to the broader economy, as well as how tightly connected the financial institutions of many countries had become to each other. Similarly the emphasis given by governments and commentators to new forms of global financial architecture and global governance mechanisms as key to reform, reinforced this focus on a globally integrated financial system. The crisis followed over three decades in which the financial system evolved from the post-war Bretton Woods model of an international monetary system based on exchange rate stability, capital controls, and national autonomy over monetary policy, which Ruggie labelled as embedded liberalism (Ruggie 1998) towards a more open system of floating exchange rates, capital mobility, and the dependence of national monetary policy on international market conditions (Eichengreen 2008). Discussing these changes in 1999, Simmons wrote: 'By virtually every measure considered—the removal of institutional barriers, the flow of capital itself, the growing correlation of interest rate changes across

[1] We thank Bob Hancké and Richard Whitley for insightful discussions and comments.

national markets—financial markets are more integrated now than they have been at any point since the nineteenth century' (Simmons 1999: 62). For example, in 1973, average daily turnover in foreign currency markets was $15 billion; by 2010 it was $3.8 trillion. In 2007 before the financial crisis, FDI inflows had reached nearly $2 trillion, having been around $50 billion annually for most of the early 1990s and only achieving $200 billion per year by 1993.

Under conditions of embedded liberalism, societies were able to pursue their own economic models subject to the broad constraints of managing their current account deficits and surpluses. Finance, which for Keynes, in its unregulated form, lay at the root of the economic chaos of the inter-war years, was to be subordinated to the requirements for steady economic growth guided by national governments and the international institutions set up under the Bretton Woods system. Short-term flows of funds which destabilised currencies and economies were constrained by capital controls (Goodman and Pauly 1993). This left leeway for the initial development of different forms of social settlement across the developed societies (Eichengreen 2007). These settlements would later provide the basis for the development of institutional diversity across advanced capitalist economies—processes which were conceptualized in a variety of ways in approaches such as regulation theory (Boyer 1990), national business systems (Whitley 1999), and varieties of capitalism (Hall and Soskice 2001). Financial systems were crucial parts of these models, working in relatively self-enclosed contexts to support and reinforce particular forms of capitalism (Zysman 1983; Amable 2003).

The collapse of Bretton Woods, however, and its gradual replacement by a system based on floating currencies (in part stabilized through the use of currency pegs or, as in the EU case, the coordination of currencies through the EU snake system, later the EMS, and eventually the creation of the euro), free mobility of capital, and deregulated financial markets began to change this context. A prevalent view of this process was that it created a new international system of financial globalization which was likely to corrode differences between forms of capitalism by enabling investors to shift their funds across national boundaries and different asset classes according to a logic of short-term returns (Cohen 1996). Over the period from the 1970s onwards through to the Asian financial crisis, pressures to allow free capital mobility between countries did indeed grow. Membership of OECD became conditional on allowing this; the EU became a zone of free capital mobility, the US sought in bilateral trade treaties to make this one of the features, and the IMF increasingly recommended it in its structural adjustment programmes, coming close in the late 1990s to making it a condition of membership and assistance (Abdelal 2007). Such increasing cross-border capital mobility was seen as weakening the significance of national differences in socio-economic organization and forms of capitalism in the twenty-first century.

In this chapter, we challenge this view by arguing that national differences remain important and are key to explaining why we have the particular form of financial globalization that has recently emerged. In our view, this is best seen as the product of these differences, acting more to reinforce them than to undermine them (for an analogous discussion of how supranational integration can reinforce national states as opposed to undermining them, see Milward, Brennan et al. 2000). In this chapter, we explore the seeming paradox of deeper financial integration accompanied by deepening national differences. In the first section, we separate out the various elements that underpin the notion of financial integration, in particular distinguishing between financial flows, financial markets, and financial institutions. We argue that in each case, characterizing the phenomenon in terms of 'globalization' is both misleading and unhelpful because it overstates the geographical diversity and dispersion of these processes and actors. It also occludes from view key features of the interconnections between these phenomena.

In the second section, therefore, we return to the national level and consider how the emergent financial system grew out of and reinforced particular institutional complementarities which had evolved in national contexts. This relates to understanding better what Rajan describes in his analysis of the financial crisis as 'the clash of systems' (Rajan 2010). Most discussions of national varieties of capitalism have concentrated on this clash from the point of view of its effect on trade in goods and services. The recent financial crisis highlights that this clash is also deeply related, not just to the organization of finance in different sorts of banks and financial institutions, but to institutional complementarities between savings, consumption, wage policies, the welfare system, and the role of the central bank. The second section of the chapter examines these issues in more detail.

Finally the chapter addresses what this means for the future if as seems likely this clash of systems does not disappear but indeed deepens with the rise of the BRIC economies, especially China. Is it the case, as Germain has suggested, that 'the high point of globalization has now been reached and that the tide of globalization is about to be rolled back, led most importantly by the containment of financial systems through efforts to tighten how banking systems and capital markets are regulated' (Germain 2010: 3)? What sort of a global financial system is likely under these circumstances?

Unpicking financial globalization

In this section, we explore the three themes of financial flows, financial institutions, and financial markets. Our aim is to move beyond the rhetoric of globalization and specify in more detail what is flowing and where to, the channels through which the flows occur (i.e. the financial institutions), and the transformation processes which take place in the financial markets.

Financial flows

The gradual reduction and eventual termination of capital controls amongst the developed countries and in varying ways amongst emerging economies signalled the end of the Bretton Woods era (Abdelal 2007) and a huge expansion of capital flows across national boundaries. It is helpful to distinguish three types of flows and their interconnections (Frieden 1991; Cohen 1996). The first is the flow of funds into foreign direct investment (FDI). FDI is usually characterized as a long-term, relatively illiquid, form of investment in productive capacities in overseas locations. The second is foreign portfolio investment into shares, bonds, and other financial instruments. This has the capacity to be short term or long term, but in general, the investor has the potential to sell at any point, subject to the existence of market makers providing prices (conditions which may be absent in some extreme circumstances, e.g. financial crisis as in 2008). The third arises from trade imbalances between countries and the development of foreign currency reserves by central banks. Over the medium term, financial balances from trade on a nation's current account are meant to even out through adjustments to currencies and price. In theory, the currency of a surplus nation will increase in value, reducing the competitiveness of its traded goods whilst for a debtor nation, the opposite process will occur.

How have these flows evolved over the last decade leading up to the financial crisis of 2008? In a series of Annual Reports from 2002, the McKinsey Global Institute (MGI) has provided valuable data for understanding this process, and the figures which follow are drawn from these reports unless otherwise stated. In their 2009 report, they showed that cross-border capital inflows declined from a peak of \$5.3 trillion in 2000 to \$3 trillion in 2002, increasing to \$10.5 trillion in 2007 (before collapsing in the aftermath of the financial crisis to \$1.9 trillion). At the 2007 peak, capital inflows were 20.7 per cent of global GDP (McKinsey Global Institute 2009: 14). MGI define capital inflows as net purchasers by foreigners of FDI, equity, and debt securities, as well as deposits and loans to local banks.

In terms of total flows, the UK and the US top the lists by some margin. In 2006, the UK exported \$1198bn of capital and imported \$1246bn; in the same year, the USA exported \$1052bn and imported \$1860 (reflecting the extraordinary and growing indebtedness of the US in this period). Comparable figures for France are \$632bn outflow, \$707bn inflow, and for Germany \$528bn outflow, \$359bn inflow. In 2006, the UK accounted for 15 per cent of total global capital outflows and 15 per cent of total global capital inflows; the US accounted for 23 per cent of inflows and 13 per cent of outflows (McKinsey Global Institute 2008: 45–46). Although these figures were down from 1996 due to the growing importance of the Eurozone and the East Asian economies in the global flows of capital, they demonstrate the centrality of these two countries to the overall process. China, by comparison, had an outflow of $382bn and an inflow of $166bn.

A crucial finding of the reports is that since 2002, emerging markets have been net providers of capital to the world. In 2006, emerging markets (including China and Russia) invested $332bn more in developed countries than they received. Other significant net exporters of capital from amongst the developed countries were Germany, Japan, and Switzerland as can be seen from Table 5.1.

MGI data also reveals the destination of these capital outflows. In country terms, the USA has absorbed the majority of the world's net capital flows, averaging $597bn per year between 2001 and 2006 (5.2 per cent of annual GDP). Eastern Europe was the second largest absorber of funds, averaging $40bn per year (4.8 per cent of GDP) with the UK third ($34bn per year; 1.6 per cent of GDP).

How are global flows divided between different categories of assets? MGI data again reveals some crucial findings. Take, for example, China in 2006: 80 per cent of its foreign investment assets were in the form of central bank reserve assets. By September 2010, China's foreign reserves totalled $2.65 trillion and were the world's largest (FT 13/10/10). This reflected its balance of trade surplus, particularly with the United States. The Chinese central bank (the People's Bank of China, PBC) holds these reserves in highly liquid form, using them among other things to intervene in the currency markets, to ensure that the Chinese currency stays within its required range and does not rise in ways which would increase the price of Chinese goods and thereby reduce the trade surplus (MGI 2008: 69).

Table 5.1. Countries with largest net capital outflows in 2006

Country	Net capital outflow 2006 in $bn	% of country GDP
China	217	8.2
Germany	169	5.8
Japan	137	3.1
Russia	101	10.2
Saudi Arabia	99	28.6
Switzerland	85	22.3
Kuwait	52	54.6
Norway	43	12.9
Singapore	38	28.6
Sweden	34	8.9

Figures adapted from McKinsey Global Institute 2007

Conversely, these manoeuvres contribute to stabilizing (or at least reducing the steepness in the decline of the value of) the US dollar at a time when it might be expected that as a debtor nation, the US would be undergoing an uncomfortable period of adjustment promoted by a decline in its currency. Schwartz states that 'China held 16 per cent of all foreign holdings of US portfolio debt by 2007 and closer to 18 per cent in 2008. Virtually all this was US Treasury and agency debt where China and Hong Kong accounted for 28 per cent of this sort of US foreign debt' (Schwartz 2009: 64). Of China's holdings of US securities in June 2008, 87 per cent were in long-term, low-yield agency (Fannie Mae and Freddie Mac) securities and long-term Treasury securities. Only 8 per cent were in long-term equities, 2 per cent in corporate securities, and 3 per cent in short-term debt (figures calculated from Morrison 2009).

Developed countries have a different pattern. Only Japan maintains significant levels of foreign reserves (around 20 per cent of foreign investment assets according to MGI 2008: 75), though again this mainly derives from a surplus trade balance with the US and is held predominantly in dollars. In the cases of the two countries with the largest outflows, the UK and the USA: for the former, 59 per cent of the capital outflow is in lending and deposit accounts, the great bulk of which involves maturities of less than one year duration (MGI 2009). It is therefore primarily short-term investment dependent on a combination of exchange rate and interest rate arbitrage for its level of profitability. Additionally, 28 per cent of the UK capital outflows is in debt securities. Only 3 per cent is in equity investment and 11 per cent in FDI, the classic sites of long-term growth. By comparison, US investment in lending and deposits was 37 per cent, in debt 27 per cent, in equity 13 per cent, and in FDI 22 per cent.

It is worth considering this in the context of inflows into the UK and the US as detailed in MGI (2009): 66 per cent of inflows into the UK were into lending and deposits. This points to the centrality of the UK as an intermediary; short-term funds enter the UK searching for yield and from there are passed on to other countries. In comparison, only 36 per cent of inflows into the US were into lending, whilst 47 per cent were placed in debt securities (predominantly into mortgage based securitizations at this period, with some into government debt); 8 per cent went into equity investments and 10 per cent into FDI; in the UK, FDI was 11 per cent, whereas in equity investment there was actually withdrawal in 2006. In these terms, the UK is a highly important node in the circulation of funds; in particular it acts as a funnel for relatively short-term lending and deposits which are seeking quick returns. Its financial sector is built on fees from acting as intermediaries for these funds, many of which are re-placed overseas. It is also built on trading and market-making on its own account and for clients in the financial markets. It is highly dependent on its ability to continue to attract short-term funds which in turn requires that it can offer high profits to such funds over a variety of short to medium-term time horizons. For these reasons, the collapse of financial flows as occurred in the financial crisis immediately and devastatingly affected the City of London (see Tylecote in this volume).

The US, however, plays a different role, first because of the position of the dollar as a global currency and secondly because of its significance as a trading nation—both features which characterized the UK in the nineteenth century but have long since ceased to do so. As a number of authors have pointed out (Schwartz 2009; Rajan 2010), the US was borrowing at low cost from international investors to fund its deficit and it was able to do so in part because of the 'exorbitant privilege' of the dollar as the predominant world currency (Eichengreen 2011). As described by Helleiner and Kirshner (2009: 3–4):

> The dollar continued to be used on one side of about 86 per cent of all foreign exchange transactions (BIS 2007 survey of foreign exchange trading) whereas its nearest rivals, the euro and yen, have shares of only 37 per cent and 16.5 per cent respectively. As a store of value, the dollar still made up 64 per cent of the world's official foreign exchange reserves at the end of 2007, compared to about 26.5 per cent for the euro and below 5% for the yen. The dollar's shares in 2006 of international bank deposits (48%) and the stock of international debt securities (44%) also remained above those of the euro (28% and 31%) with the yen again very far behind. In addition the dollar continues to be by far most popular currency in which to denominate international trade... As an official unit of account, the dollar is used as the anchor currency in almost two-thirds of all countries in the world that peg their currency in various ways.

The 'seignorage' benefits of being the dominant world currency are significant:

> Where foreigners have held dollars, they have provided the equivalent of an interest-free (in the case of Federal Reserve notes) or low-interest (in the case of US Treasury securities) loan to the United States. (ibid: 5)

Other obvious effects in relation to recent events are that the US was able to carry on having current account deficits because foreigners were willing to lend the dollars which they had earned on traded goods back to the US. The dollar was seen as a relatively safe and secure hedge even though there were phases when it was depreciating and their assets were therefore declining in value. Countries, and this has most obviously affected China in recent years, have developed a strong interest in the maintenance of the dollar's position as a result of greater interdependence with the American economy. The plentiful abundance of dollars fed into low interest rates and into the credit boom that fuelled the sub-prime housing market and the explosion of residential asset prices in the period up to 2006–7.

In terms of the US as a trading nation, the same processes had two interconnected effects. First, the dollar was a strong currency broadly held, highly liquid and supported, not just by the Fed, but by all the other Central Banks around the world which were accumulating dollar reserves. Whilst the dollar could float downwards, this required both coordinated central bank action (and inaction) as well as propitious circumstances amongst other currencies, that is, that some of them (particularly the euro) were moving upwards and therefore offered an alternative to the dollar. Overall, therefore what Kirshner describes as 'the inescapable politics of money' (Kirshner 2003) at the global level meant that devaluation as a strategy to improve the competitive position of US firms against companies from emerging economies, which pegged their currencies to the dollar was unlikely to succeed over the long term.

As a result, jobs in many standardized and relatively low technology industries were gradually lost over the period from the 1980s even though other forms of adjustment characteristic of liberal market economies were tried, such as holding down wages, increasing the flexibility of the workforce, and increasing the intensity of work. The struggle to replace these jobs for semi-skilled and unskilled workers in the US has led to a greater fragmentation of the labour force (where those with existing financial capital or high skills, technical knowledge and expertise have become more differentiated from the bulk of the workforce), stagnating real wages for many employees, heightened exploitation in the workplace, insecure contracts, and the threat of a rapid descent into poverty if the economy fails to continue to grow (Hacker and Pierson 2010). As many commentators have pointed out, the provision of easy credit which could enable house purchases contributed to an increasing sense of wealth even when incomes were stagnating (Davis 2009). So long as house prices rose, the possibility of 'equity withdrawal' existed to fund large consumer purchases; rising prices also encouraged moving houses every few years to build up 'wealth' and the possibility of equity withdrawal. As in the UK, though on a greater scale, this generated jobs in finance, real estate, building and construction and the retail sector in terms of furnishings, decorations, and electronic goods (Schwartz 2009). It was the financial flow that provided the resources for this even if it was the financial institutions and the financial markets that devised and created the panoply of financial instruments that actually allowed this to happen. In turn, this internally generated credit-driven growth pattern actually contributed to boosting the rate of growth for the US economy as a whole at the same time as the Fordist manufacturing sector was in decline and real wages were stagnating for many middle and lower income sectors (Schwartz 2009: ch. 4).

These global financial flows have enabled capital outflows from the US to earn greater returns for the US than capital inflows from other countries into the US. Schwartz, for example, states (2009: 39) that:

> US investments are generally in longer-term, higher return venues. Even within specific types of investment venue, US investments tend to be longer term and higher return. Overall, US holdings are disproportionately invested in FDI, whereas foreign holdings are disproportionately passive instruments such as bonds. But even within passive instruments, US holdings are disproportionately long-term corporate bonds, whereas foreign holdings are disproportionately short-term government securities. This creates superior aggregate returns for US international investment, despite the huge US net international debt. The concentration of foreign holdings in passive portfolio debt and particular US Treasury and agency bonds, helps power US differential growth at home and expansion by US MNCs abroad.

He also argues that US multinational firms, borrowing these funds, have consistently achieved strong returns on their overseas activities and that 'US firms have been able to expand their control over leading sectors in world markets' (Schwartz 2009: 133). He emphasizes the internationalizing efforts of firms in what Whitley has described as 'the New U.S. model' (in comparison to the production of standardized commodities based on Fordist production principles). The New US model is one based on 'commercializing radically new products and services as fast as possible... combining shallow hierarchies, extensive external linkages, limited diversification and a strong "change culture"' (Whitley 2009: 16; see also Whitley 2010 for an analysis of different competition models). This goes along with the ability of US multinationals to manage global supply chains in increasingly sophisticated and complex ways in order to maximize advantages of scale, scope, and learning (Herrigel 2010; Herrigel and Zeitlin 2010). Their reliance on formal management procedures that enable arm's length control of complex relationships (as described, for example, in Almond and Ferner 2006) in primarily modularized production chains contrasts with the sort of relationship-based forms of MNC organization that characterize both Japanese and German multinationals (Whitley, Morgan et al. 2003). Schwartz argues that these differences lie at the root of the fact that the average annual return on assets for FDI invested in the US (the bulk of which was British, German, and Japanese) was only 4.3 per cent in the period 1997–2005 whilst for the roughly comparable period of 1998–2006, return on assets for US FDI abroad was 9.5 per cent. It is, of course, important to note that these returns flowed back to the US not into the wage packets of US employees but into the dividends of US shareholders, thus serving not to narrow but to enlarge the gap between rich and poor (see also Lazonick 2009).

To summarize the argument so far, financial flows cannot be understood separately from the source of those flows, their direction, and their effects. In particular, the period from around 2002 to 2007 was characterized by distinctive patterns of flows from countries with balance of payments surpluses into the US and the UK. As the MGI reports show, in the UK investments were predominantly in short-term lending, and deposits acted as an intermediary both in the further internationalization of these funds and in their investment in financial markets. In the US, which remained a debtor throughout this period but also retained its position as a global currency and the predominant form of currency reserve held by other central banks, the funds were used for two things. First, there was considerable investment in financial markets but there was also, second, huge expansion in investment in providing credit for housing reflected in the significance of debt securities in the US capital inflow. This was crucial to enabling the expansion of the US economy and providing middle and low-income groups with a sense of increasing wealth at a time when employment income was stagnating. What was also crucial in the US context was that this inflow kept interest rates low, facilitating the further internationalization of US companies (particularly in the rapidly expanding science-based industries and services industries described by Whitley as part of the new US model) and through the borrowing of funds at a time when profits were being redistributed to shareholders (see also Thompson this volume) and firm-level growth was increasingly dependent on bond markets. These American companies earned higher returns on their foreign investments than did those groups investing in the United States, not just because much of this investment into the US was in safe, low-risk, low-yield areas but also because FDI into the US was not as profitable as American FDI overseas, at least in part to do with the capabilities of managing international firms and global supply chains that was being developed in the United States over this period.

Financial institutions

The post Bretton Woods system was built on managed floating exchange rates and relatively high levels of capital flows between countries (Frieden 1991). Such a system requires a material and organizational infrastructure; that is, it requires banking systems, clearing and settlement systems, financial markets, technology systems, calculative devices, legal contracts, etc. that can link, in a relatively stable manner, diverse actors across the financial system. Whilst it might be possible to think of a variety of infrastructures, the one which has emerged is characterized by, first, locational concentration and, secondly, organizational concentration. In this section, we examine these two features of the system.

In terms of location for funds which are moving across national boundaries, as the previous section has described, the UK and the US are the main destinations. In this section, however, we go further to focus on the predominant 'global places' of their financial centres—New York and London. Both of these locations have developed significant agglomeration advantages which make their markets, liquid, deep, innovative, and above all profitable. Shared features of these locations include a long historical tradition as a centre of finance associated in part with domestic strength (in terms of wealth, savings capacity, and consumption, and in part with the dominance of the global economy that came from this domestic strength). Clearly the UK's position changed from the nineteenth to the twentieth centuries; in the nineteenth century there was arguably a synergy between the international orientation of the financial sector and export-driven growth when the UK was the 'workshop of the world'. In the twentieth century those synergies declined and, as many authors have argued, finance and manufacturing were at odds (Ingham 1984; Erturk, Froud et al. 2008; Talani 2011; Tylecote in this volume). Finance and the City continued to pursue an international trajectory which in the inter-war years led to the UK going back on the gold standard, pricing much UK manufacturing and production out of world markets and leaving it dependent on imperial markets (where sterling remained the dominant currency). This history, however, created an infrastructure of financial institutions and supporting organizations such as lawyers, accountants and, later, technologists, economists, advertising and PR agencies that supported the industry to innovate and develop new ways of making money.

These historical advantages were reinforced by the lack of any substantive bureaucratic or legal regulation of the markets through to the mid 1980s. Up until this point, financial markets in the UK were governed primarily through what Moran refers to as a system of 'clubs', where the insiders led, in the case of the City, by the Bank of England set their own rules and the government of the day endorsed them with very little challenge (Moran 1991, 2003). Even when this moved towards a more formal system of regulation, 'self-regulation' remained the mantra, accompanied by the idea of a 'light regulatory touch'. Increasingly in the period from the 1980s, the City became seen as central to the economic growth of the UK as manufacturing continued to decline. Governments became active in providing what the City wanted in terms of interest rates, fiscal and monetary policy, tax systems, and regulation as well as a supportive broader business and social environment, through for example privatization give-aways, the introduction of personal pensions requiring stock market investment and the broader financialization of everyday life via credit cards, mortgage loans, pension provision, etc. (Froud, Johal et al. 2006; Erturk, Froud et al. 2008; Langley 2008).

The City also changed form from the small, privately owned partnerships, segmented into distinctive niche markets with highly protective barriers to competition from outsiders and fixed commission fees. Deregulation of the stock exchange and other financial markets ushered in a phase of mergers and consolidations into large-scale investment banks, often based outside the UK and working across Wall Street, the City, and certain key European and Asian financial centres (Moran 1991, 2003). Whilst the City had clear weaknesses, not least that it was located in a relatively weak economy, the currency of which was subject to uncertain declines and upsurges, it still remained attractive to international financial institutions and investors because of its organizational, political, and regulatory infrastructures, and its capacity to find innovative ways of making money out of financial markets.

Wall Street had reached a similar position of attraction to international investors but through a different route, part of which has been described previously. Unlike the UK, the US had the legacy of the New Deal regulatory system, which provided a substantial structure of rules and regulation over financial activity. However with the growth of neo-liberal ideology and deregulatory policies, this was significantly watered down in the period from the 1970s to 2000s, in spite of momentary crises that led to sharp reversals in the market, fraud charges against individuals and companies, and some new legislation, for example Sarbanes-Oxley after the Enron collapse. Thus, the Glass-Steagall rules established under the New Deal which restricted banking across state lines and separated wholesale and retail banking institutions were increasingly ignored by creating complex structures of legal ownership and organizational structuring (see, for example, the critique of this period and these processes in Stiglitz 2004, 2006, 2010). The regulatory environment bolstered by the Fed, Alan Greenspan, and the influence of investment bankers over the Clinton and George W. Bush administrations was not just open to innovation but encouraged it. The emergence of over-the-counter derivatives markets, the creation and structuring of CDOs (collateralized debt obligations) and CDS (credit default swaps) proceeded at an exponential rate of growth with very little oversight or control, allowing the development of highly complex systems of interdependence between actors and instruments that became central to the 2007–8 crash. These innovations and contracts made on this market were legally enforceable in the United States, any uncertainty having been removed under the Commodity Futures Modernization Act of 2000 (Davis 2009; Ho 2009; Tett 2009; Morgan 2010).

Both in the UK and the US, then, these developments nurtured an array of financial institutions, including those formally regulated and those which became known as the 'shadow banking system', that is, hedge funds, off-balance sheet vehicles, and private equity. Activities ranged from traders and dealers in markets on behalf of others and on their own account, financial advisers to companies seeking funds on the market for expansion including merger and acquisitions activity, and buy side institutional investors including insurers and pension funds. Specialist markets in futures, initially linked to agricultural and raw material commodities also emerged in both countries that provided the basis for the later broader development of derivatives trading.

However, capturing those financial flows in a global world and funnelling them into these two locations and then out from there back to various parts of the world as particular financial contracts and obligations is itself a task of huge organizational and technological complexity. It requires that financial firms locate branches in all the significant economies in the world. The task of these branches is three fold. First, they attract funds and business into the various products and services of the bank from local wealthy individuals, institutional investors (or their equivalents), corporations, and the state (whether in the form of sovereign wealth funds or managing currency exchange and short-term money market funds). Secondly, they sell into these economies their products such as corporate and sovereign bonds, stocks and shares, derivative products, insurances, etc. Thirdly, they participate in local financial markets leveraging their economies of scale and scope to dominate local stock markets, bond issuance, and derivative markets.

Establishing an international structure on this scale in the banking industry is an expensive and risky task. On the organizational side, it requires a high level of investment in people, processes, and technologies. The obverse of risk diversification is that internationalization places the bank in many different markets with different regulations, different economic cycles, different politics, and different weaknesses. Many banks have failed to make this transition, rushing into acquisitions in the expectation of quick profits (see, for example, the series of books by Philip Augar which expose the failings of the British—and other—banks in the City of London: Augar 2000, 2006, 2010). Expensive forays into the United States based on mistaken valuations of the acquired businesses caused large losses and effectively undermined the independence of two of the largest UK banks in the 1980s—the Midland and NatWest. The Midland was absorbed into what is now HSBC, and NatWest was taken over by the Royal Bank of Scotland. Barings Bank collapsed because of its failure to control the activities of Nick Leeson in its Singapore branch. Barclays also has made efforts to establish itself in the US and this led to large losses, and its first effort to build an investment bank on a large scale, known as BZW, was sold to Credit Suisse First Boston in 1998.

In France in the late 1980s, Credit Lyonnais, which was at the time the biggest bank in the country, crashed due to a similar rapid over-expansion and has shrunk back behind rivals such as BNP-Paribas and Société Générale as a result. In Germany, Dresdner Bank sought to make this expansion and also failed after making large takeovers in London and New York, eventually being sold off to Commerzbank supported by its dominant shareholder, the insurance company Allianz. In the US, whilst there were multiple forms of consolidation particularly as Glass-Steagall restraints weakened, a tier of what were known as bulge bracket investment banks emerged and dominated the market without major disruptions until the financial crisis.

By 2010, six of the ten largest international investment banks were US based, two from Switzerland (UBS and Credit Suisse) and one each from

Germany (Deutsche Bank) and the UK (Barclays). Each of these have full branch offices (rather than what are termed 'representative offices') in all five continents. Just outside of this group are a number of other large European banks such as the two largest French banks, BNP Paribas and Société Générale, the second largest German bank, Commerzbank, and two Dutch banks, ING and ABN-AMRO, plus the Spanish bank Santander. These banks vary in their scale but tend to have less geographical coverage and also less engagement with the full range of wholesale financial markets.

Nevertheless, it is important to identify the key advantages which these firms have. The first is that of scale; in many financial markets, margins are relatively small and firms make money by investing in infrastructure that keeps the cost of transactions low, and then utilizing this as strongly as possible, through operating on a large scale, for example in terms of trading shares and bonds. The second is that of knowledge and being able to draw on diverse and distributed pools of knowledge in order to identify trends in markets and arbitrage prices to their own advantage. The result has been that a small number of large investment banks from a small number of countries have become the major conduits for the global flow of funds; furthermore the locations in which they have conducted these funds have been primarily limited to the UK and the US.

From an organizational perspective, therefore, the globalization of capital flows was coordinated through a limited number of investment banks that had transnational networks for the sale, marketing, and distribution of financial products. Again, this is a constrained form of globalization; basically only around ten large international banks act as the intermediaries for these flows and there are two main locations in which this occurs. There are many more diverse financial institutions and actors working within the financial markets as will be discussed in the next section, but they depend on these international banks to do what might be termed the 'heavy lifting and carrying' of collecting and distributing the funds and making the key markets by providing liquidity, prices, and trades. Entry to this top tier is highly restricted as it requires massive capital to fund the technology, the network systems, and the expertise necessary. This is not, however, an insuperable barrier and it may be likely that one or more Chinese banks joins this group in the next few years, given the scale of their operations and the political will to push China into the centre of the global economy.

Nor are there insuperable barriers to the emergence of new locations to rival New York and the City of London. Tokyo, which had briefly threatened to become one of the centres of global finance (Sassen 2001), is no longer a likely candidate, but within Europe, Paris and Frankfurt are significant, and within the context of the EU and the Eurozone, may become more so, whilst potential Asian challengers in Hong Kong, Singapore, and more recently Shanghai have emerged. However at present, even after the crash, Wall Street and the City remain dominant with a number of satellite, linked regional financial centres (Sassen 2002).

Financial markets

The reason for this locational specificity goes beyond the historical and agglomeration factors previously discussed. It is important to consider how, in a specific period of time and with particular sets of resources and assets, these locations had markets and institutions that seemed capable of generating extra yield. Williams and colleagues have done much to illuminate how what they term the 'bricolage' associated with high-risk forms of financial innovation generated such profitable opportunities (Engelen, Erturk et al. 2010). In particular, many of these funds went into credit creation processes previously discussed, primarily around the expansion of the sub-prime mortgage property market in the US but also into commercial property and funding other forms of personal debt (Lounsbury and Hirsch 2010). They additionally went into funding highly leveraged buyouts and private equity deals in the UK and the US, as well as into hedge funds and large-scale leveraged speculations on price movements through the use of derivative instruments.

All these processes fed the financial boom in asset prices of the period up to 2007, sucking in more funds. There is not space here to describe how these markets worked, and more particularly how they gave rise to the financial crash (for a recent authoritative and comprehensive account see Financial Crisis Inquiry Commission 2011, as well as Bitner 2008 and Tett 2009) but what is crucial to emphasize here, however, is that this process was not global. It was massively concentrated in New York and London. In 2007, for example, London accounted for 80 per cent of hedge funds managed in Europe and 20 per cent of the world's hedge fund assets, 47 per cent of the turnover of cross border derivatives, and 46 per cent of global equity trading (Talani 2011). New York accounted for the bulk of other forms of trading. The two centres had dominant positions in initial public offerings (IPOs), in cross border lending, and in assets under management. Not surprisingly banks that wanted to participate in these markets had to come to these locations. Talani states that London hosted 250 foreign banks, New York about half that number. Both locations hosted hedge funds with barely any regulation to constrain their activities. Other countries in Europe and elsewhere were much more cautious, both in terms of the conditions under which foreign banks and particularly 'shadow banking institutions' (mainly hedge funds) could be established. They were also much more constraining in terms of how new markets and new financial instruments could be set up.

In the UK and the US, partly as a result of the dominance of common law, financial innovations did not require legal approval before they could be put into the market. In most civil law countries, positive approval generally had to be enacted into law (Morgan 2008), slowing down the whole process. It was much easier to set up a branch in London and participate in the market there than try to reform domestic law. For EU banks, the single European passport meant that they could trade in London whilst remaining under the supervision of their home regulator. As a result, some financial institutions from institutional-legal contexts that were prohibitive in terms of the development of new financial instruments were able to participate by setting up the appropriate legal subsidiary in London and/or New York.

In conclusion, the global financial system was heavily structured by the dominance of a particular pattern of flow of funds, a small number of international banks, and a concentration of markets in just two locations. In the following section, we focus more explicitly on the national contexts that shaped this flow.

National capitalisms and financial systems

In this section, we examine in more depth the institutional complementarities within national systems, particularly in terms of how the financial system relates to other aspects of society, and how this in turn shapes capital outflows, inflows, and participation in financial markets (Campbell 2011). In particular we draw out more strongly the difference between, on the one hand, the UK and the US, and on the other hand, more coordinated forms of economy. For reasons of space, we focus particularly on Germany.

Important institutional differences between advanced capitalist economies emerged sharply as policy responses to the breakdown of the Bretton Woods system and the decline in effectiveness of Keynesian demand management (Hall 1999). In the United States and the United Kingdom, the policy responses were dominated by the deregulation of financial, labour and product markets. In particular, the power of organized labour was challenged and the power of the financial markets was increased. In many other market economies, the response was different. The use of redeployment of skills inside companies constituted an alternative to the deregulation of labour markets that were prevalent in liberal market economies. These differences are important since shifts in policies in liberal market economies resulted in the sorts of stark distributive consequences discussed in the previous section (see Davis 2009). Income disparities rose and workers without transferable skills faced uncertain job prospects. Wage levels for the middle and lower income groups stagnated. This is the context in which privatized Keynesianism, based on increasing personal credit and inflating the value of key assets such as housing, emerged (Crouch 2008). To maintain high levels of aggregate demand, as well as to mobilize political consent for deregulatory policies, governments promoted access to housing, favoured the import of cheap consumer goods from low-income countries, and supported the expansion of credit through the deregulation of the financial sector (see Hall 2012). People with median or below-median salaries could keep on consuming despite the stagnant character of real income. Privatized Keynesianism, however, proved unsustainable, given the limits to indebtedness.

In Germany, the important contribution of exports to GDP has been interdependent with both conservative monetary policies and coordinated wage bargaining (Soskice and Iversen 2000). The German central bank (and more latterly the European Central Bank which has been strongly influenced by the Bundesbank approach) has been particularly concerned about controlling internal inflation in order to maintain global competitiveness. Trade unions in the traded sectors have shared this concern, seeing tight control over inflation as a way of securing overseas markets and therefore jobs for their members. Using interest rates to control inflation, even where this constrains the growth of the overall economy, has therefore been an accepted policy framework (Hall and Franzese 1998). Maintaining low inflation provides a form of protection to the export sector of the economy and for the firm-specific skills of their employees (Estevez-Abe, Iversen et al. 2001), as well as providing incentives against indebtedness (Iversen and Soskice 2010). These bargaining processes in the export sector lead to a pattern of low real wage increases. Furthermore, in the German context, this settlement provides the pattern for wage agreements in the state and non-tradable sectors through coordinated bargaining (Hancké and Soskice 2003; Johnston and Hancké 2009). The restrictive ECB monetary policy from a German perspective (see below) has inadvertently contributed to this process—lower rates of economic growth served to dampen domestic demand as a whole. This in turn prevents the growth of labour shortage across the economy as a whole, which might lead to more competition amongst firms for employees and associated spiraling wages. Restraining demand, however, leads to the creation of a relatively high permanent pool of unemployed as well as an increasing call on state welfare provision, creating pressure for reform of the tax and welfare systems (see Kitschelt and Streeck 2004: Streeck 2009).

As a result, personal incomes stagnated in Germany despite relative stability in employment—an outcome that shares some similarities with the American and British experiences. Unlike the US and the UK, however, there has been no credit boom fuelled by house price rises to promote internal consumption. The structure of the housing market in Germany differs, as does the mode of funding which requires large down payments in comparison to the US and the

UK (Schwartz and Seabrooke 2008). Funding for house purchase has come mainly through retail deposits. In so far as there has been any form of securitization it has followed a distinctively German model, the so-called 'covered bond', where the issuer remained liable for the asset pool, unlike the US system where issuers transferred all liability for the assets as part of the sale of the bonds. It was this ability to shed liability for assets that led US lenders to ignore the weak credit position of mortgage borrowers in the knowledge that once they had securitized the deal it was no longer their concern. German lenders were unable to shed these liabilities.

Consumption in Germany remained relatively flat in the 1990s and 2000s due to limited growth in wages and was further constrained by a regime that inhibited credit provision and the growth of personal indebtedness, as well as the restrictive European Central Bank (ECB) monetary policy. Other ways of freeing up earnings for different forms of consumption, such as by increasing the productivity of the service sector, for example by introducing flexible labour market rules that would have affected the position of core employees, were blocked by the existing system of labour regulation. Instead, flexibility was limited to the periphery—rules for part-time work and fixed-term contracts were liberalized (Palier and Thelen 2010).

Many of the dollars earned from export surpluses were not returned to Germany since return on investment outside the export sector was low and there was little demand to increase provision of credit. The Bundesbank, and later the ECB, sought to resist the general securitization boom for fear that it would lose control of the money supply, and more credit would be created that would stoke inflationary pressures, thus reducing the competitive advantage of German industry in global markets. Internal demand, therefore, continued to stagnate, keeping the position of labour even in the export industries weak and helping to hold down wages there, a process reinforced by German MNCs either threatening to move to lower wage areas (in Eastern Europe or China) or actually doing so, leading to pressure on works councils and trade unions to accept further wage restraints and employment restructuring (Streeck 2009). Investing the surplus overseas, much of it in the US as described earlier, became the standard response, rather than expanding production or consumption in Germany itself. Schwartz describes a number of countries including Germany and Japan operating in this way as the 'repressed rich' 'whose growth was decidedly below the OECD average.... Elites in ... these countries benefited from a politics that depressed local consumption and ... thus made their economies reliant on external demand for growth ... Foreigners opted to recycle their trade surpluses with the United States by purchasing various forms of US debt securities rather than increasing domestic consumption or ... investment' (Schwartz 2009: 7).

It is worth noting that in the German case this had particular effects on the financial sector itself. Hardie and Howarth point out that in the German context a 'fragmented domestic market restricted competition and profits, pushing both private banks and the LB increasingly abroad to increase profitability' (Hardie and Howarth 2009: 1020). The case is clearest for the largest commercial banks which found that their previous close relationships with German multinationals were becoming more arm's length as those firms raised funds from internal cash flows and directly from capital markets, going to London and New York when necessary. The possibilities of growth in the home market through increasing their levels of service to personal customers was constrained by the strong position of the Sparkasse in the retail banking markets, the limited willingness of German consumers to expand consumption through increasing credit, and a pension system that remained to a significant extent invested in collective funds following low-risk investment strategies. To survive, prosper, and grow, the commercial banks needed to internationalize, to access the funds and profitability opportunities in London and New York. Deutsche Bank was the most aggressive builder of investment banking capacity on the lines of the US bulge banks. As discussed previously, Dresdner Bank's efforts in the same direction were unsuccessful, whilst Commerzbank was more conservative until it agreed to rescue Dresdner in the light of its collapse post-Lehman.

What is less expected is that these imperatives also reached further down into the German financial system. Some of the Landesbanken (especially Bayerische LB, LB Sachsen, NordLB, and WestLB) as well as in some of the more specialist German financial institutions such as DZ Bank (which served the same function for the German cooperative banking sector as Landesbanken did for the Sparkasse), Hypo Real Estate (HRE) (a specialist bank for real estate lending) and IKB (a specialist bank for corporate financing) saw the opportunity to increase their profitability.

In contrast to big investment banks such as Deutsche or more high-risk entities such as hedge funds, these institutions were generally engaged in a simple trade known as 'securities arbitrage', which they mistakenly thought was relatively low risk. This was a common trade during the boom years for many mid range financial institutions,who were strongly sold these types of products as low risk by the big investment banks. In its analysis of IKB's demise, for example, the US Financial Crisis Inquiry Report (pp. 246–8) describes how IKB created an off-balance sheet entity which would borrow commercial paper, that is, relatively short-term unsecured lending (maximum of 270 days) with which it would buy higher yielding securitized products such as CDOs. The spread between the interest paid on commercial paper and the interest received from the CDOs would constitute the profit to be made. As the Financial Inquiry report makes clear it was Goldman Sachs that sat at the centre of these trades, constructing the CDOs, selling them to entities like IKB (even when they knew that the CDOs were likely to collapse: Lewis 2010), providing lines of credit in the commercial paper market to fund the purchase of the securitized assets. Purchasers of CDOs such as IKB, the Landesbanken, HRE, etc. were in retrospect naively reliant on the advice of the big investment banks. Since commercial paper had to be periodically renewed, once lenders felt that the assets which underpinned the payment of the interest would be failing (as was the case with CDOs etc. by late 2007 as the extent of the subprime crisis became obvious), they refused to roll over the lending, placing the borrower in a near bankruptcy situation. This was the fate which befell most of these middle-sized German financial institutions which had become dependent on the income from securitized assets both for their own growth and to facilitate a rollover of commercial paper. IKB in effect became the first victim of this when Deutsche Bank refused to renew its credit lines in July 2007 and it had to be rescued by its largest shareholder, KfW Bankengruppe (a financial institution created by the German state to promote financing for SMEs and provided with a federal guarantee against default).

Hardie and Howarth state that 'this analysis shows that the view of the German banks as more conservative as befits a bank-based financial system, does not hold' (ibid: 1028). Many of the banking institutions were risk-taking in a way that might not have been expected. However, it is important to note that they were risk-taking in the international financial markets, not risk-taking in terms of their relationship with the German companies that they were dealing with. Although the financing of the largest firms in German industry had changed from the predominant model of the 1960s and 1970s in terms of such firms seeking funding elsewhere than from their 'hausbank', ownership of them remains fairly concentrated in Germany (see Kogut and Walker 2000; Culpepper 2011; Kogut forthcoming). Similarly, relationships between German SMEs and their main providers of funding, the Sparkasse, remain relatively stable. Thus this process of internationalization in certain segments of the banking sector and the crisis which followed has not yet disrupted other aspects of the German system. In particular, in spite of pessimistic accounts of the German future, the post-crisis period has shown the resilience and the continued (indeed growing) success of German manufacturing in export markets built on the specific and well-known relationships between the institutions of skill formation, labour and product regulation, and management practice that have long been identified.

In terms of the wider response in Germany to the downturn, this reinforced existing complementarities and the importance of the firm-specific character of skills (Hall 2009 and 2012). The focus of the initial demand package stimulus was on the preservation of existing, highly skilled jobs. A key element of the rescue package was the award of subsidies to companies (in some limited number of export-oriented industries) for covering the costs of retaining employees who were put on a part-time schedule. Preventing job losses for employees with firm-specific skills is important for two reasons. The first concerns the credibility of commitment associated with the provision of skills that are limited to specific settings. Not only would dismissed employees find it hard to secure new employment, given the limited transferability of their skills, but the willingness of future cohorts of workers to invest in firm-specific skills could be negatively affected (see e.g. Estevez-Abe, Iversen, and Soskice 2001). The second issue is the restrictive macroeconomic regime of job creation in Germany. Interest rates set at the EU level represent an average for the Euro Zone, the latter increasingly being perceived as a non-optimum currency area. The issue is that rates of inflation in Germany are lower than in other EU member states, with the result that interest rates do not reflect the German situation and are set at a too high level (Hancké and Soskice 2003), holding back domestic consumption and investment. The implication therefore is that Germany cannot count on high rates of domestic economic growth to lower unemployment—except through exports, which takes us back to the complementarities originally identified! Whether the restructuring of the banking sector as described earlier might impact on that is uncertain but currently appears unlikely.

The German example reveals the complexity of the financial system. At a global level, the system is shaped by decisions such as those of the German government, the Bundesbank (and now the ECB, although inadvertently for the latter), and social partners to maintain employment and competitiveness in the export sector of the economy through holding down wages, inflation, and credit. This set of institutional complementarities may be under pressure (Streeck 2009), but it retains considerable resilience to set the terms under which the German system participates in the global financial system. This set of relationships results in the growth of surpluses with the US, helping fuel the credit boom there which, in turn, maintains a growing market for German exports. At home, however, consumption stagnates unaided by the sort of credit relaxations in the UK and the US, which fuelled the housing boom and the associated employment growth. This stagnation also pushes German financial institutions with limited opportunities for growth in their home market to expand into the more open financial markets of the US and the UK, where many of them suffered huge losses.

We are not seeking to present the German example as a general model of how more coordinated economies have evolved in relation to the characteristics of global finance which we have described. There are some similarities with China and Japan in terms of how surpluses have been built up with the US and left in the US financial markets, for example in terms of holding down wages and consumption in the home economy to sustain export competitiveness (see Rajan 2010). Clearly, however, the politics of these processes varies hugely. China is attempting to manage a massive transition from a rural to an industrial, even post-industrial economy, under conditions of leadership via the Communist Party, with all the problems of labour discipline and governmentability which that involves (see Krug in this volume). Japan remains stuck with high levels of savings and low growth in consumption due to a range of factors such as demography, the continuing impact of the crash of the bubble economy, and the decades of control of government by the Liberal Democratic Party. Also unlike Germany, even though the financial systems of both countries suffered huge losses in the crash, in neither case was the participation in the US markets so great as to bring down major players in their banking sectors.

Discussion and conclusion

Is there a global financial system? Our argument has been that there is such a system but that first, it consists of a very particular structure of flows, institutions, and markets, and secondly, it is driven by the interaction of different forms of national capitalisms and does not exist *sui generis* beyond the reach of these structures. Indeed, in many ways, the extension of finance through deregulation has reinforced national differences rather than removed them. The analysis in the previous sections has shown how specific characteristics of these different systems led to the particular flow of funds that was described, and how these funds were directed into different assets exacerbating the possibilities for further differentiation.

From this point of view, it would be a mistake to use the undoubted interdependences that came to light in the financial crash to construct a different and more diffuse notion of financial globalization. The economic downturn that has followed the financial crisis has also affected many economies that were characterized by different politics of consumer credit, lower levels of personal debt, and different positions in the global economy. It has spread across advanced capitalist economies and, moreover, has generated a flurry of responses by national governments, whether or not they were initially hit by the problems of financial institutions. However, this contagion arises because these other systems were connected to the source of the crash in various ways, some financial, some more trade-based forms of connection, but these other systems were not causally involved in the crash. Whilst some countries participated in this process by freeing up credit and creating a property boom, most noticeably Iceland and Ireland, other large economies in Europe organized key aspects of their housing system and its connection to financial market differently (Schwartz and Seabrooke 2008). Thus their domestic system was cushioned from the direct impact of this speculative bubble even if their financial institutions through their London and New York subsidiaries participated in the self-same bubble.

As Thompson points out, politicians, particularly in the UK, were quick to use the discourse of globalization as a means of shifting blame to forces beyond their control (Thompson 2009). Yet this is to ignore the basic fact that the crisis exploded precisely in the US and the UK because of the interrelationships described earlier. Placing the resolution of these problems into the hands of multilateral institutions such as the G20, the IMF, etc. shifts attention from what are first, the large political issues of international adjustment and secondly, the creation of adequate regulatory mechanisms at the national level.

With regard to the first set of issues, the continued role of the US dollar as a world currency remains problematic and is central to creating an imbalanced system of fund flows. So too, however, are the particular policies of the large saving countries such as Germany, Japan, and China, where the politics of managing potential conflicts is achieved through maintaining steady growth through prioritizing exports and holding down personal consumption, a policy only viable as long as elsewhere the opposite is occurring, which was the case with the US credit boom. There are fundamental issues of international politics and economics that are yet to be worked out and that cannot be worked out within the realms of multilateral institutions.

With regard to the second, connected set of issues, the question is how far and in what ways politicians are capable of constraining the activities of those in the financial markets. Can there be regulatory reform, not at the international level but at the national level where law and legitimacy can be drawn on by governments to shape financial markets as was done in the New Deal era in the US? In the US, whilst the Dodd-Frank Act has been passed, its operational details are still being hotly debated in the Securities and Exchange Commission (SEC), Congress, and on Wall Street. In the UK, the response has been to restructure the regulatory bodies and commit the new structure to a tighter form of regulation, though how this will work in practice is unclear. In the European Union, the new EU regulatory authorities have been set up and have begun work, but their impact is still very unclear. What is revealed, however, is that institutional reform at the level of the nation-state offers a prospect, even if it is tempered by private interests and lobbying power, of democratic debate over the financial markets, whereas international bodies suffer both from a democratic deficit and from an inability to reach agreement.

In conclusion, the argument here is that the future of financial globalization is going to be determined largely by the actions of states (Berger 2009; Gourevitch forthcoming; Hall 2009). These states are constrained both by the balance of inter-state power but also by the institutional complementarities which bind their populations and governments in various ways. Financial globalization does not exist in and of its own accord, no matter the scale of transactions or the existence of transnational rules about open markets (see Gessner and Whitley in this volume). Financial globalization is an outcome of relations between forms of capitalism which are reproduced in the process, but not always in ways which can be predicted.

References

Abdelal, R. (2007) *Capital Rules: The construction of global finance*, Cambridge, Mass.: Harvard University Press.

Almond, P. and A. Ferner (2006) *American Multinationals in Europe: Managing employment relations across national borders*, Oxford: Oxford University Press.

Amable, B. (2003) *The Diversity of Modern Capitalism*, Oxford: Oxford University Press.

Augar, P. (2000) *The Death of Gentlemanly Capitalism*, London: Penguin Books.

—— (2006) *The Greed Merchants: How the investment banks played the free market game*, London: Penguin Books.

—— (2010) *Reckless: The rise and fall of the City, 1997–2008*, London: Vintage.

Berger, S. (2009) 'Troubleshooting Economic Narratives', pp. 103–9 in A. Hemerijck, B. Knapen, and E.V. Doorne (eds) *Aftershocks: Economic crisis and institutional choice*, Amsterdam: Amsterdam University Press.

Bitner, R. (2008) *Confessions of a Subprime Lender: An insider's tale of greed, fraud, and ignorance*, Hoboken, N.J.: John Wiley & Sons.

Boyer, R. (1990) *The Regulation School: A critical introduction*, New York: Columbia University Press.

Campbell, J. L. (2011) 'The US Financial Crisis: Lessons for theories of institutional complementarity', *Socio Economic Review* 9(2): 211–34.

Cohen, B. (1996) 'Phoenix Risen: The resurrection of global finance', *World Politics* 48(2): 268–96.

Crouch, C. (2008) 'What will follow the Demise of Privatised Keynesianism?' *The Political Quarterly* 79(4): 476–87.

Culpepper, P. (2011) *Quiet Politics and Business Power: Corporate control in Europe and Japan*, Cambridge: Cambridge University Press.

Davis, G. F. (2009) *Managed by the Markets: How finance reshaped America*, Oxford: Oxford University Press.

Eichengreen, B. J. (2007) *The European Economy since 1945: Coordinated capitalism and beyond*, Princeton, N.J.: Princeton University Press.

—— (2008) *Globalizing Capital: A history of the international monetary system*, Princeton, N.J.: Princeton University Press.

—— (2011) *Exorbitant Privilege: The rise and fall of the dollar*, Oxford: Oxford University Press.

Engelen, E., I. Erturk, et al. (2010) 'Reconceptualizing Financial Innovation: Frame, conjuncture and bricolage', *Economy and Society* 39(1): 33–63.

Erturk, I., J. Froud, et al. (2008) *Financialization at Work: Key texts and commentary*, London: Routledge.

Estevez-Abe, M., T. Iversen, et al. (2001) 'Social Protection and the Formation of Skills: A Reinterpretation of the Welfare State, pp. 145–83 in *Varieties of Capitalism*, P. A. Hall and D. Soskice, Oxford: Oxford University Press.

Financial Crisis Inquiry Commission, T. (2011) *The Financial Crisis Inquiry Report: Final report of the national commission on the causes of the financial and economic crisis in the United States*, New York, NY: Public Affairs.

Frieden, J. (1991) 'Invested Interests: The Politics of N ational Economic Policies in a World of Global Finance', *International Organization* 45(4): 425–91.

Froud, J., S. Johal, et al. (2006) *Financialization and Stratgegy: Narrative and numbers*, London: Routledge.

Germain, R. D. (2010) *Global Politics and Financial Governance*, Basingstoke: Palgrave Macmillan.

Goodman, J. B. and L. Pauly (1993) 'The Obsolesence of Capital Control? Economic management in the age of global markets', *World Politics* 46(1): 50–82.

Gourevitch, P. (forthcoming) 'Yet more Hard Times?' in M. Kahler and D. Lake (eds) *Politics in the New Hard Times: The Great Recession in comparative perspective*, Ithaca, NY: Cornell University Press.

Hacker, J. S. and P. Pierson (2010) *Winner-Take-All Politics: How Washington made the rich richer-and turned its back on the middle class*, New York: Simon & Schuster.

Hall, P. A. (1999) 'The Political Economy of Europe in an Age of Interdependence', pp. 135–63 in H. Kitschelt, P. Lange, G. Marks, and J. D. Stephens (eds) *Continuity and Change in Contemporary Capitalism*, Cambridge: Cambridge University Press.

—— (2009) 'The Significance of Politics', pp. 93–102 in A. Hemerijck, B. Knapen and E. V. Doorne (eds) *Aftershocks: Economic crisis and institutional choice*, A. Hemerijck, Amsterdam: Amsterdam University Press.

—— (2012) 'The Political Origins of our Economic Discontents: Contemporary adjustment problems in historical perspective', in M. Kahler and D. Lake (eds) *Politics in the New Hard Times: The Great Recession in comparative perspective*, Ithaca, NY: Cornell University Press.

—— and R. Franzese (1998) 'Mixed Signals: Central Bank independence, coordinated wage bargaining and European monetary union', *International Organization* 52(3): 502–36.

—— and D. Soskice (eds) (2001) *Varieties of Capitalism The Institutional Foundations of Comparative Advantage*, Oxford: Oxford University Press.

Hancké, B. and D. Soskice (2003) 'Wage-Setting and Inflation Targets in EMU', *Oxford Review of Economic Policy* 19(1): 149–60.

Hardie, I. and D. Howarth (2009) '*Die Krise* but not *La Crise?* The financial crisis and the transformation of German and French Banking Systems', *Journal of Common Market Studies* 47(5): 1017–39.

Helleiner, E. and J. Kirshner (eds) (2009) *The Future of the Dollar*, Ithaca: Cornell University Press.

Hemerijck, A., B. Knapen, et al. (eds) (2009) *Aftershocks: Economic crisis and institutional choice*, Amsterdam: Amsterdam University Press.

Herrigel, G. (2010) *Manufacturing Possibilities: Creative action and industrial recomposition in the United States, Germany and Japan*, Oxford: Oxford University Press.

—— and J. Zeitlin (2010) 'Inter-Firm Relations in Global Manufacturing: Disintegrated Production and its Globalization', pp. 527–61 in G. Morgan, J. L. Campbell, C. Crouch, O. K. Pedersen, and R. Whitley (eds) *The Oxford Handbook of Comparative Institutional Analysis*, Oxford: Oxford University Press.

Ho, K. Z. (2009) *Liquidated: An ethnography of Wall Street*, Durham NC, Duke University Press.

Ingham, G. K. (1984) *Capitalism divided? The city and industry in British social development*, Basingstoke: Macmillan.

Iversen, T. and D. Soskice (2010) 'Real Exchange Rates and Competitiveness: The political economy of skill formation, wage compression, and electoral systems', *American Political Science Review*, 104(3): 601–3.

Johnston, A. and B. Hancké (2009) 'Wage Inflation and Labour Unions in EMU', *Journal of European Public Policy* 16(4): 601–22.

Kirshner, Jonathan (ed.) (2003) *Monetary Orders: Ambiguous economics, ubiquitous politics*, Ithaca: Cornell University Press.

Kitschelt, H. and Streeck, W. (eds) (2004) *Germany: Beyond the stable state*, London: Frank Cass.

Kogut, B. (ed.) (forthcoming) *The Small Worlds of Corporate Governance*, Cambridge, Mass.: MIT Press.

Langley, P. (2008) *The Everyday Life of Global Finance: Saving and borrowing in Anglo-America*, Oxford; New York: Oxford University Press.

Lazonick, W. (2009) *Sustainable Prosperity in the New Economy?: Business organization and high-tech employment in the United States*, Kalamazoo, Michigan: W.E. Upjohn Institute for Employment Research.

Lewis, M. (2010) *The Big Short: Inside the doomsday machine*, London: Allen Lane.

Lounsbury, M. and P. M. Hirsch (2010) *Markets on Trial: The economic sociology of the U.S. financial crisis*, Bingley: Emerald.

McKinsey Global Institute (2008) *Mapping Global Capital Markets: Fourth annual report*, London/New York: McKinsey & Company.

—— (2009) *Global Capital Markets: Entering a new* era, London/New York: McKinsey & Company.

Milward, A. S., G. Brennan, et al. (2000) *The European Rescue of the Nation-State*, London: Routledge.

Moran, M. (1991) *The Politics of the Financial Services Revolution: The USA, UK and Japan*, Basingstoke: Macmillan.

—— (2003) *The British Regulatory State: High modernism and hyper-innovation*, Oxford: Oxford University Press.

Morgan, G. (2008) 'Market Formation and Governance in International Financial Markets: The case of OTC derivatives', *Human Relations* 61(5): 637–60.

—— (2010) 'Legitimacy in Financial Markets: Credit default swaps in the current crisis', *Socio-Economic Review* 8(1): 17–45.

Morrison, W. M. (2009) 'China and the Global Financial Crisis: Implications for the United States', *Congressional Research Service*.

Palier, B. and K. Thelen (2010) 'Institutionalizing Dualism: Complementarities in and change in France and Germany', *Politics & Society* 38(1): 119–48.

Rajan, R. (2010) *Fault Lines: How hidden fractures still threaten the world economy*, Princeton: Princeton University Press.

Ruggie, J. G. (1998) *Constructing the World Polity: Essays on international institutionalization*, London; New York: Routledge.

Sassen, S. (2001) *The Global City: New York, London, Tokyo*, Princeton: Princeton University Press.

—— (2002) *Global Networks, Linked Cities*, New York; London: Routledge.

Schwartz, H. (2009) *Subprime Nation: American Power, Global Capital and the Housing Bubble*, Ithaca, NY: Cornell University Press.

—— and L. Seabrooke (2008) 'Varieties of Residential Capitalism in the International Political Economy: Old Welfare States and the New Politics of Housing', *Comparative European Politics* 6(3): 237–61.

Simmons, B. A. (1999) 'The Internationalization of Capital', pp. 36–69 in H. Kitschelt, P. Lange, G. Marks, and J. D. Stephens (eds) *Continuity and Change in Contemporary Capitalism*, Cambridge: Cambridge University Press.

Soskice, D. and T. Iversen (2000) 'The Nonneutrality of Monetary Policy with Large Price or Wage Setters', *Quarterly Journal of Economics* 115(1): 265–84.

Stiglitz, J. E. (2004) *The Roaring Nineties: A new history of the world's most prosperous decade*, New York: W.W. Norton & Co.

—— (2006) *Making Globalization Work*, New York: W.W. Norton & Co.

—— (2010) *Freefall: America, free markets, and the sinking of the world economy*, New York: W.W. Norton & Co.

Streeck, W. (2009) *Re-Forming Capitalism: Institutional change in the German political economy*, Oxford: Oxford University Press.

Talani, L. S. (2011) 'The Impact of the Global Financial Crisis on the City of London: Towards the end of hegemony?' *Competition and Change* 15(1): 11–30.

Tett, G. (2009) *Fool's Gold*, London: Little, Brown.

Thompson, G. F. (2009) 'What's in the Frame? How the financial crisis is being packaged for public consumption', *Economy and Society* 38(3): 520–4.

Whitley, R. (1999) *Divergent Capitalisms: The social structuring and change of business systems*, Oxford: Oxford University Press.

—— (2009) 'U.S. Capitalism: A tarnished model?', *Academy of Management Perspectives* 23(2): 11–22.

—— (2010) 'Changing Competition Models in Market Economies', pp. 363–97 in G. Morgan, J. L. Campbell, C. Crouch, O. K. Pedersen, and R. Whitley (eds) *The Oxford Handbook of Comparative Institutional Analysis*, Oxford: Oxford University Press.

—— G. Morgan, et al. (2003) 'The Changing Japanese Multinational: Application, adaptation and learning in car manufacturing and financial services', *Journal of Management Studies* 40(3): 643–72.

Zysman, J. (1983) *Governments, Markets, and Growth: Financial systems and the politics of industrial change*, Ithaca N.Y.: Cornell University Press.

6

Enabling Global Business Transactions

Relational and Legal Mechanisms

Volkmar Gessner

1. Business and institutions

As all other areas of law, business law has two faces: *regulation* and *support*. These faces or functions should be clearly separated when one is interested in their sociological description. *Regulation* of business concerns tax issues, environmental protection, labour standards, etc. The *support* function of law is currently not at the centre of the debate but will be the main focus of the remaining part of this paper. In nation states' jurisdictions, 'enabling law' is supporting economic transactions with its contract law, company law, insolvency law, and offering conflict resolution in civil procedures. From the time of Roman Law until the nineteenth century this support was almost the only task of state law. Still today, in legal practice (lawyers, courts, legal education) this is predominant, whereas regulatory aspects play a relatively minor role. The reason behind state support for the economy is, as Max Weber prominently emphasized, legal certainty:

> The modern capitalist enterprise rests primarily on *calculation* and presupposes a legal and administrative system, whose functioning can be rationally predicted, at least in principle, by virtue of its fixed general norms, just like the expected performance of a machine. (Weber 1968: 1394)

Although this core idea of sociological and economic theory on law is generally accepted as a justification for the centrality of legal reasoning in Western societies and seems to support legal initiatives in developing countries aimed at creating legal structures for global exchanges, the 'one-size-fits-all' models developed by global agents like the World Bank, the IMF, the United States Agency for Economic Development (USAID), the EU PHARE (orginally the

Poland and Hungary Assistance for Restructuring their Economies), the Trans-European Mobility Scheme for University Studies (TEMPUS) programmes, and the Deutsche Gesellschaft für Technische Zusammenarbeit (GTZ) are severely criticized (the debates are reported in Gessner 2007; Gessner (ed.) 2008a). It is possible to raise doubts about whether law is the only or the most important instrument for achieving legal certainty. The centrality of law in Weber's theory has been questioned because of his 'England problem' and because of his empirical assumptions which hold true neither for developing countries nor for countries undergoing transformation. Weber himself argued on various occasions that England was a deviant case in his theory. The observation that England, the birthplace of capitalism, lacked the calculable, logically formal, legal system that he identified as necessary for capitalist development, was troubling (Weber 1968: 719, 724, and 1036). His discussion on that issue is often considered ambiguous and contradictory (Trubek 1972). The case of England with its common law system does certainly not confirm the idea that formal legal rationality is a prerequisite for the development of a capitalist economy. Weber criticized the English common law for its lack of formal rationality and its class bias, but he recognized its importance for the English economy. Due to strong links between the capitalist class and English lawyers and the lawyers' crucial role in generating precedents, he also recognized that the English legal system was to an extent predictable—if only for social and economic elites (Weber 1968: 1049; Francis 1983).

Weber's empirical assumptions leading to his thesis regarding the centrality of law is that the 'modern economy' has destroyed conventions and customs in particularistic structures which previously had guaranteed contract enforcement and the protection of property. The enlargement of markets led to anonymous exchanges where small-scale, particularistic regulation was replaced by universalistic coercion. Weber in principle recognized informal norms and institutions as equivalent to legal coercion in providing calculability and legal certainty. His historical and comparative analyses show many variations of business cultures governed by non-legal institutions. However, he believed that those non-legal norms and non-state institutions had ceased to be relevant in a modern economy.

It is questionable whether this assumption is in fact correct for modern Western economies. Economic sociology, legal sociology, and anthropology have produced numerous examples of particularistic regulatory and support structures as well as informal universalistic rules in developed and efficient markets. Moreover, the absence and irrelevance of non-state rules within the economy can definitely not be assumed for all varieties of capitalism, for economies in the North and the South, for Asian economies, or the global trade. Weber's main thesis on the central role of law proves not to be universally applicable. If—which is questionable—predictability is the only problem for economic actors, law is not the only remedy available in most societies.

As regards informal and formal governance structures Institutional Economics' main interest is in the reduction of transaction costs in business dealings. Douglass North (1990) explains profitable economic performance as a dependent variable of efficient institutions. Economic actors can be, and in reality generally are, supported by institutions which limit the alternatives of action and reduce the investment (of time, of expertise, etc.) required in situations of open choice. Economic rationality works best when the choices of the players are most limited. 'Markets rest upon institutions' (Greif 2005: 727). Markets may be particularistic or anonymous. Whereas private, informal rules structure large sectors of the face-to-face economy in impersonal markets, formal legal institutions tend to predominate. This balanced view that private rules and formal rules co-exist in any economy tends to get somewhat lost in the literature where North's followers focus their attention on formal institutions (for a critical discussion, see Knowles 2005; Evans 1995). It also gets lost in the course of research commissioned by policy-makers and international development institutions. As North modestly notes, there is no such bias in his approach, and not even a clear opinion as to which type of institution is best for a particular market: 'We do not yet know how to structure markets and institutions so that they are adaptively efficient... It would be nice to have a model, but we do not have one' (North 1999: 12). Institutional economists, together with sociologists of law, are currently striving for a realistic picture of the choices made by business people or consumers between formal and informal modes of conflict resolution, and the role in that decision of the transaction costs of engaging in court proceedings and consulting a lawyer. This interdisciplinary research reveals that 'law' is a lively social field, changed or reproduced continuously; in this respect the sphere of law does not provide predictability across different commercial activities and across business cultures, but rather provides a diverse set of legitimate procedures, processes, social spaces, and actors within which agreements can be reached and conflicts resolved. The 'law in the making' as described, for example, by Morgan and Quack (2010) can hardly be understood as a stable structure of the market which offers rules of the game and enforcement mechanisms that are sufficiently clear and unambigous for efficiently guiding economic decisions. This is even more the case at the global level. There is consensus that global trade lacks a single stabilizing legal mechanism: 'When we talk about property rights and structuring markets in a given country, there must be an institutional structure that can define a set of rules of the game, can specify those rules, and can provide enforcement mechanisms. We do not have such an institutional structure for the global economy' (North 1999: 5). But (as North's 'must be' reveals) the difference to domestic markets is only relative.

In most social systems of production and exchange the *coordination* (*support*) function of institutions occupies an important position, whereas regulatory aspects play in fact a minor role. In some sectors of economics and in sociology it is common knowledge that market exchanges are not only contractually organized. They are embedded in social relationships and in addition largely dependent on external coordination (governance). In this perspective state law is one although not the only coordination structure, and current debates on public-private modes of regulation (Grande 2005) also apply. Some states have established such structures of coordination or are in the process of creating them, and other states on purpose or due to lack of resources refrain from building legal structures for market exchanges, leaving room for non-legal institutional support. Comparative economic sociology (Hollingsworth and Boyer 1997) has provided many examples of cultural differences in organizing markets. Support structures are in some cultures predominantly established by horizontal modes, whereas in others by vertical modes of economic coordination. Horizontal modes of coordination are markets and communities; vertical modes of coordination are firms and the state. In addition—placed between the horizontal and vertical modes—networks and associations contribute to the governance system. Regulatory States, Dominant Developmental States, Business Corporatist States and Inclusive Corporatist States (Hall and Soskice 2001) each develop distinctive ways of organizing the institutional environment of the economy. Frequently made assumptions that the models can be ranged on efficiency and rationality scales are not supported by comparative economic research. There does not seem to exist a single best way to economic growth. In addition to the 'varieties of capitalism' observed by comparative economic sociology (Hollingsworth and Boyer 1997; Hall and Soskice 2001; Whitley 2007), we expect the emergence of more varieties in globalized systems of exchange.

2. Global business and institutions

Empirical research on global legal phenomena does not support arguments offered by modernization (Friedman 1996) or rationalization (Weber 1968) or legalization (Hirschl 2004) theories that a global, formal, rational system of law is emerging to provide support for international business. Business on the Internet, for example, is 'modern' but weakly supported or regulated by global law. International Law Firms act 'rationally' but do their utmost to escape from (or manipulate) state or global law. Some elements of global trade are 'legalized' (WTO, EU) but at the same time more non-legal institutions (standards, soft law, business usages) and relational bonds are emerging in the global economy. All three of these theoretical assumptions suffer from a strong 'Western' bias. Given the complexities of legal cultures in global regimes, in some 180 different nation states, in an indefinite number of economic sectors, any unidirectional hypothesis would be hard to defend. Western legal cultural dominance (as implemented by Transnational Corporations; in the practice of International Law Firms; in the law and development activities or in the conditionalities of global financial institutions, in particular the International Monetory Fund) has been effective to a certain degree in implanting some elements of Western legal cultures in most non-Western societies, but this is strongly resisted by locals and criticized by most Non-Governmental Organizations (Antons and Gessner 2007). They point to many instances where Western legal values like social solidarity, human rights, due process, or nature conservation are consistently violated within all (including Western) legal cultures, and more so in global confrontations. Given the current gap between legal theory and Realpolitik, the recent financial crisis and the damage caused by neoliberal politics, the Western model is severely questioned as a model for an emergent World Society.

Power structures, inequalities, discrimination, protection, and distribution effects are predominantly discussed within the *regulatory* function of law. This is true for tax law, environmental law, criminal law, competition law, etc. Within legal *support* structures, privileges and discriminations are somewhat hidden but equally discernible. Legal support structures not only have a facilitative function but also a distributive effect (Wai 2002). Contract law may favour the supplier (*caveat emptor*), insolvency law the secured creditor (like the banks), procedural law the repeat players (like insurance companies), etc. Tort law is not only concerned with compensation to injured individuals but also aims at the deterrence of damage in the future. These examples, which cannot be further elaborated in our context, show the important regulatory effect of many legal support structures. Hence, any separation of regulation and support is to a certain degree 'ideal-typical' in Weberian terminology.

On the nation-state level, legal science, lobbies, and courts, together with the legislatures, largely control the power distribution effects of law. These entities provide a counterbalance to economically powerful actors and to a certain degree succeed in ensuring that the less powerful receive 'justice'. This is true neither in global legal orders nor in non-legal global orders—an observation which has led to the critique of globalization in general and of global actors like IMF or WTO in particular. Again, the debate is currently mainly dealing with regulation and less so with support. Global legal support structures will equally have to come under critical examination. Mainly the non-state character of informal support structures is currently discussed (Teubner 1997), providing an illustration for the so-called autopoiesis (the regeneration of organizations by self-reproduction of its own elements) of collective actors such as trade, scientific communities, or religions in the world system. But the retreat of the nation state is only a symptom of what is empirically going on in the reconstitution of power relations by global actors involved in the production of support structures, such as trade associations, arbitrators, and large law firms. Global actors, an elite mix of lawyers, merchants, and corporations which is sometimes labelled a mercatocracy (Cutler 2003), escape from public oversight.

In this highly disputed global sphere there are a number of emergent ways of coordinating global trade.

The MNC solution: Borders are a constant temptation for opportunism and make exchanges across firms vulnerable. The firm's economic standing may be disclosed or overstated, problems may be easily excused by pointing to bureaucratic hurdles, or contractual obligations remain disregarded simply because legal control and enforcement is difficult and expensive. By contrast, in the Multinational Enterprise, goods and services move across borders through intra-firm trading. Unlike what may happen in a market exchange situation, a subsidiary of a multinational enterprise finds it difficult to take advantage of legal uncertainties, for example in disputes with the headquarters or with other subsidiaries because of its position within a hierarchically coordinated structure. Borders become relatively insignificant in regard to the risk of opportunism since transactions occur within the Multinational. The very reason to create these big enterprises is their command structure, which not only reduces the transaction costs (as emphasized by Ronald Coase 1960) of drafting and enforcing contracts, but also minimizes the effects of legal and cultural diversity. Economic transactions are internalized within hierarchically organized firms rather than performed by market processes across firms. Since it is estimated that 50–70 per cent of global trade takes place within Multinational Enterprises, the weakness or absence of enabling law for global trade has no negative consequences for the larger part of the global economy that involves intra-firm trading.

Trade associations: Much research has been done on trade associations as support structures for international commerce. European trade only began on a considerable scale when medieval merchants created institutions that fostered long-distance trade by providing mechanisms for contract enforcement within their own network, in the absence of state structures for legal enforcement (Greif 2006). Bernstein (1992) describes the diamond trade where dealers and brokers 'opt out of the legal system' by creating a completely autonomous normative community with merchant rules, blacklisting, reputational bonds, and—as a last resort—arbitration (see also Teubner 1997, for additional examples of law merchant communities). The diamond trading merchants may be exceptional due to very particular social, economic, and even religious bonds. In general, the autonomy of these communities seems to be overestimated: there are persisting state law effects. This was convincingly demonstrated by Bernstein (1996) in another study, where she observed the arbitration practice of the US National Grain and Feed Association. Arbitration awards never refer to the autonomous norms and usages of this trade: they apply contract law strictly and even more formalistically than state courts. Bernstein's suggestive conclusion is that autonomous norms are used to *preserve* the relationship, whereas legal norms offer solutions for *ending* the relationship. The interplay of law merchant rules, private contracts, state law, and uniform law has also been impressively demonstrated in the securitization business, which was supposed to bridge the gap between the demands for risk protection of borrowers, and savers achieving this goal by different mechanisms from the banking sector (Frankel 1998) but which now has to be reorganized (i.e. regulated) after the financial crisis in 2008/9 (Morgan 2010).

The crucial role of trade associations has also been studied empirically in the international timber trade (Konradi 2009). A considerable number of associations are active in the timber industry which develop standard contracts and write down commercial customs, offer arbitration, and continuously attempt to improve normative solutions for changing realities of global trade. But Konradi concludes that, despite the powerful position of trade associations, an intensive cooperation between state and private actors and institutions of the timber industry is indispensable in order to secure complex transactions in the long term.

International arbitration: International arbitrators have also been the target of empirical studies (Dezalay and Garth 1996; Dasser 2001; Sosa 2009). They are competent and neutral but only accessible for big businesses. A case of say less than US$10m is hardly worth taking to arbitration considering the fees of the arbitration panel and of the lawyers, and the cost of procedure. Historically, international arbitration was created for the Western oil industry in order to get protection from jurisdictions in Arabic countries. This historical background has been generalized in the sense that arbitration favours, not only big business, but in particular big Western business. As regards the substance of their work, on the one hand, arbitrators mostly have to deal with contractual clauses selecting state law. On the other hand, they also deal with complex contracts that do not leave much room for resorting to applicable national or unified law. The predominant position of lawyers is shown in Sosa's (2009) empirical study: the transactions which may at some point of time lead to arbitration never left the law firm's sphere of influence. Lawyers draft complex contracts, advise their clients on all matters concerning the arbitration procedure and participate in arbitration procedures as representatives of the parties or else as arbitrators.

Mega-law firms: We also know what big 'mega' law-firms do (Flood 1996; Flood and Sosa 2008; Morgan and Quack 2010). They advise big business, some private billionaires, and even states, providing expert knowledge on national and global legal cultures and billing US$500 and more per lawyer/hour. Freshfields, a mega law-firm with 2400 lawyers in twenty-seven countries, describes itself as giving advice on taxation of domestic and international groups of companies, partnerships, joint ventures, and financial institutions, their directors and employees, financing, leasing, and property transactions, the structuring of mergers, acquisitions, and company flotations and reorganizations. Since the big (US-American and English) mega law-firms have subsidiaries all over the world, there may not be a significant north–south bias, but their clients are large international companies which are predominantly Western. The mega law-firms' creative power not only derives from their wealthy clients but also from the common law understanding that the state is not superior to a civil society, but rather the outcome of the actions of social groups (Morgan and Quack 2006). This understanding motivates them to take regulatory initiatives, rather than just giving advice and legal assistance in litigation and in dealings with state bureaucracies and courts.

Middle-sized and small business and consumers remain mostly without competent legal advice whenever they happen to have a legal claim of a cross-border nature. We have such a bias also within nation states but this privilege in legal advice for big business and the hopeless legal vacuum for the rest of economic actors is much more accentuated in global circumstances. Hence, the lack or the weakness of institutional support for the average business, the availability of legal advice and of arbitration procedures only for the top actors, and a very limited role of domestic courts in enforcing cross-border claims (see contributions in Gessner 1996a) signify an important power shift away from normal citizens and toward large international enterprises. We know that global business is predominantly based either on power or personal trust (relationships). But what are the sources of security and confidence in the remaining (small?) part of the global economy, the world of anonymous, sporadic, and low-value business transactions? There is scattered research on, for example, Ebay transactions (Pitta 2002), on the strategies of debt collection agencies in enforcing cross-border claims (Budak 1999), on civil courts in average international cases (Gessner 1996b), and on the consular services (Petzold 1998). Although some innovative structures have been discovered, the overall picture is general uncertainty due to weak institutional support.

This observation of a power shift from support for all economic actors as in Weber's theory of legal certainty toward support only for a few wealthy actors in a global legal culture may be explained by the 'needs' of global business as in transaction costs theory, or by purposeful behaviour and planning within the clubs of international managers. As an alternative we will discuss the potential of more sociological approaches which emphasize the 'agency' aspect of institution building (rather than the image of institutions as external to and merely coercive of social action). The basic argument is that actors (1) do not 'follow' rules but constantly create and re-interpret rules, and (2) they act rationally only in a limited way. Rational Choice theories have a limited value in explaining structural developments and evolutionary processes (Freiling 2009). No matter how rationally or purposefully actors might initially behave, they are unable to fully control the structural consequences of their actions.

3. Global business within networks and relationships

'Intra-community exchange' (Greif 2005) or networks (for a literature review see Holton 2005) are considered either as an alternative to or as a particularistic variant of institutional support. Networks appear in many forms: commodity exchanges, Internet auction sites, Peer to Peer and Business to Business Exchanges, etc. (Aviram 2003). Breaches of contract are sanctioned by the loss of social bonds. From a theoretical perspective this 'organic' support for market exchanges seems sub-optimal since information, monitoring and enforcement requires social investment. Any change within the community (new members, new commodities, new supplies) may reduce the efficiency of coordination. But empirical research provides a different picture (see an overview in Grandori and Soda 1995). Medieval long-distance trade, global exchanges within Chinese business networks, Mafia communities, networks within the financial sector, and many other close-knit varieties of doing business seem to support their members efficiently and over long periods of time (Appelbaum, Felstiner, Gessner 2001).

Personal trust is emphasized as an alternative to institutional and legal support by anthropologists (e.g. Yang 1994; Wiessner 2002), economists (e.g. Landa 1981; Gulati 1995), legal sociologists (Macaulay 1963) and sociologists (Granovetter 1985; Appelbaum 1998). This well-established knowledge has led to practical consequences in relational management training of business people, and in attempts to adopt relational elements in contracts and even in contract law (Macneil 1980; Gottlieb 1983). Granovetter's term 'embeddedness' is widely used in approaches which study the importance of personal relations as an overlay in economic transactions and which criticize the dominant framework of 'atomized' profit-seeking actors. The trade of Chinese business people is 'embedded' in family solidarity and ethnic networks (Landa 1981), the Sicilian mafia operates in affinal kinship and ritual friendship (blood brotherhood) (Blok 2002), the diamond trade is socially secured by the Jewish religion (Richman 2006, 2008; Bernstein 1992). Granovetter's 'personal embeddedness' is based on inter-firm mobility, interlocking directorates and other contacts among business elites, long-term associations between contractors and subcontractors and between purchasing agents and suppliers, and generally on past dealings with the trusted person. These past dealings according to him provide better information than the more abstract notion of 'reputation' as frequently used in institutional economics: '(1) it is cheap; (2) one trusts one's own information best—it is richer, more detailed, and known to be accurate; (3) individuals with whom one has a continuing relationship have an economic motivation to be trustworthy, so as not to discourage future transactions; and (4) departing from pure economic motives, continuing relations often become overlaid with social content that carries strong expectations of trust and abstention from opportunism' (Granovetter 1985: 490).

Sosa (2007: 196–254) seems to have used this approach for the first time specifically in the area of international business. In his empirical study on German export and import trade in three different sectors (machinery, chemistry, agriculture and food) personal trust became one of the central explanatory elements. There was variation between the sectors and between long-term and short-term business relations. Relationship aspects influenced business behaviour more in daily exchanges and minor conflicts than in the resolution of serious controversies (Bernstein's endgame situation). Thus the picture is more complex than available theoretical approaches are suggesting. Contracts are important as a governing device during ongoing business deals and as an endgame structure. But personal trust is complementary and in most cases prevents the actors from resorting to law or litigation.

4. Global business and legal support

The Treaty of Westphalia (1648) initiated a long period where state law assumed a central role among the norms and rules in European and some other Western societies. Globalization has changed the situation. The emergence of norms and rules above the level of the nation-state is forcing legal norms to compete with other societal norms on an equal footing. Global actors, in particular business actors, define and limit the relevance of law. This certainly holds true for enabling law. As regards regulatory law, global actors often have a choice between regulatory regimes, preferring a tax haven for financial transactions, a Third World country for low labour standards, and the US state of Delaware for a liberal law of incorporation. But escaping from regulation is generally not as easy as selecting the most appropriate governance form if a business deal needs to be structured and secured against opportunism. To be sure, in addition to criminal behaviour, the above mentioned aspects of legal pluralism, such as powerful actors, influential lobbies, creative lawyers, and in-house counsels have always limited the nation states' legislative autonomy and efficiency. The difference from global problems of regulation is not of a fundamental nature but a matter of degree. Gradually and quantitatively there is more competition for rule making on the global than on the national level.

The situation of global enabling law in particular also requires an important qualification. Business, however global it appears in its dealings, is always grounded in one single domestic jurisdiction where its property rights are established and defined. This jurisdiction may have been chosen on purpose. But afterwards the choice carries consequences which are not any more under the control of the investor. These aspects are somewhat under-researched in economic discussions of the determinants of foreign direct investment locations where only some obvious legal prerequisites, like a strong court system, taxation, labour regulation, environmental protection, or protection against crime (in particular corruption), are taken into account (but see Perry 2000; Hadfield 2009). There are many more local legal determinants which either support or hinder the market performance of global business actors.

a) Domestic law supporting international business: property rights

It has been frequently observed (Riese 1996: 422; Stiglitz and Walsh 2002: 494; Dixit 2004: 2) that economists take the institutional infrastructure underlying a market economy for granted. This infrastructure is mainly or exclusively of a legal nature (Wai 2002; Fligstein 2002). Although not a single author in economic and sociological literature tries to offer a complex picture of the legal infrastructure offered for a market economy, in a previous publication (Gessner 2009b: 182) a long list of elements from the existing literature is provided: Land registry is mentioned by Barzel (2002: 186) and Ogus (2004: 7), protection and/or registration of intellectual property rights, patents, copyrights, and trademarks by Barzel (2002: 186), Riese (1996: 431), Ogus (2004: 2), and Swedberg (2003: 201, 204), protection of trade secrets by Riese (1996: 431), mortgages, transaction documents, and transportation documents by Swedberg (2003: 201), corporations as a legal entity by Swedberg (2003: 201), Ogus (2004: 5), and Dietz (2002: 69), bankruptcy procedures by Carruthers and Halliday (2007), Webb (1999: 167), and Ogus (2004: 5), effective principles of accountability by Ogus (2004: 4), private institutions such as banks and insurance companies by Dietz (2002: 69), credit bureaus and credit card companies by Greif (2006: 49), state guarantees of bank deposits by Webb (1999: 167), and regulatory agencies governing securities' exchanges by Whitley (2003: 20). No doubt, more examples could easily be produced with additional research. Relatively comprehensive but on a more abstract level is the following list provided by Ogus (2004: 8):

- rules published and thus readily accessible
- rules which are reasonably certain, clear, and stable (thus excluding decisions of unconstrained discretion)
- mechanisms ensuring the application of rules without discrimination
- binding decisions by an independent judiciary
- limited delay in judicial proceedings
- effective judicial sanctions
- compliance by, and accountability of, the government and its officials in relation to relevant rules.

b) Private International Law and global law supporting global business transactions

In addition to, or instead of, autonomous rules, transnational business actors have recourse to state or global law and legal institutions. For many actors there is no substitute for the security provided by state-based support structures and many disputes (torts, property) remain in most cases outside relational or network protection. This recourse is organized either through 'global law' or private international law (the former being multi-state law, the latter single state law).

Wai (2002) emphasizes the remaining (in his view even increasing) relevance of private international law for the protection of property rights and the effective enforcement of contractual agreements. He points to a set of reforms in an internationalist vein: doctrinal innovations, legislative reforms, international conventions, and court decisions which all foster the efficiency of transnational dispute resolution. Empirical research shows the frequency of international cases in domestic courts—by far exceeding the number of international arbitration cases (Gessner 2009b). National courts are in fact reforming to make it easier for them to deal with international cases. Special international chambers are created, English is more and more accepted as a working language, foreign attorneys may appear in court, and the use of Internet sources for legal information on foreign law is becoming common practice.

Equally dynamic is the development of global law, consisting of international conventions, uniform laws, codes, and rules of conduct that attempt to meet practical needs by means of global or international or only binational uniform rules (Bonell 1990). In this contribution, instead of giving a necessarily incomplete and inaccurate overview, we can provide some examples of the range of ways in which global business dealings are facilitated by making use of existing legal mechanisms at the international level:

- A contract is drafted or a disagreement arises in the performance of a contract: the business people or their lawyers may agree on and recognize as the applicable law the CISG (UN Convention on Contracts for the International Sale of Goods).
- A contract may also be drafted with a choice of law clause or else a judge refers to his/her Private International Law which defines the applicable law in the particular case. This is state law coordinated to a considerable degree with other states' law or even harmonized as in the European Union.
- A business uses the instruments of international money transfers which are regulated by the UN Convention on International Bills of Exchange and International Promissory Notes.
- An export business is facilitated by several Conventions on the Carriage of Goods by Sea or by Road or by Rail or on Inland Waterways. Other rules of transport law are drafted by the Chicago Convention on International Civil Aviation.
- Businesses claiming liabilities in ship collisions, trans-boundary effects of nuclear accidents, industrial accidents, or oil spills are equally supported by a number of international conventions.
- Intellectual Property is a valuable asset of most economic actors. Licenses are regulated and claims are facilitated by the World Intellectual Property Organization which represents no less than 184 member states.
- If a trans-border case is taken to a domestic court (there are no international courts for commercial matters), most elements of the procedure are somehow coordinated by international agreements on issues such as jurisdiction, service of process, taking of evidence, and recognition and enforcement of judgments.

The legal qualification of such conventions in the area of enabling law is subject to doctrinal debates (international commercial law, transnational economic law, law merchant, etc.). More interesting in our economic context is their practical relevance. There are some observations that unified contract law is rarely used, either because lawyers regulate all possible risks autonomously in complex contracts, or because cases are not taken to court, or because judges prefer to apply domestic state law (Bonell 1990; Gordon 1998; Ziegel 2005; Gessner 1996b). But empirical research is scarce, and any generalization from available studies is difficult due to the diversity of global economic actors and of legal mechanisms for supporting the global economy. It should also be emphasized that most legal mechanisms have at least an indirect effect as points of reference for creative lawyering. Law merchant rules, arbitration awards and, in particular, contracts drafted by international law firms often use international law as a background structure which is partly adopted without further change and partly adapted to the specific situation of the trade, the industry, or individual clients. Adaptation is used mainly to mitigate negative effects or even to reverse the balance of power established by legal provisions.

The problem with unified law's practical relevance is that experts who develop rules for the global economy are mostly legal academics without business experience and without interest in doing empirical research (Hartnell 2007). They do not take notice or discuss existing socio-legal studies: interdisciplinary efforts are considered a waste of time.[1] All efforts of legal academics are oriented towards establishing and maintaining a consistent normative system—although consistency may not be the most relevant requirement and even may be counterproductive in a world characterized by legal pluralism, by a multitude of forms of capitalism, and by rapid change of social and economic structures. Sociological theory discourages such efforts of legal rationality (Luhmann 1982). A universal generalization and system building (like codification) of normative expectations, which has been accomplished to a certain degree on the nation state level, cannot be achieved in an emerging world society. Luhmann (1971) believes that such legal efforts on the world society level are doomed to failure (*Fehlspezialisierung der Menschheitsentwicklung*—a failed specialization in the history of mankind). Successful developments of European Union law may disprove such a harsh statement. But his critical position certainly leads to an increasing interest in non-legal mechanisms for regulating and supporting the global economy (this is further elaborated in Gessner 1998).

Among other initiatives for catching up with non-legal support structures for global business many nation states are—as mentioned before—currently opening their judicial systems to international cases. Also legal education has changed. Silver (2008) reports new courses in US law schools where students are introduced to foreign (legal) cultures, to core financial concepts, and the terminology and basic concepts of economic analysis that will allow lawyers to understand the business aspects of their clients. European legal education

[1] Hartnell (2007: 754) who has spent two years in a German law faculty (Cologne) and who worked with prominent German scholars in international commercial law resumes her observations: 'My German colleagues advanced three major arguments against interdisciplinary work by legal scholars. The first is that considerations of labour efficiency (*Arbeitsökonomie*) preclude anything beyond minimal borrowing across disciplinary lines. Second, institutional concerns caution against such endeavours. And third, some argue that the principal task of the legal academic is to address normative questions, and in particular to stay 'close to practice' and seek solutions to real problems'. This last argument sounds promising but legal academics only have legal practice (court decisions, arbitral awards) in mind rather than business practice. Another justification for ignoring social-science knowledge (as opposed to economic analysis of law) is its non-prescriptive orientation (Basedow 2001).

may still lag behind. Hartnell (2007) observes in Germany (but the same can be said of all other countries with a civil law tradition) the emphasis on legal skills rather than a 'scientific' approach. The subjects of German legal education have been extended to international commercial and international public law, but the doctrinal orientation in legal education has remained as it has been before. Law is taught 'as a purely analytic, intellectual construct, a sealed system of logically interconnected propositions impermeable to the economic pressures of the business world' (Osiel, cited in Morgan and Quack 2006: 9). This adds to the above-mentioned problem of the creation of highly elaborated and consistent legal mechanisms in an inconsistent, diverse, and pluralistic world of global business dealings. Doctrinal legal education partly explains the insignificant international role of European (except UK) legal professions, whereas the global success of US lawyers and US law firms partly derives from a less intellectual and more down-to-earth experience in law school education (for additional—structural—reasons see Morgan and Quack 2006).

5. Conclusions

The patchwork character of institutional support for the global economy is the main argument of this chapter. Businesses may organize themselves in multinational enterprises or in complex contract relationships. They may also avoid opportunistic behaviour through the establishment of trust and by building close communities and networks. External support is offered by domestic courts, mega law firms, arbitrators, and trade organizations which apply either domestic and global law or non-state rules developed within the economy. The only stabilizing element which is largely mandatory in a world otherwise full of choices is the legal infrastructure of property rights. State law offers this basic security for domestic as well as global trade.

As opposed to the largely deficient regulation of the global economy, the protection (governance) of international commercial transactions is fairly successful (except for small businesses or the consumer). Global trade wouldn't constantly grow in a business culture dominated by opportunism and uncertainty. There is widespread practical knowledge within the economy as regards the most efficient ways for carrying out mutually beneficial trade relationships. Future research should uncover these successful practices empirically rather than proceed with theoretical debates of the future development of legal vs non-legal institutions. Empirical research reported in this chapters suggests already two insights. One observation leads to a reconsideration of the concept of institution. If law or any other governing structure of the economy is—in particular in globalizing business cultures—the outcome of permanent innovation, change, and power struggles, its stabilizing function and its role in reducing transaction costs assumed by institutional economics is rather doubtful. This brings us to a second consideration. Calculability, the indispensable element of economic action in Max Weber's theory, may not be any more the primary goal in the processes of coordination of commercial transactions. Modern communication facilities which allow permanent online exchange of information substitute largely for institutional enforcement. Business people in a pluralist and transparent institutional environment may prefer a non-normative and non-institutional approach. They may in their daily interaction with the trading partner adapt to new situations rather than insist on their contractual expectations. This requires some investment, but may in the long run better reduce transaction costs than reliance on institutional support for contractual claims. An interdisciplinary debate and further empirical research on those lines will enrich our knowledge in the emerging field of global legal and economic studies.

References

Antons, Christoph and Volkmar Gessner (eds) (2007) *Globalization and Resistance: Law reform in Asia since the crisis*, Oxford: Hart.

Appelbaum, Richard P. (1998) 'The Future of Law in a Global Economy', *Social & Legal Studies*, 7(2): 171–92.

——William L. F. Felstiner, and Volkmar Gessner (eds) (2001) *Rules and Networks: The legal culture of global business transactions*, Oxford: Hart.

Aviram, Amitai (2003), 'Regulation by Networks', *Brigham Young University Law Review*, 2003(4): 1179–1238.

Barzel, Yoram (2002) *A Theory of the State: Economic rights, legal rights, and the scope of the state*, Cambridge: Cambridge University Press.

Basedow, Jürgen (2001) 'Der Standort des Max-Planck-Instituts: Zwischen Praxis, Rechtspolitik und Privatrechtswissenschaft', pp. 3–16 in Jürgen Basedow et al. (eds) *Aufbruch nach Europa—75 Jahre Max-Planck-Institut für Privatrecht*, Tübingen: Mohr Siebeck.

Bernstein, Lisa (1992) 'Opting Out of the Legal System: Extralegal contractual relations in the diamond trade', *Journal of Legal Studies*, 21(1): 115–57.

——(1996) 'Private Commercial Law in the Cotton Industry: Creating cooperation through rules, norms, and institutions, *Michigan Law Review*, 99: 1724–90.

Blok, Anton (2002) 'Mafia and Blood Symbolism', pp. 109–28 in Frank K. Salter (ed.) *Risky Transactions: Trust, kinship, and ethnicity*, New York: Berghahn Books.

Bonell, Michael Joachim (1990) International Uniform Law in Practice—or Where the Real Trouble Begins, *American Journal of Comparative Law*, 38: 865–88.

Budak, Ali Cem (1999) *Making Foreign People Pay*, Aldershot: Dartmouth/Ashgate.

Carruthers, Bruce G. and Terence C. Halliday (2007) 'Law, Economy, and Globalization: Max Weber and how international financial institutions understand law', pp. 128–51 in Victor Nee and Richard Swedberg (eds) *On Capitalism*, Stanford: Stanford University Press.

Coase, Ronald H. (1960) 'The Problem of Social Cost', *Journal of Law & Economics*, 3(1): 1–44.

Cutler, Claire (2003) *Private Power and Global Authority: Transnational merchant law in the global political economy*, Cambridge: Cambridge University Press.

Dasser, Felix (2001) 'Lex Mercatoria—Critical Comments on a Tricky Topic', pp. 189–200 in Richard P. Appelbaum, William L. F. Felstiner, and Volkmar Gessner (eds) *Rules and Networks: The legal culture of global business transactions*, Oxford: Hart.

Dezalay, Yves and Bryant Garth (1996) *Dealing in Virtue: International commercial arbitration and the construction of a transnational legal order*, Chicago: University of California Press.

Dietz, Markus (2002) 'Zur Bedeutung des Rechts für die Ökonomik', pp. 64–71 in Ingo Pies and Martin Leschke (eds) *Walter Euckens Ordnungspolitik*, Tübingen: Mohr Siebeck.

Dixit, Avinash K (2004) *Lawlessness and Economics: Alternative modes of governance*, Princeton and Oxford: Princeton University Press.

Evans, Peter (1995) *Embedded Autonomy—States and Industrial Transformation*, Princeton: Princeton University Press.

Fligstein, Neil (2002) *The Architecture of Markets: An economic sociology of twenty-first-century capitalist societies*, Princeton and Oxford: Princeton University Press.

Flood, John (1996) 'Megalawyering in the Global Order: The cultural, social and economic transformation of global legal practice, *International Journal of the Legal Profession*, 3: 169–214.

——and Fabian Sosa (2008) 'Lawyers, Law Firms, and the Stabilization of Transnational Business', *Northwestern Journal of International Law and Business*, 28: 489–525.

Francis, Clinton W. (1983) 'The Structure of Judicial Administration and the Development of Contract Law in Seventeenth-Century England', *Columbia Law Review*, 83: 35–137.

Frankel, Tamar (1998) 'Cross-Border Securitization: Without law, but not lawless', *Duke Journal of Comparative & International Law*, 8: 255–82.

Freiling, Jörg (2009) 'Institutional Design in International Transactions—An Evolutionary Economics Perspective, pp. 257–87 in Volkmar Gessner (ed.) *Contractual Certainty in International Trade: Empirical studies and theoretical debates on institutional support for global economic exchanges*, Oxford: Hart.

Friedman, Lawrence M. (1996) 'Borders: On the emerging sociology of transnational law', *Stanford Journal of International Law*, 32: 65–90.

Gessner, Volkmar (ed.) (1996a) *Foreign Courts: Civil litigation in foreign legal cultures*, Aldershot: Dartmouth.

——(1996b) 'International Cases in German First Instance Courts', pp. 149–207 in Volkmar Gessner (ed.) *Foreign Courts: Civil litigation in foreign legal cultures*, Aldershot: Dartmouth.

——(1998) 'Globalization and Legal Certainty', pp. 427–50 in Volkmar Gessner and Ali Cem Budak (eds) *Emerging Legal Certainty: Empirical studies on the globalization of law*, Aldershot: Ashgate. Reprinted in David Held and Anthony McGrew (eds) *The Global Transformations Reader: An introduction to the globalization debate*, pp. 172–80, Cambridge: Polity Press 2000.

——(2007) 'Legalization and the Varieties of Capitalism', pp. 27–51 in Christoph Antons and Volkmar Gessner (eds) *Globalization and Resistance: Law reform in Asia*, Oxford: Hart.

——(ed.) (2009a) *Contractual Certainty in International Trade: Empirical studies and theoretical debates on institutional support for global economic exchanges*, Oxford: Hart.

——(2009b) 'Theories of Change: The governance of business transactions in globalizing economies', pp. 175–213 in Volkmar Gessner (ed.) *Contractual Certainty in International Trade: Empirical studies and theoretical debates on institutional support for global economic exchanges*, Oxford: Hart.

Gordon, Michael Wallace (1998) 'Some Thoughts on the Receptiveness of Contract Rules in the CISG and UNIDROIT Principles as Reflected in One State's (Florida) Experience of (1) Law School Faculty, (2) Members of the Bar with an International Practice, and (3) Judges', *American Journal of Comparative Law*, 46: 361–77.

Gottlieb, Gidon (1983) 'Relationism: Legal theory for a relational society', *University of Chicago Law Review*, 50: 567–612.

Grande, Edgar (ed.) (2005) *Complex Sovereignty: Reconstituting political authority in the twenty-first century*, Toronto: University of Toronto Press.

Grandori, Anna and Guiseppe Soda (1995) 'Interfirm-Networks: Antecedents, mechanisms and forms', *Organization Studies*, 16(2): 183–214.

Granovetter, Marc (1985) 'Economic Action and Social Structure: The problem of embeddedness', *American Journal of Sociology*, 91: 481–510.

Greif, Avner (2006) *Institutions and the Path to the Modern Economy: Lessons from medieval trade*, Cambridge: Cambridge University Press.

——(2005) 'Commitment, Coercion and Markets: The nature and dynamics of institutions supporting exchange', pp. 727–86 in C. Ménard and M. Shirley (eds) *The Handbook of New Institutional Economics*, Berlin: Springer.

Gulati, Ranjay (1995) 'Does Familiarity Breed Trust? The implications of repeated ties for contractual choice in alliances', *Academy of Management Journal*, 38: 85–112.

Hadfield, Gillian (2009) 'The Public and the Private in the Provision of Law for Global Transactions', pp. 239–56 in Volkmar Gessner (ed.) *Contractual Certainty in International Trade*, Oxford: Hart.

Hall, Peter and David Soskice (eds) (2001) *Varieties of Capitalism: The institutional foundations of comparative advantage*, Oxford: Oxford University Press.

Hartnell, Helen E. (2007) 'Living La Vida Lex Mercatoria', Golden Gate University School of Law, Faculty Scholarship Publications (available at http://digitalcommons.law.ggu.edu/pubs/79), also in *Festschrift Horn* (2006), 'Zivil- und Wirtschaftsrecht im Europäischen und Globalen Kontext', Klaus Peter Berger, Georg Borges, Harald Herrmann, Andreas Schlüter, Ulrich Wackerbarth (eds), Berlin/New York: de Gruyter.

Hirschl, Ran (2004), *Towards Juristocracy: The origins and consequences of the new constitutionalism*, Cambridge, Mass. and London: Harvard University Press.

Hollingsworth, J. Rogers and Robert Boyer (1997) Coordination of Economic Actors and Social Systems of Production, pp. 1–47 in J. Rogers Hollingsworth and Robert Boyer (eds) *Contemporary Capitalism: The embeddedness of institutions*, Cambridge: Cambridge University Press.

Holton, Robert John (2005) 'Network Discourses: Proliferation, critique and sythesis, *Global Networks*, 5: 209–15.

Knowles, Steven (2005) 'Is Social Capital Part of the Institutions Continuum?' Working paper No 05/11, *Center for Research in Economic Development and International Trade*: University of Nottingham.

Konradi, Wioletta (2009) 'The Role of Lex Mercatoria in Supporting Globalized Transactions: An empirical insight into the governance structure of the timber industry', pp. 49–86 in Volkmar Gessner (ed.) *Contractual Certainty in International Trade: Empirical studies and theoretical debates on Institutional Support for Global Economic Exchanges*, Oxford: Hart.

Landa, Janelle (1981) 'A Theory of the Ethnically Homogeneous Middleman Group: An institutional alternative to contract law', *Journal of Legal Studies*, 10: 349–62.

Luhmann, Niklas (1971) 'Die Weltgesellschaft', *Archiv für Rechts- und Sozialphilosophie*, 57: 1–35.

——(1982) 'The World Society as a Social System', *International Journal of General Systems*, 8: 131–8.

Macaulay, Stewart (1963) 'Non-Contractual Relations in Business: A preliminary study', *American Sociological Review*, 28: 55–67.

Macneil, John (1980) *The New Social Contract*, New Haven: Yale University Press.

Morgan, Glenn and Sigrid Quack (2006) 'Global Networks or Global Firms? The organizational implications of the internationalisation of law firms', pp. in Ferner, Quintanilla, and Sanchez-Runde (eds) *Multinationals and the Construction of Transnational Practices: Convergence and diversity in the global economy*, London: Palgrave (Macmillan).

—— ——(2010) 'Law as a Governing Institution', pp. 275–308 in Glenn Morgan, John Campbell, Colin Crouch, Ove Kai Pedersen, and Richard Whitley (eds) *The Oxford Handbook of Comparative Institutional Analysis*, Oxford: Oxford University Press.

North, Douglass C. (1990) *Institutions, Institutional Change and Economic Performance*, Cambridge: Cambridge University Press.

——(1999) 'Dealing With a Non-Ergodic World: Institutional economics, property rights, and the global environment', *Duke Environmental Law and Policy, Forum*, 10: 1–12.

Ogus, Anthony (2004) 'The Importance of Legal Infrastructure for Regulation (and Deregulation) in Developing Countries', Working Paper No. 65 of the *Centre on Regulation and Competition, Institute for Development Policy and Management*, Manchester: University of Manchester.

Perry, Amanda (2000) 'Effective Legal Systems and Foreign Direct Investment: In search of the evidence', *International and Comparative Law Quarterly*, 49: 779–99.

Petzold, Andreas (1998) 'Information on Foreign Legal Systems', pp. 283–321 in Volkmar Gessner, Ali Cem Budak (eds) *Emerging Legal Certainty: Empirical studies on the globalization of law*, Aldershot: Dartmouth.

Pitta, Julie (2002) 'Banking on Reputations', *Relationship Journal*, 1, 10.

Richman, Barak D. (2006) 'How Community Institutions Create Economic Advantage: Jewish diamond merchants in New York', *Law and Social Inquiry*, 31: 383–420.

——(2008) 'Ethnic Networks, Extralegal Certainty, and Globalisation: Peering into the diamond industry', pp. 31–47 in Volkmar Gessner (ed.) *Contractual Certainty in International Trade: Empirical studies and theoretical debates on institutional support for global economic exchanges*, Oxford: Hart.

Riese, Hajo (1996) 'Institutionenökonomie und Marktökonomie', pp. 409–47 in Reinhard Penz, Holger Wilkop (eds) *Zeit der Institutionen: Thorstein Veblens evolutorische Ökonomik*, Marburg: Metropolis.

Silver, Carole, David Van Zandt, Nicole De Bruin (2008) 'Globalization and the Business of Law: Lessons for legal education', *Northwestern Journal of International Law and Business*, 28: 399–414.

Sosa, Fabian (2007) *Vertrag und Geschäftsbeziehung im grenzüberschreitenden Wirtschaftsverkehr*, Baden-Baden: Nomos.

——(2009) 'Cross-Border Dispute Resolution from the Perspective of Mid-sized Law Firms: The example of international commercial arbitration', pp. 107–55 in Volkmar Gessner (ed.) *Contractual Certainty in International Trade: Empirical studies and theoretical debates on institutional support for global economic exchanges*, Oxford: Hart.

Stiglitz, Joseph E. and Carl E. Walsh (2002) *Principles of Macroeconomics*, New York: W.W. Norton.

Swedberg, Richard (2003) *Principles of Economic Sociology*, Princeton and Oxford: Princeton University Press.

Teubner, Gunther (1997) 'Global Bukowina: Legal pluralism in the world society', pp. 3–108 in G. Teubner (ed.) *Global Law without a State*, Aldershot: Dartmouth.

Trubek, David M. (1972) 'Max Weber on Law and the Rise of Capitalism', *Wisconsin Law Review*, 3: 720–53.

Wai, Robert (2002) 'Transnational Liftoff and Juridical Touchdown: The regulatory function of private international law in an era of globalization', *Columbia Journal of Transnational Law*, 40: 207–63.

Weber, Max (1968) *Economy and Society*, New York: Bedminster Press & Berkeley U. of California P.

Whitley, Richard (2003) 'How National are Business Systems? The Role of Different State Types and Complementary Institutions in Constructing Homogeneous Systems of Economic Coordination and Control', pp. 190–231 in Glenn Morgan, Richard Whitley and Eli Moen (eds.) *Changing Capitalisms? Internationalization, Institutional Change and Systems of Economic Organization*, Oxford: Oxford University Press.

——(2007) *Business Systems and Organizational Capabilities: The institutional structuring of competitive competences*, Oxford: Oxford University Press.

Wiessner, Polly (2002) 'Taking the Risk out of Risky Transactions: A forager's dilemma', pp. 21–43 in Frank K. Salter, *Risky Transactions:Trust, kinship, and ethnicity*, New York: Berghahn Books.

Yang, Mayfair Mei-hui (1994) *Gifts, Favors, and Banquets: The art of social relationship in China*, Ithaca, NY: Cornell University Press.

Ziegel, Jacob (2005) 'The Scope of the Convention: Reaching out to Article One and beyond', *Journal of Law and Commerce* 25: 59–73.

7

Transnational Governance through Standard Setting

The Role of Transnational Communities

Marie-Laure Djelic and Sigrid Quack

Introduction

Over the last decades, we have seen a multiplication of transnational standard-setting initiatives. We live today more than ever in a transnational 'world of standards' (Brunsson and Jacobsson 2000). Multi-stakeholder arrangements, with a varying combination of public and private actors, come together and produce rules or 'soft laws' often with a transnational ambition if not reach (Djelic and Sahlin-Andersson 2006; Graz and Nölke 2008; Tamm Hallström and Böstrom 2010; Brunsson, Rasche, and Seidl 2011; see, also, Gessner in this volume). Transnational standard setting entails complex dynamics of standard elaboration and negotiation, standard implementation and monitoring, which we can follow in many different domains of economic activity—with an impact on production, research and development, marketing and distribution, finance, audit, and litigation.

Those dynamics involve a variety of actors. Quite striking are the role, presence, and clout of private actors of different kinds (Graz and Nölke 2008). But even more striking is the fact that the strong involvement of many different private actors does not necessarily imply a 'retreat of the state' (Strange 1996). The idea of the 'emergence of private authority' (Hall and Biersteker 2002) is partly misleading, at least in the sense that it would suggest a simple transfer of governance power from public to private actors. The reality, in fact, is more complex and subtle. Quite often, state or government representatives are directly or indirectly involved in transnational standard setting—not necessarily as drivers but as actors amongst others in a process where consultation, deliberation, confrontation, and negotiation all play an important role. Hence, governance arrangements associated with transnational standard setting generally go beyond simple state-to-state or firm-to-firm interactions. Civil society actors (NGOs and social movement activists in particular) have a tendency to target both states and firms, together and at the same time, demanding action and responsibility in initiatives that go well beyond the borders of any single country (Prakash and Gugerty 2010). As a result, governance through standard setting involves a significant blurring of classical dividing lines—between the public and the private but also between the national and the transnational. Interestingly, transnational standard setting also generally means a partial overlapping of the categories of 'regulators' and 'regulatees'. At least some of those actors who will/may have to conform to a particular standard are likely to be involved already in the process of standard setting.

We suggest in this chapter that the complex multi-stakeholder dynamics associated with transnational standard setting can be effectively captured through conceptualizing it as a particular form of transnational governance that both generates, and is facilitated by, the structuration of transnational communities (Djelic and Quack 2010). Typologies of governance forms have tended to associate communities with primary groupings based on solidarity (Crouch 2005; Jessop and Ngai-Ling 2006). We argue here, though, that communities based on territory and physical proximity constitute only one particular form amongst others. In modern societies, a variety of forms of communal organization have evolved that need no longer be based on kinship and propinquity. They can be structured around a shared cognitive, epistemic, practice or value base and/or through the mutual orientation to a common project. A collective 'imagined identity' emerges in the process that translates into strategies and actions on the ground. In analytical terms, communities differ from other forms of governance (markets, hierarchies, or networks) in the nature of their coordination.

While markets are coordinated through exchange, hierarchies function through command and control, and networks are stabilized through multidirectional negotiation. Communities, on the other hand, are coordinated through conscious common orientation and shared identity (Morgan 2001; Djelic and Quack 2010; Mayntz 2010). Yet, empirically, such communities often overlap with and develop in parallel to organizations or networks (Mayntz 2010). The line separating, in particular, social networks as interconnected nodes from communities as defined above may sometimes be thin and fluid and we often encounter hybrid arrangements (Crouch 2005). As a consequence, transnational communities as social groups emerging from mutual interactions across national boundaries, oriented around a common project and or 'imagined' identity, can be difficult to grasp empirically.

Nevertheless, as we argue in this chapter, a focus on transnational communities is helpful in order to explore the neglected cognitive and cultural dimension of transnational standard setting.

Building upon earlier work on transnational governance, we explore the interplay between processes of transnational standard setting and processes of transnational community building (Djelic and Sahlin-Andersson 2006; Djelic and Quack 2010). We illustrate these processes and their interplay through the comparative analysis of two empirical cases that each exemplify a distinct pattern of transnational community development. The first case is the transnational setting of standards for the regulation of competition and the parallel structuration and development of a transnational community—embodied in particular in the International Competition Network (ICN). The second case is the development and dissemination of Creative Commons licence by a non-profit organization, here also paralleled and sustained by the structuration of associated transnational communities. In both cases, we find that transnational processes of standard setting are co-evolving with transnational processes of community building. Transnational standard setting triggers and fosters processes of community building beyond national boundaries. But transnational communities can also themselves be important facilitators of standard setting initiatives. In particular, those communities contribute, over time, to the alignment of the cognitive and normative orientations of members. Hence, they can help stabilize and ground fragile standard setting projects by turning them into behavioral patterns applicable and legitimate in many diverse and distant locales. In the conclusion, we try to learn from those similarities but also from differences between those two cases, indicating directions for further research.

Transnational communities and standard setting

We live in a (transnational) 'golden era of regulation', characterized by the multiplication of rules that reach over and beyond national boundaries (Levi-Faur and Jordana 2005). Our well-entrenched national 'rules of law' increasingly have to confront the progress of a transnational 'law of rules' (Djelic 2011). Those 'rules' are often described as 'soft laws'. The difference between 'hard' and 'soft' law lies essentially in the fact that 'soft law lacks the possibility of legal sanctions . . . and hence is not legally binding' (Mörth 2004: 1; see, also, Gessner in this volume). Various forms of so-called 'soft law' become consequential and effective through non-legal mechanisms of inducement and persuasion, and yet, not infrequently, 'soft laws' can be a first step towards and an input for 'hard' law-making (Djelic and Sahlin-Andersson 2006: 377; Quack 2007).

Standards as 'soft laws'

'Soft laws' can take different forms—principles, guidelines, directives, codes of conduct, 'white books', best practice and evaluation schemes, or standards. Typically, the term 'standards' is used to identify highly formalized sets of rules but with a high degree of specificity—in contrast to, on the one hand, broader and more general principles and, on the other hand, more informal guidelines or best practices (Ahrne and Brunsson 2006: 82; Braithwaite and Drahos 2000: 20). Still, the lines separating these different types of non-legally binding rules can be rather fuzzy and they become even more so if we look at standard setting as a process rather than at standards as outcomes.

This fuzziness translates into significant variability when it comes to definitions. On the one hand, The International Organization for Standardization (ISO) proposes a rather narrow definition of a standard as

> a document, established by consensus and approved by a recognized body, that provides, for common and repeated use, rules, guidelines or characteristics for activities or their results, aimed at the achievement of the optimum degree of order in a given context. (ISO/IEC 2004)[1]

On the other hand, Brunsson and Jacobsson call for a broader and more encompassing understanding where standards are 'pieces of general advice offered to a large number of potential adopters' (Brunsson and Jacobsson 2000: 2). Drawing on Timmermans and Epstein (2010: 71), we position ourselves somewhere in between. We propose to focus on standard setting rather than standards. We understand standard setting as a process of constructing and implementing agreed-upon rules, usually backed by some external body, with the aim of creating uniformities across time and space between different localized activities. Standard setting understood in this sense can also encompass attempts to formulate guidelines, codes of conduct, or to work out best practices as intermediary steps in the process of formulating and implementing standards.

The international standards that emerge from complex production processes in principle tend to be voluntary. Some of these standards, such as quality and technological standards, aim at better coordination of economic activity in global markets. Others strive to build social and environmental concerns into the constitution of markets, as in the case of standards relating to labour rights, human rights, corruption and ethics, or environmental protection. In order for standards to be effective, they have to be associated with a whole range of mechanisms and processes that target adoption on the

[1] It is clear that this definition has become itself a 'standard' for the definition of standards. It has been appropriated word for word by most national or transnational normalizing or standardizing organizations.

ground across and beyond local differences and contexts—norms of transparency and accountability, incentive systems, persuasion, socialization and monitoring mechanisms, if not more coercive tools such as exclusion from access to resources, markets, benefits, or even banishment from a valued community or 'league'. To understand how and why some standards develop a quasi-binding character and others do not, the process perspective needs to be broadened beyond the defining phase to subsequent phases of diffusion and implementation. Botzem and Dobusch (2009) argue that such an approach to standard setting should grant particular attention to reciprocal interactions between standard formation and standard diffusion, and how those two stages generate different forms of legitimacy. Processes of legitimacy building around particular standards are likely to invoke the participation of a variety of groups and interests that often started from a national base (Black 2008; Quack 2010). These processes also contribute in time to the structuration and stabilization of those same groups into a broader collective—and in time, community—with a transnational reach and scope.

Transnational communities and their role

When it comes to transnational standardization, transnational communities can play a variety of analytically distinct roles that can combine in different ways. First, transnational communities, particularly in the form of epistemic or practice communities, can be initiators of formal standard-setting processes. Cutting pragmatically across entrenched perceptions and interests, whether public or private, transnational communities can draw on diverse pools of knowledge and expertise and bring them together in a unique manner. Secondly, transnational communities can contribute to the creation of a transnational public problem space, where issues in need of standardization can be identified and agreed upon. Creating and framing a common problem is clearly an important first step towards collective mobilization and action. Thirdly, transnational communities can mobilize collective action to support transnational standard setting projects, but also to help diffuse standards and convince local actors to adopt them. By addressing diffuse and unorganized actors as potential users and adopters, standard setters often galvanize processes of community formation among previously isolated actors, which in turn positively feed back on diffusion and adoption rates.

Fourthly, transnational communities shape and delineate a public arena where a multiplicity of actors can actively search for a common solution or standard. In so far as communities nurture discussion and deliberation, or provide social space for contained contention and conflicts over standard setting, they structure public arenas where compromise solutions to complex standard setting problems can emerge. Fifthly, and partly as a consequence of their previous roles, transnational communities can over time foster preference transformation in some or all of their members; this can be the result of learning, mutual adjustment, socialization, or inducement by threat of exclusion. As a consequence they can contribute to the progressive convergence of preferences between participants coming from many different national institutional and cultural backgrounds, and this throughout the process of standard setting. Finally, transnational communities can have a profound impact on standard setting as they exert their capacity for informal sanctioning of and social control over their members. The probability of 'conversion' and real adoption will increase through peer pressure, the sharing of information, and more formal socialization mechanisms. Ultimately, the strongest source of sanctioning is the threat of exclusion from or refusal of admission into an existing community—particularly if this community is associated with significant resources and/or legitimacy.

While it is clear that structured transnational communities are likely to be powerful facilitators of transnational standard setting, a partial reverse influence can also be assumed. Transnational standard setting is likely to involve and invoke processes of community formation at a transnational level. A successful standardization process is bound to come together with the stabilization, deepening, and broadening of one or several transnational communities. Those communities may even construct and crystallize their collective 'imagined identity' through and around the standard-setting project itself.

We conceptualize transnational communities as being actively constructed and shaped by people with multiple group affiliations interacting across societal and national borders. This conceptualization makes it possible to envision different patterns of community formation, development, and maintenance, as well as community decline. We distinguish three dimensions that are likely to influence the development of transnational communities, and hence could serve to structure a typology (Table 7.1). A first dimension is the nature of the goals fostering community building, which itself reflects the relative power of members in a given regulatory field. Transnational communities can start out from a small base of powerful actors with the goal to enlist others in following their proposed (and existing) standards. Yet, transnational communities can also emerge through a challenger project where less resourceful actors target the development of an alternative standard. A second dimension refers to the nature of the rules

Table 7.1. Dimensions of transnational community development

DIMENSION 1: Nature of Goals/Power	Enlisting ——— Challenging
DIMENSION 2: Mode of Access	Elite-exclusionary ——— Grass-roots-inclusionary
DIMENSION 3: Nature of Actors	State ——— Business ——— Civil Society

governing access for new members. While elite communities apply selective and exclusionary rules when it comes to access, grass-roots communities follow a more inclusive mode of community building. A third dimension concerns the nature and the mix of actors involved in community building. The range would go here from transnational communities formed exclusively of state or quasi-state actors to transnational communities made up of only private actors. In private transnational communities, a distinction also needs to be made between those communities made up exclusively of powerful, often organizational, business actors and those communities that are constructed through the aggregation of multiple individual or organizational actors drawn from civil societies. Naturally, somewhere between the different extremes we have the possibility of many different hybrids.

In theory, different combinations are possible that would suggest different patterns of transnational community development. Table 7.2 suggests the two analytically most relevant combinations along those three dimensions and moves us towards a classification of transnational community development.[2] Transnational communities consisting of powerful actors in a given field of governance aiming at enlisting other actors to follow their standards are likely to employ a selective if not exclusionary mode to recruit new members. Such communities can consist of regulatory state agencies of a few powerful countries aiming to enlist regulatory agencies from other parts of the world; they also can be formed by business actors aiming to enlist others of a similar kind to produce standards as a 'club common good'. In both cases, the mode of access is selective if not exclusionary—members of the emerging community recruit their peers and exert strong control about who is able to join. In contrast, transnational communities that are formed with the goal of

Table 7.2. Classification of transnational communities development

		Goals	
		Enlisting	Challenging
Mode of access	Elite/Exclusionary	TOP DOWN (State/Business)	—
	Grass-roots/Inclusionary	—	BOTTOM UP (Civil society/mixed)

[2] This typology elaborates further on a distinction drawn in earlier work that contrasted a bottom-up approach by which a transnational community is built up and stabilized through multiple and repeated interactions between members of diverse national or local communities with a top-down approach according to which a small, generally elite, transnational group tries to disseminate its particular project or agenda to audiences in multiple nations and localities (Djelic and Quack 2011).

challenging dominant rules in a given field of governance are likely to follow a grass-roots approach which is more inclusionary and targets a broad variety of actors from civil society or mixed background (state as well as business).

Elsewhere (Djelic and Quack 2011) we have suggested that different types of transnational communities have their specific strengths and weaknesses. Transnational communities consisting of powerful actors following an elite approach with a top-down trajectory are likely to constitute more unified actors in terms of standard setting. Yet, they might lack the ability for broad mobilization on implementation, monitoring and control. Transnational communities challenging dominant rules and recruiting members via an inclusionary approach, often following a bottom-up trajectory, might find it difficult to come to a unified position on rule-making. Yet, they will have a greater capacity to mobilize varied resources and collective action. One way for those different types of communities to deal with their respective weaknesses, we furthermore suggested, would be to develop complementary strategies.

In order to examine the value of this typology for the analysis of the co-evolution between transnational standard setting and transnational community building, we now turn to a more detailed analysis of two case studies. The Competition/ICN and Copyleft/Creative Commons cases were chosen because they represent a good mix of striking differences and parallel roles in processes of transnational standard setting. The communities involved in each case display significantly different characteristics with respect to their goals and their modes of access, as well as the nature of membership. The International Competition Network (ICN) consists predominantly of officials from governmental or transgovernmental competition agencies reaching out periodically to small numbers of private actors (non-governmental advisors—NGAs). By contrast, the Creative Commons community counts a majority of non-state actors, essentially lawyers and civil society groups. While the former developed out of and in interaction with a transnational network of governmental agencies, the latter emerged and evolved in tight connection to an international non-profit organization with national affiliates. Finally, while the former started out with the objective of fostering convergence at the global level around common understandings and practices, the latter set out to develop a private licence, both as an alternative to, and as a critique of, existing international and national laws.

Our two cases are contrasting on all three dimensions, and therefore one could expect different trajectories, reflecting distinct strengths and weaknesses. Still, in spite of those striking differences, the emergent transnational communities in both cases turned out to perform, through time, quite similar functions. They both significantly contributed to the elaboration, diffusion, and adoption of shared standards. In order to do so, they both relied on softer mechanisms of persuasion and socialization. And in the end, they both came to allow for a certain degree of flexibility and local adaptability—combining formal standard setting with a degree of 'informed divergence'.

The International Competition Network (ICN) and standard setting for the regulation of competition

The International Competition Network (ICN) was officially launched in October 2001. Thirteen national antitrust agencies and the European Union competition agency were its founding members.[3] From the start, membership was both open and restricted to all national, regional, or multinational antitrust agencies. Numbers rose fast and, by the spring of 2002, the ICN already had fifty members. Today, the ICN has close to a global reach—ninety-nine jurisdictions are represented that together account for more than 90 per cent of world GDP (ICN 2010).

From transnational network based on common interest...

The 2001 Founding Memorandum defined the ICN as

> a project oriented, consensus-based, informal network of antitrust agencies that will address antitrust enforcement and policy issues of common interest. (ICN 2001)

As a network, the ICN has three main characteristics—it is virtual, inclusive, and open in a selective manner. First, the ICN is a virtual network—with no offices, legal status, employees, or even budget. The ICN does not have a geographic hub or permanent secretariat. A Steering Group of fifteen members sets agendas and work plans, identifying priorities that then have to be approved by members during the yearly conference. The work itself is done within ad hoc and temporary working groups that each focus on a particular issue and meet rarely, relying instead on modern technologies. Second, the ICN is an inclusive network, based on voluntary membership. Any national or multinational competition authority can easily become a member without having to fit any specific criteria. At the same time, though, it is important to note that throughout the last ten years, the Steering group of the ICN has been and remains dominated by representatives from the more established antitrust agencies—with an overwhelming weight of developed countries.[4]

[3] The thirteen countries were Australia, Canada, France, Germany, Israel, Italy, Japan, Mexico, South Africa, South Korea, the United Kingdom, United States, and Zambia.

[4] In 2008, the list of countries represented in the Steering Group was quite telling and not very different from the list of founding members: US (2 representatives), UK, Mexico, Japan, Canada, Russia, Brazil, Australia, Korea, Germany, Turkey, Netherlands, France, EU, South Africa, Italy, Switzerland.

Finally, the ICN is a network that is selectively open. While membership in the full sense of the term is strictly restricted to competition agencies, the ICN keeps a number of doors open to other parties interested in or connected to issues of competition and antitrust. In principle, the ICN wants to 'maximize cooperation with non-governmental antitrust experts from the relevant international, industry, consumer, legal, economic and academic communities' (Ugarte 2002). In practice, this means that member agencies, and in particular members of the Steering Group, can invite non-governmental experts to the annual ICN conferences or to working group events.

From the start, the central focus of the ICN transnational network was competition—'all competition all the time' (Finckenstein 2003). Initially, the ICN emerged as an initiative to foster dialogue amongst antitrust officials and beyond. Ultimately, though, a more ambitious objective was to create, deepen, and spread worldwide, a 'culture' of antitrust and competition—which, as key actors recognized, was part of a 'broader mosaic' and came together with a culture of 'markets' (Kolasky 2002: 3–5). A forum for dialogue, exchange, and collaborative work could generate in time a common culture around competition policy. It would also build up progressively a dense social and cognitive space and, hopefully, beyond simply the network, a real 'community of interest' (Finckenstein 2002).

The structuring logic behind the ICN was to start with the creation of an inclusive, tight and in fact exclusionary network of insiders and to combine and articulate it progressively, with a number of weaker external networks reaching out to important constituencies, both nationally and transnationally. Such a combination would be likely to increase the scale and scope of the double effort at transnational culture-building and transnational culture-spreading. That one of the three original working groups focused on 'advocacy' says enough about the centrality of that double project. The Advocacy working group defined its mission in the following way:

> Competition advocacy refers to those activities conducted by the competition authority related to the promotion of a competitive environment for economic activities by means of non-enforcement mechanisms, mainly through its relationships with other governmental entities and by increasing public awareness of the benefits of competition. (AWG 2002)

The Advocacy working group (AWG) began with a systematic comparison of the situation of member agencies and with an exploration of their embeddedness in unique national institutional contexts. The AWG sent a questionnaire to each ICN member to build up the empirical base for such a comparison and exploration. The first report was presented during the 2002 Naples conference. This report underscored different perceptions on the importance of advocacy in each member agency, as well as variation in the types of obstacles and challenges that member agencies faced in their competition advocacy activities. Following this analysis, the AWG defined its mission as 'recommending best practices to ICN members and providing them with information to support their advocacy tasks' with a consideration for the variability of national conditions and local politics (AWG 2002).

... to transnational community of governance

While building itself up progressively as a 'community of interest', the International Competition Network was from the start doing much more. With hindsight, it is obvious that the structuring of the ICN through the last ten years has largely contributed to the framing of competition and antitrust as a public problem space with transnational scope and reach. The ICN has been actively involved in shaping and delineating a transnational public arena around those issues. It has played the role, if we can use this image, of a central 'magnetic' forum—attracting and involving, around its member base, a multiplicity of other actors with an interest or a stake in competition and antitrust.

The ICN does not define itself as a regulatory actor—although many of its members could be defined in this way within their respective jurisdictions. Still, its role and impact since 2001 show the progress of an ambition that goes well beyond dialogue, information, and exchange. Members of the Steering Group are conscious of—and claim in fact—such broadening of their ambitions through time. From a transnational network, the ICN has transformed into a 'transnational community of interest', and progressively it has even been imposing itself as a highly active 'transnational community of governance'. The ICN is increasingly targeting, in its various forms of official and less official communication, a real transformative impact on competition regulation, both nationally and transnationally.

Transnationally, the ICN increasingly sees its role as contributing to best practice definition and standard setting. It is, in other words, increasingly claiming an identity as a 'transnational community of governance'. The ICN has the capacity and the resources to mobilize widely and broadly—if only because of its significant reach—around different projects targeting the elaboration of partial best practices and standards. The different ad hoc and temporary working groups are particularly well designed for this kind of purpose. As David Lewis, then Chairman of the ICN Steering group, said in his introductory remarks to the 2009 Zurich annual conference, 'we (the ICN) are clearly in the business of making "soft law" and this is what we must continue' (Lewis 2009). 'Soft law', he made clear, is qualitatively different from 'hard law'—and not just a 'less binding, pale version' of it (see also Mörth 2006). The ICN does not follow a logic of constraint or coercion. 'Soft law', Lewis continues,

> is rooted in consensus rather than majority; in persuasion through shared experience rather than coercion; in understanding and celebrating differences rather than suppressing them. (Lewis 2009)

Even though the ICN defines itself today as a transnational community of governance and is thus, as such, targeting some form of transnational standard setting, it also sets itself the objective of having a local or national impact. It hopes to do that through two different but complementary paths—that follow respectively a trickle-down and a trickle-up trajectory (Djelic and Quack 2003). First, members of the Steering Group are hoping for a trickle-down impact. ICN work should come to reflect upon national competition regimes in a direct way, through the involvement of representatives from member agencies. The idea is not that members comply with recommended practices right from the outset. Rather, the hope is that they 'will consider them as aspirational goals in the context of evolving national competition frameworks' (Finckenstein 2003: 13). Members are, in other words, in no obligation to ensure that domestic laws reflect ICN guidelines and recommendations. Each agency will decide whether and how to implement the recommendations—adapting its strategies to local politics and constraints (Fingleton 2009b: 21). Still, members of the ICN Steering Committee expect, on a practical level, that 'as best practice proposals are acted upon by members, a natural peer influence will come to bear on other jurisdictions to do the same' (Finckenstein 2002: 4). The ICN Steering Group hopes that such trickle-down impact will combine with a trickle-up one. By opening the network of insiders to representatives of relevant and important constituencies, the Steering Group wants to build bridges with those constituencies. Non-governmental experts are co-opted and involved in the work of the ICN at many different stages, with the idea that they will then become themselves important agents of the fight for competition and antitrust in their respective constituencies. Once a number of local constituencies—or parts thereof—become champions of competition and antitrust, they can push those ideas back up at the national or regional governmental level and thus reinforce the impact and influence of competition authorities.

Hence, throughout its evolution over the last ten years, the ICN has emerged as an increasingly significant and powerful 'transnational community of governance'. As such, it has been fulfilling most of the functions such communities are expected to fulfil (Djelic and Quack 2010). The ICN has shaped a transnational problem space and interactive arenas around the issue of competition. It has played a role in the mobilization around competition regulation. It has directly contributed to the setting of rules and standards and to the monitoring of their implementation. It has helped transform preferences along the way and has certainly exerted a certain kind of social control over its members.

While the ICN was progressively moving away from being a simple transnational network to becoming a 'transnational community of interest' and in time even a 'transnational community of governance', the various steps it took were not always easy ones. Members of the ICN, and particularly members of the Steering Group, have had to realize in the process the complexities of transnational 'soft governance'. And while they persisted in their ultimate ambition of being an important actor of transnational governance for competition and its regulation, they have had to dampen a bit early hopes of easy convergence and homogenization. As Lewis recently acknowledged, 'the evidence is that "best practices", even in relatively uncontroversial areas, usually have to be tailored to national circumstances and so implementation will always be uneven at best' (Lewis 2009). The Steering Group appears to have come to the realization that 'convergence is not possible' and its members are now talking about 'informed divergence' instead, as a less ambitious, more realistic but also more complex goal (Fingleton 2009a: 6). 'Informed divergence', according to them, implies to identify the 'nature and sources of divergence and to understand and respect the divergent underlying rationale' in each national jurisdiction (Fingleton 2009b: 27).

This 'softer' stance, though, should not blind us to the consequential politics and power issues that are at work here. As members of the Steering Committee underscore, a 'culture of antitrust' goes together with a 'culture of markets'. As such, the project of the ICN belongs to, and has been integrated from the start in, the broader wave of neoliberalism that has diffused across many shores (Campbell and Pedersen 2001; Dezalay and Garth 2002; Fourcade-Gourinchas and Babb 2002; Djelic 2006). The structuration of a transnational community around competition and antitrust would not have been even thinkable without the striking missionary activism of American (but also European) competition authorities that took place from the 1990s on. Between 1990 and 1998 only, American Antitrust Authorities (Antitrust Department, Department of Justice and Federal Trade Commission) alone sent 390 expert missions around the world to help countries across all regions set up a national competition regime. They also provided training in the United States for around 300 foreign (future) experts (Djelic and Kleiner 2006). Effectively, this suggests that what might really be at stake is not the convergence of many different standards but the progressive and 'soft' imposition of a certain model of competition—a standard pioneered in the United States and relayed to a degree by the European Union (see, also, Whitley in this volume). Interestingly, those background politics and power issues have reflected less than could be expected on internal debates within the ICN. Regularly, a few members within the ICN worry that it should be made 'clear that all members of the competition family are the actors of the initiative and that they all play an equal role' (Tesauro 2002). But this is as far as it seems to go—softly expressed worries addressed by the formal re-assurance that 'of course, consistently sound antitrust enforcement policy cannot be defined and decreed for others by the United States, not that you would presume to do such a thing' (Kolasky 2002: 3).

Creative commons and standardized copyright licences for a digital commons[5]

In 2001, a group of US legal academics founded Creative Commons (CC) as an American non-profit organization. In the context of the TRIPS (Agreement on Trade-Related Aspects of Intellectual Property Rights), the US media industries ran a powerful lobbying campaign to extend copyright in order to protect their traditional business model. This new organization instead was targeting a middle ground between the Internet practice of freely sharing content and the traditional 'all rights reserved' setting that copyright law provides.[6] The Creative Commons organization set itself the objective to develop standardized licences. Those licences would enable creative individuals and organizations to easily grant copyright permissions to freely copy, distribute, and recombine contents, thereby contributing to a digital commons. By 2010, Creative Commons had developed into an international organizational network with more than 100 affiliates. The licences it has produced have been 'ported', that is, translated and legally adapted to local requirements, in about seventy different jurisdictions. Cautious estimates of the total number of works licensed under Creative Commons worldwide added up to about 350 million by then.[7]

From emergent epistemic community to organizational capacities

Creative Commons was not born out of nowhere. The idea of fostering a public commons for all kinds of contents had been nurtured during the late 1990s by a community of legal academics in the United States (Dobusch and Quack 2010a). The TRIPS agreement in 1994 and the US Copyright Term Extension Act in 1998 spurred this group to react in critical terms to the extension of copyright terms. Similarity in professional backgrounds was certainly an important foundation for the emergence of a community around this critical opposition. Of equal importance, though, were shared norms and

[5] Details of the following section are, unless stated otherwise, based on Dobusch and Quack (2010a).

[6] http://creativecommons.org/about [accessed: 25 April 2011]

[7] See http://wiki.creativecommons.org/Metrics [accessed: 7 January 2011]

the commitment to a common policy project. In so far as this group was a network of professionals and opinion leaders 'with recognized expertise and competence in a particular domain and an authoritative claim to policy-relevant knowledge within that domain or issue-area', they constituted what Haas (1992) calls an 'epistemic community'.

This epistemic community significantly contributed to the framing of a public policy argument that portrayed existing copyright regulations based on 'all rights reserved' as highly problematic. The extension of copyright terms was presented as socially undesirable because it hampered a free use of the Internet for research, educational, and cultural purposes. Founding members of the Creative Commons organization published articles and books that denounced the shortcomings and problems of the dominant copyright doctrine (Lessig 1999, 2001). In 2003, one member of this community, Stanford law professor Lawrence Lessig, challenged the constitutionality of the US Copyright Term Extension Act in the Supreme Court. Acting then as the legal advisor in the trial of an online publisher of public domain texts, his plea was, however, not heard. Several members of the community attempted to convince policy-makers of the advantages of securing tax deductions for individuals who would be willing to relinquish their property rights in texts.[8]

In their role as public intellectuals, these members of the community called on a form of 'cultural environmentalism' to protect the public domain (the 'cultural commons') from all types of infringements (Boyle 2006). They put forward the notion of a 'free culture' to overcome outmoded doctrines of copyrights (Lessig 2004). While the epistemic community was originally based in the US, the statements and publications of its members rapidly diffused through old and new media to like-minded people in other countries. Progressively, a transnational public problem space emerged. Virtual arenas were established and actors from different backgrounds became mutually aware of each other. They engaged in common discussions and became gradually oriented towards a common policy project.

With the Creative Commons organization, the founding members in fact had set up an infrastructure that provided a home for ongoing discussions on digital commons. Their vision built on principles developed by a larger and more established practice community and social movement in the open source software sector (Weber 2004). In the process, they emphasized the broader applicability of the open source licensing approach to all kinds of creative works. In the words of Lawrence Lessig, Creative Commons was founded

[8] Interview with Lawrence Lessig 2007.

> to produce copyright licenses that artists, authors, educators, and researchers could use to announce to the world the freedoms that they want their creative work to carry. If the default rule of copyright is 'all rights reserved,' the express meaning of a Creative Commons license is that only 'some rights [are] reserved.[9]

The Creative Commons organization was established to provide a 'brand' for the Creative Commons copyright licences. Its purpose was also to raise funds and create the administrative capacities necessary for the realization of the community's vision of a 'digital commons'. Financial support came from law centres at Universities and public foundations. Since the early days, the board of directors of the Creative Commons organization (with a strong representation of lawyers) has worked together with a technical advisory board (with a strong presence of computer scientists) and an audit committee. Creative Commons started as a rather minimalist organization with only a few staff members employed.[10] The first main task was to develop a legal toolbox: machine-readable licence modules and corresponding iconographic markers that could be combined to form different standardized copyright licences. In December 2002, the first versions of Creative Commons licences were issued in the US.

Towards transnationalization—of communities and of organization

Transnationalization originated mainly from bottom-up initiatives and queries. Soon after the first launch of the licences in the US, foreign lawyers and experts contacted Creative Commons to obtain the right to port the licences into their own national legal systems. These foreign contacts often belonged or were inspired by the free/open source software movement. As early as the spring of 2003, Creative Commons opened an international office in Berlin with a view to coordinate the activities of volunteers in different countries. Creative Commons had become a model for audiences in many different countries searching for alternatives to the existing copyright.[11] Creative Commons' approach to transnationalization of their model combined community building with the setting up of an international organizational network. This approach emerged out of a series of ad hoc decisions and personal interactions with activists pursuing a similar cause in other countries. Among those foreign nodes, a number had been socialized into the Creative

[9] Interview with Lawrence Lessig 2007.

[10] Ten years later, the organizational chart lists 41 staff members (20 full-time, 10 part-time paid staff and unpaid) (http://mirrors.creativecommons.org/cc-org-chart.pdf [accessed: 13 January 2011]).

[11] Braithwaite and Drahos (2000: 539) highlight that modelling can be a 'potent weapon' for relatively weak actors because it involves learning based on conceptions of practical actions—actions which pursued by a large number of people can make a change.

Commons spirit through participation in seminars run by some of the founding members in major American law schools.[12]

The Board of Directors of Creative Commons encouraged like-minded individuals with professional legal credentials and a reputation in the copyright debate to become so-called 'project leads' in their country. These project leads were typically critical copyright lawyers or experts in open source software with a base in public universities or research institutes. The latter then became 'affiliate institutions' in the Creative Commons organizational network. Creative Commons signed a memorandum of understanding (MOU) with the affiliate institution with the intent to 'work together to advance public education, access and the use of knowledge by translating and legally adapting the Creative Commons licenses and/or amendments to the Creative Commons licenses . . . and to explain the mission and the purpose of Creative Commons'.[13] Restrictions and constraints stated in the MOU related exclusively to the use of Creative Commons as a trademark and to the formal licence porting processes. The organization of local events, funding, or thematic priorities were up to the discretion of local organizations. Hence, they could take into consideration and adapt to the different local and national social and political contexts.

A close look at the individuals and at the affiliate organizations involved in translating the licences shows that transnationalization during the first years (2003–2005) was fuelled predominantly by the absorption into the epistemic community of critical open source and Internet lawyers from outside the US. The pre-existence in a given country of a free/open source software movement was then and there a clear accelerator of licence porting. Even though not all lawyers involved were copyright experts, legal professionals clearly dominated the transnationalizing epistemic community during the early expansion phase of Creative Commons.

Once licences were in place, the activities of Creative Commons and its affiliates expanded from developing legal tools (which still continued in the form of upgrading and revising licence versions in response to feedback from users) to a wider set of tasks related to public advocacy and user mobilization. For example, Creative Commons engaged in courting well-known artists or widely recognized public institutions to adopt their copyright licences as one strategy to promote them as a standard. At the local and national level, project

[12] The project leads, for example, of two pioneer countries—Japan and Finland—had been at the same seminar at Stanford where they met Lawrence Lessig. Ronaldo Lemos, the Brazilian project lead, first came into contact with Creative Commons at Harvard's Berkman Center. Those early socialization opportunities hence played a big role in the transnationalization of the community (Dobusch and Quack 2010a).

[13] Template of a memorandum of understanding, see http://wiki.creativecommons.org/images/9/9f/CCMOU.pdf [accessed: 13 January 2011]

leads and affiliate organizations became contact-points for loosely coupled individuals and practice groups from many different fields of cultural production (e.g. music, education, public archives) and provided opportunities for them to engage in shared projects of collaborative production of digital content under the CC licence standard. Creative Commons therefore also gave rise to the formation of new collective actors within the field of digital production, as well as shaping the common identity of these actors. Project leads in jurisdictions which joined the network after 2005 often came from civil society or educational fields, thereby reaching out to potential users from the start.

Advocacy, publicizing, and mobilizing quickly yielded fruit. The use of Creative Commons licences increased exponentially after their release[14] with the double effect of enhancing attractiveness to future potential users and bringing many new individuals and practice groups to the Creative Commons community. This clear trend towards a broadening of the community was partly fuelled by the building up, globally, of social movements targeting the protection of civil rights to information on the Internet and promoting a 'digital and cultural environmentalism'. This translated in the dynamism of online discussions on various mailing lists and public events associated with the Creative Commons community.

While the multiplication of practice and user groups was instrumental for Creative Commons to prosper, it also made management structures and functions much more complex in the still young organization. Local affiliates and user activists asked for more participation and decision-rights in the organization, while Board members like Lawrence Lessig emphasized that developing CC licences as a brand required 'expertise rather than democratic motivation'.[15] In 2005, the Board initiated an organizational overhaul at both the international and national levels. At the international level, Creative Commons actually split into two parts when it hived off 'iCommons' in November 2005 as a separate legal and organizational entity headquartered in London. At the same time, the internationalization project in Berlin was renamed Creative Commons International (CCi) and remained as 'just an office' of the US non-profit organization.

At the national level, Creative Commons introduced a differentiation between legal and public project leads. The legal lead continued to provide legal expertise and work in close cooperation with the CCi office in Berlin on both licence porting and licence development. The public project lead, on the

[14] By 2009 Creative Commons had become the standard licence for open content in the Internet, as evidenced by the move of Wikipedia from an open source software licence to the use of Creative Commons licences in the same year.

[15] Interview with Lawrence Lessig 2007.

other hand, was meant to take over all the 'community work'—above all organizing events, marketing the licences, and networking among and across different groups of licence users. Legal and public project leads could be based in the same or in different affiliate organizations. While this division of labour was implemented in most jurisdictions, ICommons as a separate organization never lived up to the expectations of its founders. After having organized iSummits in Rio de Janeiro in 2006, in Dubrovnik in 2007, and in Sapporo in 2008, it silently suspended its activities after four years of existence. Today, it only continues to operate as a webpage for the posting of events, while debates on more democratic participation in Creative Commons periodically re-emerge on mailing lists and in other virtual and public arenas.

Creative Commons is therefore a community that has evolved, over the past ten years, from a small, mostly national epistemic community into a transnational community of interconnected communities (of practice, episteme, or interest). In many respects, it seems to be able to benefit from its internal plurality and diversity. It has clearly become a transnational community with an impact on governance. It plays, as such, different roles. It is involved in the framing of public problem spaces and arenas. It contributes to the structuring and the mobilization of collective actors. It plays a significant role in rule setting and in the monitoring of rule implementation. It has unmistakably shaped and transformed the preferences of many members in the process. And it certainly exerts a degree of social integration and control.

The development of the Creative Commons community has to be seen in the context of the political and social controversies surrounding transnational copyright regulation as revealed, initially, through the TRIPS negotiations. Its organizational and framing strategy has been successful in the face of a much more resourceful opposition, essentially because it resonated with widespread social practices of Internet use. By addressing and mobilizing both, authors that have no or only a limited interest in the commercial exploitation of their creations and users of commons-based goods or file-sharing software they fostered the creation and expansion of a collectively experienced, transnational community of practice (Dobusch and Quack 2010b). By way of this shared self-image, they can be mobilized and because they daily use and champion the CC licence, they in fact have a regulative impact. Still, it remains to be seen to which extent the Creative Commons community, which evolved as a countermovement to a copyright coalition, will be able to exert equal impact in the area of commercial cultural production (see Elkin-Koren 2005). Currently, Creative Commons is generating fiercer opposition amongst copyright collecting agencies, that is, private bodies established in different countries to collect royalty payments from various individuals and groups for established artists as copyright holders, than within multimedia companies whose advocacy campaigns address predominantly Internet piracy.[16] Creative Commons is pursuing coordinated negotiations with copyright collecting agencies in different countries, the outcomes of which will be important for the further diffusion of its licence. Overall, thus, the case study of the Creative Commons shows how a community of challenging civil society actors reached out to a wider constituency of actors from the public and private sector and, through organizational and framing strategies, built a collective identity for a mixed set of producers and users of Internet content in the public domain.

Discussion and conclusion

We have argued, in this chapter, that the analysis of transnational communities provides a fruitful new perspective on the complex constituencies and dynamics of transnational standard setting. We define transnational communities as social groups emerging from interactions across national boundaries and bound together through mutual recognition and a common sense of belonging (Djelic and Quack 2010). We have argued that those transnational communities contribute to standard setting processes and hence have a significant impact when it comes to transnational governance. They foster collective mobilization, particularly of the kind cutting across different dividing lines—public and private, transnational and national, 'regulators' and 'regulatees'. We also underscored the potential role of transnational communities when it comes to the launching of standard setting projects. Transnational communities, we argued, help shape and transform the preferences of their members, with partial alignment through time as a consequence. Finally, transnational communities unmistakably exert social control in a more or less formal way.

Our two case studies differed from each other in significant ways along the three dimensions identified above—goals and power, mode of access, and nature of actors. On the one hand, the ICN case pointed to an elite top-down pattern where powerful public agencies strove to enlist and mobilize others around an existing standard. The Creative Commons case reflected a more grass-roots pattern of community development led by private and civil society actors with the project to develop an alternative or challenger standard. We hypothesized that each of these types of community development patterns might have specific strengths and weaknesses. The two cases studied in this chapter illustrate this quite nicely. They also show that, in each case, the community came to deploy complementary strategies. In spite of clear

[16] http://governancexborders.com/2010/06/27/declaring-war-on-free-culture-collecting-society-confronts-creative-commons[accessed: 25 April 2011]

differences, transnational communities came to perform through time strikingly similar roles in those two cases. This suggests that we should explore the developmental trajectories of different communities rather than simply doing static comparisons. In time, the elite ICN community has come to open up in a selective and controlled manner to connect with certain important stakeholders, mostly in the private business and academic spheres. In parallel, the challenger and grass-roots based Creative Commons came to differentiate from within in order to deal with an increasing internal heterogeneity.

A comparison of the enlisting and challenging types of transnational community has highlighted the contribution of cognitive and cultural factors to the stabilization and institutionalization of transnational standards. Naturally, the concrete ways in which the communities in each case fulfilled those parallel roles differed in part. The ICN tended to privilege peer pressure and inclusivity pressure as mechanisms of socialization. The Creative Commons, on the other hand, was better characterized by the use of modelling as a strategy aiming at persuasion and learning. Another difference was quite striking at the start but, interestingly, did come to wither away in part through time. Initially, the ICN strove to impose general standards to be adopted locally. The Creative Commons, by contrast, fostered diversity in the local adaptation of a general standard. Yet, as the ICN community became through time more aware of and reflexive about the limits of convergence, it moved towards a philosophy of 'informed divergence' that included quite a bit of room for local adaptation. In parallel, as the Creative Commons community came to realize that too many jurisdictional variants of their licences could create undesirable compatibility and convertibility problems, they amplified the promotion of the generic licences. Hence, the initial differences in philosophy between our two cases appear to be diminishing over time. Whether this is also true of differences in terms of socialization mechanisms remains an open question to be explored in further studies. To test this empirically would call for a different research design and different data-gathering methods. Equally, it would be interesting to explore whether elite communities constituted of business actors exhibit the same kinds of features and dynamics as those characteristic of the ICN, which is made of public or quasi-public regulatory agencies.

Finally, while the systematic comparison of our two cases underscored the importance of transnational communities in the ongoing process of transnational governance through standard setting, it also pointed to the potential significance of a reverse impact. As transnational standard setting is deployed and developed, the networks, organizations, and individuals involved increasingly come to exhibit community features and properties. The exploration of this proposition, again, would call for an extension of our research design and for now, this remains an interesting but tentative proposition.

References

Ahrne, G. and N. Brunsson (2006) 'Organizing the World', pp. 74–94 in Djelic and Sahlin Andersson (eds) *Transnational Governance*, Cambridge, UK: Cambridge University Press.

AWG (2002) 'Advocacy and Competition Policy', *Report prepared by the Advocacy WorkingGroup for the First ICN Conference, Naples*, http://www.internationalcompetitionnetwork.org/uploads/library/doc358.pdf

Black, J. (2008) 'Constructing and Contesting Legitimacy and Accountability in Polycentric Regulatory Regimes', *Regulation and Governance*, 2: 137–64.

Botzem, S. and L. Dobusch (2009) 'The Rule of Standards Codifying Power in the Transnational Arena', Paper presented at 25th EGOS Colloquium, July 2–4, 2009. Barcelona Sub-theme 13: The Social Dynamics of Standardization.

Boyle, J. (2006) 'Cultural Environmentalism?' *Financial Times*, 20 February.

Braithwaite, J. and P. Drahos (2000) *Global Business Regulation*, Cambridge: Cambridge University Press.

Brunsson, N. and B. Jacobsson (eds) (2000) *A World of Standards*, Oxford: Oxford University Press.

——A. Rasche, and D. Seidl (eds) (2011—forthcoming), 'The Dynamics of Standardization', Special Issue *Organization Studies*.

Campbell, J. and O. K. Pedersen (eds) (2001) *The Rise of Neoliberalism and Institutional Analysis*, Princeton, NJ: Princeton University Press.

Crouch, C. (2005) *Capitalist Diversity and Change*, Oxford: Oxford University Press.

Dezalay, Y. and B. Garth (eds) (2002) *Global Prescriptions*, Ann Arbor, MI: University of Michigan Press.

Djelic, M. L. (2006) 'Marketization: From intellectual agenda to global policy making', pp. 53–73 in Djelic and Sahlin-Andersson (eds) *Transnational Governance*, Cambridge: Cambridge University Press.

——(2011) 'From the Rule of Law to the Law of Rules', *ISMO*, 41(1): 35–61.

——and T. Kleiner (2006) 'The International Competition Network: Moving towards transnational governance', pp. 287–307 in Djelic and Sahlin-Andersson (eds) *Transnational Governance*, Cambridge: Cambridge University Press.

——and S. Quack (eds) (2003) 'Globalization as a Double Process of Institutional Change and Institution Building', pp. 302–33 in Djelic and Quack (eds) *Globalization and Institutions*, Cheltenham: Edward Elgar.

————(eds) (2010) *Transnational Communities: Shaping global economic governance*, Cambridge, UK: Cambridge University Press.

————(2011) 'The power of 'limited liability'—Transnational communities and cross-border governance', in Greenwood, Lounsbury, and Marquis (eds) *Communities and Organizations*, Research in the Sociology of Organizations, Emerald Publishers.

——and K. Sahlin-Andersson (eds) (2006) *Transnational Governance*, Cambridge, UK: Cambridge University Press.

Dobusch, L. and S. Quack (2010a) 'Epistemic Communities and Social Movements: Transnational dynamics in the case of Creative Commons', pp. 252–66 in Djelic and Quack (eds) *Transnational Communities,* Cambridge, UK: Cambridge University Press.

Dobusch, L. and S. Quack (2010b) 'Urheberrecht zwischen Kreativität und Verwertung: Transnationale Mobilisierung und private Regulierung', MPIfG Discussion Paper 6/2010, http://www.mpifg.de/pu/dp_abstracts /dp10-6.asp.

Elkin-Koren, N. (2005) 'What Contracts Cannot Do: The limits of private ordering in facilitating a Creative Commons', *Fordham Law Review,* 74: 375–422.

Finckenstein, K. (von) (2002) 'Introductory Remarks' at the First ICN Conference, Naples.http://www.bureaudelaconcurrence.gc.ca/eic/site/cb-bc.nsf/vwapj/ct02433e.pdf/$file/ct02433e.pdf

——(2003) 'Recent Developments in the International Competition Network', *An Address to the Forum in International Competition Law,* New York, 6 February.

Fingleton, J. (2009a) 'Closing Speech to International Competition Network Conference, Zurich', http://www.oft.gov.uk/shared_oft/speeches/2009/spe0909.pdf

——(2009b) 'Competition Agencies and Global Markets: The challenges ahead', http://www.oft.gov.uk/shared_oft/speeches/2009/spe0909paper.pdf

Fourcade-Gourinchas, M. and S. Babb (2002) 'The re-birth of the Liberal Creed: Path to neoliberalism in four countries', *American Journal of Sociology,* 108(3): 533–79.

Graz, J. C. and A. Nölke (eds) (2008) *Transnational Private Governance and its Limits,* Milton Park: Routledge.

Haas, P. M. (1992) 'Introduction: Epistemic communities and international policy coordination', *International Organization,* 46(1): 1–35.

Hall, R. B. and T. J. Biersteker (eds) (2002) *The Emergence of Private Authority in Global Governance,* Cambridge, UK: Cambridge University Press.

ICN (2001) 'Memorandum on the Establishment and Operation of the International CompetitionNetwork', http://www.internationalcompetitionnetwork.org/uploads/library/doc579.pdf, lastdownloaded December 10th, 2010.

——(2010) International Competition Network Website, http://www.international-competitionnetwork.org/, last downloaded December 10th, 2010.

ISO/IEC (2004) 'Rules for the Structure and Drafting of International Standards', 3.1Standard http://www.iec.ch/tiss/iec/Directives-Part2-Ed5.pdf, last downloaded January 2nd, 2011.

Jessop, B. and S. Ngai-Ling (2006) *Beyond the Regulation Approach: Putting capitalist economies in their place,* Cheltenham: Edward Elgar.

Kolasky, W. (2002) 'International Convergence Efforts: A US perspective', *Address by the DeputyAssistant Attorney General, Antitrust Division, US DoJ, before the International Dimensionsof Competition Law Conference,* Toronto, 22 March, http://www.justice.gov/atr/public/speeches/10885.pdf

Lessig, L. (1999) *Code and Other Laws of Cyberspace,* New York: Basic Books.

——(2001) *The Future of Ideas,* New York: Random House.

——(2004) *Free Culture,* New York: Penguin Press.

Levi-Faur, D. and J. Jordana (eds) (2005) *The Rise of Regulatory Capitalism: The global diffusion of a new regulatory order, The Annals of the Americal Academy of Political and Social Science,* 598, London: Sage.

Lewis, D. (2009) 'Introductory Address to ICN Conference, Zurich', http://www.internationalcompetitionnetwork.org/news-and-events/newsroom-2009/intro-address.aspx

Mayntz, R. (2010) 'Global Structures: Markets, organizations, networks—and communities?' pp. 37–54 in Djelic and Quack (eds.) *Transnational Communities*, Cambridge: Cambridge University Press.

Morgan, G. (2001) 'Transnational Communities and Business Systems', *Global Networks: A Journal of Transnational Affairs*, 1(2): 113–30.

Mörth, U. (2004) *Soft Law in Governance and Regulation*, Cheltenham: Edward Elgar.

—— (2006) 'Soft Regulation and Global Democracy', pp. 119–38 in Djelic and Sahlin-Andersson (eds) *Transnational Governance*, Cambridge: Cambridge University Press.

Prakash, A. and M. K. Gugerty (eds) (2010) *Advocacy Organizations and Collective Action*, Cambridge, UK: Cambridge University Press.

Quack, S. (2007) 'Legal Professionals and Transnational Law-Making: A case of distributed agency', *Organization*, 14(5): 643–66.

—— (2010) 'Law, Expertise and Legitimacy in Transnational Economic Governance: An introduction', *Socio-Economic Review*, 1: 3–16.

Strange, S. (1996) *The Retreat of the State: The diffusion of power in the world economy*, Cambridge, UK: Cambridge University Press.

Tamm Hallström, K. and M. Boström (2010) *Transnational Multi-StakeholderStandardization: Organizing fragile non-state auhtority*, Cheltenham, UK: Edward Elgar.

Tesauro, G. (2002) 'Opening Speech at the International Competition Network First Annual Conference', Naples, 28 September.

Timmermans, S. and S. Epstein (2010) 'A World of Standards but not a Standard World: Toward a sociology of standards and standardization', *Annual Review of Sociology*, 36: 69–89.

Ugarte, F. (2002) 'International Competition Network', Speech in Cape Town, South Africa, 18 March, available at http://www.internationalcompetitionnetwork.org/news/march182002.pdf.

Weber, S. (2004) *The Success of Open Source*, Cambridge MA: Harvard University Press.

8

Innovation versus Going South

A Strategic Challenge for Capitalism in the Early Twenty-First Century

Andrew Tylecote

Introduction

Technological innovation—and the diffusion of the innovations of others—has long been the main source of growth in per capita output. On the other hand, for an individual firm any real innovation is expensive and uncertain. It will make sense from the point of view of shareholders, and still more so managers, to find the least innovative means possible to expand markets and reduce costs. Financiers are in a similar position: lending to or taking equity in a truly innovative firm must be highly risky, and so will generally be avoided if there are reasonably attractive alternative outlets for capital.

These general statements are true always and everywhere to some extent, but not to the same extent. One factor affecting the extent is (I shall argue) the point reached within the *technological long wave*. This is a succession of techno-economic paradigms each of which crystallizes, diffuses, becomes established, diffuses rapidly, then becomes exhausted. When the latest *techno-economic paradigm* has become established (as for example Fordism in the 1940s and 50s), it offers a relatively safe, certain, and profitable trajectory of technological change. Firms have established routines for using capital for innovation; capitalists have established routines for providing it. When a techno-economic paradigm is more or less exhausted and/or the latest one is too new for 'innovative routines' to have become established, there is no such safe trajectory, and thus the aversion to innovation, and the financing of it, is relatively intense. I argue in this chapter that our latest techno-economic paradigm is indeed not yet 'established' in this sense.

The extent of aversion to innovation is only half the issue. The other half is the availability—or *perceived* availability—of other profitable outlets for expansion and investment. One outlet can be defined as classic for firms and capitalists in developed countries: less-developed countries. Product X which is 'mature' in developed economies—with little prospect of rapid growth in sales—is likely to find fast-expanding sales in less-developed economies. Firms based in developed countries will have competences in producing and marketing X, and indeed in making modest improvements in it, which are superior to those of firms based in less-developed countries. They will, on the other hand, have higher wage costs—but only to the extent that they produce at home. As multinationals with operations in low-wage economies—perhaps the same ones in which they are building up their sales—they can have their cake and eat it. Financiers will look in the same direction. They may finance—and drive—the MNCs' expansion, as lenders or shareholders, or they may take advantage of the classic gradient between developed and less-developed: relative abundance of capital in the one, relative shortage (and thus high returns to it) in the other. The obvious investment opportunities are in infrastructure—directly, if it is privately owned, or via government bonds, if state-owned.

For firms, the opportunities are currently exceptional. Less-developed economies have for long been growing faster than developed ones, and there are almost unprecedented differences in labour costs between them in general and developed countries. Moreover there has been since around 1990 a dramatic opening up of the (ex-) communist countries, as markets and as 'production platforms'. China alone, through its entry into the world market, has transformed the world economic situation and provided extraordinary opportunities for profit via its market and its labour force. For financiers, however, the situation is more complex. Operating independently, they have confronted a perverse situation: since 2000, the classic gradient between developed and less-developed has been reversed, so far as the main 'emerging economies' are concerned. China has a huge balance of payment surplus on current account and accordingly needs to export, not import capital. Many others among the more successful less-developed countries are in a similar situation. One can sum up the current situation of less-developed economies, from the perspective of Northern finance, as every banker's nightmare: the prospective customers they would like to have, don't want to borrow; the ones who would like to borrow are obvious bad risks. Financiers can, however, share the opportunities just described for firms, as their shareholders and lenders; and when they are the ultimate masters of a firm, they can press firms to take them.

This chapter follows the sequence of argument above. We begin by setting out the concepts of techno-economic paradigms and technological long wave, and defending the view outlined above as to the current position. We go on to describe the alternative—'going South'– first for firms and then for finance. The terms North and South are here used to refer to advanced and less-developed economies. There is of course the usual objection to using two categories when reality lies on a continuum. Poland is not 'South' in any sense, but it is not yet advanced either, and there are similar issues involved when (say) a German firm takes advantage of low Polish wages or a developing Polish market, as when (say) a US firm does the same in China. We shall treat such economies as Poland as 'semi-South'. We show from interview material that British finance, as of *c.*2000, was firmly attached to routines which were highly adverse to innovation. We discuss in a concluding section what will be required to tilt the financial system—and thus the businesses in which it invests—towards innovation.

The unfinished technological revolution: information and communication technology

Technological development in modern capitalism is of course continuous, but that does not mean that it necessarily moves always at much the same speed. A number of authors, including the present writer, have argued for at least thirty years that since the Industrial Revolution, it has followed a 'long wave' rhythm, in which approximately every half-century a new 'techno-economic paradigm' or 'technological style' has appeared or 'crystallized.' This follows the cumulation of a number of radical process innovations, leading to certain key factors of production becoming drastically cheaper than before, with clear prospects of further cheapening. The possibilities of the new technologies are *pervasive,* and thus a new broad trajectory of technological advance becomes apparent (Perez 1983, 2002; Tylecote 1992, 1994; Freeman and Louçã 2001; and see also Schumpeter 1939).

The character of the latest techno-economic paradigm is now clear: it is based on information and communication technology (arguably with biotechnology also playing a subsidiary and related role) (Freeman and Louçã 2001, ch. 9). 'Machine intelligence' based on computing, is brought together with advanced telecommunications travelling through optical fibres as well as by established wireless methods—and the combination is made seamless by digitalization. The Internet raised to a global level the possibilities of almost instantaneous interaction among computers and their human users. The opportunities for the transformative application of this new paradigm extend to every sector and indeed every firm (at least in the North), and thus ICT is far more pervasive than its predecessor

Fordism, which could be applied only in a minority of sectors and firms (Freeman and Louçã 2001).

Although much of this is widely known, it is striking how little the wealth of innovative opportunity the ICT revolution offers has been, or is being, exploited. Of course the 'motive branches' of the new paradigm—software, IT hardware, and telecommunications—have seen spectacular innovation, investment, and growth. But a pervasive technology should have pervasive effects. After making no visible impact at all on the statistics for the overall rate of growth of productivity during the 1980s and 90s, ICT appears now to be having a modest effect, but the growth of productivity in developed economies is still slower than in the heyday of Fordism (for the United States record, 1940–2002, see Bivens and Weller 2006, Figure 2). That wealth of innovative opportunity should have stimulated spending on innovation, and consequent physical capital investment. The intensity of R&D spending by developed country firms has risen modestly over the last two decades, but their physical capital investment spending has fallen, as Weller (2004) shows for the United States.

Two sectors provide illustrations of this phenomenon: pharmaceuticals and energy. The initial breakthroughs in biotechnology were made in the late 1970s (Tylecote 1992) and followed up with the birth of genomics in the 1990s; ICT has greatly facilitated the processes of drug discovery and testing. The potential for new drugs and medical advances is clearly huge, yet the large investments in new biotechnology firms have not yet, overall, yielded a profit, while the big research-intensive pharmaceutical firms which dominate world markets have found increasing difficulty in bringing new drugs to market, with the result that they have begun to cut back on their R&D spending, to the approbation of the stock market (Economist 2011b). The energy market—including the production and distribution of fuels and electricity—is huge (estimated at $6trn. per annum—10 per cent of the world's economic output—Economist 2008), yet it is still based on technologies which were familiar in the 1960s at latest. Biotechnology is still scarcely applied to the production of fuels; the immense possibilities of the smart grid remain to be exploited (Economist 2008).

There should be nothing surprising about this. As first argued in Perez (1983), when the new paradigm appears there is a tension between the techno-economic subsystem (which has made a sharp, discontinuous advance) and the socio-institutional framework (which has not, and in most countries is decidedly *mismatched* with the new paradigm). There is no particular reason to expect all the main mismatches to have been resolved by now. There are specific mismatches affecting specific sectors: thus innovation in the energy sector will respond marvelously to carbon taxation; pharmaceuticals, which relies heavily on patenting, is finding its intellectual property rights regime ill-matched with the opportunities of genomics.[1] One can also expect to find more general mismatches; Tassey (2007) argues that the state currently does not understand, let alone discharge, its responsibilities for providing the public base on which profitable private innovation must be built. But the place where one may expect the worst mismatch is at the heart of the machine: finance.

Finance has to find ways of funding innovation profitably under the new dispensation—that is both the establishment of new innovative firms, and the support and guidance of existing firms even where they are merely recycling their own cash into innovation. This is inevitably hard, now that innovation in the new paradigm, unlike its predecessors, requires above all investment in human and intellectual capital—intangible capital. How can such intangible capital be monitored, measured—and made profitable? There must be ways—including the use of finance's unparalleled influence on government to get it to make changes in tax and IPR regimes and fill the infrastructural gap that Tassey identifies. But such convulsions are inevitably a last resort. One can count on finance, as Churchill wrily remarked about the Americans, always to do the right thing—once they have exhausted all the alternatives. As we see in the next section, there is still a lot of money to be made out of one of the alternatives.

'Going South': The preferred option for firms

This section will focus on China, which is very much the most important destination for firms taking the option of Going South—and the one most familiar to the present writer. According to an UNCTAD survey in September 2005, 87 per cent of multinational firms ranked China 'the world's most attractive place to do business' (Economist 2005). 'According to the UN Conference on Trade and Development (UNCTAD), global inflows of foreign direct investment (FDI) in 2010 totalled $1.12 trillion, a shade more than the $1.11 trillion recorded during 2009. Last year was the first, UNCTAD reckons, in which rich countries received less than half of global FDI. More than $100 billion of FDI poured into China, making it the world's second-largest recipient of such investment' (Economist 2011a). Meanwhile China had become, during 2009, the world's largest exporter (Economist 2010a).

[1] The greatest immediate opportunity arising from genomics to improve the drug portfolio is to review drugs already tested, found effective in early trials, but rejected due to serious side effects for a limited part of the population: genomics can identify which genetic type(s) this subset belongs to, making the drug safely prescribable for the rest of the population. However the patent will have expired before, or soon after, the 'rescued' drug can be marketed (Ray Hill, President of the British Pharmaceutical Society, personal communication).

The gains from going South

The opportunities for profit in, and from, less-developed economies can be grouped into at least six categories, of which the first two relate to them as markets:

Brand strengths and marketing skills. Western visitors to China soon encounter a conspicuous example of this type. The novice visitor who accepts an offer of coffee may receive a product of a well-known Swiss multinational which he or she may not recognize as this beverage. Close inspection reveals that coffee, or an extract of it, is listed as the seventh or eighth ingredient. It can be inferred that market research revealed that the Chinese did not drink coffee because they did not like its taste, but they were quite attracted by the idea of a fashionable Western drink. A drink distantly related to coffee was then concocted which they *could* be persuaded to drink, and the advertising department did the rest. One aspect of brand strength which is particularly effective in developing countries is trust in quality and specifically safety, by contrast with local firms' products; vide the Sanlu baby milk scandal (Economist 2010b).

Technological advantage. Usually allied with brand strength is technological advantage, which applies particularly in high and medium-high technology sectors. A classic case of profit from the technological gradient between developed and less-developed economies is VW's joint venture with Shanghai Automotive, which involved the production of the Santana model using an assembly line which had been moved from the United States, where the model had failed (Jürgens 1994). Production took place throughout the life of the model under very tight control, which prevented Shanghai Automotive from getting any substantial technological capability from the experience (Liu and Tylecote 2009).

The remaining four categories relate to the attraction of the South as a production location—production in the broadest sense:

1. *Resource extraction.* This is the oldest-established source of profit from less-developed countries—take silver from Peru, for example, immediately after the Spanish conquest in the sixteenth century. It is, however, limited by the desire of Southern governments to control their own natural resources, as with oil. The Chinese government fully shares that desire, and accordingly FDI into China for resource extraction is negligible. FDI into other Southern countries for sale of minerals and agricultural commodities to China may not be negligible, however.

2. *Cheap manufacturing platforms, (i): operations by 'foreign-invested enterprises'.* The development of the container during the 1960s and the subsequent 'container revolution' in cargo transport paved the way for the exploitation of

large differences in wage costs between countries. The opening up of China and other 'socialist' economies to the market, and the progressive reduction in tariffs by (in particular) developed countries, provided the institutional complement to wage differentials and logistical possibility. However, as we shall see, foreign direct investment is not always necessary in the exploitation of low-wage economies as production platforms. Where it *is* generally necessary is in high-technology goods, where the protection of intellectual property demands that the foreign owner of it maintain tight control of the production process. The much-lauded ascent of China as an exporter of high-tech products—the share of high-technology exports in total (fast-rising) exports rose from 7.9 per cent in 1995 to 29.9 per cent in 2004 [www.stats.gov.cn/tjsj/qtsi/zgktjnj]—turns out on inspection to be mostly the rise of exports from operations owned in whole or part by foreign firms.[2]

3. *Cheap manufacturing platforms, (ii): operations by domestic firms.* Where low and medium-low technology is concerned, there is little to gain from owning and directly controlling production operations in any Southern country where there are competent local entrepreneurs—as, manifestly, in China. Better to buy from the latter. Who then is the Northern buyer? In a squarely low-technology sector, the Northern retailer, like Walmart, may simply get 'own brand' goods made in China to its own designs. Further up-market, a Northern firm may design and market under its brand, goods manufactured by a Chinese firm (the OEM mode). In higher-technology sectors, a multitude of relatively low-tech components will be bought from Chinese suppliers. In all these cases manufacturing is going South as certainly as when a Northern multinational (re-)locates a factory there. And whether it involves FDI or not, there must be a switch of emphasis in the search for competitive advantage. With expensive Northern labour (including wages, benefits, and payroll taxes) increased labour productivity is the key to cost reduction. Now lower Southern wages provide labour cost reductions beyond the dreams of any Northern manufacturer, and the emphasis must shift to design for lower transport costs, design for clarity of requirements, and design for protection of intellectual property.

An example from Finland: the Finnish timber products industry has long been organized in a cluster, as is common in Finland, with the main paper manufacturers such as UPM-Kymmene displaying a good deal of vertical integration and quasi-integration (very close cooperation with machinery

[2] In 2003 61.9 per cent and 21.4 per cent of high-tech exports were produced by fully foreign-owned and partly foreign-owned firms respectively (Gu and Lundvall 2006). Between 1998 and 2005 the share of Chinese-owned firms (aside from joint ventures) in exports of high-tech products fell by more than half (www.sts.org.cn/sjkl/kjtjdt/data2006, Fig 2-10) while that of wholly foreign-owned rose year by year.

builders (such as Metso) and engineering consulting companies (Pöyry). Now the world's largest single line pulp mill is owned by UPM, but it is not in Finland, but in Uruguay. Its cost advantage over Finland arises largely from the fact that eucalyptus trees in Uruguay are ready for cutting after seven years, compared with 70 for conifers in Finland. The close Finnish cluster is now rather stretched by the fact that Metso and Pöyry, et al., are providing machinery and services at some 10,000 kms distance. Moreover there is very little vertical integration in the production process, because most of the pulp output is not processed for paper in Uruguay—much of it goes to a large paper mill owned by UPM in China. Both these mills are highly profitable. Meanwhile Western markets for paper are over-supplied, and plant closures are the order of the day in Finland, as elsewhere.

Consider the implications for innovation. With the pulp mill paying Uruguayan wages, and the paper mill, Chinese, the incentive for labour-saving innovation is drastically reduced; but more to the point, with the remoteness of new production capacity and the loss of vertical integration, the potential for product innovations related to by-products—wood fibres and other particles of wood (particularly lignin as opposed to the cellulose which is used in paper)—has received little attention. This is true for all pulp and paper companies in Western countries (Kari Lilja, University of Aalto, Finland, personal communication).

4. *Cheap research and development platforms for Northern firms*. With rapid growth of Southern universities—most notably the science and engineering disciplines in China and India—highly educated and highly skilled labour is the latest low-cost input to become available to Northern firms. It is therefore becoming increasingly attractive to re-locate to the South, the element of Northern firms' activities that makes most intensive use of highly-qualified labour: research and development (Asakawa and Som 2008). There are broadly three categories of R&D which are candidates for re-location: first in time and still most important, development work to 'customize' existing products for the local market; second, development work to deal with problems of production at local MNC manufacturing plants; third, and most recent, strategic R&D with value for the whole firm, globally (Sun et al. 2006).

There are, however, two drawbacks: first, this is the part of the firm where most of the intellectual property is generated. Locating it in the South, notably in that alleged hotspot of IP theft, China, may seem dangerous. For category 1 and 2, the advantages are probably so clear that they outweigh the risks. For category 3, the risks are likely to be the greatest—if the cat gets out of the bag, it is a most valuable cat. Second, for category 3, putting R&D centres thousands of miles away from headquarters, and probably from lead users, and very likely from lead production operations, is another form of vertical disintegration, one which may impact very badly on the effectiveness of the innovation process. The vertical disintegration may be exacerbated by the need to protect intellectual property: the safest strategy is to make sure that no one individual or group in the Southern R&D centre has a view of the whole picture of an innovation (or even, perhaps, invention).

All three categories of R&D relocation to the South, then, are essentially means to cut costs: there is no reason to suppose that this relocation is a way to accelerate innovation.

The movement Southwards

It is not possible to give a fully-disaggregated statistical picture of the developments outlined in this section. Overall, however, the importance and rate of growth of the 'Going South' phenomenon can be gauged from aggregate data:

FDI inflows to developing countries have risen from 5.4 per cent of their GDP during the 1980s, to 27.3 per cent in 2005 (Nurse 2010, citing UNCTAD 2007). Export processing zones—areas of Southern economies specifically designated as 'cheap production platforms'—have expanded from 79 zones in 25 developing countries employing 800,000 people, in 1975, through 176 zones in 47 countries employing 1.7million, in 1986, to 3,500 zones in 130 countries, employing 40 million, in 2006. (The figures given for the first two dates do not include China (which had not yet set up export processing zones (EPZs)); in 2006 more than half of the EPZ employment, 26m, was in China, while 9 years earlier it had been exactly a quarter, at 4.5m.). (See Nurse 2010 citing Boyenge 2007.) Feenstra (1998) finds that what he calls the integration of trade, and the dis-integration of production—to take advantage of low costs in the South—has contributed handsomely to the improvement of profitability in the United States.

Finance and the preference for going South[3]

In one respect, 'going South' may be unattractive—as unattractive as innovation. It will often involve major organizational reconfiguration. UPM's 'Southern strategy' and concurrent plant closures at home have involved the largest lay-offs ever seen in Finland. Meanwhile there are no doubt Finnish managers in Uruguay and China who would much rather be in Finland. One can hardly then say that going South allows firms to maintain comfortable organizational routines. (The least uncomfortable will be the Japanese, German, and Swedish

[3] This section draws on interviews carried out by Paulina Ramirez and the author in London in 1999–2000 and 2004–5 and largely reported in Tylecote and Ramirez (2008).

firms which have Southern, or semi-Southern, economies on their doorsteps: China, Poland, and Estonia respectively.) For their shareholders, it may be otherwise. It depends who their shareholders are. If they belong to the founding family, particularly if they are themselves involved in management, they may well be attached to the firm as it is and where it is. Outside shareholders, with no connection or attachment to the firm, are on the other hand likely to be entirely comfortable with any reconfiguration which offers reasonable assurance of profit. The category of shareholder most clearly recognizable as 'outsiders' are financial institutions, except for (commercial) banks, which may have longstanding connections with, and large stakes in firms. These 'outsider institutions' are mostly pension funds, insurance companies, and mutual funds; the mutual funds and smaller pension funds being managed mainly by investment banks. In the economies largely without 'funded' pensions (notably Germany, Italy, and France) their deficiency of 'outsider' capital is largely made up by inflows from abroad. It is significant, therefore, that the proportion of non-bank institutional shareholders has been rising virtually everywhere in the North. They have dominated share registers in the UK since at latest the early 1980s, and they now do so in the United States—rising from less than 10 per cent in 1952 to over 50 per cent by 2004 (Bivens and Weller 2006). With the reduction of bank shareholdings in Germany and France, and the unwinding of inter-firm shareholdings, and privatizations, outsider influence is growing there too, though founding families generally maintain their power (Tylecote and Visintin 2008).

The impact of outsider shareholders has been obscured by the slogan under which they operate: 'shareholder value' (Lazonick and O'Sullivan 2000). 'Shareholder value' on the face of it means profitability, which it is hardly surprising to find to be an aim of the owners of capital. Perhaps large firms under management control—if there were ever many of those—might have veered away from prioritizing profit, but scarcely for long. The key feature of 'shareholder value' as an aim of 'outsider capital' is precisely that outsiders wish to ensure that it is pursued by managers, and at the same time they wish *to remain outsiders*. Outsiders hold shares in a firm as pieces of paper, of which they may sell some or buy more as profit beckons. If the representative of an outsider institution becomes a non-executive director (as Warren Buffett by contrast normally does in a firm in which he takes an ownership stake), the outsider status is legally compromised, and with it the freedom to buy or sell shares. As the Head of UK Investments at Mercury Asset Management explained,

> But even if we bought 27% of a company we are only the financial owners of that company. We wouldn't demand a place on the Board and we wouldn't have a say in strategy. If we did we would receive insider information and we wouldn't be able to deal in that share until the information became public.

On the other hand, without such representation on the board, the power of the outsider shareholder, and the effectiveness of its monitoring, is questionable. The apparent solution to the problem—or so it is believed—is the alignment of interests through suitable remuneration policies: give top managers the incentive to think and behave like shareholders through stock options and stock grants (O'Sullivan 2000), or even tie executive pay to dividend pay-outs (Ferreira White 1996). The beauty of remuneration policies is that they are something that outsider shareholders can unite to press on managers, without the expenditure of effort that good monitoring requires. What City of London investors do *not* want is any obligation to develop expertise in a sector's technologies, or deep understanding of a firm's affairs:

> You go through your [financial] training and after 9–12 months you will be analysing a sector and managing funds. Every fund manager changes sector every 1–2 years. (Head of UK investments MAM)
>
> The City and the analysts can't do this [develop a deep understanding of technologies and markets]. This knowledge is too specialised. However, management should be able to explain it so that the City can understand. (Senior manager Prudential Insurance)

After all,

> Why should the analyst want to spend a lot of time trying to find out what is going on down there? [inside the firm] Why should the fund manager who has access to global markets and who has a remit to maximise the returns on his assets, bother about the company down the road? (Senior investor, Association of British Insurers)

A further problem is that even if the fund manager does 'bother about the company down the road' and find out about its prospects for successful innovation in (say) two to three years' time (not long at all, for any innovation to pay off) she or he may not dare to invest accordingly:

> We have to see our clients (for example the pension funds) every three months to show them how the portfolio is performing, and that puts a lot of pressure on fund managers. You feel that you have to show out-performance every quarter, and that is a relatively short time horizon. If you are buying a share with a two-year view, then you may have some period of under-performance in that time, but your clients are demanding quarterly out-performance. (Fund Manager MAM)

Under these circumstances the slogan of 'shareholder value' is far from indicating simply an interest in profit. In effect it indicates an interest in the impression of profit, subject to severe information asymmetry between managers and outside shareholders; an interest advanced by the remuneration policies just outlined. Bivens and Weller (2006) offer a persuasive way of measuring what they call a 'corporate governance variable': the share of internal resources dedicated to dividend payouts and share repurchases. Dividend payouts naturally rise when executive pay is tied to them (and Ferreira White established that this happens); share repurchases are a simple way for managers to raise the firm's share price and thus raise the value of their stocks and options. They found for the United States that their 'corporate governance variable' rose from 16.8 per cent to 30.5 per cent between 1952 and 1978 and 1978 and 2004. Between the same two periods, the after-tax profit share with net interest earnings rose from 9.3 per cent to 13.6 per cent (Bivens and Weller 2006, Table 4). Moreover in their time-series regressions using data for all quarters from 1952 to 2004, they found that a 1 per cent increase in the corporate governance variable was associated with a rise in the profit share by 0.1 per cent in the subsequent quarter.

How is manager behaviour then changed? The more they spend on dividends and share repurchases, the less capital they have available for investment of any kind, including innovation. The more pressure they are under for profit, soon, the more they need to focus what they do spend, on projects which offer fast pay-back—and while that payback is pending, can be easily explained and justified to their poorly informed outsider shareholders. From this point of view, the Go South option is ideal: it is generic, well-tested and clearly profitable.

Reflections after the second bubble

The interviews quoted above took place in 1999–2000. The bursting of the share price bubble in 2000–1 was a severe shock to the financial institutions of the City of London, as the bursting of the most recent bubble has been. What was learnt from it, and what changed as a result? We returned to the City in 2004–5 to find out.[4] We found that, in the face of declining returns, the shareholding institutions had become more set on their course than ever: more determined to remain outsiders, but at the same time more activist, more determined to get management to sing to their tune. An activist outsider investor may demand changes in strategy such as the selling of a division—or indeed of the whole firm—whose value (to the share price) can be gauged without any need to *engage* with the firm (Young and Scott 2004; Tylecote and Ramirez 2006).[5] One category of new activist investor is hedge funds—some at

[4] We conducted two further interviews in the City of London in winter 2004–5. One was with a senior adviser in a major pension fund, the other with a recently-retired director of two FTSE 100 companies—thus one on the City side, the other on the industry side.

[5] They can gauge it without engagement because the value to the share price depends on what their peers think.

least; but conventional investors have moved in the same direction, and their pressure can be irresistible: 'If Y [a senior industry analyst] says we should get rid of a particular business, we will most likely get rid of it' (Young and Scott 2004: 173). The obvious conduits of pressure are the chairman of the board—normally, in the UK, a non-executive director—and the finance director. Neither of these individuals needs to have any background in the firm or even its sector, so they can more easily represent 'City' interests—or be replaced by someone who will. But even CEOs can be chosen for their receptiveness to City pressures:

> There is a definite bias towards external appointments... we found a well-developed belief... in the financial markets and the executive search community that top managers should not remain in post for too long... five years in a CEO post is about right. A typical process of recruitment... will start with the selection of an executive search consultant... the shortlist will be compiled... The absolutely key question 'What will the City think?' has to be answered... if there is more than the slightest hint of hesitation from influential figures in the investment community, the chances of an individual being appointed decrease markedly. (Young and Scott 2004: 171–2.)

Just under two-thirds of CFOs of FTSE100 firms had been appointed from outside their companies, half of chairmen, and approximately one third of CEOs. This is new: 'Twenty years ago, the norm was for top managers to spend the bulk of their careers with one company, and if they moved, to do so in the early part of their careers' (Ibid.: 187). In the UK, almost all large listed firms have their headquarters in central London, so the pressure can be constant, and personal.

So why should not the Going South strategy be followed with all the greater determination, now, after the bursting of another bubble? It is more familiar than ever to outsider shareholders, and to the extent that it involves selling on Southern markets, more attractive than ever, as Southern and Northern growth rates diverge. The British economy may desperately need innovation to fuel investment and exports, but British financial institutions merely need the firms they invest in to make profits, and where they get them from is quite immaterial.

How far can we generalize these arguments to the North as a whole? The United States certainly has redeeming features absent in the UK: a powerful venture capitalist community with a track record of funding new high-technology firms and making money out of them (in ICT at least); a community of industry analysts on Wall Street with considerably more industry expertise in markets and technology than their London counterparts have (Tylecote and Visintin 2008). But Bivens and Weller's findings make clear that the dominant current is much as in the UK, sceptical of the returns to be had from heavy investment in innovation or anything else at home, optimistic of profit from squeezing costs at home and investment in the South. Lazonick (2009) argues similarly for the ICT industry in the United States. Germany too has redeeming features: ingrained routines of training and investment in R&D, protected by the special nature of its corporate governance. But (like Japan) these routines are applied, and bear fruit, in medium-high technology firms whose technological progress is steady and sustained—incremental innovation which causes few surprises and involves modest risk (Tylecote and Visintin 2008).

And for German as for Japanese firms, the nearness of low-cost production locations ensures that going South (or 'semi-South') is indeed a reasonably comfortable organizational routine, particularly once the pattern of division of labour is established and the firm is successful enough to be able to maintain employment at home while expanding it abroad. We might then find a dynamic equilibrium between relocation and innovation, in which relocation goes as far as convenient and then the main tendency is innovation. But neither Germany nor Japan shows any sign that innovation provides a 'macro-dynamic' force, stimulating investment in the economy as a whole: on the contrary, demand in these economies depends heavily on an export surplus, which is the greater in Germany because it has exchanged the appreciating DMark for the steady euro.

So the key actors are content to continue in their established routines.

Conclusion: How can we switch emphasis to innovation?

This chapter has argued that major firms, and financial systems, in developed economies face a broad strategic choice between 'innovation' on the one hand, and 'relocation' or 'Going South' on the other. For the opportunities of the new 'techno-economic paradigm,' based on information and communication technology, to be realized, 'innovation' has to be emphasized. This will require large sums to be invested in new high-technology enterprises, and within existing firms the concentration of financial and managerial resources on innovation. However when a new 'techno-economic paradigm' is not yet established, it does not present routes to profit which are reassuringly familiar from the point of view of finance; at the same time, *this* new TEP is particularly challenging because of the intangibility of investment and capital within it. In consequence, in order for finance to do its job properly with respect to innovation, it must develop particular strengths in both industrial expertise and in engagement with firms. Now there has for decades been a clear trend within finance, throughout Northern economies, towards 'outsider' capital—capital which deliberately keeps its distance from industrial management.

Outsider capital in its nature is disengaged, although it may (or may not) be industrially expert. The British financial system is dominated to an unusual extent by outsider capital, and those outsiders, as we saw, are unusually inexpert, so it presents an extreme case which would be particularly averse to the financing of innovation; but the tendencies it displays are presumably general.

While the strategic option of innovation has been unusually unattractive, that of 'relocation' to the South has been unusually attractive, due notably to the large cost gradient between North and South and the freedom to produce in and export from the South. From the point of view of outsider finance, 'going South' has the particular merit of a rather routine, generic strategy which can be replicated across a wide range of sectors.

What can be predicted—and/or prescribed? The implication of the argument above is that a new TEP will become more favourable to heavy spending on innovation as it becomes more established. But does 'becoming more established' arise automatically from the passage of time or through the reform of institutions during that time? Tylecote (1992) finds a good deal of the latter in the historical record of previous TEPs, notably Fordism, as do Tylecote and Vertova (2007). Certainly energy innovation, discussed in Section 2, is a case in point: the key requirement for 'take-off' there is carbon taxation, which would tilt the balance of profitability at last against the established technologies of fossil fuel extraction and combustion. Likewise, Tassey's (2007) argument with respect to innovation generally suggests that the public sector must play a much more assertive, and expensive, role in future. Finance learns from experience, and alas its experience of heavy investment in high technology in the late 90s dotcom and telecom boom was highly discouraging. It would appear that there is no alternative to the state (so to say) widening the goal posts and raising the crossbar.

Postscript: on 'varieties of offshoring?'

There is a striking overlap of subject matter between chapters, and, and indeed much agreement: 'Varieties of Offshoring' (Chapter 11) is concerned with Going South, albeit only that part of it aimed at Northern markets ('fragmentation'). Both chapters recognize differences between varieties of capitalism in this connection. Bair and Muhutga expect CMEs (coordinated market economies) such as Germany, Sweden, and Japan to be more restrained in Going South/fragmentation than LMEs (liberal market economies) such as the UK and the US (their hypothesis 4b). This is entirely consistent with the argument in this chapter that the outsider shareholders which dominate LMEs drive harder for relocation than do insider shareholders (which dominate CMEs). However this chapter takes account of geography where Bair and

Muhutga do not. Take Volkswagen for example, whose dominant shareholders (the government of Lower Saxony and now the Piech and Porsche families) are as unlike 'outsiders' as one can imagine. Its HQ and main production base, Wolfsburg, is as near to the Czech Republic and Poland as it is to Baden Wurttemberg, the main automotive *Land* of Germany. Small wonder that Skoda of the Czech Republic has become a wholly-owned subsidiary of VW. How could VW *not* 'fragment' production between Germany and the Czech Republic to take advantage of the large labour cost differences between them? Much the same applies, as pointed out above, to Japan's relationship with China, Sweden and Finland's with the Baltic States. It is therefore not surprising that H4b is not (strongly) supported by the data. No doubt it would be, but for geography.

Indeed geography can explain another slight surprise in Bair and Muhutga's findings: Why did Japan's transport equipment industry fragment more slowly than Germany's, while the fragmentation rate was much the same in Japan as in Germany for Bair and Muhutga's other two industries? Because in garments and electronics every Northern country's main 'fragmentation partner' was and is China, which dominates the more labour-intensive operations in these sectors. Japan's opportunities to make use of China as a production platform are at least as good as Germany's. But China has been a relative laggard in transport equipment, so in this industry Japan lacked a neighbouring low-wage 'fragmentation partner'—while German auto firms had the opportunity to link German, Polish, and Czech operations a hundred or so kilometers apart. However, Bair and Muhutga's own explanation, in terms of institutional differences between Japan and Germany, is also credible. Their insistence on differentiating within the CME (or 'stakeholder capitalist') category seems sound, and the Japan-Germany differences can be matched by US–UK differences within the LME (or 'shareholder capitalist) category (Tylecote and Visintin 2008). The fact that the empirical work reported in this chapter was restricted to the UK is a limitation which needs to be lifted.

References

Asakawa, K. and A. Som (2008) 'Internationalization of R&D in China and India: Conventional wisdom versus reality', *Asia Pacific Journal of Management*, 25(3): 375–94.

Bivens, N. Josh and Christian E. Weller (2006) 'The 'Job-loss' Recovery: Not new, just worse', *Journal of Economic Issues*, 40(3), September, 603–28.

Boyenge, J-P.S. (2007) *ILO Database on Export Processing Zones (Revised)*, Geneva: ILO.

Economist (2005) 'China', 27 October.

—— (2008) 'The Power and the Glory', 19 June.

Economist (2010a) 'China's Export Prospects: Fear of the dragon', 7 January.
—— (2010b) 'Product Liability in China: Redress by relocation', 3 June.
—— (2011a) 'Foreign Direct Investment', 20 January.
—— (2011b) 'American Business: Never had it so good', 5 February.
European Fund for the Improvement of Living and Working Conditions (2007) *Restructuring and Employment in the EU: The impact of globalisation*, Brussels: ERM Report.
Feenstra, Robert (1998) 'Integration of Trade and Dis-integration of Production', pp. 31–50, *Journal of Economic Perspectives*, 12(4) (Fall): 31–50.
Ferreira White, Lourdes (1996) 'Executive Compensation and Dividend Policy', *Journal of Corporate Finance: Contracting, Governance, and Organization*, 2(4): 335–58.
Freeman, C. and C. Perez (1988) 'Structural Crises of Adjustment: Business cycles and investment behaviour', pp. 38–66 in G. Dosi et al. (eds) *Technical Change and Economic Theory*, New York: Pinter Publishers, London and Columbia University Press.
Freeman, C. and F. Louçã (2001) *As Time Goes By: From the Industrial Revolution to the Information Revolution*, Oxford: Oxford University Press.
Gu, S. and B. Lundvall (2006) 'China's Innovation System and the Move Towards Harmonious Growth and Endogenous Innovation', *Innovation: Management, Policy & Practice*, 8(1–2): 1–26.
Jürgens, Ulrich (1994) 'VW at the Turning Point: Success and crisis of a German production concept', pp. 91–108 in Groupe d'Étude et de Recherche Permanent sur l'Industrie et les Salariés de l'Automobile (GERPISA), Programme International 'Emergence de Nouveaux Modeles Industriels', 1992–1995, Actes du GERPISA No. 10, Des Trajectoires des Firmes aux Modèles Industriels, Paris.
Kirkegaard, J. F. (2007) 'Offshoring, Outsourcing and Production Relocation: Labor market effects in the OECD countries and developing Asia', Working Paper 07-02, Washington, DC: Peterson Institute for International Economics.
Lazonick, W. (2009) *Sustainable Prosperity in the New Economy? Business Organization and High-Tech Employment in the United States*, Kalamazoo, MI: Upjohn.
—— and M. O'Sullivan (2000) 'Maximizing Shareholder Value: A new ideology of corporate governance', *Economy and Society*, 29(1): 13–35.
Liu, Jiajia and Andrew Tylecote (2009) 'Corporate Governance and Technological Capability Development: Three case studies in the Chinese auto industry', *Industry and Innovation*, 16(4): 525–44.
Nurse, K. (2010) 'Techno-Economic Paradigms and the Migration (Relocation) of Industries to the Peripheries', pp. 287–306 in *Techno-Economic Paradigms: Essays in honour of Carlota Perez* (eds) W. Drechsler, R. Kattel and E. S. Reinert, London, N York, Delhi: Anthem.
Organization for Economic Cooperation and Development (1995) *National Systems for Financing Innovation*, Paris: OECD.
Perez C. (1983) 'Structural Change and Assimilation of New Technologies in the Economic and Social Systems', *Futures*, 15(5): 357–75.
—— (2002) *Technological Revolutions and Financial Capital: The dynamics of bubbles and golden ages*, Cheltenham: Edward Elgar.

Ramirez, P. and A. Tylecote (2004) 'Hybrid Corporate Governance and Its Effects on Innovation: A case study of AstraZeneca', *Technological Analysis and Strategic Management*, 16(1) (March): 115–37.

Schumpeter, J. A. (1939:1982) *Business Cycles* (2 vols.), Philadelphia: Porcupine Press.

Sun, Y., D. Du, and L. Huang (2006) 'Foreign R&D in Developing Countries: Empirical evidence from Shanghai, China', *The China Review*, 6(1) (Spring): 67–91.

Tassey, G. (2007) *The Technology Imperative*, Cheltenham: Elgar.

Tylecote, A. (1992) *The Long Wave in the World Economy*, London and New York: Routledge.

—— (1994) 'Long Waves, Long Cycles, and Long Swings', *Journal of Economic Issues*, 28(2) (June): 477–88.

—— (2007) 'The Role of Finance and Corporate Governance in National Systems of Innovation', *Organization Studies*, 28(10) (October): 1461–81.

—— and P. Ramirez (2006) 'Corporate Governance and Innovation: The UK compared with the US and "Insider" economies', *Research Policy*, 35(1): 160–80.

————(2008) 'Finance, Corporate Governance and the New Techno-Economic Paradigm', *Recherches économiques de Louvain* 74(4) Special Issue: 'Corporate Governance in Advanced Economies: Lessons in a post financial crash era', 583–613.

—— and G. Vertova (2007) 'Technology and Institutions in Changing Specialisation: Chemicals and motor vehicles in the US, UK and Germany in the 20th Century', *Industrial and Corporate Change*, 16(5) (October): 875–901.

—— and F. Visintin (2007) 'A New Taxonomy of National Systems of Corporate Governance', pp. 71–122 in L. Mjøset and T. Clausen (ed.) *Capitalisms Compared*, Amsterdam: JAI-Elsevier Science Comparative Social Research Yearbook.

————(2008) *Corporate Governance, Finance, and the Technological Advantage of Nations*, London: Routledge.

UNCTAD (2007) *The Least Developed Countries Report, 2007: Knowledge, technological learning and innovation for development*, Geneva: United Nations.

Weller, Christian (2004) *Lagging Investment: The cost of the 'upside-down' economy*, CAP Policy Brief, Washington, DC: Center for American Progress.

Young, D. and P. Scott, (2004) *Having their Cake: How the City and big bosses are consuming UK business*, London: Kogan Page.

Section 3

The Organization of Firms and Markets in Twenty-First Century Capitalism

9

Internationalization and the Institutional Structuring of Economic Organization

Changing Authority Relations in the Twenty-First Century

Richard Whitley

Introduction

The removal of many market entry barriers to foreign companies and investors during the second half of the twentieth century has created a form of 'semiglobalization ... [that] ... involves situations in which barriers to market integration at borders are high, but not high enough to insulate countries completely from each other' (Ghemawat 2003: 139). It enabled many firms to access much larger markets for their products and services and to expand managerial coordination and control of economic activities across national borders. This increase in transnational corporate integration has also been supported by the widespread adoption of regulatory principles that prevent discriminatory support for domestic firms and provide greater transparency of national market rules (Braithwaite and Drahos 2000).

In some political economies, this growth of foreign direct investment (FDI) has contributed to a decline in the national homogeneity and specificity of prevalent patterns of economic coordination and control relative to those established in the period dominated by the Bretton Woods System. In particular, the more that leading firms invest significant resources in operations and strategic assets abroad, on the one hand, and foreign companies establish or take over major subsidiaries within a political economy, on the other hand, the weaker the authority of domestic institutions and interest groups over strategic managers of the companies operating within a country may become.

In such cases, firms in different sectors and localities within national boundaries can be expected to develop more varied patterns of organization, collaboration, and competition than was common in many countries during the heyday of the Bretton Woods System. In the longer term, this may well mean that the sectoral specialization of different forms of capitalism may decline as the capabilities developed by major firms become less nationally specific and more attuned to competitors and markets in varied institutionalized settings. As the size of product markets grow through internationalization, and capital markets support transnational mergers and acquisitions, some companies based in more collaborative kinds of institutional regimes are narrowing the scope of their activities while enlarging their customer base within particular sectors (see, for example, the account of some Danish firms in Meyer 2006). With institutional regimes in some national economies becoming less homogenous and complementary, leading firms in those countries could become more sectorally heterogenous, while international companies in general become more technologically specialized and focused on a limited range of product markets.

These developments have been seen by some as heralding the 'end of diversity' (Yamamura and Streeck 2003) and the weakening of nationally specific institutional regimes that supported non-liberal or more highly coordinated forms of capitalism, as well as reducing the national distinctiveness of particular kinds of production systems such as diversified quality production. However, while they may indicate a reduction in the national homogeneity and complementarity of dominant institutions governing economic activities in some countries, this need not imply a worldwide convergence to a neoliberal variety of capitalism. Rather, they suggest that leading economic actors in many market economies could become increasingly heterogeneous in their governance and strategies as well as gaining greater autonomy from domestically dominant institutions and interest groups, especially the largest firms that are able to access international capital markets.

It is important to note, though, that the conduct of economically rational strategies and operation of competitive markets across national borders remain dependent on largely national institutional frameworks governing property rights, contracting practices, limited liability, and other features of the business environment, which are maintained through states' legal infrastructures (Gessner 2009a). Furthermore, although pressures from international capital markets and foreign portfolio investors may have become more significant influences on large firm behaviour in recent decades, the extent of cross-border capital market integration varies between different types of financial instruments and remains subject to the decisions of nation states (Ghemawat 2003; Pauly 2002; Weiss 2003). As the recent financial crisis has amply demonstrated, states remain the primary agents dealing with the consequences of market failure, and predominantly national legal systems, corporate governance practices, and political pressures continue to play the central role in supporting transnational economic coordination. Additionally, growing sovereign and counterparty risk fears in the wake of the 2008–10 financial crisis, together with increasing national control over banks' behaviour, may well reduce private cross-border capital flows and 'mark the start of the deglobalisation of capital markets' (Bowers 2010).

The increasing variety of many firms' institutional environments as they internationalize key assets and activities, coupled with the growing diversity of competitors from different kinds of home economies as cross-border competition intensifies, do, however, raise a number of questions about the nature of leading economic actors and prevalent forms of economic coordination and control in the twenty-first century. In particular, if some companies are becoming less constrained by domestic institutions and less dependent on national collective competition goods, such as easy access to cheap capital, skilled labour, and new knowledge, in their home economy, what factors influence their choice of international strategies and how they integrate different activities across borders? If more firms are able to select how and where they develop their distinctive firm-specific organizational capabilities that provide significant competitive advantages, how will different kinds of companies do so, and how are they likely to take advantage of the semiglobalized nature of the world economy? Additionally, insofar as new and more influential forms of transnational governance are being developed by both private and public actors (Hall and Biersteker 2002; Djelic and Sahlin-Andersson 2006; Quack 2007), how would we expect them to affect the internationalization of different kinds of economic organization and the emergence of new kinds of cross-border systems of economic coordination and control?

In this paper, I suggest a way of approaching such questions, focusing particularly on the role of corporate and institutional authority in coordinating economic activities in different institutional environments. Institutional authority here refers to the role of societal institutions in legitimizing and regulating particular kinds of economic actors and behaviour. I first summarize the key characteristics of the expanding transnational business regulations that have become established since the collapse of the Bretton Woods System, and then consider the major differences in how authority can be distributed between MNC centres, their foreign subsidiaries, and dominant national and international institutions as many companies internationalize their operations and develop some autonomy from domestic institutions. These variations enable us to distinguish six ideal types of MNC. In the following section, I consider the key factors that are likely to encourage and restrict both the extent of corporate authority and worldwide economic integration and the authority of home and host economy institutions and interest groups in the twenty-first century.

The expansion of arm's length transnational governance

The decline of many national barriers to competition and investment since the collapse of the Bretton Woods System has been accompanied by an expansion of cross-border governance and of new forms of public and private regulation in many sectors (Braithwaite and Drahos 2000; Djelic and Sahlin-Andersson 2006; Morgan and Engwall 1999; Porter 1994). Much of this growth of international business regulation reflects the influence and interests of dominant states and their leading businesses, in a similar manner to the historical development of transnational governance of economic exchange and competition in earlier periods. For example, in the nineteenth century much international trade and investment became governed by the national institutions of the major colonial powers that were extended over their dependent territories. As Braithwaite and Drahos (2000: 50) put it in the case of the *Bills of Exchange Act* of 1882: 'The Act applied to the whole of the UK and was subsequently adopted, usually with very little change, by colonies or former colonies of the British Empire.'

To some extent, this pattern has continued through the twentieth century and into the twenty-first century as the dominant powers of the UK and, more significantly, the USA played major roles in establishing and managing key international regulatory organizations such as the IMF, World Bank, and WTO, exemplified perhaps by the critical influence of Keynes and US Treasury official Dexter White in the establishment of the Bretton Woods' institutions (see, e.g. Obstfeld and Taylor 1998). Towards the end of the twentieth century, to quote Braithwaite and Drahos (2000: 63) in connection with the inclusion of rules governing intellectual property rights in worldwide trade negotiations:

> The US had the support of Europe, Canada and Japan for including intellectual property in the (Uruguay) Round, but basically, it was a US initiative. It was the US, or more specifically the US business community, which had made all the running on the matter of intellectual property.

Similarly, in considering the development of cross-border legal rules and especially the role of large law firms in establishing conventions that facilitate cross-border business transactions, Gessner (2009a: 189) suggests:

> there is a clear trend towards the Americanisation of international lawyering, law as big business and creative lawyering, the strategic and aggressive use of law in

> business relations, and highly commercial and pragmatic approaches.... International law firms...indicate the power of common law and the hegemony of the United States in the global market.

To the extent, then, that private companies rather than nation states have played an important role in the institutionalization of 'global law'—which is mostly focused on trade regulation and contractual certainty as Gessner emphasizes—this entrepreneurial activity of law firms resembles their proactive role in common law regimes rather than any radically novel system of international regulation.

As Quack (2007) emphasizes, the lack of any central state governing the development and enforcement of international law means that non-state actors, especially law firms from common law jurisdictions, have more political-economic space to develop innovative transnational contracts and influence cross-border regulation of economic transactions more generally. Many aspects of the emerging system of global business regulation, and especially its pluralist, multi-actor, and less hierarchical nature, reflect the primarily custodial role of the state (Evans 1994) in the twentieth-century USA and other influential Anglophone economies, as well as private companies' concern to increase the transparency of business regulation in different national economies, and ensure that foreign firms are treated on the same basis as domestic ones (Braithwaite and Drahos 2000: 24–30, 507–15).

Relatedly, much of the economic integration in the European Union has been dominated by arm's length institutions that encourage the removal of barriers to product market competition, deregulating national markets and establishing common rules of the game across Europe, as opposed to those that support more positive forms of integration (Amable 2003; Majone 2005). The relative weakness of corporatist agencies and institutions at the European level, which is not too surprising given the lack of EU-wide political integration, competition, and accountability, has limited the effectiveness of national constraints on economic opportunism and of institutions encouraging mutual collaboration between firms and other actors. Furthermore, the judicial activism of the European Court of Justice in pursuing the equalization of market conditions throughout the EU 'has weakened or eliminated the nation-state's control over the balance of contributions and benefits...and...(ensured that)...Existing economic institutions in (social market economies) will be systematically weakened by the deregulatory effect of negative integration and the competitive pressures resulting from mutual recognition' (Sharpf 2010: 238).

Insofar as the emerging international institutions do indeed make cross-border transactions more reliable and enable companies to invest in a wider range of locations, they reduce the risks of making strategic investments abroad and accessing collective competition goods in foreign locations. In the absence of such institutions, the systematic integration of foreign assets and competences with domestic ones to generate new kinds of knowledge and skills might well have been considered too risky if it rendered key capabilities partially dependent on foreign subsidiaries and their environments. This kind of transnational integration involves greater commitment to foreign economies than the conventional MNC investment in raw materials or cheap labour because it seeks to use host economy assets to develop and enhance firm-specific capabilities and competitive advantages across the MNC, and so makes core components of the firm more interdependent with subsidiary partners and contexts.

This is especially the case when such assets are significantly supported by host economy institutions to the extent that their strategic value would be severely diminished if the MNC attempted to detach them from this context. An obvious example is R&D expertise that is closely dependent on a particular country's public science system and relatively accessible through local labour market institutions. In these cases, foreign companies can become significantly dependent on host economy collective competition goods and the institutional regimes that support them.

However, not all, or perhaps most, international companies do attempt to gain long-term advantage through the organizational integration of assets and competences located in different kinds of business environments. Indeed, given the limited institutionalization and power of transnational regulations governing property rights and transactions as well as their predominantly arm's length nature, it seems reasonable to assume that much foreign investment tends to be more opportunistic and focused on short-term goals. Even where MNCs do undertake investments in training and the improvement of suppliers' competences for longer-term advantages than the immediate reduction of input prices, these are unlikely to be as wide ranging and long term as are inter-firm relationships in economies dominated by strong, collaborative institutions.

Variations in authority relations governing cross-border coordination and control

In considering how different firms change their governance, capabilities, and cross-border links with business partners as they internationalize, it is useful to distinguish between their degree of authoritative integration of activities, resources, and strategies across markets and institutional regimes, on the one hand, and their dependence on different institutional regimes and their collective competition goods in their home and host economies, on the other hand. While in general many international companies may have increased their strategic autonomy from domestic interests and institutions, the extent to which they remain constrained and supported by business partners, employees, and dominant institutions in different market economies continues to vary considerably, as does their authoritative integration of activities, assets, and commitments across different territorial entities. In the more internationalized business environment, we can, then, compare patterns of economic coordination and control in terms of three sets of authority relations:

- the degree of cross-border authoritative integration of economic activities through both managerial hierarchies and various kinds of alliances and partnerships;
- the interdependence of MNCs with domestic institutions, interest groups and collective competition goods;
- their interdependence with dominant institutions and groups in host economies.

Cross-border authoritative integration

Beginning with corporate authority, the degree and scope of ownership integration of operations and systematic coordination of activities in different locations to achieve international economies of scale and scope remains highly variable across MNCs, albeit generally increasing as regulatory environments in host economies become more predictable and supportive of foreign investors, and technological changes reduce communication and transport costs. The more that companies are able to control subsidiary strategies, routines, and processes in accordance with some corporate-wide logic that takes little heed of national market differences and variations in business partner and employee characteristics and preferences, the more international corporate authority they can be said to have. In contrast, where local market conditions, business partners, and employees differ so much that products and services have to be more customized and subsidiaries have to adapt much more to local circumstances if they are to be successful and to access key locally provided collective competition goods, the less corporate authority the MNC as a whole has.

The more MNCs attempt to gain advantages over their less internationalized competitors by integrating the distinctive kinds of knowledge, capabilities, and other assets in different host economies that developed interdependently with particular business partners and institutional logics specific to those societies, the more difficult it becomes for them to exert full corporate authority over such units. The more successful and innovative are foreign subsidiaries embedded in societally specific markets and institutional contexts, the more autonomous they tend to be, at least with respect to market and technology strategies (Forsgren et al. 2005). In practice, then, very high levels of corporate authority over the strategies and practices of managers of successful subsidiaries in different kinds of political economies are difficult to achieve in most MNCs (Kristensen and Zeitlin 2005).

In addition to encouraging FDI and the managerial coordination of economic activities across national borders, regulatory changes and the growth of transnational governance have increased contractual certainty (Gessner 2009b), and arguably encouraged more extensive inter-firm commitments between suppliers and customers in different countries. At least in some parts of the car industry and mechanical engineering sectors, firms seem willing to go beyond spot market contracting and invest in longer-term relationships with business partners abroad (Herrigel and Zeitlin 2010; Kristensen et al. 2011). Whether this leads to more widespread transnational alliances and authoritative integration of value chains through shared commitments between business partners to the extent found in some national markets dominated by collaborative institutional regimes remains to be seen.

The interdependence of MNCs with domestic institutions, interest groups, and collective competition goods

There are two important aspects to analysing the authority of institutions over the nature and behaviour of firms. The first aspect is the constitutive nature of the rules and norms governing corporate existence, rights, and duties in a particular society. These specify the kinds of entities that can exercise legitimate authority over economic resources and activities and how they are to be established, governed, and granted particular powers, as well as how they are to be held accountable to other groups and agencies. They therefore determine who and what becomes a legitimate economic actor in the market economy.

While these constitutive rules and norms remain largely nationally specific and formalized in national legal systems (Gessner 2009a), the role of international authorities and organizations, such as the European Commission and the Bank for International Settlements, in developing transnational forms of incorporation and modifying national laws has grown over recent decades. However, as the history of the European Union highlights, most such transnational systems have to be incorporated into domestic legislation to become effective, and usually rely on variously organized national administrations to implement and police them, often in rather variable and diverse ways (Duina 1999; Knill 2001).

The second aspect of institutional authority over firms concerns how such rights and duties are to be exercised in competitive markets, how relationships between investors, managers, and employees are to be organized, and what sorts of behaviour are regarded as acceptable and what kinds are not. These regulatory institutions encompass both formal rules and procedures governing firm behaviour and informal customs and norms about appropriate and effective managerial practices. They additionally govern the production of collective competition goods, such as skilled labour, formal knowledge, and various forms of financial and political support, and how firms can gain access to, and control, these.

The extent and scope of such institutions' authority over the constitution and behaviour of firms varies considerably between different home and host economies, as the comparative capitalisms literature has emphasized (Amable 2003; Crouch 2005; Whitley 2007, 2010). At least three levels of institutional authority can be distinguished. First, in societies where institutional regimes exert relatively high levels of authority over companies, both the degree and scope of institutional influence over the nature and behaviour of companies within particular territorial entities is considerable. Not only do the institutions governing capital, labour, and product markets, in addition to the state regulatory structures, exercise effective authority over who becomes a significant economic actor and how they behave in competitive markets in such societies, but they also extend that authority over a considerable range of responsibilities and behaviours, including employment policies, as in many inclusive corporatist political economies (Whitley 2007: 46–55). Quite often firms' responsibilities to different groups and institutions, as well as their rights to autonomous decision-making, are specified, such that the ability of companies to develop idiosyncratic forms of corporate governance and identities are relatively restricted. Similarly, informal norms and conventions governing managerial practices and competitive actions within and between companies have high levels of influence over firm behaviour in such cases.

Second, medium levels of institutional authority combine effective influence over firm constitutions and behaviour, but with a narrower scope of the range of actions and relationships being subject to dominant norms and regulations. In such cases, formal rules of incorporation and access to capital and labour markets may constrain and direct companies' strategies, but their discretion and ability to act opportunistically and idiosyncratically with respect to a range of economic relationships and actions are greater than in the previous case. As a result, the variety of firms' strategies and policies can be considerable, especially with regard to employment relations and in federal states, such as the USA, where corporate governance rules differ between jurisdictions.

Third, low levels of institutional authority refer here to societies where the predictability and reliability of both formal and informal institutions are limited and the business environment in general is highly uncertain. While formal rules of the game governing legal incorporation, rights, and duties may exist, their impact on firms and major interest groups remains slight and inconsistent. Distinctive economic rationalities based on coherent institutional logics separate from political and personal pressures and loyalties remain weakly established in these kinds of societies, as in many industrializing economies and those where radical institutional change is taking place, such as the former state socialist countries of Eastern Europe and elsewhere (Fafchamps 1996; Humphrey and Schmitz 1998; Whitley and Czaban 1998; Whitley et al. 1996).

The interdependence of MNC with host economies

In considering the authority of host economy institutions on firms' governance and capabilities, a particularly important aspect concerns the extent to which they govern access to, and the use of, assets, skills, and knowledge that foreign firms seek to appropriate in developing their organizational capabilities and competitive competences. The more MNCs wish to learn from abroad and gain competitive advantages from operating in different environments that provide novel ways of working and other knowledge, and the more such learning involves adapting to the dominant institutions in host economies that support these capabilities, the greater the authority of these institutions becomes.

In many cases, of course, MNCs seeking market access and/or labour and material inputs have to adapt to host state regulations and interests as well as local labour market conventions, but this does not usually involve changing business practices elsewhere or developing transnational organizational capabilities on the basis of host economy policies and competences. Some Japanese pharmaceutical companies investing in the UK and USA research communities, for example, have found it difficult to integrate such foreign operations with their domestic R&D activities, let alone to change the latter effectively (Lam 2003).

Just as Malnight (1995) distinguished between the participant and contributor roles of foreign subsidiaries of Eli Lilly, so too we can separate those MNCs that adapt to local institutions for primarily local purposes from those that generalize such adaptations across their international operations, as when some US car firms attempted to learn lean production techniques from Japan, and German banks developed their investment banking capabilities in the UK and USA, and then expanded these on a worldwide basis. A simple contrast can, then, be drawn between three MNC approaches to the management of their foreign subsidiaries in different contexts. First, there are those that adapt very little to host economy institutions and largely impose their standard way of working on foreign operations, usually because they are powerful enough to ignore local pressures. Second, those that adapt locally but not more widely, and, third, those that learn from abroad by changing routines and strategies in other organizational units as a result of adapting to particular host economy partners and institutions.

Different forms of MNCs

Multinational companies often experience all these levels of home and host economy institutional authority, and combine them with varying degrees of corporate authority and cross-border integration. We can, though, distinguish a number of ideal types in terms of the relative authority of domestic and host economy institutions and corporate integration, and consider how the changes outlined above could affect their development. In Table 9.1, I characterize six of these in terms of three dichotomies.

First, it is necessary to distinguish whether MNCs exercise considerable authority over how their foreign subsidiaries operate and integrate their operations systematically across national borders or whether they prefer to run them more at arm's length as separate organizations with their own profit and loss accounts primarily controlled through financial targets and outcomes. Second, is the authority of domestic institutions and interests over MNC constitution and capabilities considerable in both degree and scope—or is it

Table 9.1. Six ideal types of MNC

		Degree of Corporate Integration and Control			
		Largely limited to financial controls	Considerable procedural and sequential interdependence		
	Some	**Fragmented,** e.g. APV, franchized MNCs	**Detached,** e.g. interwar Ford	Low	
Degree and Scope of Domestic Interdependence with institutions, agencies, and business partners			**Federal,** e.g. Unilever for much of the 20th century	Some	Degree of Subsidiary Contribution to MNC
	Considerable	**Delegated,** e.g. locally adaptive banks such as HSBC before the 1970s	**Domestically dominated,** e.g. many Japanese firms	Low	
			Hybrid, e.g. some German banks	Some	

more limited to that of the regulatory and custodial state? Third, are foreign subsidiaries able to develop distinctive capabilities and knowledge that contribute to the enhancement of transnational organizational competences? Alternatively, do foreign subsidiaries either have little or no autonomy, or is any autonomy which they have restricted to developing largely local capabilities? Since such transnational contributions are improbable when the overall level of corporate integration is low, two of the eight possible combinations are empirically unlikely.

Considering initially MNCs that are quite integrated with domestic institutions and interests, as in highly coordinated market economies, there are three distinct types that differ in their openness to learning from abroad and their transnational coordination of activities and knowledge. *Hybrid* companies combine strong ties to home economy governance structures and groups with a willingness to adapt to different institutional regimes and business partners' practices in order to appropriate strategic assets and the benefits from novel capabilities in overseas contexts, and to use them, not only in particular subsidiaries, but also more widely across the organization. They actively seek to develop new kinds of firm-specific competences from the systematic coordination of economic activities conducted in diverse institutional environments with varied business partners. When successful, this should lead to the generation of new hybrid competition models, organizational routines, and competitive advantages that reflect, and modify, the variety of collective competition goods and institutional interdependences that they acquire and become involved with. To the extent that this does occur, we would expect these firms to become more detached from domestic institutions and interest groups, as seems to have happened with some German banks and car manufacturers, although political pressures may restrict this.

Probably more common, given the difficulties of balancing home and host economy institutional pressures and interests while accessing collective competition goods and other resources in diverse societies, are *domestically dominated* and *delegated MNCs*. The first are similar to those characterized as national firms with foreign operations in that they are highly integrated into their domestic society's institutions and dominant business system, such that their distinctive capabilities and dominant growth strategies are similar to those of other leading firms in that market economy, and reliant on domestic collective competition goods. Foreign subsidiaries are tightly controlled by head office in these MNCs, with little opportunity to develop their own competences or adapt to local market and institutional conditions. Many Japanese companies in the postwar period seem to be close to this ideal type (Westney 2001; Whitley et al. 2003).

Delegated MNCs combine considerable domestic dependence and integration with some delegation to major foreign subsidiaries to adapt to local business partners, institutions, and ways of doing business, but limit the degree of such delegation and learning to predominantly local entities and markets. Organizational integration of locally developed knowledge and competences remains relatively low in these types of MNC compared to their home economy capabilities and strategies. This pattern seems likely to develop when MNCs derive most of their competitive competences and knowledge from their domestic operations and institutional context but are increasingly operating in a number of quite different and complex environments that require them to adapt to local practices and institutions if they are to be successful, as in commercial and retail banking before communication costs became drastically reduced and regulatory barriers were weakened.

Three other kinds of MNC are less integrated with their home economy institutions but vary in their degree of corporate integration and willingness to learn from abroad. *Detached* MNCs combine a considerable level of corporate authority with less interdependence with domestic institutions, business partners, and employees, and more limited reliance on domestically generated collective competition goods. They also exhibit some reluctance to adapt to a foreign country's institutions and adopt novel practices and approaches developed in foreign subsidiaries. Often, these are tightly controlled by head office and have little opportunity to develop their own competences or adapt to local market and institutional conditions, as in the case of Henry Ford's European subsidiaries during the interwar years (Tolliday 2000). Such companies seek high levels of strategic autonomy from national institutions and actors, and are rarely willing to engage in long-term commitments or authority-sharing with business partners and employees, whether domestic or foreign. International expansion is usually focused on achieving market access, acquiring low cost inputs, and/or obtaining strategic assets that are not highly interdependent with national institutional arrangements and actors.

Focused on realizing economies of scale and scope through the managerial integration of activities across the world, such firms resemble the Chandlerian corporation subject to varying degrees of international capital market pressures, but largely controlled by a self-selected managerial elite. While this ideal type may be popular in much consultancy and strategic management literature, not to mention amongst many senior MNC managers, its empirical manifestations are not as widespread as often claimed. This is not least because the ability of top managers to organize and control such detached firms in a coherent and 'rational' manner is limited. Resources, skills, and facilities can rarely, if ever, be moved around the world as discrete organizational units isolated from their societal contexts, and their corporate governance remains tied to largely national legal systems and patterns of ownership. Additionally, as Ghemawat (2003, 2007) has emphasized, the world economy is scarcely globalized, and MNCs can often make as much money from realizing economies of arbitrage that take advantage of, and help to reproduce, national differences in factor costs, institutions, skills, and knowledge as from economies of aggregation.

More *federal* MNCs, on the other hand, invest resources in developing new knowledge and competences from operating in different host economies and adapting to some of their institutionalized conventions. Authority here is more equally shared between home and host economy interests and institutions and the corporate organization as companies attempt to generate distinctive transnational capabilities by integrating economic activities across a variety of contexts that provide different kinds of collective competition goods. This is more likely when attractive foreign markets differ widely in their organization of competition and cooperation and offer a considerable range of strategic assets such that firms have to invest major resources in learning how to do business successfully in them and to gain significant advantages from doing so.

Fragmented MNCs, finally, delegate considerable authority to their foreign operations with little cross-national integration of their activities or attempt to learn from different ways of doing things. Here, the degree of ownership coordination and control of activities in different contexts is lower than in the two previous types, and subsidiaries have greater strategic autonomy to adapt to local circumstances. They therefore are able to develop more varied and distinctive competences in conjunction with local institutions, collective competition goods, and business partners, but these are only weakly integrated into the MNC as a whole, and the global head office functions as much as a financial holding company as an authoritative integrator of different activities and competences. To some extent, the portrayal of APV in Kristensen and Zeitlin's *Local Players in Global Games* (2005) resembles this kind of MNC. Some professional services companies also seem to operate in much the same way, not least because legal constraints and highly nationally specific institutional contexts limit corporate authority and encourage an international structure more akin to a franchized organization than a fully integrated managerial hierarchy (Morgan and Quack 2005, 2010).

These combinations of different degrees of authority of corporate head offices, home economy and host economy institutions, and business partners reflect variations in the strength and cohesion of national institutions and collective competition goods, as well as in the nature and effectiveness of international institutions governing cross-border coordination and control. As an extensive literature has shown, companies from different kinds of domestic economy internationalize their operations to varying degrees and in contrasting ways (see, e.g. Doremus et al. 1998; Westney 2001; Whitley et al. 2003), and the growth of cross-border competition, investment, and governance can be expected to affect firms in different sectors and countries in different ways.

Changing institutions, authority relations and forms of international coordination and control

Turning now to consider some of the key factors that are likely to affect how such variations in internationalization occur and change these kinds of authority relationships, it is first worth emphasizing that the present state of semiglobalization (Ghemawat 2003, 2007) of the world economy means that national product, capital, and labour markets remain partially segmented, and the nature and organization of economic activities, resources, and knowledge are quite location-specific. Consequently, although transnational corporate authority and integration may have grown considerably in the late twentieth century, the worldwide standardization of product and service development, production, and distribution to achieve global economies of aggregation has been difficult, and arguably strategically irrational. Instead, the location-specificity of key resources and competences enables MNCs to achieve economies of arbitrage by acquiring and controlling different kinds of economic activities, skills, and assets in different political economies. These resources range from low-cost inputs and culturally specific brand advantages to nationally specific collective competition goods provided and enhanced by key institutions, as in the case of state-supported new knowledge development in US biotechnology.

Insofar as MNCs do pursue these kinds of international arbitrage strategies, they will reinforce the centrifugal limits to very high levels of corporate integration that stem from successful adaptation of foreign subsidiaries to foreign markets, business partners, and institutions. The more that subsidiary growth and profitability depend on their embedding strategies and routines in distinctive local and national business environments, the more difficult it becomes for MNC head offices to impose standard approaches and procedures on them, and this will be reinforced where companies seek to take advantage of arbitrage opportunities arising from institutional differences and the provision of particular kinds of collective competition goods. Both the degree and the scope of corporate integration of economic activities across national borders may well, then, be rather less than some enthusiasts for global firms suggest, as global markets encourage sectoral specialization rather than diversification, and arbitrage opportunities become as significant as aggregation economies.

Considering next how more alliance-based cross-border economic coordination and control might be likely to develop as transnational governance becomes more established, the increasing level of contractual certainty (Gessner 2009b) in international commerce has additionally facilitated cross-border integration though various forms of inter-firm agreements and partnerships, as several recent accounts have emphasized (Herrigel and Zeitlin 2010; Kristensen et al. 2011). While largely remaining dependent on national legal systems for enforcement, and constraining economic opportunism only to the extent found in many Anglophone societies, the growing reliability of transnational business regulation has enabled many companies to undertake international collaborations that appear to be more long lasting and involve greater mutual commitments than spot market transactions based mostly on economic power.

Especially where product architectures are highly integrated so that modularization is difficult, and competitiveness depends greatly on the organizational integration of problem-solving and continuous improvement activities, firms facing increasing pressures to respond to foreign customers' demands are investing in upgrading their suppliers' capabilities in lower-cost locations so that they can become more flexible in foreign markets (Herrigel and Zeitlin 2010; Sako 2003). Although some MNCs may have originally intended to operate at arm's length from their new suppliers in low-cost economies, and focus on price reductions, as local foreign markets become more important and differentiated, many are developing more collaborative and responsive capabilities in their operations abroad.

The extent to which such integration of key tasks leads to risk sharing and mutual trust more generally remains highly variable, though, as MacDuffie and Helper point out (2006: 428–56). Close collaboration and technology sharing between large assemblers and their suppliers on operational matters such as design and engineering can be quite high without necessarily implying that the purchasing regime is equally cooperative and mutually trusting. A similar distinction between operational collaboration and strategic or governance cooperation was found in a study of customer–supplier relations at a British airport where the airport authority, baggage handling companies, airlines, and air traffic control agencies were forced to work closely together on day-to-day tasks, but were much more adversarial and antagonistic in their strategic dealings with each other (Lelievre-Finch 2008). It is a mistake, then, to assume that increasing international customer-supplier cooperation and information-sharing on task matters automatically means closer trust on governance matters. These latter seem much more affected by institutional constraints and what MacDuffie and Helper (2006: 453) term 'legacy modes of exchange', that is, effective practices that have largely been developed in firms' domestic environments.

Insofar, then, as the emerging system of international governance remains primarily concerned with ensuring regulatory transparency, equal treatment for domestic and foreign firms and contractual reliability, and is opposed to both restrictions on competitive behaviour and collaboration between companies, it is unlikely to encourage strong cross-border alliances of the kind found in Japanese business groups, or substantial cooperation within trade associations, as in some continental European societies. Rather, inter-firm cooperation across national boundaries seems likely to be quite narrowly focused on a limited range of activities and to be more restricted in time than that common in highly coordinated economies where there are relatively strong institutional constraints on free riders and similar forms of short-term opportunism.

The internationalization of regional industrial districts similar to those found in postwar Italy, Jutland, and elsewhere in Europe is, then, going to be difficult to sustain in the absence of strong cross-border institutions that limit predatory pricing, poaching, and so on. Although firms in some Italian industrial districts have tried to establish collaborative relationships with suppliers and competitors in low-cost countries such as China (Bellandi and Caloffi 2008), this has met with limited success so far. Furthermore, some Chinese firms are establishing units with emigrant Chinese labour in Italy to be able to label their products as being 'Made in Italy' and undercut Italian producers' prices considerably, thus threatening the continued viability of certain local industrial district patterns of collaboration and competition in towns such as Prato (Dinmore 2010).

Instead, project team forms of international cooperation seem more likely, such as those found in some technology intensive and highly dynamic sectors, in which firms and groups of skilled workers collaborate on specific tasks and purposes for limited periods (Whitley 2006). For instance, cross-national teams are increasingly providing problem-solving services in consultancy and other knowledge-intensive business services (Miozzo and Grimshaw 2006). The formation and coordination of such teams are greatly facilitated by mutual recognition, if not international standardization, of skills as well as by the modularization of production and service chains. This last feature of sectoral organization enables relatively small groups to collaborate in developing specific components or parts of systems, rather than having to integrate the development, production, and sale of large complex systems such as commercial aircraft.

The significance of modularization for cross-border integration highlights the importance of sectoral variations in patterns of international economic coordination and control. To the extent that transnational governance is becoming both stronger and more reliable in supporting distinctive economic rationalities that are relatively separate from political economic dominance, and largely reflects the institutions of liberal market economies, we would expect considerable differences to arise in how firms in different industries manage relationships with suppliers, customers, and competitors.

As Herrigel and Zeitlin (2010) emphasize, where product architectures are highly integrated, such that component specifications cannot be readily altered in isolation, and modularization is limited, cross-border collaboration tends to be wider ranging and more extensive than in some parts of the electronics industry where modularization is more common and arm's length, spot market like contracting more frequently practised (Ernst 2006; Sturgeon 2002). Overall, then, the degree and scope of transnational alliance coordination and control are unlikely to be greatly increased by the recent expansion of transnational governance, and in any case will vary between sectors.

Considering next the changing relationships between MNCs and their domestic institutional context as internationalization of markets and regulation increases, the more leading firms internationalize major parts of their operations, the more the authority of domestic institutions and groups over their competitive strategies can be expected to decline. This is especially likely if they actively seek to learn from abroad and locate key activities in quite different kinds of institutional environments where the rules of the competitive game vary considerably from those in their home economy. German banks competing with Anglophone investment banks in London and New York, for instance, are much more likely to become relatively detached from their home economy than those focused on domestic customers and networks. This detachment will be reinforced when foreign investors increase their shareholdings, and firms become quoted on major foreign stock markets.

However, there are a number of factors that are likely to limit such separation from domestic institutions and interests. First, the more a firm's distinctive competences are seen by managers to depend on its domestic business environment and the collective competition goods it provides, the less it is likely to pursue internationalization strategies that weaken its domestic ties. This is especially so where, second, home economy institutions also provide security against hostile takeovers and radical changes in corporate governance. The combination of strong, cohesive, and complementary institutions that encourage the collaborative development of effective organizational capabilities with a weak market for corporate control and relatively low rates of inward FDI seems likely to inhibit managers' wishes to detach themselves from their home economy, as well as limiting their delegation of key competences to foreign subsidiaries.

In any event, firms from supportive home environments can, and do, invest in foreign operations without necessarily withdrawing from domestic alliances, as numerous companies from corporatist economies have done in the past thirty or so years. In some cases, they have experimented with novel working practices and managerial strategies in environments that were more supportive of such innovations than their domestic ones. Arguably, many German car manufacturers have combined incremental changes in their home society with such experiments abroad as international competition for high quality goods has intensified (Boyer 1998; Lane 2001).

A third factor restricting MNC detachment from domestic institutions and actors is the size and attractiveness of the home market. Where firms have developed successfully in a large domestic market that remains attractive, it seems unlikely that they will wish to distance themselves from it, or to search for quite new knowledge and competences from other societies. Despite Japanese banks being involved with foreign capital markets for some decades, for example, few have actively sought to transform themselves into radically different kinds of enterprises and detach themselves from their domestic environment and business partners.

Indeed, hardly any have tried to integrate their experience of foreign markets with their home operations, or to use internationally experienced employees' expertise to improve domestic practices (Morgan et al. 2003; Sakai 2000; Whitley et al. 2003). Nomura's recent acquisition of some Lehman Brothers staff and assets in Europe and Asia represents perhaps the most determined effort of any Japanese bank to 'learn from abroad'. It is only when companies become clearly uncompetitive and/or the domestic environment changes substantially through, for instance, major regulatory shifts that they might seek alternative collective competition goods and to learn from abroad, as perhaps has been the case for some Japanese pharmaceutical firms (Lam 2003).

In contrast, firms that develop their distinctive capabilities and competitive competences in greater isolation from business partners, domestic skilled workers, and institutions in the broader socio-economic environment are likely to be more willing to detach themselves from home economy institutions and groups, and to extend domestically developed capabilities and business models internationally. Especially in capital market dominated financial systems that are becoming more internationalized, such firms have limited ties to domestic banks and investors, and will be encouraged by the emerging system of international business regulation to separate themselves further from domestic economy actors and long-term interdependence with their institutions. Even here, though, MNCs often rely on their home state agencies to support their interests, particularly where those states are large and powerful as in the case of the USA, and take care to maintain their connections with domestic political and other allies.

Considering finally the changing authority of host economy institutions and actors over MNCs, this can be expected to grow as increasingly effective transnational governance makes it more feasible for some companies to engage in institutional arbitrage and invest in assets and capabilities abroad to improve their overall competences. Such increasing involvement with foreign agencies and authoritative groups seems most likely when, on the one hand, domestic institutions weaken in their cohesion, complementarity, and provision of collective competition goods, and the domestic market becomes too limited and/or competitive, and, on the other hand, foreign markets, assets, and collective competition goods grow in significance. Thus, firms from: a) smaller economies and/or, b) whose capabilities seem to decline in their effectiveness and/or, c) whose domestic institutions fail to provide appropriate and highly valued support compared to foreign ones will probably be the most willing to learn from abroad and adapt to prevalent norms and practices in other markets.

Additionally, considerable delegation of operational and some strategic autonomy to foreign subsidiaries is more likely when firms make substantial investments in large and wealthy political economies dominated by cohesive and strong, established institutional regimes that pressure MNCs to adapt to the local context and business partners. To become successful in these kinds of societies, foreign firms have to adjust their practices and business models to suit customers and employees, as well as local regulatory institutions, as many firms have found in Japan. This need not necessarily, though, lead to MNCs integrating such novel ways of working in other parts of the firm. That would depend on the extent to which such foreign markets become crucial for firm growth and domestic institutions are seen as too constraining and/or failing to provide appropriate collective competition goods. A further feature of the environment that can affect such adaptation and learning concerns the ownership and control of MNCs, especially the interests and power of domestic shareholders who may be unwilling to accept foreign corporate governance structures or strategic shifts that imply a weakening of domestic commitments.

Concluding remarks

In summary, the postwar opening of product markets to foreign competition and investment, coupled with the liberalization of capital markets in many countries and expansion of international business regulation limiting discriminatory support for domestic firms, have encouraged cross-border managerial integration of economic activities and greatly enlarged markets for many goods and services. These developments, in turn, have enabled internationalizing companies to narrow the range of different kinds of products they offer while acquiring strategic assets and competences in foreign economies. Such corporate integration of economic activities and resources across national boundaries can potentially enhance MNCs competitive capabilities and ability to realize economies of arbitrage, while reducing their dependence on domestic institutions, interest groups, and collective competition goods. It increases the variety of different kinds of firms operating in national political economies, how they compete and cooperate, and reduces the homogenizing authority of nationally specific institutional regimes governing economic coordination and control. As a result, the coherence and distinctiveness of some national business systems and varieties of capitalism that became established after the end of the Second World War have declined.

This pattern of increasing internationalization of firms and product and capital markets since the collapse of the Bretton Woods System, and greater sectoral heterogeneity of firm governance and behaviour in some national economies remains, though, limited in degree and scope. Despite the considerable growth in FDI and capital mobility compared to the 1950s, most markets remain governed by predominantly national legal systems and other institutions regulating economic activities. The establishment of a fully autonomous global system of economic coordination and control governed by supranational institutions in which globally integrated MNCs compete in worldwide markets as independent strategic actors pursuing transnational economic logics seems as improbable in the twenty-first century as the construction of a stable system of world political integration. Rather, the degree and scope of corporate and institutional authority over economic activity within and between national economies seem likely to continue to vary considerably.

In the case of corporate authority, the more that MNCs seek to improve their organizational capabilities and competitive competences through accessing knowledge, skills, and collective competition goods in foreign locations by adapting to local business partners and institutions, the more limited becomes their ability to impose central control over subsidiary strategies and procedures. This is especially so when key competences are closely dependent on national institutions and patterns of collaboration, as in, for instance, the German skills machine (Culpepper and Finegold 1999). While realizing economies of arbitrage and organizing a vertical division of labour of activities between particular locations, as Ghemawat (2003) urges, do imply considerable MNC corporate authority and transnational integration, the degree and scope of such control are inherently limited by the need for units to adapt to, and take advantage of, location-specific opportunities. Thus, while the general level of cross-border corporate authority may have increased in the late twentieth century as a result of changing ICT, opening of markets, and regulatory shifts, it is restricted by the continuing institutional variety and location-specificity of strategic assets and opportunities of national markets, as well as the continued dominance of national legal systems, forms of corporate governance, and market rule-setting.

A fortiori, similar arguments apply to cross-border cooperation and partnerships. Increasing contractual certainty and regulatory reforms may support the development of longer-term collaboration between companies than spot market contracting based on political economic power, but the arm's length nature of most transnational governance institutions and their ultimate dependence on diverse national legal and administrative systems for enforcement limit their ability to constrain opportunistic behaviour, such as free riding, and are unlikely to encourage intensive mutual commitments. At least as long as global law and similar institutions remain largely constructed by shifting—and often unstable—coalitions of law firms, MNCs, different national regulators and court systems, this situation seems unlikely to change.

Turning next to consider the changing nature of domestic institutions' authority over firms, product, capital and labour markets, this seems likely to have declined as many firms become able to access collective competition goods elsewhere. Firms are also more able to resist the demands of local interest groups, especially those of organized labour, as their share register becomes more open to foreign investors and they make major investments abroad. However, many internationalizing companies remain interdependent with domestic business partners and agencies when improving their key capabilities, and are unlikely to become fully detached from their home base. This is especially so when it: a) supports the position of strategic managers, b) provides a large market in which they continue to thrive and have considerable influence, and, c) continues to provide critical assets.

Furthermore, increasing exposure to foreign markets and learning from abroad need not always, or indeed very often, imply a rejection of domestic institutions and interests. MNCs are quite capable of continuing to draw on home economy-supported capabilities and knowledge whilst benefiting from foreign partners and institutions. However, the diversity of leading companies' governance, growth strategies, and competitive behaviour within national borders does seems likely to grow in the twenty-first century as long as most markets remain open, especially between firms in different industrial sectors and with different degrees of investment in foreign locations.

Finally, increasing foreign involvement in different host economies need not necessarily lead many firms to adapt greatly to their dominant institutional arrangements and respond to their interest groups' concerns, as the behaviour of some MNCs in emerging economies illustrates. However, the more important such foreign markets become to inward investors, and the more their key strategic assets gain much of their value from being embedded in the local business environment and partnerships, the more significant the authority of host economy institutions and groups seems likely to become. This is especially so where dominant institutions are mutually reinforcing with respect to the behaviour of firms and market rules, and there is a stable political-economic dominant coalition pursuing distinctive national economic goals. Thus, as MNCs invest more in accessing collective competition goods abroad to develop their own competences, and the more these are closely interdependent with national institutions and interests, the more willing they should be to adapt to them. However, such adaptation may remain nationally specific, even when the host economy is large and attractive, if its dominant political economic system is highly idiosyncratic and/or remains unattractive to the wider MNC. Additionally, MNCs may limit their exposure to a particular regime by locating complementary assets in third countries to reduce political and commercial risks, as some have done in China.

References

Amable, Bruno (2003) *The Diversity of Modern Capitalism*, Oxford: Oxford University Press.

Bellandi, M. and A. Caloffi (2008) 'District Internationalisation and Trans-local Development', *Entrepreneurship and Regional Development*, 20: 517–32.

Bowers, David (2010) 'Greece will leave its mark long after the dust has settled,' *Financial Times*, 29 April, 32.

Boyer, Robert (1998) 'Hybridization and Models of Production: Geography, history and theory,' pp. 23–56 in R. Boyer, E. Charron, U. Jurgens and S. Tolliday (eds) *Between Imitation and Innovation: The transfer and hybridization of productive models in the international automobile industry*, Oxford: Oxford University Press.

Braithwaite, John and Peter Drahos (2000) *Global Business Regulation*, Cambridge: Cambridge University Press.

Crouch, Colin (2005) *Capitalist Diversity and Change: Recombinant governance and institutional entrepreneurs*, Oxford: Oxford University Press.

Culpepper, Pepper and David Finegold (1999) (eds) *The German Skills Machine: Sustaining comparative advantage in a global economy*, New York: Berghahn Books.

Dinmore, Guy (2010) 'Tuscan town turns against Chinese immigrants', *Financial Times*, 9 February, 12.

Djelic, Marie-Laure and Kerstin Sahlin-Andersson (eds) (2006) *Transnational Governance: Institutional dynamics of regulation*, Cambridge: Cambridge University Press.

Doremus, P. N., W. W. Keller, L. W. Pauly, and S. Reich (1998) *The Myth of the Global Corporation*, Princeton, N. J.: Princeton University Press.

Duina, Francesco (1999) *Harmonizing Europe: Nation-states within the Common Market*, Albany, New York: State University of New York Press.

Ernst, Dieter (2006) 'Searching for a New Role in East Asian Regionalization-Japanese Production Networks in the electronics Industry', pp. 161–87 in P. J. Katzenstein and

T. Shiraishi (eds) *Beyond Japan: The dynamics of East Asian regionalization*, Ithaca: Cornell University Press.

Evans, Peter (1994) *Embedded Autonomy: States and industrial transformation*, Princeton, N. J.: Princeton University Press.

Fafchamps, Marcel (1996) 'The Enforcement of Commercial Contracts in Ghana', *World Development*, 24: 427–48.

Forsgren, Mats. U Holm and J. Johansen (2005) *Managing the Embedded Multinational*, Cheltenham: Edward Elgar.

Gessner, Volkmar (2009a) 'Theories of Change—The Governance of Business Transactions in Globalising Economies', pp. 175–213 in Gessner (ed.) *Contractual Certainty in International Trade*, Oxford: Hart.

—— (ed.) (2009b) *Contractual Certainty in International Trade*, Oxford: Hart.

Ghemawat, Pankaj (2003) 'Semiglobalization and International Business Strategy', *Journal of International Business Studies*, 34: 138–52.

—— (2007) *Redefining Global Strategy: Crossing borders in a world where differences still matter'*, Boston: Harvard Business School Press.

Hall, R. B. and T. J. Bierstecker (eds) (2002) *The Emergence of Private Authority in Global Governance*, Cambridge: Cambridge University Press.

Herrigel, Gary and Jonathan Zeitlin (2010) 'Inter-Firm Relations in Global Manufacturing: Disintegrated Production and Its Globalization', pp. 527–61 in G. Morgan et al. (eds) *Oxford Handbook of Comparative Institutional Analysis*, Oxford: Oxford University Press.

Humphrey, John and Hubert Schmitz (1998) 'Trust and Inter-firm Relations in Developing and Transition Economies', *Journal of Development Studies*, 34: 32–61.

Knill, Christoph (2001) *The Europeanisation of National Administrations*, Cambridge: Cambridge University Press.

Kristensen, P. H., M. Lotz, and R. Rocha (2011) 'Denmark: Tailoring flexicurity for changing roles in global games', pp. 86–140 in P. H. Kristensen and K. Lilja (eds) *Nordic Capitalisms and Globalization: New forms of economic organization and welfare institutions*, Oxford: Oxford University Press.

—— and Jonathan Zeitlin (2005) *Local Players in Global Games: The strategic constitution of a multinational corporation*, Oxford: Oxford University Press.

Lam, Alice (2003) 'Organisational Learning in Multinationals: R&D networks of Japanese and U.S. MNEs in the U.K', *Journal of Management Studies*, 40: 673–704.

Lane, Christel (2001) 'The Emergence of German Transnational Companies: A theoretical analysis and empirical study of the globalization process', pp. 69–96 in G. Morgan, P. H. Kristensen and R. Whitley (eds) *The Multinational Firm: Organizing across institutional and national divides*, Oxford: Oxford University Press.

Lelievre-Finch, Dominique (2008) *Changing Forms of Inter-firm Governance within Supply Chains and the Building of Firms' Capabilities*, unpublished PhD thesis, Manchester Business School, University of Manchester.

MacDuffie, John Paul and Susan Helper (2006) 'Collaboration in Supply Chains: With and without trust', pp. 417–66 in C. Heckscher and P. Adler (eds) *The Firm as a Collaborative Community*, Oxford: Oxford University Press.

Majone, Giandomenico (2005) *Dilemmas of European Integration: The ambiguities and pitfalls of integration by stealth*, Oxford: Oxford University Press.

Malnight, Thomas W. (1995) 'Globalization of an Ethnocentric Firm: An evolutionary perspective', *Strategic Management Journal*, 16: 119–41.
Meyer, Klaus (2006) 'Globalfocusing: From domestic conglomerate to global specialists', *Journal of Management Studies*, 43: 1109–44.
Miozzo, Marcela and Damian Grimshaw (eds) (2006) *Knowledge Intensive Business Services: Organizational forms and national institutions*, Cheltenham: Edward Elgar.
Morgan, Glenn and Lars Engwall (eds) (1999) *Regulation and Organizations: International perspectives*, London: Routledge and Kegan Paul.
—— Bill Kelly, Diana Sharpe, and Richard Whitley (2003) 'Global Managers and Japanese Multinationals: Internationalisation and management in Japanese financial institutions', *International Journal of Human Resource Management*, 14: 1–19.
—— and Sigrid Quack (2005) 'Internationalization and Capability Development in Professional Service Firms', pp. 277–311 in G. Morgan, R. Whitley and E. Moen (eds) *Changing Capitalisms?* Oxford: Oxford University Press.
—— —— (2010) 'Law as a Governing Institution', pp. 275–308 in G. Morgan et al. (eds) *The Oxford Handbook of Comparative Institutional Analysis*, Oxford: Oxford University Press.
—— Richard Whitley, and Eli Moen (eds) (2005) *Changing Capitalisms? Internationalisation, Institutional change and systems of economic organisation*, Oxford: Oxford University Press.
Obstfeld, Maurice and Alan Taylor (1998) 'The Great Depression as a Watershed: International capital mobility over the long run', in M. D. Bordo, C. Goldin and E. N. White (eds) *The Defining Moment: The American economy in the twentieth century*, Chicago: University of Chicago Press.
Pauly, Louis (2002) 'Global Finance, Political Authority, and the Problem of Legitimation', pp. 76–90 in *The Emergence of Private Authority in Global Governance*, edited by Rodney Bruce Hall and Thomas Biersteker, Cambridge: Cambridge University Press.
Porter, Tony (1994) *States, Markets and Regimes in Global Finance*, London: Macmillan.
Quack, Sigrid (2007) 'Legal Professionals and Transnational Law-making: A case of distributed agency', *Organization*, 14: 643–66.
Sakai, Junko (2000) *Japanese Bankers in the City of London*, London: Routledge.
Sako, Mari (2003) 'Modularity and Outsourcing: The nature of co-evolution of product architecture and organization architecture of the global automobile industry', pp. 229–53 in A. Prencipe, A. Davies and M. Hobday (eds) *The Business of Systems Integration*, Oxford: Oxford University Press.
Scharpf, Fritz (2010) 'The Asymmetry of European Integration, or why the EU Cannot be a "Social Market Economy"', *Socio-Economic Review*, 8: 211–50.
Sturgeon, Timothy (2002) 'Modular Production Networks: A new American model of industrial organization', *Industrial and Corporate Change*, 11: 451–96.
Tolliday, Steven (2000) 'Transplanting the American Model? US Automobile Companies and the Transfer of Technology and Management to Britain, France, and Germany, 1928–1962', pp. 76–119 in J. Zeitlin and G. Herrigel (eds) *Americanization and its Limits: Reworking US technology and management in post-war Europe and Japan*, Oxford: Oxford University Press.

Weiss, Linda (ed.) (2003) *States in the Global Economy: Bringing institutions back in*, Cambridge: Cambridge University Press.

Westney, Eleanor (2001) 'Japan', pp. 623–51 in A. Rugman and T. Brewer (eds) *Oxford Handbook of International Business*, Oxford: Oxford University Press.

Whitley, Richard (2006) 'Project-based Firms: New organisational form or variations on a theme?' *Industrial and Corporate Change*, 15: 77–99.

—— (2007) *Business Systems and Organisational Capabilities*, Oxford: Oxford University Press.

—— (2010) 'The Institutional Construction of Firms', pp. 453–95 in G. Morgan et al (eds) *The Oxford Handbook of Comparative Institutional Analysis*, Oxford: Oxford University Press.

—— and Laszlo Czaban (1998) 'Institutional Transformation and Enterprise Change in an Emergent Capitalist Economy: The case of Hungary', *Organization Studies*, 19: 259–80.

Whitley, Richard, J. Henderson, L. Czaban, and G. Lengyel (1996) 'Trust and Contractual Relations in an Emerging Capitalist Economy', *Organization Studies*, 17: 397–420.

—— Glenn Morgan, William Kelly, and Diana Sharpe (2003) 'The Changing Japanese MNC', *Journal of Management Studies*, 40: 639–68.

Yamamura, Kozo and Wolfgang Streeck (eds) (2003) *The End of Diversity? Prospects for German and Japanese Capitalism*, Ithaca, New York: Cornell University Press.

10

Public Research Systems, Career Structures, and the Commercialization of Academic Science in Different Capitalisms*

Steven Casper

Introduction

Within advanced industrial economies, universities are increasingly viewed as an important source of societally useful knowledge, and many states have initiated policies encouraging them to play a more active role in commercializing research results (Stokes 1997; Hage 2011). Significant national differences in the extent and manner in which universities engage in such commercialization activities and contribute to technological innovations do, however, remain. While much research on national systems of innovation has shown how the embeddedness of universities within broader economic and political institutions can explain these variations (Lundvall 1992; Nelson 1993), the existing literature on commercialization processes lacks an organizational component linking macro-institutional analyses with more micro-organizational processes, such as those discussed by Whitley (2003).

The premise of this chapter is that the processes through which academics successfully engage in commercialization activities are primarily conditioned by organizational incentives and constraints structured by national research systems. Regulatory frameworks, such as the US Bayh-Dole Act, establish a legal foundation for establishment and ownership of intellectual property surrounding university discoveries, and have been used by universities as the basis to create strong financial incentives for professors to become active

* Acknowledgement: I thank Richard Whitley for insightful comments and editorial help that had a major impact on the development of this chapter.

in commercialization. It seems unlikely, however, that professors would dedicate resources to commercialization activities, especially time-intensive projects such as launching a university spin-off, unless doing so had a neutral and more likely a beneficial effect on the core non-market goals of the laboratory. The chapter explores how involvement in commercialization activities can be used to improve the competitiveness of scientific laboratories to varying degrees within different national research systems, and thus to contribute to our understanding of the continuing contrasts in patterns of research commercialization between differently organized public science systems.

A large comparative institutional literature has examined variations in commercial innovation that are linked to different 'models of capitalism' (Amable 2003; Hollingsworth and Boyer 1997; Whitley 1999; Hall and Soskice 2001; Crouch 2005). Within this literature, micro-foundations have been created linking national institutional frameworks to organizational strategies of managers, skilled workers, and other actors across different types of economies (see e.g. Casper and Whitley 2004). This approach has explored, for example, how in the United States—shareholder-based corporate governance institutions, capital market oriented financial institutions, and largely deregulated labour markets support organizational strategies associated with Silicon Valley type new technology start-ups, which can be conducive to radical innovation (see Casper 2007a, ch. 3). In Germany, by contrast, a stake-holder oriented corporate governance framework, primarily credit-based system of corporate finance, and more regulated markets facilitate credible commitments between highly skilled employees and firms to invest in tacit, firm-specific knowledge investments that are not easily tradable on an open marketplace. Such skill investments have been linked to Germany's long-term competitiveness in many medium-technology or 'incrementally innovative' industries, such as machine tools or automobiles (see Streeck 1992, 2009).

In this chapter, I apply a similar mode of institutional analysis to understand how differences in the organization of labour markets and public science systems structure the commitment and effectiveness of academic commercialization activities cross-nationally. Initially, I summarize Whitley's synthesis of different types of public research systems, and then consider how this framework can be applied to the United States and Germany, countries with strongly contrasting national research systems.

The bulk of the chapter then analyses key patterns of competition across scientific laboratories within contrasting national research systems, and explores how the development of commercial ties could enhance the capabilities of a particular laboratory within a given institutional context. Across most countries, scientific research takes place with primarily hierarchically organized scientific laboratories, employing a senior professor and any number of junior scientists. National research systems have a fundamental impact on how such laboratories are funded, on career progression patterns for junior scientists, and on broader labour market organization. The analysis here pays particular attention to labour market dynamics within different research systems, exploring at a micro-level how national research system institutions affect patterns of competition at the laboratory level within the United States and Germany. To provide empirical support for key claims, the chapter also presents short empirical case studies of the organization of labour markets within the cell biology field in the United States, and labour market ties between academic labs and spin-offs in Germany.

The impact of research system institutions on public knowledge production

In recent years sociologists of science have linked the organization of research systems to the production of different types of public knowledge. A premise behind such thinking is that some types of public knowledge are particularly useful to society. Hollingsworth (2009), for example, has adopted an organizational sociology perspective to explore the link between organizational structures within universities, primarily at the department level, and the development of interdisciplinary research environments linked to the production of major research discoveries. Jong (2006) has applied a similar perspective to help explain why, during the 1970s, the University of California San Francisco, but not the University of California at Berkeley, took an early lead in applying genetic engineering techniques to medical problems, which led to early commercialization efforts in the field of biotechnology (for similar comparisons focused on engineering see Kenney and Goe 2004 and Adams 2009).

While important, such research focused at the organizational level of analysis either ignores, or implicitly controls for, institutional factors surrounding the organization of research systems that vary at the national level and can help explain important differences in the production of science and technology across countries at particular historical junctures. The German research system during the early twentirth century, for example, is commonly claimed to have fostered numerous discoveries in physics, chemistry, and other basic science fields (Murmann 2003; Lehrer et al. 2009), while the US research system during the post-World War II period has gained pre-eminence in many fields, but particularly the life sciences.

How do national research systems affect the pattern by which knowledge is commercialized? A useful starting point is Whitley's (2003) typology of the institutional organization of different types of research systems, and the influence such institutional structures have on types of public knowledge production. Whitley's starting point on knowledge production is broadly analogous to the distinction between 'radical innovation' and 'incremental innovation' that has been popularized within comparative business system research. Whitley focuses on two outputs of public research systems: the intensity of reputational competition and the level of intellectual pluralism or flexibility within a given research system. He argues that research systems with intense reputational competition across researchers and high intellectual flexibility will encourage 'intellectual risk taking and varied, changeable approaches to common problems' (pg. 1019; Table 1)—which in turn can lead to discontinuous or radical innovations within a scientific field. Research systems with lower levels of intellectual competition and less pluralism, on the other hand, encourage longer-term investments and planning, which conduce towards 'incremental intellectual innovation' (pg. 1919; Table 1).

In a mode of analysis analogous to comparative institutional studies of business systems, Whitley explores several elements of public research systems. Institutional factors highlighted by Whitley (2003: 1021–4) include:

1) The extent to which funders and employers delegate control over research goals, performance, and assessment to practitioners through competitive peer review procedures.
2) Institutional differences in how work is organized and controlled within universities, as well as in the procedures governing promotion and other rewards.
3) Degree of concentration of intellectual prestige and control over the allocation of resources across research organizations.
4) Organizational rigidity and segmentation of goals and resources between different employment units.

Whitley is careful to point out that variation over these four factors exists across numerous research systems, and dominant ideal-typical institutional designs applicable across numerous country examples may not exist empirically in any one public science system. Nonetheless, to describe these concepts in more detail and help anticipate the more detailed examination of academic commercialization incentives below, it is useful to characterize the United States and German research systems using Whitley's dimensions. Table 10.1 and the short discussion below summarize the two systems for much of the postwar period using the Whitley framework.

Within the United States competitive peer-review systems are widely used to allocate research funding, evaluate research articles for publication, and assess career performance (see Geiger 1986). Department structures within the US are highly decentralized and routinely employ several senior professors who rotate administrative responsibilities. While many elite research universities do exist, there is no stable and long-term hierarchy of institutions, and

Table 10.1. Whitley's public research system characteristics, applied to Germany and the United States

Research System Characteristic	US Research System	German Research System
Extent to which funding, assessment and performance decisions are made through competitive peer review	**High**; most funding from competitive grant processes; extensive use of peer reviews for performance assessment and hiring decisions	**Low to medium**; Full professors have long-term funding and control most hiring and promotion within departments; modest competition for peer reviewed grant funding
Work organization and labor markets	**Decentralized** department structures; rotating department heads; several full professors; fragmented research programs within departments	**Centralized**; 'full professor' controls department hiring and research program over the long-term
Hierarchy of prestige across universities	**Low to medium**; no fixed hierarchy, universities compete for status and prestige	**Low**; little hierarchy or status differentials across universities
Organizational rigidity and segmentation of goals and resources	**Low**; little segmentation between	**High**; division of labor between research universities; specialized research institutes, and applied technical universities

Sources: Categories and terminology from Whitley 2003. Characteristics of US and German systems from Ben-David 1968; Enders 2001; Geiger 1986.

competition for funding and the recruitment of professors, junior scientists, and students is fierce. Finally, there is relatively low segmentation of goals and labour markets between universities. The same university may have both strong basic science departments and strong industry-related research schools in engineering and other technological fields. Within Whitley's framework the postwar United States public science system is a good example of a research system encouraging a high amount of reputational competition and intellectual pluralism, the antecedents of radically innovative knowledge production.

The German system has changed considerably over the last century (Ben-David 1968; Lehrer et al. 2009), developing in the post World War II era into a relatively homogeneous model, in the sense that funding mechanisms, organizational structures, and career patterns are relatively uniform across most universities. The central unit of analysis in the German system is the full professor (Enders 2001), who controls long-term funding for research and hiring surrounding his or her area of specialization (see Schimank 2005; Harley et al. 2004). As a result, competitive peer reviewed funding for research projects has been less important within the German system. Additionally, partly because universities are controlled by the states or *Laender*, they are not organized into a strong hierarchy of prestige. However, there is a strong division of labour across different types of research organizations. Most basic research is concentrated within research universities and stand-alone research institutes such as those of the Max Planck Society, while technical universities and polytechnic universities (*Fachhochschuhlen*) carry out more applied, industry-focused research (see Ben-David 1968). In sum, Germany is a strong example of a system which, again according to Whitley's framework, conduces towards more long-term knowledge production within scientific laboratories.

The comparative institutional analysis of knowledge production helps shed light on the availability of different kinds of academic knowledge within a given country, that is available for commercialization. However, this analysis does not examine the mechanisms by which such commercialization takes place, nor does it explore how research system incentives and support shape scientists engaged in commercialization activities. The next sections of the paper explores in more detail how patterns of competition within a particular research system, especially those surrounding career structures of scientists, help to shape incentives for professors to become involved in commercialization.

Career dynamics and incentives for professors to commercialize

While national research systems most strongly shape the competitive dynamics of university laboratories, in recent years market forces have created new opportunities for professors. In many research fields, but especially those areas that affect medical research, companies increasingly view academic research findings as directly relevant to corporate R&D (see Lam 2007). Technology oriented firms have strong incentives to develop collaborations with leading university scientists. Research on new technology ventures has shown that firms founded by prominent university scientists tend to be more successful than firms without such ties. Zucker et al. (1998), for instance, have shown in the case of biotechnology that companies founded by 'star scientists', measured by forward citation counts to their publications, have a higher likelihood of achieving initial public offerings on stock markets, an important milestone in the development of entrepreneurial technology firms. This argument rests partly on the assumption that scientific research linked to prominent scientists has a higher commercial potential compared to research of lesser-known scientists. However, association with a star-scientist may also help raise the status of a fledging start-up (Higgins and Gulati 2003). Doing so might help a company raise financing from venture capitalists and attract talented personnel. For these reasons, entrepreneurs and venture capitalists have a strong motive to cultivate relationships with prominent professors, helping to institutionalize the role of professors within the biotechnology industry.

While companies may have strong incentives to forge collaborations with prominent university scientists, less well understood are the incentives motivating scientists to become involved in commercialization. To explore this theme, this section examines how commercialization opportunities affect patterns of competition to produce public knowledge within different national research systems. The analysis will show how the increased opportunity of university laboratories to interact with established companies or, at times, engage in entrepreneurial processes of 'spinning-off' technologies into new companies, affects the competitive capabilities of labs.

Research within many of the natural sciences is commonly conducted by teams of scientists within laboratories. The modern scientific laboratory is an organization (see e.g. Knorr-Cetina 1999). Within most research systems laboratories are organized in a relatively hierarchical manner. The professor running the lab, or principle investigator, is responsible for setting the broad research priorities within the laboratory, raising research funding, and recruiting junior scientists, both PhD students and Postdoctoral Fellows (or postdocs) into the laboratory. While numerous factors influence the ability of a professor to develop a successful scientific research programme, it is useful to focus on two key competences: acquiring research funding and attracting talented junior scientists. The laboratory organizations managed by professors must compete for these resources. Professors able to secure sustainable funding necessary to equip and staff large laboratories with exceptional junior scientists are more likely to perform well in creating public knowledge that is valued within scientific communities.

While labs compete for money and scientific staff members, this is primarily within a non-market setting that is structured differently in different national research systems. These strongly influence (and often legally determine) the organization of universities, departments, and the career structures of academic scientists (Whitley 2003). Commercial ties may, however, provide opportunities for professors to heighten the competitive position of their laboratories, though within an institutional context strongly shaped by national research systems. The following revisits the US–Germany comparison. A brief overview of institutional frameworks governing commercialization is provided within both country contexts, followed by an analysis of how the development of intellectual property, and commercial ties surrounding it, can impact a lab's reputation and competitive position within each research system.

a) Commercialization dynamics within the United States research system

The United States government has established legal frameworks that encourage the commercialization of university research. Widespread efforts by universities to commercialize research began after the passage, in 1980, of the Bayh Dole Act by the United States Congress (for an overview, see Mowery et al. 2004). This legislation established property rights over all federally funded research and, in most cases, transferred ownership to universities. In exchange for receiving ownership of federally funded research, universities are expected to steward this intellectual property and guide its effective commercialization. Most universities responded to the passage of Bayh-Dole by developing technology licensing and transfer offices (TLOs), which assumed responsibility over commercialization processes. Typical duties of TLOs include working with faculty in creating invention disclosures that form the basis for patent applications, filing applications, and then licensing the resulting intellectual property to either existing companies or to start-up companies that are 'spun off' from the university.

Universities within the United States, both public and private, routinely raise substantial endowments, primarily through gifts from alumni. Some US universities have raised endowments of over a billion dollars, while most universities have endowments ranging from tens to hundreds of millions of dollars (Pope 2006), which have supported the initial operations of technology transfer offices. This includes hiring professional staff who can work with scientists to develop invention disclosures and then negotiate licences with companies. In addition to human resource expenses, licensing offices must cover patenting costs, which can run as high as $50,000 to $100,000 for patents with international coverage (Rauber 1997).

The establishment of technology licensing offices at most major universities within the US, coupled with the establishment of national rules governing intellectual property for university research, has helped drive closer university–industry relationships. Research on university licensing has found that the majority of university technology licences generate little or no profits (AUTM 2008). However, a small number of licences, often surrounding patents for successful drugs or important enabling technologies, can be worth tens, even hundreds of millions of dollars in yearly revenue (see Scherer and Harhoff 2001). Universities can also earn substantial revenue from equity holdings in spin-off companies that become successful. The allure of such profits creates an incentive for universities to encourage commercialization (see Shane 2004 for an overview of university patenting trends).

Most US universities have created financial incentives for university professors to become active within commercialization processes. While variations exist, many universities have copied Stanford University's system, which divides any profits from licensing into thirds, split between the university, department, and professors (Kenney 1986; Colyvas 2007). Commercialization activities are also encouraged by universities through allowing professors, within employment contracts, to spend up to a day a week on consulting activities. Many universities also encourage professors to become active in the creation of start-up companies. Universities often license the founding technology for a start-up to the new company in exchange for equity. Professors active in the founding of the company also receive equity, and typically serve as scientific advisors to the new firm.

A by-product of university commercialization efforts is that many faculty members have benefited financially from their research. While an important incentive, it is unlikely that professors would engage in commercialization activities if doing so damaged the ability of their labs to vigorously compete within basic science fields. What, then, are the mechanisms by which commercialization activities can increase the capabilities of a university lab, and does the organization of the US research system impact the terms of university–industry relationships (see Murray 2004 and Lam 1997 more generally).

CAREER PATTERNS AND LABORATORY ORGANIZATION

A useful starting point is to explore the size and organization of the labour market for scientists within the United States. Within the US system senior professors do not control long-term funding from universities to hire junior scientists. Instead, professors must compete for grant funding, which derives primarily from the federal government and is awarded through competitive peer review processes. Principal investigators commonly request funding for graduate students and postdoctoral fellows within research grants. Tuition and stipends for most PhD students, particularly within established research universities, are thus provided by federal funding. As a result, the size of the labour market for junior scientists is strongly influenced by federal funding of university scientists.

How large is the labour market pool for junior scientists? In recent decades the US federal government has provided large-scale funding to scientific research. Over the 1995–2010 period federal research budgets for the US National Institutes of Health have averaged between $25 and 31 billion a year (National Institutes of Health 2011). A further $6.5 billion of research funding flows through the National Science Foundation (National Science Foundation 2010), and other federal agencies such as the Department of Energy are also active in supporting university research. While generous federal funding for research exists, particularly in the life sciences, competition for funding is fierce. Only about 20 per cent of NIH and NSF grant proposals, for example, are funded (National Science Foundation 2010;

National Institutes of Health 2011. Professors compete for funding, with the result that professors who are adept at fund raising can organize larger and possibly more productive laboratories.

Competition for funding is related to career dynamics. Academic careers within the United States are organized in a manner similar to 'up or out' partnership structures commonly used within law practices and consultancies. The labour market within such systems resembles a pyramid, with numerous jobs at entry level positions but relatively few senior positions associated with job security. Due to the availability of PhD training grants and postdoctoral opportunities, the US trains far more scientists than there are long-term academic jobs. Junior scientists compete for positions within the laboratories of senior academics. Only when hired as assistant professors are scientists able to run their own laboratory. While junior faculty are usually provided with 'start-up' funding from their universities, assistant professors must successfully use these funds to develop a federally supported programme. Only then can funding be secured to sustain a sizeable research laboratory capable of creating a successful research programme likely to win the professor tenure within a major research university.

Career dynamics within the US science system are, thus, highly competitive, but also to an important degree meritocratic. While there is no doubt that status, in the form of endorsements from well-known professors, is an important currency within the US science system, career progression is to a considerable extent driven by achievement. Referring back to Whitley's description of research systems, peer review committees play an important role in evaluating funding proposals and tenure decisions, and most scientific journals use blind reviewing processes. Scientists capable of developing successful research programmes can develop long-term academic careers. However, the academic career process produces many PhD level scientists who are unable to develop careers as professors within research -intensive universities.

INCENTIVES TO COMMERCIALIZE

The establishment of commercial ties can affect the competitive performance of a laboratory. Most directly, collaborations with industry can provide sponsored research funding and, at times, access to industry research and development platforms that can, in either case, increase the research productivity of the laboratory. Companies are typically better capitalized than academic laboratories and often have superior equipment. In some competitive research fields, access to industry resources can be a crucial advantage in races to make discoveries. In the life-sciences, for example, researchers with support from industry have been shown to publish more frequently, file more patents, and earn higher salaries (Blumenthal et al. 1986). However, there are disadvantages created by direct collaborations with companies. Most controversially, corporations often ask university collaborators to refrain from presenting or publishing results until intellectual property claims are filed (Van Looya et al. 2006). Corporate sponsors also have an obvious bias towards more applied rather than basic research (more generally see Krimsky 2004; Mirowski and Sent 2002).

While understanding the motives underpinning the increase in university-industry collaborations is an important issue (see Lam 1997), industry ties may affect labour market dynamics surrounding the careers of junior scientists in ways that can improve the performance of a laboratory. This second feature has been less explored in research on academic commercialization dynamics and is likely to vary across research systems.

From the perspective of competitive laboratory dynamics, senior scientists must vigorously compete for the services of the most talented junior scientists. What factors affect the ability of a lab to attract high-profile recruits? Comparing the career paths of both the perceived 'winners', presumed to be those securing tenured faculty positions at major research universities, and 'losers', presumed to be those who exit the competitive academic science system at some point in their career, can help to understand the interdependences between academic laboratories and science-based industry. Starting with the 'winners', one obvious factor is a senior scientist's ability to place lab members in subsequent high-profile jobs (PhD students to high profile postdocs; postdocs to junior faculty jobs). However, given that even in the best labs many junior scientists will fail to achieve significant academic results, a reputation of placing 'losers' of the competitive science game in a variety of other career paths, particularly within industry, can be an important advantage.

Sociologists have long demonstrated that social networks can provide a decisive edge in obtaining jobs (Granovetter 1974). Collaborations between labs and companies can generate direct social ties linking junior scientists to company scientists, ties that can lead to job opportunities if needed. More broadly, senior professors with ties to companies forged through licensing or advisory activities can directly recommend junior scientists for open jobs at the company, again providing a likely labour market edge. While a laboratory's history of placing students within high-profile academic jobs is most important, a reputation for moving students into high-status industry jobs, particularly research oriented labs within biotechnology, can heighten the attractiveness of a laboratory as a place to work.

The ability of a professor to signal to junior scientists that a lab has strong ties to industry is especially strong when a professor has successfully 'spun out' science-based start-ups developed around the lab's discoveries. Professors who have successfully launched companies frequently become high-status individuals within science (Zucker et al. 1998). Such status can be leveraged to recruit both funding and high-quality scientists to the professor's academic lab. Moreover, when a spin-off firm is launched, PhD students and postdocs who were instrumental in developing the firm's founding technology are frequently recruited to the new company (see Murray 2004). This can be lucrative, as such scientists can obtain leadership positions within the new company and usually receive company stock. Moreover, junior scientists attached to spin-offs are frequently named as founders of the new company, an important signifier of status within the academic and corporate world.

Within highly competitive scientific labour markets, the ability of a professor to place students within start-up jobs creates an additional career option for junior scientists working within the lab. Moreover, even though most junior scientists in such laboratories will not end up working in a start-up, the professor has 'proven' links with venture capitalists and senior managers of other companies through participation in start-ups: ties that can be used to help move junior scientists into lucrative industry careers. Doing so makes the lab a more attractive place to work, especially to students potentially interested in forging industry careers.

In sum, while financial incentives to commercialize within the United States research system are strong, it is unlikely that senior professors would readily engage in such activities unless doing so had a neutral or positive effect on the core goals of academic research—achieving status within the highly fragmented and competitive US research system. This review suggests that senior professors engage in commercialize because doing so can increase the attractiveness of working in his/her laboratory, from the career dynamic perspective of junior researchers.

ILLUSTRATIVE CASE STUDY: LABOUR MARKET DYNAMICS WITHIN CELL BIOLOGY LABS

Little systematic research exists on labour market competition for research-oriented jobs within industry. However, anecdotal evidence suggests that within the biotechnology industry competition for research jobs at leading companies can be fierce, especially at companies known to engage in 'serious' research, frequently linked to allowing their scientists to publish and hence participate in 'open science' (Stern 2004). Genentech, a leading biotechnology company that also has a reputation for allowing scientists to publish research results, routinely receives hundreds of applications for open staff science positions.[1] Given the large supply of PhD scientists trained in the United States, it is likely that competition is intense for research jobs at science-based companies.

Data from a survey of employment dynamics surrounding laboratories working in the field of cell biology further support the point that the market

[1] Interview with Judy Heyboer, former Senior Vice President of Human Resources, Genentech.

for industry jobs in R&D within the United States is highly competitive. From the early 1990s through to the present a major emphasis within the biotechnology industry has been to understand the molecular basis of disease in order to locate targets for new drugs (see Werth 1995). As a result, scientific findings from the cell biology field have become particularly germane to the biotechnology industry, suggesting a high commercialization potential. Data was collected in 2003 as part of a survey of thirty-one labs listed within an Internet directory of cell biology research. This directory listed over 100 laboratories. Only those laboratories listing the names of alumni were included in the survey. This selection criteria is a possible source of bias, as more successful laboratories may be more likely to list the names of past lab members. The names of 929 former laboratory members were found. For each of these individuals, Internet searches were conducted to determine the type of job held in 2003. Cell biology has a number of disciplinary sub-fields; labs were placed within a particular sub-field within the Internet directory. Table 10.2 displays summary data from this project, organized by scientific sub-field.

A first finding is that laboratories within the cell biology field vary strongly in terms of size. Table 10.2 only lists the average laboratory size within each sub-field. However, across individual labs the largest laboratory surveyed employed forty-five junior scientists and the smallest just three. The average laboratory size is ten people. This finding helps substantiate the claim that scientific laboratories within the United States can differ dramatically in terms of size, and is consistent with the claim that laboratories compete for the services of talented junior scientists.

Table 10.2 contains data on the percentage of junior scientists within each disciplinary sub-field that took subsequent employment as faculty members, postdoctoral fellows in a different lab, industry positions, physicians, or other fields. About 20 per cent of laboratory alumni were in postdoc positions, and presumably had yet to find longer-term employment. Over 45 per cent of scientists surveyed were in faculty positions. This is a higher percentage than is commonly cited in research on the academic job market. Note, however, that within this survey no distinction was made between faculty running laboratories at major research universities and faculty jobs at universities or colleges outside the competitive science field, such as liberal arts colleges, teaching oriented state colleges, or community colleges. The percentage of alumni actively pursuing competitive academic research careers is likely to be much lower than 45 per cent. Slightly less than 25 per cent of scientists had moved to industry. This figure substantiates the claim that a sizeable number of academically trained scientists move into industry. Considerable variation in the percentage of scientists who moved to industry exists across sub-fields. About one third of the alumni in the chemical cell biology field, for example,

Table 10.3. Career dynamics of alumni of Howard Hughes medical institute laboratories, 2003

	Current Lab Size	Total Alumni	Faculty (%)	Postdocs/RAs (%)	Industry (%)	Physicians (%)	Other (%)
Robert Horvitz (MIT; also Nobel Winner)	16	65	61.5	12.3	12.3	0	0
Stuart Schreiber (Harvard)	35	166	39.2	10.1	34.3	1.2	3.6
Tim Stearns (Stanford)	7	12	8.3	33.3	41.7	8.3	8.3
Gerald Crabtree (Stanford)	14	43	53.5	9.3	30.2	2.3	4.7
All HHMI Labs	18 (avg)	286	45.1	11.2	29.0	1.4	3.1
Non-HMMI Labs	9.4 (avg)	623	44.9	22.9	21.7	3.6	3.2

Source: World Wide Web of Cell Biology and Internet searches of laboratory home pages, conducted in November 2003

ties to San Francisco Bay biotechnology firms, and also send a sizeable number of alumni to industry jobs. While more systematic research needs to be conducted on this topic, this trend supports the notion that professors with links to industry may use such ties to help place students in company jobs.

A final way to examine the relative competitiveness of the industry laboratory market is to measure and rank the scientific output of junior scientists while they worked in a particular lab and then examine the types of jobs that high performers in a lab moved into compared to lower performers. Scientific output is typically measured using bibliometric tools and is controversial (see Osareh 1996). Hence the data presented here should be considered preliminary. Bibliometric measures of performance were captured for thirty-four alumni of Gerald Crabtree's HHMI lab at Stanford University. This laboratory was chosen because its website contains detailed career histories for all alumni. In order to measure the performance of each scientist, the ISI Web of Science was used to download information about all publications of each lab alumnus from the time they worked in the Crabtree lab. Data was then collected on the total number of publications for each scientist, the number of publications in which the scientist was the first author, the number of publications in the prominent journals *Nature* and *Science*, and the number of forward citations to each article, both total and adjusted for publication year.

Table 10.4 summarizes the results of this analysis. Scientists were bundled into three groups depending on the type of subsequent job they moved into after leaving the Crabtree Lab. The "faculty" category refers to scientists who have moved into academic faculty positions within major research universities and are now principle investigators within their own lab. Within the Crabtree laboratory all scientists that took industry jobs moved into research positions within biotechnology companies, mostly within Silicon Valley start-ups in close proximity to Stanford. Scientists also took a range of "other" jobs,

Table 10.4. Bibliometric performance of crabtree lab members sorted by career path, 2003

Job Type		Publications	First Author	Prominent Publications	Total Forward Citations**	Adjusted Forward Citations***
Faculty	Avg.	7.0	2.9	1.8	977.2	17.8
(n = 14)	Median	6.5	3	2.0	891.0	15.7
Biotech	Avg.	4.5	1.7	1.2	726.8	22.6
(n = 11)	Median	4.0	2	1.0	445.0	17.5
Other	Avg.	3.8	1.1	0.78	428.7	12.2
(n = 9)	Median	3.0	1.0	1.0	384.0	8.3

Source: Crabtree Lab Website, access December 2003 and ISI Web of Science, accessed December 2003. *Prominent Publications = *Nature* or *Science* publications while employed at the Crabtree Lab; **Total Forward Citations = Number of citations from the year of publication to 2003. ***Adjusted forward citations = (forward citations/2003-year of publication)

which include vocations such as Wall Street analyst, high school teacher, patent agent, and lecturer type positions in state colleges that did not involve running a laboratory. While varied, the alumni within the "other" category have left the competitive science field.

Not surprisingly, the fourteen people who found faculty jobs have the most impressive bibliometric performance records. They have published the most, including an average of two co-authorships in *Nature* or *Science*, and have the most forward citations to their research. Within Crabtree's high-status HHMI funded laboratory, the most successful junior scientists are moving into faculty careers. However, the scientists who moved to the biotechnology industry jobs have stronger bibliometric impact factors across all bibliometric variables compared to lab alumni who chose to take jobs in the 'other' category. While it isn't known whether this was by choice, the evidence that the scientists who did take biotechnology industry jobs performed more strongly as junior scientists than those who did not do so suggests that a competitive labour market exists within the biotechnology industry. The weaker performers within Crabtree's laboratory did not take research jobs within companies. Instead, they left competitive science.

The evidence from cell biology laboratories is limited in scope and needs to be expanded in terms of the number of laboratories studied, and applied to different scientific fields. That being said, the analysis supports the theoretical analysis of competitive lab dynamics presented earlier. Obtaining a faculty position within a research university is likely to be the overarching career objective for most junior scientists. However, junior scientists within high-profile HHMI labs were more likely to find jobs in industry than those working in less high-profile jobs. Moreover, the three HHMI labs with known ties to industry sent far more scientists to companies than the lab without industry ties. Finally, career dynamics within the Crabtree lab suggests that when examining the performance of the 'losers' of the highly competitive job market for academic faculty appointments, there appears to be competition also for the jobs within industry. Taken together, this evidence supports the general claim that senior professors cultivate commercial ties in part to improve career outcomes for junior scientists, and through doing so increase the attractiveness of their lab within the labour market for the best junior scientists.

b) Commercialization dynamics within the German research system

Referring back to Whitley's characterization of research systems, a key feature of the postwar German system affecting the organization of university-industry ties is the high amount of functional segmentation across higher education institutions. Basic research is carried out within universities and specialized research institutes, such as those of the Max Planck Society. Applied research is focused primarily within a network of technical universities and *Fachhochschule* (similar to polytechnic universities within the UK). Germany is also well known for its strong network of applied technology transfer organizations that play an intermediary role between industry and applied university research, and in particular the sixty institute strong Fraunhofer Society (for an overview see Abramson et al. 1997).

The relationship between the technically oriented universities and the private sector in Germany is strong, but the primary technology link has been the licensing of technology to established firms rather than the 'spinning out' of new companies that is common in the United States (Abramson et al. 1997). The system of intellectual property ownership surrounding university research in Germany has traditionally been oriented towards sponsored research. Prior to 2002 professors owned intellectual property generated within universities. Applied research has been primarily commercialized through relationships with established firms. The system is oriented towards applied technology fields, such as engineering. Firms would sponsor a professor's research, which often included the provision of stipends for graduate students, in return for the opportunity to license any intellectual property that resulted. Graduate students funded by firms would then commonly take research positions in the company sponsoring their research.

Lacking ownership of intellectual property, German universities have had little incentive to establish technology transfer offices. Moreover, due to the centrality of the chaired professor, German universities are traditionally hollow organizations lacking strategic autonomy or capacity (see e.g. Meier and Schimank 2010; Schimank and Lange 2009 and more generally Clark 2006). Professors would typically negotiate directly with companies, often trading intellectual property rights for sponsored research funds, graduate stipends, or consultancy fees. This framework creates poor incentives for the commercialization of more basic research, in which venture capital funded university spin-off companies typically spend several years commercializing new research findings, often in close contact with founding university labs, before technology can easily be applied to product markets. As a result, in Germany research within the bio-medical sciences and other basic research fields has until recently been conducted with minimal attention to possible commercial spin-offs (see Asakawa and Lehrer 2004 for a broader discussion).

During the late 1990s, however, technology policy within Germany became more oriented towards creating institutions better supporting high-technology industries (see Casper 2000, 2007a; Lehrer 2000). Increased support for the commercialization of basic research, particularly within the biomedical sciences, became a core goal of German technology policy. This led to the establishment of government-supported technology development agencies within many German states or *Laender*, often intentionally located in close proximity to major research universities. Technology development agencies often worked closely with university professors to promote the commercialization of research into new ventures, often paying patenting costs, deploying consultants to help develop business development plans, and organizing incubators and technology parks to help nurture entrepreneurial technology start-ups (Casper 2000). Federal and local governments have also been active in channelling venture capital to university start-ups, allocating several hundred millions of funding for an array of grants and 'public venture capital' aimed at companies during the 1995 to 2002 period (see Adelberger 2000; Casper 2007a, ch. 4).

To create stronger incentives for commercialization within universities, in 2002 the German parliament adopted a revised patent law covering university research. Following the US Bayh-Dole framework, the new law transferred ownership of intellectual property surrounding publicly supported research to universities (Kilger and Bartenbach 2002). The new law also mimicked the Stanford University incentive structure surrounding university intellectual property by guaranteeing 30 per cent of any eventual revenues from licensing to the university scientists listed as inventors on patents. Recognizing the lack of university funding to support technology licensing offices, in 2002 the German federal government developed a programme to organize and fund a network of university licensing offices in order to better support licensing (OECD 2003, ch. 9).

Both legal frameworks surrounding the development and licensing of intellectual property and resources available to universities and professors in support of the commercialization of basic research have evolved towards a US-inspired model. Less clear, however, is how professors in basic research fields, operating within a highly centralized and hierarchical research system, will respond to these new incentives. Mirroring the earlier analysis of the United States, it is useful to explore how the introduction of commercial ties within the German basic research system, and particularly the widespread promotion of spin-out companies, is likely to interplay with career dynamics within laboratories.

CAREER PATTERNS WITHIN THE GERMAN BASIC SCIENCE RESEARCH SYSTEM

A key factor in examining career patterns within German universities is the role of the full professor. Within the ideal-typical German academic model (see e.g. Enders 2001), senior professors assume responsibility for most activities within their particular sub-field within their institute. Professors receive long-term funding for graduate students and the German equivalent of post-doctoral fellows, often referred to as senior assistants, who typically perform some teaching as well as directed research towards a second dissertation (*Habilitation*), which is needed to compete for professor level jobs. Undergraduate degrees in Germany (the *Diplom*) have a dissertation component that in some respects is similar to a Masters level degree in the US or UK and take an average of six to seven years to complete (Federal Ministry of Statistics 2003). As a result, German professors also typically engage late stage *Diplom* candidates as researchers in their laboratories.

The German university system has historically conformed to this highly centralized departmental model, though in the last decade the German federal government has increased the proportion of research funding that is allocated through peer-reviewed selection processes, while some state or *Laender* governments have begun instituting performance reviews of professors based on peer reviews and bibliometric measures (see Meier and Schimank 2010; Schimank 2005). It is important to note, however, that the overall percentage of university research funding that is provided through competitive grant funding in Germany is much lower than in the United States, as is the level of competition for such grants. The percentage of research proposals funded by the German Federal Research Ministry (DFG) has decreased over the past decades, but from a very high rate of 84.5 per cent in 1974 to 58.7 per cent in 1997 and 55.5 per cent in 2009 (Hornsbostel 2001; Deutsche Forschungsgemeinschaft 2010). Most research funding within German universities comes from the government, but through long-term, non-competitive funding through universities. A study of funding within German physics departments, for example, found that during 1995–1997 less than 40 per cent of funding was from competitive DFG grants (Hornsbostel 2001). While the percentage of research funding derived from external funding might have increased through the 200s, it is most likely less than in the United States. A study of research funding within US universities found that in the early 2000s about 80 per cent of R&D expenditures were funded through external budgets (Ehrenberg et al. 2003).

High levels of departmental centralization mutes the degree of reputational competition and pluralism, but allows senior faculty to develop long-term, cumulative research trajectories within preferred scientific areas. To the extent that cumulative research programmes create organization (or laboratory) specific skill-sets or develop tacit skills, particularly across teams of workers, professors have an incentive to promote longer-term employment tenures of junior scientists within their laboratories. This argument parallels comparative institutional analysis of knowledge investments linked to different innovation trajectories within companies (see Casper and Whitley 2004; Casper 2007a, ch. 2; and more broadly Winter 1987 and Milgrom and Roberts 1993).

In order to facilitate cumulative patterns of knowledge development within their laboratories, German professors may have an incentive to refrain from external searches when appointing junior scientists to doctoral and senior assistant positions within their lab, and instead promote current lab members who have developed laboratory specific skills. The organization of careers for junior scientists in Germany has been structured primarily through internal labour markets (see Enders 2001). While there is a modest amount of movement between labs after the PhD, the dominant model within Germany is for a junior scientist in most fields to stay within the same laboratory throughout their early career. Professors frequently invite talented undergraduate *Diplom* students to stay within a laboratory to complete doctoral studies. Such students receive fixed-term contracts for up to six years to complete their PhDs. Professors can also sponsor postdoctoral students to complete a second dissertation or *Habilitation*, again on fixed-term contracts for up to six years. When completing the *Habilitation*, scientists officially become *PrivatDozents* or lecturers and can apply for full professor positions. German law prevents individuals from applying for professor jobs at the university where they completed their *Habilitation*, creating a more open labour market (Harley et al. 2004). However, the average age of individuals completing the *Habilitation* is 38 years (Federal Ministry of Statistics 2003); individuals often compete on an open labour market only after spending some twelve to eighteen years within the same laboratory.

Given the longer-term employment of junior scientists in one laboratory, the labour market for junior scientists resembles a relational contracting model (McNeil 1973). Junior professors are strongly dependent on the full professor at all early career stages up to the *Habilitation*. In contrast, while most junior scientists in the USA must repeatedly apply for positions, they can do so within the large external labour market for PhD and postdoc positions that is fuelled by expansive federal grant funding. They are therefore less likely to invest in lab specific skills, and may develop a portfolio of generalizable scientific skills over their early years through working on projects at different labs. However, the external labour market for junior scientist positions is less developed in Germany, while investments in lab-specific skills could prove less valuable if applying for jobs at other laboratories. Moreover, if a junior professor is able to successfully compete for a full professor position, the research programme of their senior scientist mentor could plausibly be extended to a new university, an important outcome in terms of extending the professor's reputation within German science. From this perspective, senior professors have a strong incentive to promote scientists from their lab within the more open competition for full professor positions.

INCENTIVES TO COMMERCIALIZE

A key question surrounding the German system is how professors regulate the flow of junior scientists into and out of a lab. From the point of view of the full professor, it seems important to only take in as many PhD students as one can plausibly move into *Lehrstelle* type positions, though some attrition might be expected as some PhD students will choose to exit competitive science after completing the PhD or could apply for postdoctoral positions in laboratories outside the traditional German academic system—possibly within the Max Planck system or in the US or UK. Within a relational contracting system, a professor will face pressure to place students within subsequent jobs. Control over long-term funding helps ameliorate this problem, as a professor will know with reasonable certainty the number of doctoral research and senior assistant positions available over coming years. Within the German system, relying on external funding can, though, be problematic. While it can be used to increase the size of labs and hence their output, if a professor engages more junior scientists than he or she can eventually place in subsequent jobs, then the attractiveness of the laboratory as a place of employment may decline.

The public policy push within Germany for basic science labs to develop stronger commercialization activities can improve the competitive position of German labs through allowing professors to 'safely' engage more junior scientists. Professors may choose to mimic the long-established industry sponsored PhD research tradition from engineering and other applied sciences. Doing so would allow their laboratory to expand, under the assumption that industry-sponsored PhD students could move to industry. The incentive for professors in Germany to establish ties with industry may be stronger than it is for US professors, since under a relational contracting system the pressure for professors to help junior scientists find jobs is higher, and industry links can commonly be used to locate job opportunities.

Of particular interest is the establishment of spin-off companies. German policy from the mid 1990s onwards has strongly encouraged the creation of university start-up firms, and many of the financial and organizational obstacles to starting companies have been reduced through state programmes, especially during the 1995 to 2002 period. While companies were required to have private investors, state subsidies doubled and sometimes tripled private investments and also provided free or low cost consultancy services and space in incubators and technology parks.[2] During this period full professors, particularly in the life sciences, who were interested in starting a spin-off company could do so with relatively little effort. Hundreds of biotechnology companies were launched in Germany during the 1995–2003 period, almost all linked to basic science laboratories in German universities.

[2] The information in the next five paragraphs on the German biotechnology industry draw from Casper (2007a), chapter 4.

German professors have financial and reputational incentives to invest resources in start-ups so that they succeed. That being said, given the relational contracting system within German labs, control of a start-up provides a direct source of potential employment for a lab's junior scientists. Through launching a start-up a professor will have a strong say in the hiring decisions of the new company, particularly during the company's early launch phase. Professors also hold private information on the quality of junior scientists in their laboratory, information not immediately known to investors in the company (and particularly to government officials managing state subsidies). German professors could use the opportunity to launch new technology start-ups as an opportunity to push junior scientists who are employed within labs under the relational contracting system into corporate jobs—a 'soft exit' for junior scientists who were unlikely to succeed longer term in the German academic system.

ILLUSTRATIVE CASE STUDY: EMPLOYMENT LINKS TO 'FOUNDER LABS' WITHIN GERMAN BIOTECHNOLOGY

Between 1994 and 2000 the size of the German biotechnology sector grew from less than 50 companies to over 350. Research on the German biotechnology industry has generally demonstrated that the new sector has performed poorly. While a small number of internationally competitive firms have developed, particularly in the Munich region (see Lange 2009), German firms have been able to move very few drug candidates through clinical trial pipelines and have not matched the research productivity of the longer-established UK industry, and lag far behind the US industry.

Research on the poor performance of German biotechnology has emphasized institutional constraints within the country's business system that impede the formation of 'Silicon Valley' type entrepreneurial companies (see Casper, Lehrer, and Soskice 1999; Casper and Whitley 2004). Long-term employment patterns within established companies, and in particular the pharmaceutical industry, block the development of an active labour market of managers with commercial pharmaceutical development skills to work within the hundreds of new start-ups. While financial markets appeared to support the growth of new technology firms during the 1995–2000 period, the rapid 'bursting' of the Internet stock market bubble in the United States sent shock waves through the nascent German technology oriented stock market, which was eventually shut down in 2003 (see Audretsch and Lehmann 2008). It is also difficult to implement systems of high-powered financial incentives and short-term employment contracts for skilled scientists and engineered within the German corporate governance system.

While the institutions dominating key features of the business system are undoubtedly important explanatory factors, career dynamics within the German research system may also be a contributing influence. Facing relational contracting norms, have German professors used the founding of spin-off companies as an opportunity to shift weaker scientists from their labs to industry? To help shed light on this issue, Table 10.5 provides data on the most previous job of individuals in management positions within over two dozen German biotechnology companies during 2002, the year before the German biotechnology industry began to contract. For comparison purposes, similar data is also provided for managers working in the San Diego, California biotechnology cluster, one of the world's best performing commercial biotech hubs (Casper 2007b). One immediate conclusion from Table 10.5 is that in Germany most managers (78 per cent) have been recruited from academic laboratories, while in San Diego most came from other industry jobs (83 per cent). This trend is consistent with the explanation, from the comparative business system literature, that long-term employment patterns within German industry have muted the development of an active labour market for mid-career managers.

Note, however, that almost half of all managers within the German firms were recruited directly from the company's academic founder laboratory. While data on founder lab links is not available for San Diego, the finding that only 17 per cent of senior managers were recruited from academia implies that far fewer scientists from academic laboratories move into management positions in San Diego. The founder laboratory linkage in Germany is also strong for junior scientists moving to non-management roles within companies. A study of 299 scientists working within 44 German biotechnology companies found that 34 per cent moved directly from the academic laboratory to the new start-up. Moreover, over half of these scientists had worked within the laboratory of the senior scientist who had founded the company earlier in their career. Overall, the data from Table 10.5 helps demonstrate that German professors used the opportunity to found a start-up to move junior scientists out of the laboratory and into a company.

Table 10.5. Most previous job of science-oriented managers, German and San Diego biotechnology firms

	German biotech (2002)		San Diego biotech (2004)	
Founder Academic Lab	40	48%	n/a	
Local Academic Lab	2	2%	17	7%
Non-Local Academic Lab	24	29%	27	10%
Biotech	6	8%	168	65%
Pharma/Industry	12	14%	47	18%
Total Sample	84		259	

Source: Casper (20007a), chapter 4.

Why have so many junior scientists been moved by professors to start-up companies? A moral hazard explanation would suggest that German professors, facing a relational contracting norm to help find jobs for lab employees, are moving weaker scientists who are having difficulty finding academic jobs into start-up companies that they control. One way to investigate this claim is to measure the number of years each junior scientist worked in a particular German academic laboratory before moving a spin-off company connected to the lab. Within the German system, the longer a junior scientist worked within a laboratory, the greater the pressure facing the professor running the lab to look after that scientist's career.

Given that the time to complete doctoral studies in Germany is normally four to six years (Federal Ministry of Statistics 2003), data showing substantially longer average employment tenure would be consistent with a scientist holding multiple junior scientist positions in a laboratory, for example completing doctoral studies and then moving to a *Lehrstelle* type position to begin research on a *Habilitation*. Using the data on scientists working in German biotechnology firms from 2002, an estimate of employment tenure was found for 124 junior scientists, all of whom moved from a German academic laboratory to a start-up company founded by the full professor in charge of that laboratory. The estimate was found through using the Web of Science to locate the year of each scientist's first publication with the lab, and then subtracting this year from the year the scientist joined the start-up company. The results on employment tenure are displayed in Figure 10.1. The majority of scientists worked for a long period of time in the lab before

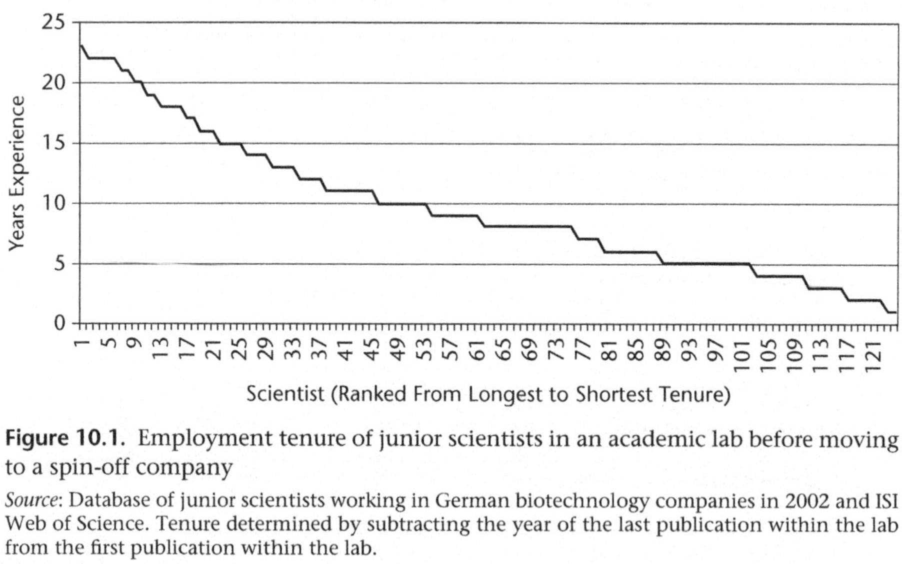

Figure 10.1. Employment tenure of junior scientists in an academic lab before moving to a spin-off company

Source: Database of junior scientists working in German biotechnology companies in 2002 and ISI Web of Science. Tenure determined by subtracting the year of the last publication within the lab from the first publication within the lab.

moving to industry. Of the 124 scientists, the median length of time employed in the academic founder lab is 9 years. Fifty-three scientists had worked in the laboratory for ten or more years, and twenty-five for over fifteen years. The data on employment tenure suggests that most of these scientists were employed in the laboratory for much longer than the time needed to complete a PhD dissertation.

German professors, when establishing start-up companies, moved many junior scientists who had worked in the laboratory for long periods of time, close to a decade or more in the majority of cases, out of the lab and into companies they controlled. This data supports the claim that German professors have created an internal labour market surrounding junior scientists. It is also consistent with a more controversial argument, that German professors took the opportunity of founding a biotechnology company to move weaker scientists to industry jobs that they controlled. If German companies were in a sense forced to take extra or weaker scientific personnel, this could help explain the sector's weak performance.

Concluding summary and implications for future research

The organization of scientific research systems varies cross-nationally. This chapter examined how national research systems impact processes by which public knowledge is commercialized. The mode of analysis adopted in the chapter is similar to that used in the comparative institutional analysis of commercial innovation across advanced industrial economies (especially Hall and Soskice 2001 and Casper and Whitley 2004). The findings developed in the paper surrounding commercialization processes across the United States and Germany support a general claim for the usefulness of comparative institutional analysis focusing on how micro-actors strategize within national research systems. While academic science is conducted by teams of scientists within laboratories across most countries, institutions structuring career structures, labour markets, funding and assessment criteria, and organizational structures within universities strongly impact the conduct of science. Commercialization activities can strongly affect career dynamics surrounding junior professors within academic laboratories within national research systems. While professors have actively become involved in commercialization in both the United States and Germany, the motives driving these activities and their outcomes of such efforts may significantly vary.

The analysis here rests on ideal-typical institutional analysis of Germany and the United States and draws primarily from empirical research on commercialization patterns within the life science industries. While the analysis of competitive laboratory dynamics within national research systems appears useful, it could be broadened through comparing commercialization dynamics within different scientific fields and, of course, across more countries. The empirical examples from cell biology and German biotech hopefully provide useful templates of how to explore the impact of commercialization dynamics and career patterns of junior scientists within a competitive research system context. However, more detailed and matched cross-national comparisons are needed to provide stronger empirical support.

Comparative institutional analysis is most useful in mapping out differences in societal organization and then tracing the effect of such differences on important societal outcomes. Due to wide cross-national variation in the institutional organization of science (Whitley 2000, 2010), it is likely that the interplay between academic and industry differs widely across societies. In recent years countries across the world have imported elements of the US system governing commercialization, and in particular the Bayh-Dole Act, with the expectation that the creation of a similar set of rules governing the ownership of university intellectual property will lead to similar patterns of commercialization as seen in the United States. A deeper comparative institutional analysis of the type developed here would predict that, given continuing underlying differences in the organization of scientific practices, commercialization outcomes are likely to vary.

A well-known criticism of some forms of institutional analysis is the difficulty of explaining change (Thelen 2004; Crouch 2005). It is important to acknowledge that research systems can change dramatically. The German research system, as described in this chapter, lacks the reputational competition or pluralism that Whitley associates with being conducive to major breakthroughs in knowledge production. However, during the early twentieth century a similar system led the world in producing important discoveries in physics, chemistry, and other fields. Moreover, the German system at present may be evolving. While both long-term funding for professors and Germany's *Habilitation* based system continue to persist, many German professors appear to be using shorter-term postdoc type positions to fill some positions (perhaps minimizing relational contracting obligations). Department structures within some universities may be becoming more fragmented, allowing several professors within a general field to be hired, and possibly creating more decentralized departmental research organizations. Such trends may ultimately lead to shifts in the structure of the German research system, with important implications on how professors choose to develop ties with industry. Understanding how patterns of knowledge production have changed in Germany and other countries is an important research topic.

References

Abramson N., J. Encarnacao, P. Reid, and U. Schmoch (eds) (1997) *Technology Transfer Systems in the United States and Germany*, Washington DC: National Academy Press.

Adams, Stephen B. (2009) 'Follow the Money: Engineering at Stanford and UC Berkeley during the rise of Silicone Valley', *Minerva*, 47(4): 367–90.

Adelberger, K. (2000) 'Semi-Sovereign Leadership? The State's Role in German Biotechnology and Venture Capital Growth', *German Politics*, 9: 103–22.

Amable, B. (2003) *The Diversity of Modern Capitalism*, Oxford, UK: Oxford University Press.

Asakawa, K. and M. Lehrer (2004) 'Pushing Scientists into the Marketplace: German and Japanese efforts to promote science entrepreneurship', *California Management Journal* V, 46(3): 55–76.

Association of University Technology Managers (AUTM) (2008) The AUTM Licensing Survey, FY 2007, Norwalk, CT: AUTM.

Audretsch, D. and E. Lehmann (2008) 'The Neuer Markt as an Institution of Creation and Destruction', *The International Entrepreneurship and Management Journal*, 4(4): 419–29.

Ben-David, J. (1968) 'Universities and the Growth of Science in Germany and the. United States', *Minerva*, VII: 3–35.

Blumenthal, D., M. Cluck, L. K. Seashore, M. A. Stoto, and D. Wise (1986) 'University-Industry Research Relationships in Biotechnology: Implications for the university', *Science*, 232: 1361–66.

Casper, S. (2007a) *Creating Silicon Valley in Europe: Public policy towards new technology industries*, Oxford: Oxford University Press.

—— (2007b) 'How Do Technology Clusters Emerge and Become Sustainable? Social network formation and inter-firm mobility within the San Diego biotechnology cluster', *Research Policy*, 36: 438–55.

—— (2000) 'Institutional Adaptiveness, Technology Policy, and the Diffusion of New Business Models: The case of German biotechnology', *Organization Studies*, 21: 887–914.

—— M. Lehrer, and D. Soskice (1999) 'Can High-Technology Industries Prosper in Germany: Institutional frameworks and the evolution of the German software and biotechnology industries', *Industry and Innovation*, 6: 6–23.

Casper, S. and R. Whitley (2004) 'Managing Competences in Entrepreneurial Technology Firms: A comparative institutional analysis of Germany, Sweden and the UK', *Research Policy*, 33(1): 89–106.

Clark, William (2006) *Academic Charisma*, Chicago: University of Chicago Press.

Colyvas, J. (2007) 'From Divergent Meanings to Common Practices: The early institutionalization of technology transfer in the life sciences at Stanford University', *Research Policy*, 36: 456–76.

Crouch, C. (2005) *Capitalist Diversity and Change*, Oxford: Oxford University Press.

Deutsche Forschungsgemeinschaft (2010) *Funding Rates in the Individual Grants Programme 2006–2009*. Internet site: http://www.dfg.de/en/dfg_profile/evaluation_

statistics/funding_statistics/facts_figures/processing_proposals/index.html. Accessed April 18, 2011.

Enders, J. (2001) 'A Chair System in Transition: Appointments, promotion, and gatekeeping in German higher education', *Higher Education*, 41: 3–25.

Ehrenberg, R., M. Rizzo, and G. Jakubson (2003) 'Who Bears the Growing Cost of Science at Universities?' Working paper, Cornell School of Industrial and Labor Relations.

Federal Ministry of Statistics (Germany) (2003) 'Basic and Structural Data', Bonn.

Geiger, R. (1986) *To Advance Knowledge: The growth of American research universities, 1900–1940*, Oxford: Oxford University Press.

Granovetter, M. (1974) *Getting A Job: A study of contacts and careers*, Cambridge, Mass.: Harvard University.

Hage, J. (2011) *Restoring the Innovative Edge: Driving the evolution of science and technology*, Stanford: Stanford Business Books.

Hall, P. and D. Gingerich (2009) 'Varieties of Capitalism and Institutional Complementarities in the Macroeconomy: An empirical assessment', *British Journal of Political* Science, 39: 449–82.

—— and D. Soskice (2001) 'Introduction' pp. 1–70 in Peter Hall and David Soskice (eds) *Varieties of Capitalism*, Oxford: Oxford University Press.

Harley, S. et al. (2004) 'From Academic Communities to Managed Organizations: The implications for academic careers in UK and German universities', *Journal of Vocational Behavior*, 64: 329–45.

Higgins, M. and R. Gulati (2003) 'Getting Off to a Good Start: The effects of upper echelon affiliations on interorganizational endorsements', *Organization Science*, 14(3): 244–63.

Hollingsworth, J. R. (2009) 'The Role of Institutions and Organizations in Shaping Radical Scientific Innovations', pp. 139–65 in Lars Magnusson and Jan Ottosson (eds) *The Evolution of Path Dependence*, Cheltenham, UK and Northampton, MA: Edward Elgar.

—— and R. Boyer (ed.) (1997) *Contemporary Capitalism: The embeddedness of institutions*, Cambridge: Cambridge University Press.

Hornbostel, S. (2001) 'Third Party Funding of German Universities: An indicator of research activity?' *Scientometrics*, V(50): 523–37.

Jong, J. (2006) 'How Organizational Structures in Science Shape Spin-Off Firms: The biochemistry departments of Berkeley, Stanford, and UCSF and the birth of the biotech industry', *Industrial and Corporate Change*, 15(2): 251–83.

Kenney, M. (1986) *Biotechnology: The university-industrial complex*, New Haven: Yale University Press.

—— and W. R. Goe (2004) 'The Role of Social Embeddedness in Professorial Entrepreneurship: A comparison of electrical engineering and computer science at UC Berkeley and Stanford', *Research Policy*, 33: 691–707.

—— and D. Patton (2009) 'Reconsidering the Bayh-Dole Act and the Current University Invention Ownership Model', *Research Policy*, 38(9): 1407–22.

Kilger, C. and K. Bartenbach (2000) 'New Rules for German Professors', *Science*, 298: 1173–75.

Knorr-Cetina, K. (1999) *Epistemic Cultures: How the xciences make knowledge*, Cambridge: Harvard University Press.

Krimsky, S. (2004) *Science in the Private Interest: Has the lure of profits corrupted biomedical research?* New York: Rowman & Littlefield.

Lam, A. (1997) 'Embedded Firms, Enbedded Knowledge: Problems of Collaboration and Knowledge Transfer in Global Cooperative Ventures', *Organization Studies*, 18: 973–96.

—— (2007) 'Knowledge Networks and Careers: Academic scientists in industry–university links', *Journal of Management Studies*, 44: 993–1016.

Lange, K. (2009) 'Institutional Embeddedness and the Strategic Leeway of Actors: The case of the German therapeutic biotech industry', *Socio-Economic Review*, 7: 181–207.

Lehrer, Mark (2000) 'Has Germany Finally Solved Its High-Tech Problem? The Recent Boom in German Technolology-based Entrepreneurism', *California Management Review*, 42: 89–107.

—— P. Nell, and L. Gärber (2009) 'A National Systems View of University Development: Towards a broadened perspective on the entrepreneurial university based on the German and US experience', *Research Policy*, 38(2): 268–80.

Lundvall, B-Å. (ed.) (1992) *National Innovation Systems: Towards a theory of innovation and interactive learning*, London: Pinter.

McNeil, I. (1977) 'Contracts: Adjustment of Long-Term Economic Relations under Classical, Neoclassical, and Relational Contract Law', *Northwestern University Law Review*, V(72): 854–902.

Meier, F. and U. Schimank (2010) 'Mission Now Possible: Profile building and leadership in German universities', pp. 211–37 in R. Whitley, J. Glaser, and L. Engwall (eds) *Reconfiguring Knowledge Production: Changing authority relationships in the sciences and their consequences for intellectual innovation*, Oxford: Oxford University Press.

Milgrom, P. and J. Roberts (1995) 'Complementarities: Industrial strategy, structure, and change in manufacturing', *Journal of Accounting and Economics*, 19: 179–208.

—— (1993) *Economics, Organization, and Management*, Eaglewood Cliffs: Prentice Hill.

Mirowski, P. and E. Sent (ed) (2002) *Science Bought and Sold: Essays in the economics of science*, Chicago: University of Chicago Press.

Mowery, D. and R. Nelson (1999) *Sources of Industrial Leadership: Studies of seven industries*, Cambridge: Cambridge University Press.

—— —— B. Sampat, and A. Ziedonis (2004) *Ivory Tower and Industrial Innovation: University-Industry technology transfer before and after the Bayh-Dole Act in the United States*, Palo Alto: Stanford University Press.

Murray, F. (2004) 'The Role of Inventors in Knowledge Transfer: Sharing in the laboratory life', *Research Policy*, 33: 643–59.

Murmann, J. P. (2003) *Knowledge and Competitive Advantage*, Cambridge: Cambridge University Press.

National Institutes of Health (2011) 'NIH Budget', http://www.nih.gov/about/budget.htm (accessed April 15, 2011).

National Science Foundation (2010) *FY2009 Performance and Financial Highlights*, Washington: National Science Foundation.

Nelson, R. (1993) *National Innovation Systems: A comparative analysis*, Oxford: Oxford University Press.

OECD (2003) *Turning Science into Business: Patenting and licensing at public research organizations*, Paris: OECD.

Osareh, F. (1996) 'Bibliometrics, Citation Analysis and Co-Citation Analysis: A review of literature II', *Libri*, 46: 217–25.

Pope, J. (2006) 'Donors Give All-Time Record to Colleges', *Boston Globe*, 16 February.

Rauber, C. (1997) 'Dr Strange Glove', *San Francisco Business Times*, 5 December.

Scherer, F. and D. Harhoff (2001) 'Technology Policy for a World of Skew-Distributed Outcomes', *Research Policy*, 59: 559–66.

Schimank, U. (2005) '"New Public Management" and the Academic Profession: Reflections on the German situation', *Minerva*, 43: 361–76.

——and S. Lange (2009) 'Germany: A latecomer to new public management', pp. 51–75 in: C. Paradiese et al. (eds) *University Governance: Western European comparative perspectives*, Dordrecht: Springer.

Shane, S. (2004) *Academic Entrepreneurship: University spinoffs and wealth creation'*, London: Edward Elgar Publishing.

Stern, S. (2004) 'Do Scientists Pay to Be Scientists?' *Management Science*, 50: 835–53.

Streeck, W. (2009) *Re-Forming Capitalism: Institutional change in the German political economy*, Oxford: Oxford University Press.

——(1992) 'On the Institutional Preconditions of Diversified Quality Production', in W. Streeck (ed.) *Social Institutions and Economic Performance*, London and Newberry Park: Sage.

Stokes, D. (1997) *Pasteur's Quadrant: Basic science and technological innovation*, Washington DC: Brookings Institution Press.

Thelen, K. (2004) *How Institutions Evolve: The political economy of skills in Germany, Britain, Japan and the United States*, Cambridge: Cambridge University Press.

Van Looya, B., J. Callaertb, and K. Debackere (2006) 'Publication and Patent Behavior of Academic Researchers: Conflicting, reinforcing or merely co-existing?' *Research Policy*, 35: 596–608.

Von Hippel, E. (1988) *The Sources of Innovation*, New York: Oxford University Press.

Werth, B. (1995) *The Billion-Dollar Molecule*, New York: Touchstone, Simon & Schuster.

Whitley, R. (2010) 'Reconfiguring the Public Sciences: The impact of governance changes on authority and innovation in public science systems', in R. Whitley, J. Glaser, and L. Engwall, *Reconfiguring Knowledge Production: Changing authority relationships in the sciences and their consequences for intellectual innovation*, Oxford: Oxford University Press.

—— (2003) 'Competition and Pluralism in the Public Sciences: The impact of institutional frameworks on the organization of academic science', *Research Policy*, 32: 1015–29.

—— (2000) *The Intellectual and Social Organization of the Sciences* (Second Edition), Oxford: Oxford University Press.

—— (1999) *Divergent Capitalisms: The social structuring and change of business systems*, Oxford: Oxford University Press.

Winter, S. (1987) 'Knowledge and Competence as Strategic Assets', pp. 159–84 in David J. Teece (ed.) *The Competitive Challenge: Strategies for industrial innovation and renewal,* New York: Ballinger.

Zucker, L., M. Darby, and M. Brewer (1998) 'Intellectual Human Capital and the Birth of U.S. Biotechnology Enterprises', *American Economic Review,* 88: 340–90.

11

Varieties of Offshoring?

Spatial Fragmentation and the Organization of Production in Twenty-First Century Capitalism

Jennifer Bair and Matthew C. Mahutga[1]

Introduction

Scholars agree that changes in economic organization reflect political and technological developments, but disagree about the extent to which these changes foster convergence in the organization of industries, the role of institutions, and the behaviour and performance of firms across industries and institutions. One view is that the *organization of transnational production networks* is a central and distinguishing characteristic of contemporary capitalism, while others emphasize the continued, or even increased, importance of *institutional context* in producing persistent cross-country or cross-regional variation in economic organization.

Those who focus on the transnational dimension contend that the development of functionally integrated but geographically dispersed production networks is an emergent and defining feature of globalization (Gereffi 1994; Feenstra 1998). Such networks express organizational dynamics that vary systematically by sector in ways that relate to the characteristics of particular production processes and the strategies and capabilities of firms. Moreover, these dynamics cannot be reduced to nationally specific patterns of economic organization or the institutional contexts that have historically fostered them. Alternatively, those who emphasize persistent heterogeneity in the institutional landscape of the global economy argue that because patterns of internationalization carry the imprint of institutional legacies, globalization is

[1] Authors' names are listed in alphabetical order.

both not only compatible with, but may even reinforce institutional diversity by increasing the salience of institutional comparative advantage in international markets (Boyer 2004; Hall and Soskice 2001; Whitley 2007, 1999 and in this volume).

We take the institutions versus sectors debate as a point of entry into analyzing the dynamics of contemporary capitalism. On one hand, we draw from the highly influential varieties of capitalism approach most closely associated with the work of Hall and Soskice (2001) in order to derive and assess empirically a set of propositions about institutional comparative advantage, as we explain below. Although this framework has been extensively criticized over the last decade (Hollingsworth and Boyer 1997; Streeck et al. 2005; Hancke et al. 2007; Taylor 2004),[2] it is useful for our purposes because it lends itself to clear and testable hypotheses. Similarly, though several frameworks for analyzing global production networks have been proposed (Henderson et al. 2002; Bair 2008; Gibbon et al. 2008), we draw on Gereffi's (1994) global commodity chain approach and the subsequent global value chain governance typology elaborated by Gereffi, Humphrey, and Sturgeon (2005). Taking the varieties of capitalism (hereafter VoC) and the global commodity/value chain (hereafter GCC/GVC) approaches as indicative of the institutional and sectoral camps respectively, we formulate and evaluate hypotheses drawn from these frameworks regarding the degree to which economic organization is shaped by institutional contexts, industry logics, or both.

The focus of our discussion is spatial fragmentation in contemporary capitalism. Feenstra (1998) describes this dimension of economic organization as the 'integration of trade and the disintegration of production': it refers to the dispersion of disaggregated manufacturing processes that were previously contained within Northern economies to multiple locations, frequently in the global South. We advance the organizational/convergence versus institutional/persistent diversity debate by examining empirically at what level variation in spatial fragmentation is greater—at the industry level or at the institutional level—by developing four specific hypotheses regarding the rate of spatial fragmentation across industries and institutional settings.[3] We find that rates of spatial

[2] For example, some argue that this approach treats firms as passive 'institution-takers' that develop strategies appropriate to the institutions that exist, failing to appreciate the extent to which organizational actors seek to create an institutional environment consistent with their goals (Allen 2004; Deeg and Jackson 2007). Other critics take issue with the static nature of Hall and Soskice's framework, though this weakness is being addressed in a vibrant subfield of comparative institutionalism focusing on institutional change (Morgan and Kubo 2005; Hall and Thelen 2009; Streeck and Thelen 2005).

[3] In keeping with the varieties of capitalism model developed by Hall and Soskice, we define institutions at the national level. However, we recognize that some approaches within the comparative capitalism literature, such as Whitley's business systems (2007) and Amable's economic models (2003) do not necessarily delimit institutional contexts by national borders.

fragmentation vary more by industry than institutional type. In particular, we identify industry-specific differences in the rate of spatial fragmentation (simply measured as an increased ratio of imports to domestic value added, as we explain below) that are more or less constant across different institutional contexts. While some of our results are attributable to a degree of industry-specific variation in spatial fragmentation *within* varieties of capitalism, our findings are ultimately consistent with the expectations of the GCC/GVC perspective. We conclude by highlighting the robust analytical space within which scholars from the GCC/GVC and institutional camps can come together to understand the determinants of variation in how the spatial fragmentation that we observe is achieved.

1. Varieties of capitalism versus global chains: competing or complementary forms of economic organization?

One can trace the origin of this debate to an exchange between Gary Gereffi and Richard Whitley in a symposium about the implications of globalization for economic organization in the journal *Competition and Change*, in which the authors staked out contending positions regarding the development of new modes of inter-firm coordination in global industries. In explicating his position, Gereffi makes three claims: 1) rising economic competition has important consequences for organizational behavior and performance at the firm, national, and regional levels; 2) a key response to the problem of rising competition is the emergence of commodity chains—that is, functionally integrated, geographically dispersed production systems coordinated by Northern-based lead firms that decide how, where, and by whom activities are carried out; and 3) commodity chains vary by industry, as a result of both product and process characteristics and policies at the national and international level.

Gereffi distinguished producer-driven (e.g. autos and aircraft) from buyer-driven (e.g. apparel and footwear) commodity chains. This distinction was based on the observation that the lead firms coordinating the latter are retailers and brands that retain activities such as product development and marketing in-house but outsource most of the actual production to networks of independent suppliers located primarily in lower-wage countries. In contrast, the lead firms of producer-driven chains are primarily manufacturers that retain a greater degree of manufacturing capabilities, both in-house and in other Northern countries, than their counterparts in buyer-driven chains. This distinction between producer- and buyer-driven chains thus has implications for the organization (hierarchy versus vertical disintegration) and the geography (less versus more spatially dispersed) of production. While GCC/GVC analysts admit that national institutions shape what happens when particular links in global commodity chains touch down, they focus on patterns of internationalization that vary by chain types. For example, Gereffi and others expect that firms having a similar position in a commodity chain will focus on similar activities in terms of the inter-firm division of labour, and will have similar relationships with other chain participants. To the extent that these sector-specific organizational patterns conflict with older, nationally specific modes of industrial organization, globalization might tend 'to diminish the influence of national origins on business systems' (1996: 427).

In contrast, Whitley took issue with the claim that commodity chains 'constitute separate coordination and control systems of economic activities', arguing that for this to be true, 'they would need to establish distinctive ways of organizing firms and markets on a worldwide scale which differed significantly from purely national and regional ones' (Whitley 1996: 416). Instead, Whitley argues that there is likely to be significant variation in the way transnational coordination is occurring across distinct institutional contexts, even in the same industry. That is, variation in how firms operate in the market, organize work internally, and coordinate interactions with one another and with other actors (e.g. labour unions and financial institutions) by institutional contexts is more important to economic organization than variation across purportedly global models of industrial organization. In short, national institutional contexts are resilient to the pressures of global economic change precisely because 'distinctive ways of coordinating and controlling economic activities... developed interdependently with key institutions' (ibid: 412).

There has been relatively little change in the essential contours of this debate over the last decade and a half. There is considerable agreement among proponents of both the VoC and GCC/GVC approaches that national-level institutions do matter for many outcomes of interest to organizational scholars, and there is also growing consensus that globalization may lead to some degree of decoupling between institutional contexts and organizational dynamics. Yet there remains a fundamental disagreement about which matters more for economic organization—national (or more rarely, regional) institutions or industry-specific systems of inter-firm coordination. In our view, this is both a theoretical and empirical question. Answering it requires us to develop a clearer distinction between the analytical foci of the GCC/GVC and VoC camps, as well as identifying measures of organizational behavior and performance that are more or less suited to these foci. Thus, our circumscribed goal is to more clearly delineate the outcomes that are of primary interest to the GCC/GVC approach, and juxtapose its explanation of them to those that can be drawn from the VoC perspective.

The empirical outcome in focus here is national variation in spatial fragmentation at the level of three broad industries—garments, electronics, and transportation equipment—that were chosen because they are the most extensively studied in the GCC/GVC tradition. Following Feenstra (1998), we measure spatial fragmentation with the ratio of imports to value added in each industry, which captures the amount of industry-specific domestic production that is augmented by imports for each country. As we discuss further in the methodological section below, our particular metric is a useful indicator of global production networks but it is also an imperfect one because it does not allow us to distinguish between arm's-length imports and coordinated trade of the sort that interests us here. Nevertheless, it is preferable to alternative measures that do not capture the full range of processes through which offshored manufacturing can be coordinated.

Our empirical analysis is guided by a set of hypotheses about spatial fragmentation drawn from the VoC and GCC/GVC literatures, which we develop in the next section. Of course, spatial fragmentation is only one dimension of economic organization that scholars refer to when they claim that organizational outcomes reflect either institutional contexts or sectoral logics. Furthermore, our analysis does not allow us to speak definitively to *how* spatial fragmentation is achieved—that is either through equity-based, market-based or network-based ties. We return to this point in the conclusion because we believe that this lacuna in our analysis provides an ideal space within which institutional and GCC/GVC literatures could engage in intellectual cross-pollination.

2. Economic organization and spatial fragmentation across industries and institutions: What do the sectoral and institutional approaches suggest?

One of the central claims of Gereffi's original commodity chains framework is that the role that firms and countries play in a global division of labour is increasingly linked to the formation of producer-driven and buyer-driven commodity chains. While it was not initially clear in Gereffi's original formulation *why* functionally integrated but spatially dispersed production networks were emerging in the manufacturing sector (e.g. Gereffi 1994, 1996), over time commodity chains scholars developed a dynamic theory in which pressure generated by heightened global competition led Northern firms to respond by offloading the parts of the production process with lower barriers to entry, and thus, higher degrees of competition (Kaplinsky 2005). Indeed, the original distinction between producer-driven and buyer-driven chains reflected this logic: Lead firms in the apparel industry (e.g. retailers) retain control over brand development and marketing, but externalize to networks of independent and/or off-shore suppliers those activities characterized by the lowest barriers to entry, the highest competition, and the lowest returns (e.g. apparel assembly). Conversely, manufacturing links in the capital intensive auto chain are protected by higher barriers to entry, which reduce the pressure on auto assemblers to externalize and/or offshore production. Thus, relative to lead firms in the apparel industry, auto companies are more likely to service the home market through domestic manufacturing operations (Mahutga 2012).

However, even the prototypically producer-driven auto industry experienced a significant degree of both organizational fragmentation (e.g. General Motors' spin-off of Delphi as an independent supplier) and spatial fragmentation in recent decades, as companies expand their production networks to include overseas component suppliers or offshore assembly plants to service both the home and foreign markets. Thus while offshore manufacturing relations may be occurring more rapidly in the apparel industry than in autos, the fact that it is occurring in both can be explained with reference to a general decline in the barriers to entry that protect manufacturing or 'tangible' activities *relative* to 'intangible' ones, such as research and development, product design, and marketing (Gereffi et al. 2001; Kaplinsky 2005). This argument about the relationship between declining barriers to entry in manufacturing and spatial fragmentation can be restated as our first hypothesis.[4]

> *H_1: Given declining barriers to entry in many production activities, rates of spatial fragmentation are increasing in all manufacturing industries.*

While a trend toward rising spatial fragmentation across the manufacturing sector is a clear implication of the GCC/GVC approach, GCC/GVC analysts pay more attention to what they argue are *industry-specific* responses to global competition. These responses reflect the fact that 'fundamental differences exist between industries in terms of technology, competitive structures, and labor-intensity, and these play a primary role in explaining industrial governance structures and the strategies countries should pursue in order to succeed in global markets' (Gereffi 1996: 433–4). Research on global industries over the course of the 1990s provided support for this view, and in fact revealed a greater degree of variety in governance structures, thus suggesting a need to move beyond the original producer- versus buyer-driven dichotomy. Accordingly, scholars are increasingly focused on developing a more comprehensive typology of coordination mechanisms and identifying the factors producing

[4] As the literature on multinational corporations has long emphasized, there are multiple reasons for a firm to establish a presence outside of its home country. These include, among others, market access, access to inputs such as labour or raw materials, and control of distribution channels (Dunning 2000).

particular forms of governance. In other words, if we take governance structure as the dependent variable, what are the independent variables that produce particular patterns of inter-firm coordination?

The theory of global value chain governance developed by Gereffi, Humphrey, and Sturgeon (2005) aims to provide such a specification. They develop a typology consisting of five governance structures, based on the possible combinations of three independent variables (measured 'low' or 'high'): the complexity of the transaction between firms, the codifiability of information relating to the production process, and the capabilities existing in the supply base. What is theoretically novel about this theory is that its fivefold governance typology includes three network forms between the poles of hierarchy and market: captive networks, relational networks, and modular networks. Rather than juxtapose a single mode of network coordination to both market and hierarchy as a 'third form' (Hall and Soskice 2001: 14), this elaboration suggests that there are multiple network logics, which, in turn, have distinct implications for spatial fragmentation. For example, while relational networks typically require frequent and extensive interactions between firms, modular networks do not; consequently, the latter are compatible with a greater degree of spatial fragmentation between exchange partners.[5] Codification is a critical independent variable in this respect because it permits the exchange of complex information across space, thus mitigating the need for spatial proximity between firms in modular networks (see Tylecote in this volume).

In sum, the GVC theory of governance conceptualizes rising competition in the global economy as an exogenous process to which firms respond with some combination of organizational and spatial fragmentation that varies by the opportunities and constraints available to them. Because these opportunities and constraints are related to the variables identified above—entry barriers, complexity, codifiability, supplier capabilities—and because the values of these variables differ across industries, so, too, do fragmentation patterns vary by industry. In contrast to the VoC's emphasis on institutional variation across advanced industrialized countries, then, the GCC/GVCs literature emphasizes the more or less similar role that developed-country firms play in globalizing industries. Thus, rates of spatial fragmentation vary across industries in relation to the number and geographic distribution of capable suppliers as well as the complexity of the production process. Specifically, fragmentation will be highest when capabilities are high and complexity is

[5] It is important to note here that the modular networks elaborated in the GVC theory of governance draws from Sturgeon's (2002) work on modularity in the electronics industry, and specifically how the development of standards affects inter-firm relations between OEMs and suppliers. There is a large literature on modularity, and some of it uses the term 'modular' more in a general way (i.e. to refer to production systems that feature subassemblies, as in autos) (Baldwin and Clark 2000; Sako 2003).

low. In industries characterized by more complex production processes, fragmentation will increase with the codifiability of product and process technology.

In terms of the three specific industries we examine here, lead firms in the garment industry would be expected to organize their manufacturing via internationally diffuse sourcing networks because apparel manufacturing is characterized by low barriers to entry and low complexity, while the capabilities of the supply base in the global South are high. Alternatively, lead firms in the transport equipment industry would be expected to internalize a larger share of the manufacturing activity than those in the garment industry because of higher barriers to entry in manufacturing. Moreover, when outsourcing does take place, auto firms should coordinate relational networks with a smaller and less globally dispersed set of sourcing partners because the complexity of the production process is high, its codifiability is low, and supplier capabilities in the global South are modest (Sturgeon, Biesebroeck, and Gereffi 2008). Finally, the electronics industry is typically conceptualized as having a modular governance structure. In this industry, spatial fragmentation is expected to be intermediate because, although the production process is more complex than in the garment industry, this complexity can be managed across long distances through codification, which is higher in the electronics industry than in the auto industry. Moreover these industry-specific governance structures apply regardless of the institutional context in which firms are embedded (Sturgeon 2009),[6] which leads us to our second hypothesis:

> *H_2: Industry-specific rates should rank as follows: garments, electronics, transportation equipment.*

While the VoC literature and related institutional perspectives comprise a voluminous and diverse body of work, we are particularly interested in the argument that a coupling dynamic exists between institutions and organizations. According to this view, the configuration of institutions that exists in a given political economy favours certain organizational capabilities and behaviours over others. For example, some institutional environments encourage high-risk, high-reward strategies, while others facilitate longer-term investments by cultivating patient capital, which reduces pressure on firms to generate immediate returns to shareholders.

[6] While institutions are formally exogenous to this framework, it is possible that institutional dynamics are important for determining the value these variables take in a given context, as suggested by the large literature on the development of international industry standards, since such standards clearly affect the 'codifiability' measure (Greenstein and Stango 2007; Langlois 2004).

Similarly, firms that conduct business in institutional environments that provide the capacity for '(i) the exchange of information among actors, (ii) the monitoring of behavior, and (iii) the sanctioning of defection from cooperative endeavors', environments that include 'powerful business or employer associations, strong trade unions, extensive networks of cross-shareholding, and legal or regularity systems designed to facilitate information sharing and collaboration', should enjoy a competitive advantage in forms of industrial organization that rely upon thick relational networks among domestic firms, rather than either vertical integration or arm's-length market ties (Hall and Soskice 2001: 10).

The relationship between institutional context and organizational capability is the basis for Hall and Soskice's claim that institutional diversity is a source of comparative advantage for firms of different national origins competing in global markets: 'the institutional structure of a particular political economy provides firms with advantages for engaging in specific types of activities there. Firms can perform some types of activities, which allow them to produce some kinds of goods, more efficiently than others because of the institutional support they receive for those activities in the political economy', which vary across nations (2001: 37). In this sense, globalization, far from eroding institutional vitality, may actually reinforce it; 'nations often prosper, not by becoming more similar, but by building on their institutional differences' (ibid: 60).

While the best procedure for identifying unique institutional regimes and the placement of particular countries within any classificatory scheme has been a subject of debate with this literature, Hall and Soskice propose a typology that divides most of the advanced, industrialized countries of the OECD into one of two categories: liberal market economies (LME) and coordinated market economies (CME). In the former, 'firms coordinate their activities primarily via hierarchies and competitive market arrangements', whereas in the latter 'firms depend more heavily on non-market relationships to coordinate their endeavors with other actors and to construct their core competencies... In contrast to liberal market economies, where the equilibrium outcomes of firm behavior are usually given by demand and supply conditions in competitive markets, the equilibria on which firms coordinate in coordinated market economies are more often the result of strategic interaction among firms and other actors' (Hall and Soskice 2001: 8–9). These distinct institutional settings shape firm competencies and inter-firm coordination in such a way as to either encourage specialization in particular industries, and/or specialization in particular kinds of inter-firm organization across industries (Casper and Whitley 2004; Amable 2003; Casper in this volume; cf. Crouch, Schröder and Voelzkow 2009).

According to the VoC literature, the CMEs feature institutions that foster long-term, trust-based relationships between firms, including 'extensive systems for what might be termed "network reputational monitoring"' (Hall and Soskice 2001: 23). By fostering communication and repeat exchange among firms, say between lead firms and suppliers, this institutional context enables firms to work collaboratively in the pursuit of the kind of incremental innovation that is important for success in industries such as car manufacturing (cf. Herrigel and Wittke 2005). Thus, firms in CMEs are more likely to use non-market ties such as long-term relational contracting, while LMEs should have a higher degree of vertical integration and/or arm's-length ties among firms. In other words, the dominant form of economic organization in the LMEs is presumed to be a mix of hierarchy and market, while the institutional milieu of CMEs is thought to encourage inter-firm coordination via relational networks.

One implication that Hall and Soskice draw from the link between institutional context, organizational competencies, and the dominant mode of inter-firm coordination found in an economy is that 'firms based in LMEs may be more inclined to move their activities abroad to secure cheaper labor than companies based in CMEs, because the former already coordinate their endeavors using the market structures that less developed nations usually provide, while the latter often pursue corporate strategies that rely on high skills and institutional infrastructure difficult to secure elsewhere' (2001: 57). The claim here is simply that, across all industries, firms in LMEs rely more heavily than firms in CMEs on market-based inter-firm relations that are easier to reproduce in developing countries than the kind of collaborative inter-firm ties that predominate in CMEs. Thus, relative to their counterparts in CMEs, firms in LMEs can more easily shift production to lower-wage locations, while firms from CMEs will 'continue to invest in their home CME even when other investment opportunities in low-cost, less-developed countries exist' (Allen 2004: 101–2). Accordingly, our third hypothesis is as follows:

H_3: Across all industries, rates of fragmentation are higher in LMEs than CMEs.

The institutional comparative advantage framework developed by Hall and Soskice is also consistent with expectations of cross-national patterns of industry-specific specialization, because certain types of industries are more compatible with the institutions that predominate in one VoC versus another. Firms in CMEs are competitive in industries based on diversified quality production, with German auto firms representing the classic example of institutional-organizational coupling for this model (Streeck 2009). Diversified quality production, which characterizes capital goods such as machine tools, consumer durables, and transportation equipment, is based on incremental innovation that improves an established product line, while securing 'continuous improvements in the production process in order to improve quality control and hold down costs' (Hall and Soskice 2001: 39). In contrast, firms in LMEs are expected to excel in industries that are based less on incremental improvements in process technology and more on radical innovation (e.g. creating entirely new product lines or making significant changes to extant products or processes). Examples include segments of the electronics industry (e.g. semiconductors, software development), telecommunications, and services such as corporate finance or entertainment.

How might we evaluate empirically the VoC claim that there is a coupling between, on the one hand, institutional configurations, organizational capabilities, and the types of innovation characterizing particular industries, and, on the other, firm performance and sectoral specialization? If patterns of internationalization reflect comparative advantage, and if the latter is shaped partially by the resources that different institutional regimes provide, then we would expect firms to be competitive in those industries that are commensurate with the VoC in which they are embedded. Where firms can draw on the comparative advantage provided by the institutional contexts within which they operate, domestic production in the context of highly embedded relational production networks should present itself as a viable functional substitute to offshoring.

For example, because CME countries should be more competitive in industries characterized by incremental innovation, and because collaborative inter-firm networks facilitate this kind of innovation, we expect spatial fragmentation to be lower in these industries. Similarly, LME countries should experience less spatial fragmentation in industries characterized by radical innovation. Thus, we derive a set of hypotheses about variation in rates of industry-specific fragmentation within and across the two institutional systems described by Hall and Soskice as coordinated and liberal market economies. Generally, we would expect that rates of fragmentation vary between LMEs and CMEs such that fragmentation is lowest in those industries for which there is a comparative institutional advantage, as the following two hypotheses suggest.

> *H_{4a}: Within the CME category, rates of fragmentation should be lower in the transportation equipment industry than in the electronics or apparel industries.*
>
> *H_{4b}: Rates of fragmentation in the transportation equipment industry should be lower for the CME countries than for the LME countries.*

3. Using spatial fragmentation to evaluate sectoral and institutional explanations: variation across and within industries and capitalisms

Data

SPATIAL FRAGMENTATION

Our dependent variable is a country-level measure of spatial fragmentation, which following Feenstra (1998) we calculate by computing the ratio of imports to value added in the garment, electronics, and transportation equipment industries and in the manufacturing sector as a whole. Our measure is one of three types of trade-based measures of spatial fragmentation; others include ratios of component to final goods trade, and two-way trade. Although the use of any one may be more or less appropriate, depending on the researcher's particular interest, none are without limitations. For example, measures of the ratio of component to final goods trade and two-way trade are either incomplete insofar as they only reflect a particular type of offshoring arrangement (i.e. trade in intermediate component imports as opposed to 'full package' offshoring), or prone to measurement error because standard trade statistics do not differentiate between components and final goods, and it is therefore impossible to accurately differentiate between them post-hoc. On the other hand, ratios of imports/exports to value added may conflate offshoring with other causes of trade (see Antras and Rossi-Hanaberg 2009 for a fuller discussion of all three types).

Although not subject to the first two sources of bias, our measure of spatial fragmentation is problematic for the third reason because we cannot determine the degree to which imports (whether they be components or assembled goods) are produced within chains coordinated by resident lead firms (either domestic firms or foreign subsidiaries). That is, our measure of spatial fragmentation is compatible with two scenarios in which lead firms are coordinating imports—1) the importation of intermediate components, which is the modal strategy in electronics and transport equipment and 2) the importation of final goods that were made offshore to specifications provided by lead firms, which is the modal strategy in the garment industry. It is also sensitive to a third scenario in which imports are not being coordinated by firms in the importing country, as when firms exit an industry entirely, leaving the domestic market to import penetration from foreign firms. Because the primary goal of our analysis is to compare fragmentation rates across industries and VoCs, we could ignore the possible conflation of scenarios 1 and 2 with 3 if we could assume the error was evenly distributed across industries and countries. Since the (in)validity of this assumption is impossible to know, our results should be read with some caution.

The trade data comes from the United Nations Commodity Trade Statistics Database (UN comtrade), and is measured at the two-digit (industry) level according to the standardized international trade classification (SITC). We use the first classificatory system (Revision 1), because it extends the farthest back in time. The categories we use for our three specific industries include 84 (wearing apparel), 73 (transport equipment); and 72 (electrical machinery). We use the sum of categories 6 (manufactured goods classified chiefly by material), 7 (machinery and transport equipment) and 8 (miscellaneous manufactured articles) for the manufacturing sector as a whole (UN 2006). The value-added data come from the United Nations Industrial Development Organization's (UNIDO) Industrial Statistics Database (UNIDO 2006), categorized according to the International Standard Industrial Classification (ISIC) system, Revision 2. We use categories 322 (Clothing), 383 (Electrical Machinery) and 384 (Transport Equipment) and 300 (Total Manufacturing) for the garment, electronics, transport equipment industries, and all manufacturing respectively.

Two of the three industry-specific categories—transport equipment and electrical machinery—are perhaps less disaggregated than would be ideal. For example, transport equipment includes autos, airplanes, bicycles, ships, and trains. Electrical machinery includes state-of-the art computers along with more standardized office equipment and appliances. All categories include both finished goods and intermediate components. However, this level of aggregation provides the greatest comparability to the value-added data, and many of the particular commodities included in these two categories are organized in similar ways, and thus approximate the ideal-typical patterns we discuss above (see Kimura 2007 for aircraft and Sturgeon and Kawakami 2010 for electronics). Thus, if we assume incorrectly that there is less variation within these categories than between them in terms of the modal GCC/GVC governance mechanisms responsible for their organization, the error of our estimates of industry-specific fragmentation rates would increase, which would increase proportionately the likelihood of insignificant industry comparisons. In other words, the possibility of measurement error in these aggregate industry categories makes it more difficult to identify significant differences in fragmentation rates across industries and thereby yields rather conservative estimates of inter-industry variation in spatial fragmentation.

VARIETIES OF CAPITALISM

In order to understand the extent to which rates of spatial fragmentation vary systematically across varieties of capitalism, we introduce indicator (dummy) variables for two varieties of capitalism. We follow Soskice and Hall (2001) in classifying countries as either coordinated market economies (CME) or liberal market economies (LME), and include only the set of advanced capitalist countries that fit neatly into one or the other category as recorded in Table 11.1.[7]

Methods

We begin by constructing five-year average levels of fragmentation for each country in each industry between the years 1963 and 2002 to smooth out any idiosyncratic year on year variation. This yields a total of eight possible observations per industry and thirty-two per country. We then pool these five-year averages across industries and countries, which yields a total of 512 possible observations. Because some countries were missing data on either trade or value added, the total number of observations was reduced to 456 in the regression models. We then regress the five-year fragmentation rates on (1) a linear time-trend, (2) indicator variables for the garment, transportation, and electronics industries, (3) the VoCs identified in Table 11.1, and (4) interactions between the three sources of variation. These regressions are ideally suited to test hypotheses involving industry and VoC specific explanations, as well as control for each in testing the other, because they allow for direct hypothesis tests of all three sources of variation from within the same model.[8]

However, interpreting regressions involving two and three-way interactions can be difficult without a careful consideration of the conditional implication of interaction terms (Kam and Franzese 2007). Thus, in order to simplify the presentation of our hypothesis tests, we report the full interaction models in Table 11.3 in the methodological appendix at the end of the chapter and confine our discussion to Table 11.2, which reports combinations of the estimated coefficients along with their variance and covariance that are relevant to our hypothesis tests. These combinations are detailed in the methodological appendix. We first test hypotheses about fragmentation rates across VoCs ignoring variation by industry. We then test hypotheses across industries ignoring variation by VoC. We conclude by testing industry-specific fragmentation hypotheses within and between VoCs.

[7] We include 18 of the 34 OECD countries in our dataset. As do Soskice and Hall, we exclude Turkey, Mexico, and the Central and Eastern European countries. We also exclude those (primarily southern) European countries (Greece, Spain, Italy, Portugal, and France), which correspond to neither the CME nor LME categories. Some studies in the VoC tradition include these western European countries, or some subset of them, as a third 'mixed' variety of capitalism (e.g. Rueda and Pontusson 2000). We restricted our analysis to the CME and LME categories because we did not feel confident formulating clear hypotheses about the relationship between economic organization and institutional context for other varieties.

[8] The regression parameters reported below are obtained with ordinary least-squares regression except that the standard errors have been adjusted to account for the clustering of the error term within the repeated country observations (Rogers 1993). The industry-country-year levels of fragmentation were logged with the base 10 logarithm prior to the analysis to adjust for skew.

Table 11.1. Country by variety of capitalism (VoC)

Country	VoC
Austria	CME
Belgium/Luxembourg*	CME
Denmark	CME
Finland	CME
Germany	CME
Japan	CME
Netherlands	CME
Norway	CME
Sweden	CME
Switzerland*	CME
Australia	LME
Canada	LME
Ireland	LME
New Zealand	LME
United Kingdom	LME
United States	LME

Notes: Categorization from Hall and Soskice (2001). *Belgium and Luxembourg's trade data has been reported at the aggregate level until only very recently. We maintained this aggregation because it is impossible to disaggregate backward in time. Switzerland is missing value-added data systematically and is excluded.

Results

Figure 11.1 displays fragmentation trends by industry using a locally weighted scatterplot smoother (LOWESS), where the level of fragmentation is logged with the base-10 logarithm and averaged across the CME and LME groups. By the second half of the period under investigation, all three of our industries—garments, electronics, and transport equipment—are more fragmented than the manufacturing sector as a whole. The fragmentation rate is highest for the garment industry, but it is difficult to identify real differences in the fragmentation rate between the transportation and electronics industries, except that the former seems to slow while the latter increases toward the end of the period. The fragmentation rate for manufacturing as a whole seems more or less constant throughout the period. In short, there appears to be a trend toward increased fragmentation across all these industries over time, but it is unclear exactly how this rate varies by industry.

Do the apparently positive industry-specific trends in Figure 11.1 together constitute a statistically significant trend toward fragmentation on average across all these industries? The first coefficient in Table 11.2 tests our first hypothesis (H_1) that rates of spatial fragmentation are increasing across all manufacturing industries, regardless of VoC type. The positive coefficient on the linear time trend in Model 1 supports this hypothesis, suggesting that the average rate of increase in the manufacturing sector as a whole is roughly 9.6

Table 11.2. Hypothesis Tests for fragmentation rates conditional on VoC, industry, and VoC-industry interactions (from Table 11.3), 1963–2002

	Model 1	Model 2			Model 3	Model 4		
	All	CME[a]	LME[a]	CME—LME[a]	All[b]	CME[c]	LME[c]	CME—LME[c]
Industry Trends								
All	0.096*** (0.009)	0.086*** (0.010)	0.112*** (0.016)	—	—	—	—	—
Garments	—	—	—	—	0.193*** (0.013)	0.200*** (0.011)	0.186*** (0.016)	—
Electronics	—	—	—	—	0.075*** (0.016)	0.057** (0.016)	0.102** (0.029)	—
Transport	—	—	—	—	0.059*** (0.014)	0.040** (0.011)	0.087** (0.026)	—
Difference between industry-specific fragmentation trends within VoCs								
Garments—Electronics	—	—	—	—	0.117*** (0.023)	0.143*** (0.016)	0.084* (0.038)	—
Garments—Transport	—	—	—	—	0.134*** (0.021)	0.160*** (0.016)	0.098** (0.031)	—
Electronics—Transport	—	—	—	—	0.016 (0.013)	0.017 (0.013)	0.015 (0.027)	—
Difference in industry-specific fragmentation trends between VoCs								
All	—	—	—	−0.027 (0.016)	—	—	—	—
Garments	—	—	—	—	—	—	—	0.014 (0.020)
Electronics	—	—	—	—	—	—	—	−0.045 (0.033)
Transport	—	—	—	—	—	—	—	−0.047 (0.028)

Notes: Coefficients are conditional unstandardized regression coefficients. Standard errors adjusted for clustering at the country level in parentheses.
* $p<0.05$;
** $p<0.01$;
*** $p<0.001$. See the appendix for notes a–c.

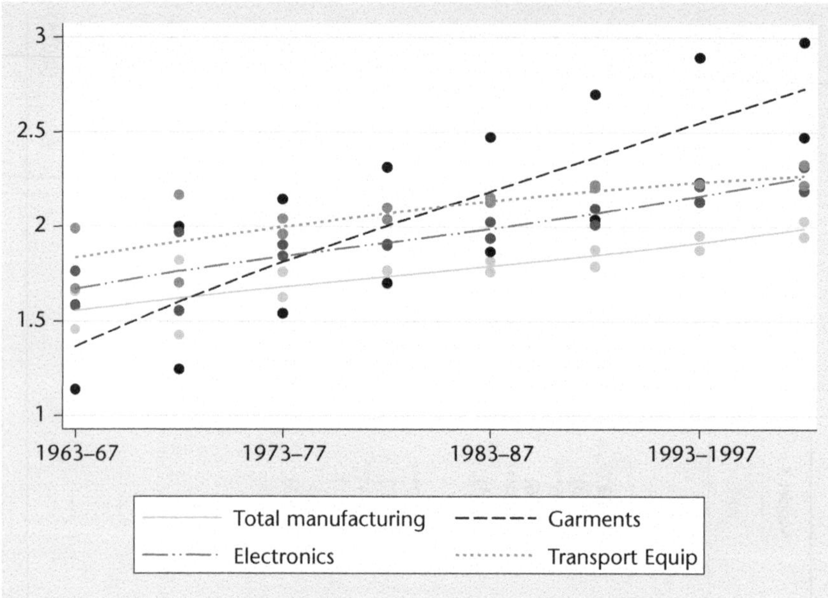

Figure 11.1. Average level of fragmentation by industry, 1963–2002

Notes: Fragmentation levels are logged with the base 10 logarithm and averaged across the CME and LME countries. Time trend fit with a LOWESS smoother.

(100 × 0.096) per cent every five years, a trend that is significantly different from zero.

Figure 11.2 displays the same trends as in Figure 11.1, but disaggregated by variety of capitalism. The positive trend for all industries in Figure 11.1 seems to hold for both VoC groups, as do the relative fragmentation rates across industries. However, it is difficult to ascertain whether or not industry-specific fragmentation rates differ systematically between industries or across VoCs on the basis of a visual inspection of Figure 11.2. Thus, we turn now to the regression models to test the hypotheses we elaborated above. The first tests appear in columns 2–4 of Table 11.2 (Model 2). The second and third columns of Table 11.2 report the average fragmentation rate across all industries for the CME and LME categories, respectively. The fragmentation rate is 8.6 (100 × 0.086) per cent every five years in the CMEs and 11.2 (100 × 0.112) per cent every five years in the LMEs, for a difference of 2.7 per cent between the two varieties. The fourth column tests our third hypothesis (H_3)—namely, that rates of fragmentation are higher in LMEs than in CMEs. The difference of 2.7 per cent in the rate of fragmentation between the two VoC groups is in the expected direction—LMEs fragment faster than CMEs—but is not significant. Thus, the evidence does not support the third hypothesis that rates of fragmentation are systematically higher in LMEs across all industries.

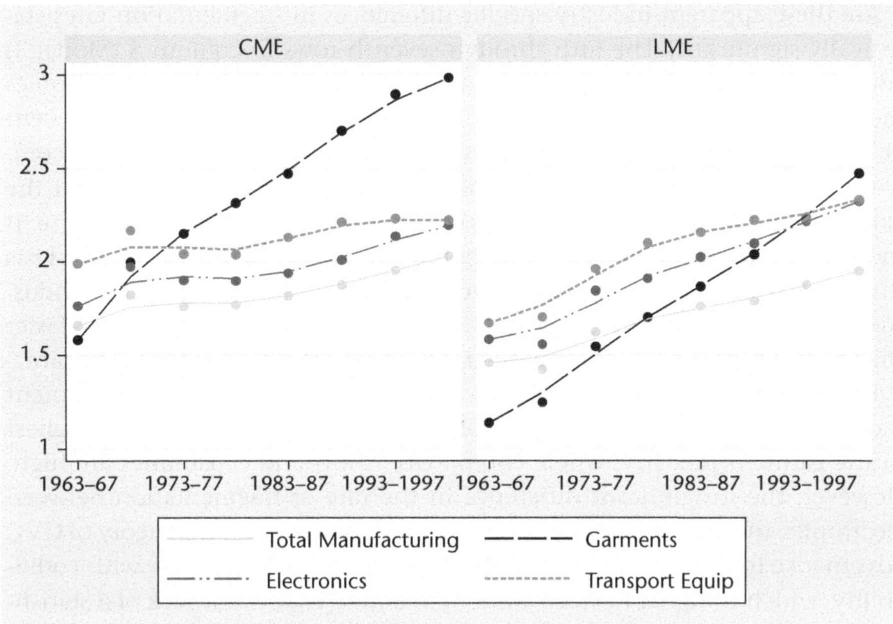

Figure 11.2. Average level of fragmentation by industry and VoC, 1963–2002

Notes: Fragmentation levels are logged with the base 10 logarithm and averaged by the CME and LME countries. Time trend fit with a LOWESS smoother.

The fifth column in Table 11.2 (Model 3) addresses our second hypothesis (H_2) that rates of fragmentation vary systematically across industries. This hypothesis tests the claim that fragmentation will be highest when the capabilities of suppliers are high and complexity is low, and otherwise increase with the codifiability of product and process technology. In terms of our three industries, this means that fragmentation is highest in the garment industry (low complexity, high capabilities) and lowest in the auto industry (high complexity, low codifiability), with the electronics industry constituting an intermediate case (high complexity, high codifiability).

The second through fourth rows in column 5 (Model 3) report the industry-specific trends. Each industry has a positive and statistically significant rate of fragmentation. Moreover, the rates of fragmentation across industries appear to vary in a manner consistent with our second hypothesis—the rate of fragmentation is highest in the garment industry (19.3 per cent every five years), where complexity is low and capabilities are high. It is intermediate in the electronics industry (7.5 per cent every five years), where both complexity and codifiability are high. Finally, the fragmentation rate is lowest in the transport equipment industry (5.9 per cent every five years), where complexity is high and codifiability is low.

Are these apparent industry-specific differences in fragmentation rates statistically significant? The fifth through seventh rows in column 5 (Model 3) address this question. The fifth row compares the garment and electronics industry, and suggests that the garment industry fragments 11.7 per cent faster that electronics, which is statistically significant. The sixth row compares the garment and transport equipment industry, and suggests that the garment industry fragments 13.4 per cent faster than the transport equipment industry, which is also statistically significant. Finally, the seventh row tests the same hypothesis for the electronics and transportation equipment industries, suggesting that the electronics industry fragments 1.6 per cent faster than the transport equipment industry, but the difference is not significant.

In short, the significantly higher rate of fragmentation in the garment industry supports our second hypothesis that fragmentation rates are highest in the garment industry, where complexity is low and capabilities are high. However, the insignificant difference in the rate of fragmentation between electronics and transport equipment may call into question the theory of GVC governance insofar as it expects spatial fragmentation to increase with codifiability, which is higher in electronics than autos. That is, the lack of a statistically significant difference between autos and electronics in Model 3 suggests that the difference between modular and relational modes of governance may be inconsequential for spatial fragmentation.

Model 4 in Table 11.2 allows us to test hypotheses comparing the VoC and GCC/GVC literatures by addressing the extent to which the between-industry variation in fragmentation rates identified above holds across VoC types, and whether or not industry-specific fragmentation rates vary across VoCs. In rows 2–4 of columns 6 and 7 in Table 11.2, we report the results of Model 4, which shows trends in industry-specific fragmentation in the CMEs and LMEs, respectively. Each industry shows a positive and statistically significant rate of fragmentation in each VoC category. In the CMEs, the five-year rate of fragmentation is 20 per cent for garments, 5.7 per cent for electronics, and 4 per cent for transportation equipment. In the LMEs, the five-year rate of fragmentation is 18.6 per cent for garments, 10.2 per cent for electronics, and 8.7 per cent for transportation equipment. These positive trends are also significantly different from zero in both varieties. Moreover, and similar to the analysis of all countries in column 5 (Model 3), the industry rank ordered fragmentation rates in both the CMEs and LMEs are consistent with the expectations of the GCC/GVC approach, where garments fragment the fastest, followed by electronics and then transport equipment.

Are these industry-specific fragmentation rates significantly different within each of the VoCs? The fifth through seventh rows of columns six and seven test whether the between-industry differences for all countries in Model

2 hold for each variety of capitalism. The results are identical to the same comparisons in column 5 for all countries. In CMEs, the garment industry fragments significantly faster than both the electronics (14.3 per cent) and transportation equipment (16 per cent) industries, but the difference between the transportation and electronics industries (1.7 per cent) is not significant. Likewise in the LMEs, the garment industry fragments significantly faster than both the electronics (8.4 per cent) and transport equipment (9.8 per cent) industries, but again the difference between the transportation and electronics industries (1.5 per cent) is not significant.

On one hand, this is consistent with hypothesis 4a (H_{4a}), which predicts that rates of fragmentation in the transportation equipment industry should be lower than those for the garment industry in countries with coordinated market economies. On the other hand, the insignificant difference between the fragmentation rate in the electronics and transport equipment industries within the CME group, coupled with the identical pattern of industry-specific rank ordered fragmentation rates in the LME group, might suggest that the low rates of fragmentation for the transport industry in the CMEs is a not function of the institutional advantage that firms in these economies enjoy but rather the industry-specific governance patterns predicted by the GCC/GVC literature. Thus, we find only mixed support for H_{4a}.

However, a cursory comparison across rows two through four in columns 6 and 7 may suggest that industry-specific rates of fragmentation vary significantly across VoCs because the estimate of the garment fragmentation rate is higher for the CMEs, while that for the electronics and transport equipment industries are lower. Significant differences in industry-specific fragmentation rates across VoCs would be consistent with hypothesis 4b (H_{4b}) which, drawing from the VoC theory of comparative institutional advantage, predicts that rates of fragmentation in the transport equipment industry should be lower in the CMEs than the LMEs. In other words, perhaps there is significant variation in fragmentation rates across VoCs once industry differences are controlled—that is, within the same industry. Thus, the final three rows in column 8 test the null hypothesis that the industry-specific fragmentation rates do not vary across VoCs. The signs on these comparisons are consistent with H_{4b}: The fragmentation rate is slower in the CMEs than the LMEs in both transport equipment (4.7 per cent) and electronics (4.5 per cent). However, none of these between-VoC differences are significantly different from zero.

While the results above indicate that the variation in spatial fragmentation across institutional types is not significantly larger than that within them, part of this might be attributable to variation within the VoC categories. Indeed, there is no shortage of criticisms regarding either the placement of particular countries in either the CME or LME camps or the need for additional categories beyond the CME and LME models. One of the more developed critiques focuses on classification of Japan and Germany within the same category. Critics point out that while these political economies are indeed distinct from those comprising the LME category, they also differ from each other in terms of how they organize relations, both with their suppliers and with their employees. For example, the industrial organization of the Japanese auto industry has long been based on very low levels of vertical integration. Historically, Japanese assemblers outsourced most of their component production to independent suppliers, who also played a major role in product development and testing. In contrast, competitor firms in Germany retained more parts manufacturing and R&D/design activities in-house (Kwon 2005). Similarly, the Japanese industrial relations system is less centralized and relies more heavily on internal labour markets at the company level than the German one (Thelen and Kume 1999).

One implication of this literature is that Japan's institutional context gives domestically co-located but vertically disintegrated firms a competitive advantage versus companies that rely more on offshore suppliers. If this is the case, we would expect lower rates of spatial fragmentation in Japanese industries than those in other CMEs like Germany. However, this outcome would not emerge from the analysis we conducted above, since we do not differentiate among the CMEs. In other words, it is possible that there is a relationship between institutional context and organizational fragmentation, but that one has to look *within* the CME group to find it, a possibility to which we now turn.

Figure 11.3 displays the industry-specific spatial fragmentation rates in both Japan and Germany. Much like the pattern in Figure 11.2, there are clear similarities across Japan and Germany: in both countries, the garment industry has the steepest slope and the electronics industry has a fairly flat slope until the early 1990s. However, Japan's transport equipment industry has a fairly flat slope that never rises above the level of spatial fragmentation for the manufacturing sector as a whole, whereas Germany's looks similar to the CME average in Figure 11.2. Thus, it is possible that Japan's institutional context allows its firms to substitute a higher degree of domestically based vertical disintegration for the relatively higher level of offshoring observed in Germany and the LMEs. In order to test this hypothesis, we conducted unreported analyses that are complementary to Table 11.2 but limited to comparisons between Japan and Germany, rather than the CME and LME groups. In both countries, all industries had a significantly positive rate of fragmentation, the garment industry fragmented significantly faster than the other two, and the fragmentation rate in the garment and electronics industry did not vary across the two countries. However, Japan's transport equipment industry did fragment significantly slower than Germany's, which is consistent with the expectations of the institutional foundations of the Japanese business system discussed above.

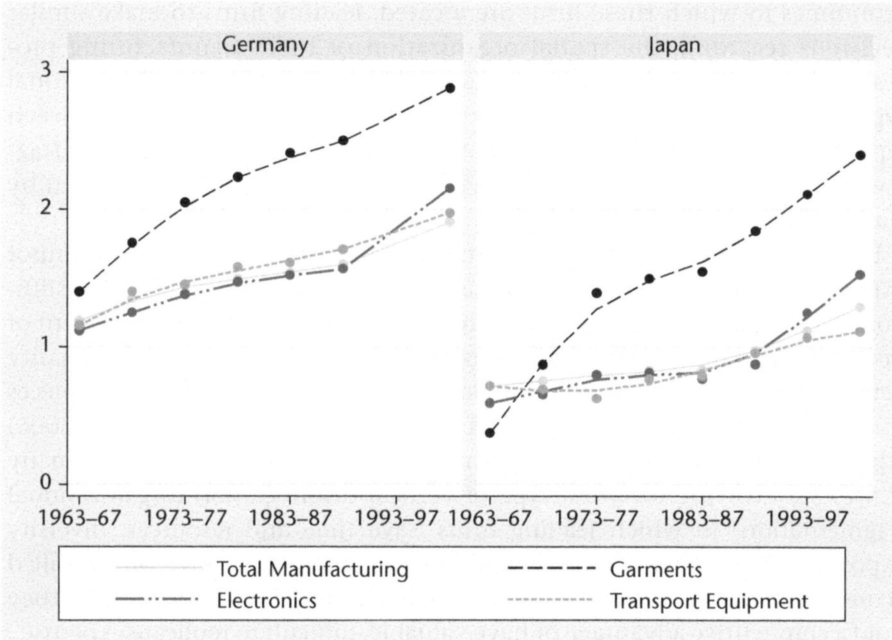

Figure 11.3. Average level of fragmentation by industry in Germany and Japan, 1963–2002

Notes: Fragmentation levels are logged with the base 10 logarithm. Time trend fit with a LOWESS smoother.

4. Conclusion

We identified two sets of hypotheses regarding the rate of spatial fragmentation in manufacturing. One set (H_1 and H_2) focuses upon the GCC/GVC literatures, and predicts significant variation in fragmentation between industries, which reflects more or less sector-specific, global models of industrial organization. Another set (H_3 and H_{4a}/H_{4b}) focuses on institutional variation between countries, and suggests instead that both overall and industry-specific rates of fragmentation should vary by institutional context. Our analysis suggests that the spatial fragmentation rate in manufacturing among advanced capitalist countries appears to vary more by industry than institutional context. We believe this is because firms in the advanced capitalist countries that are the focus of the VoC literature play similar roles in globalizing industries (i.e. as 'lead firms', in the language of GCC/GVC analysis), and because particular characteristics of these industries transcend the institutional configurations of the political economies in which these firms are located, leading firms to make similar decisions regarding the spatial organization of their manufacturing processes. Indeed, the only significant variation we observe across institutional types was in spatial fragmentation rates for transport equipment between Japan and Germany. If institutional variation is significant for spatial fragmentation, one may have to go beyond the VoC categories developed by Hall and Soskice to identify it.

Because we focus narrowly on spatial fragmentation, our findings cannot explain *how* firms across advanced capitalist countries with varying institutional types achieve spatial fragmentation. Indeed, this is a central concern of institutional perspectives and presents one possible complementarity between the GCC/GVC and VoC approaches. We highlight two recent pieces that advance the debate in this direction. First, Herrigel and Wittke (2006) argue that the auto industries in both the United States (LME) and Germany (CME) are evolving toward a type of vertical disintegration (organizational fragmentation) in which leading firms 'save time and resources, diversify exposure to risk and enhance flexibility [by concentrating] on so-called "core competence" areas—that is, on particular functions . . . for which they hold a competitive advantage or have valuable, difficult to replicate expertise', and rely on suppliers 'in all other areas' (313; also see Thelen and Kume 1999: 492). Moreover, and consistent with our discussion of the GCC/GVC approach outlined above, they find that vertical disintegration is being achieved via a markedly similar type of 'contingent collaboration' in both countries, where the links between purchasing and supplying firms oscillate between moments of conflict and cooperation. They conclude by underscoring the degree of autonomy and creativity these firms possess with respect to their national institutions, which allows them to 'respond to challenges posed by the competitive environment in ways that appear to neither be systematically constrained nor encouraged by the institutional architecture in which they are embedded' (Herrigel and Wittke 2006: 344).

On the other hand, similar comparative research on the garment industry finds some convergence in offshoring behaviour between clothing firms in the United Kingdom (LME) and Germany (CME), but a significant degree of variation between them in terms of how this offshoring is achieved. Those in the UK pursue more arm's-length, market-based ties with suppliers, and those in Germany pursue more equity-based vertical links with offshore subsidiaries (Lane 2008). Thus, both studies are consistent with our own research as far as it goes—organizational fragmentation is characterized by a higher degree of spatial fragmentation in the garment (Lane 2008) than the auto (Herrigel and Wittke 2006) industry. However, one study argues for the emergence of a modal type of inter-firm coordination in the auto industry across institutional varieties (Herrigel and Wittke 2006), while the other finds persistent diversity in inter-firm coordination across institutional varieties in the same industry (Lane 2008). This variance is a puzzle—why would institutional variation matter more in the garment industry than the auto industry, especially when the latter would seem to be more heavily impacted by national institutions than the former (Sturgeon et al. 2008)? Future research on the organization of inter-firm relations, both across institutional varieties and across industries, is needed to explicate the conditions under which firms respond to global competition through similar organizational fixes, or rather by exploiting the institutional environment that exists in their home or a foreign country.

Methodological Appendix

Table 11.3. Interaction models of five-year average level of fragmentation within and between industries and varieties of capitalism, 1963–2002

Constituent Terms	1	2	3	4
Year	0.096***	0.112***	0.057***	0.068***
	(0.009)	(0.016)	(0.009)	(0.016)
CME * year		−0.027		−0.018
		(0.019)		(0.019)
Garments * Year			0.136***	0.118***
			(0.016)	(0.025)
Electronics * Year			0.018 +	0.034*
			(0.009)	(0.014)
Transport * Year			0.002	0.019
			(0.010)	(0.020)
CME * Garments * Year				0.032
				(0.028)
CME * Electronics * Year				−0.027
				(0.017)
CME * Transport * Year				−0.029
				(0.021)
Constituent Terms				
CME		0.297		0.189
		(0.245)		(0.232)
Garments			−0.251 +	−0.454 +
			(0.119)	(0.213)
Electronics			0.099	0.096
			(0.058)	(0.094)
Transport			0.307***	0.270*
			(0.067)	(0.118)
CME * Garments				0.331
				(0.233)

(*continued*)

Table 11.3. Continued

Constituent Terms	1	2	3	4
CME * Electronics				0.005 (0.117)
CME * Transport				0.061 (0.139)
Constant	1.557*** (0.131)	1.378*** (0.173)	1.519*** (0.116)	1.406*** (0.175)
R^2	0.161	0.192	0.279	0.358
N	456	456	456	456

Notes: Coefficients are unstandardized regression coefficients. Standard errors adjusted for clustering at the country level in parentheses.

+ p⟨0.10;

*p⟨0.05;

**p⟨0.01;

***p⟨0.001.

In the annotations to Table 11.2 that follow, the 'conditional' standard errors vary by the particular industry, VoC or industry–VoC comparison being drawn, and the equations are therefore too cumbersome to reproduce here. See Kam and Franzese 2007 for a discussion of their derivation.

a. The fragmentation trend in CME countries is obtained by adding the coefficient for the interaction between time and CME with the linear term and dividing the sum by the conditional standard error. The trend for LME is equal to the coefficient on the linear term.

The difference between the trend in the CME and LME is just the interaction term.

All of these come from Model 2 in Table 11.3.

b. The industry–specific fragmentation trend is obtained by adding the coefficient for the interaction between time and the focal industry to the coefficient on the linear term.

The difference between industry trends is obtained by subtracting the coefficients on the industry–time interaction terms across the focal industries and dividing that by the standard error of the difference.

All of these come from Model 3 in Table 11.3.

c. The industry–specific fragmentation trends within the CME are obtained with the sum of the coefficients on the linear term, the interaction between the focal industry and time, the three–way interaction between the focal industry, time, and the CME group, and the interaction between time and the CME group, and is expressed over the relevant conditional standard error.

The industry–specific trends in the LME group are obtained with the sum of the coefficients on the linear term and the interaction between the focal industry and time, expressed over the relevant conditional standard error.

References

Allen, M. (2004) 'The Varieties of Capitalism Paradigm: Not enough variety?' *Socio-Economic Review*, 2: 87–108.

Amable, B. (2003) *The Diversity of Modern Capitalism*, New York: Oxford University Press.

Antras, Pol and Esteban Rossi-Hanaberg (2009) 'Organizations and Trade', *Annual Review of Economics*, 1: 43–64.

Bair, J. (ed.) (2008) *Frontiers of Commodity Chain Research*, Palo Alto, CA: Stanford University Press.

Baldwin, C. and K. Clark (2000) *Design Rules, volume 1: The power of modularity*, Cambridge, MA: M.I.T. Press.

Boyer, R. (2004) 'New Growth Regimes, but Still Institutional Diversity', *Socio-Economic Review*, 2: 1–32.

Casper, S. and R. Whitley (2004) 'Managing Competences in Entrepreneurial Technology Firms: A comparative institutional analysis of Germany, Sweden and the UK', *Research Policy*, 33: 89–106.

Crouch, C., M. Schröder and H. Voelzkow (2009) 'Regional and Sectoral Varieties of Capitalism', *Economy and Society*, 38(4): 654–78.

Deeg, R. and G. Jackson (2007) 'Towards a More Dynamic Theory of Capitalist Variety', *Socio-Economic Review*, 5: 149–79.

Dunning, J. H. (2000) 'The Eclectic Paradigm as an Envelope for Economic and Business Theories of MNE Activity', *International Business Review*, 9(1): 163–90.

Feenstra, R. (1998) 'Integration of Trade and Disintegration of Production in the Global Economy', *Journal of Economic Perspectives*, 12(4): 31–50.

Gereffi, G. (1994) 'The Organization of Buyer-Driven Global Commodity Chains: How US retailers shape overseas production networks', pp. 95–122 in Gary Gereffi and Miguel Korzeniewicz (eds) *Commodity Chains and Global Capitalism*, Westport: Praeger Press.

—— (1996) 'Global Commodity Chains: New forms of coordination and control among nations and firms in international industries', *Competition and Change*, 4: 427–39.

—— J. Humphrey, R. Kaplinsky, and T. Sturgeon (2001) 'Introduction: Globalisation, value chains, and development', *IDS Bulletin*, 32(3): 1–8.

—— —— and T. Sturgeon (2005) 'The Governance of Global Value Chains', *Review of International Political Economy*, 12(1): 78–104.

Gibbon, P., J. Bair, and S. Ponte (2008) 'Governing Global Value Chains', *Economy and Society*, 37(3): 315–38.

Greenstein, S. and V. Stango (eds) (2007) *Standards and Public Policy*, New York: Cambridge University Press.

Hall, P. and D. Soskice (2001) 'An Introduction to Varieties of Capitalism', pp. 1–69 in Hall and Soskice (eds) *Varieties of Capitalism: The institutional foundations of comparative advantage*, Oxford: Oxford University Press.

—— and K. Thelen (2009) 'Institutional Change in Varieties of Capitalism', *Socio-Economic Review*, 7(1): 7–34.

Hancke, B., M. Rhodes, and M. Thatcher (eds) (2007) *Beyond Varieties of Capitalism: Conflict, contradictions and complementarities in the European economy*, New York: Oxford University Press.

Henderson, J., P. Dicken, M. Hess, N. Coe, and H. Wai-Chung Yeung (2002) 'Global Production Networks and the Analysis of Economic Development', *Review of International Political Economy*, 9(3): 436–64.

Herrigel, G. and V. Wittke (2006) 'Varieties of Vertical Disintegration: The global trend toward heterogeneous supply relations and the reproduction of difference in US and German manufacturing', pp. 277–311 in G. Morgan, R. Whitley, and E. Moen (eds) *Changing Capitalisms? Internationalization, Institutional Change, and Systems of Economic Organization*, Oxford: Oxford University Press.

Hollingsworth, J. R. and R. Boyer (eds) (1997) *Contemporary Capitalism: The embeddedness of institutions*, Cambridge: Cambridge University Press.

Kam, C. and R. J. Franzese Jr (2007) *Modeling and Interpreting Interactive Hypotheses in Regression Analysis*, Ann Arbor: University of Michigan Press.

Kaplinsky, R. (2005) *Globalization, Poverty and Inequality: Between a rock and a hard place*, Cambridge: Polity Press.

Kimura, S. (2007) *The Challenges of Late Industrialization: The global economy and the Japanese commercial aircraft industry*, New York: Palgrave.

Kwon, Hyong-Ki (2005) 'National Model under Globalization: The Japanese model and its internationalization', *Politics and Society*, 33: 234–52.

Lane, C. (2008) 'National Capitalisms and Global Production Networks: An analysis of their interaction in two global industries', *Socio-Economic Review*, 6: 227–60.

Langlois, R. (2004) 'Competition through Institutional Form: The case of cluster tool standards', University of Connecticut, Department of Economics Working Papers 2004-10.

Mahutga, Matthew C. (2012) 'When Do Value Chains Go Global? A theory of the spatialization of global value chains', *Global Networks*, forthcoming. doi: 10.1111/j.1471-0374.2011.00322.x.

Morgan, G. and I. Kubo (2005) 'Beyond Path Dependency? Constructing new models for institutional change: The case of capital markets in Japan', *Socio-Economic Review*, 3(1): 55–82.

Rogers, W. (1993) 'Regression Standard Errors in Clustered Samples', *Stata Technical Bulletin*, 13: 19–23.

Rueda, D. and J. Pontussson (2000) 'Wage inequality and varieties of capitalism', *World Politics* 52(3): 350–83.

Sako, M. (2003) 'Modularity and Outsourcing: The nature of co-evolution of product architecture and organization architecture in the global automotive industry', pp. 229–53 in A. Prencipe, A. Davies, and M. Hobday (eds). *The Business of Systems Integration* Oxford : Oxford University Press.

Streeck, W. (2009) *Re-forming Capitalism: Institutional change in the German political economy*, New York: Oxford University Press.

—— and K. Thelen (eds) (2005) *Beyond Continuity: Institutional change in advanced political economies*, Oxford: Oxford University Press.

Sturgeon, T. (2002) 'Modular Production Networks: A new American model of industrial organization', *Industrial and Corporate Change*, 11(3): 451–96.

—— (2009) 'From Commodity Chains to Value Chains: Interdisciplinary theory building in an age of globalization', pp. 11–135 in J. Bair (ed.) *Frontiers of Commodity Chain Research*, Palo Alto, CA: Stanford University Press.

—— V. Biesebroeck, and G. Gereffi (2008) 'Value Chains, Networks, and Clusters: Reframing the Global Automotive Industry', *Journal of Economic Geography*, 8: 297–321.

—— and M. Kawakami (2010) 'Global Value Chains in the Electronics Industry: Was the crisis a window of opportunity for developing countries?' pp. 245–301 in O. Cattaneo, G. Gereffi, and C. Staritz (eds) *Global Value Chains in a Postcrisis World: A development perspective*, New York: World Bank Press.

Taylor, M. (2004) 'Empirical Evidence Against Varieties of Capitalism's Theory of Technological Innovation', *International Organization*, 58: 601–31.

Thelen, K. and I. Kume (1999) 'The Effects of Globalization on Labor Revisited: Lessons from Germany and Japan', *Politics and Society*, 27(4): 477–505.

United Nations (2006) COMTRADE, New York: United Nations.

United Nations Industrial Development Office (2006) *Industrial Statistics Database: 3-digit level of the ISIC Code, Revision 2*, Vienna: Statistics Unit, United Nations Industrial Development Organization.

Whitley, R. (1996) 'Business Systems and Global Commodity Chains: Competing or complementary forms of economic organisation', *Competition and Change*, 1: 411–23.

—— (1999) *Divergent Capitalisms: The social structuring and change of business systems*, New York: Oxford University Press.

—— (2007) *Business systems and organizational capabilities*, New York: Oxford University Press.

12

What is Happening to Corporations and What of Their Future?

Grahame Thompson

Introduction

In the wake of the financial crisis, commercial banks and other financial institutions have come under increased public scrutiny. Of course, whether this scrutiny will, in the end, make much difference to how they are regulated or operate is another matter. 'Business as usual' is likely to be a strong post-crisis reaction for banks, particularly as 'normality' descends on market sentiment and growth prospects improve (Thompson 2009b; Lall 2009). But whatever happens, non-financial corporations are likely to have to adapt differently from those operating mainly in the financial sphere, particularly in the longer term, though both of these face similar shorter-term pressures as will be outlined in a moment. However, non-financial corporations are uniquely vulnerable under present circumstances. Not only do they face the usual pressures that come from the 'market for corporate control'—takeovers and mergers activity continue to abound—but the acceleration of technological change means that even the best laid and seemingly robust business model can be quickly swept aside by a clever invention which undermines the possibility of corporate 'business as usual'. And even the largest global firms can be stalked by activist investors—hunted by private equity or sovereign wealth funds seeking added shareholder value extraction. We have come to think of large global firms as powerful and arrogant, but actually—under present conditions—they are weak and vulnerable. Part of the story to be told in this chapter is one about what large corporations are doing to try to shore up and bolster their prospects under these circumstances: how they are positioning themselves 'politically' to combat the potential plundering of their assets and unwanted attacks on their business model, as they see it.

But, of course, whilst individual companies may be weak, the commercial system as a whole looks to be as strong as ever. This is the main apparent paradox explored below.

The discussion begins by analyzing the relationships between owners and shareholders, particularly in the context of the legal constitution of corporations. It argues that this is of the first importance in sustaining the ideology of shareholder value, but is full of the most glaring ambiguities, ones that could be exploited by those seeking radical reform of corporate governance and company law. The chapter then moves on to take up the 'debate' about the divorce of ownership from control in the light of this thorough examination of the legal status of the corporation, in so doing re-visiting the terms of that debate in the 1930s and 1940s that arose in the light of Berle and Means' book *The Modern Corporation and Private Property* (1932). Subsequent to this it moves on to think about the possible future of the corporation and the potential for reform of corporate governance in the light of current circumstances and trends in a post-crisis world.

The modern corporation in law

This section concentrates upon the legal position of the company vis-à-vis its owners and its managers. By and large this discussion is confined to the Anglo-American corporate form, though it has important consequences for developments in other jurisdictional milieus. The rise of the shareholder value ideology has been a key ingredient in stimulating the discussion, and although this has had its most obvious direct impact in the UK and the USA, this discourse is also very influential in France, Germany, Japan, and elsewhere (Gourevitch and Shinn 2005; Cioffi 2010; Culpepper 2011). The example of the shareholder-driven corporation is often taken as a model for desirable corporate developments elsewhere. But this model is not as simple as it appears and is in fact riven with complexities and ambiguities which need to be considered in order to have a proper debate about the nature of the corporation—a debate which would undermine simplistic arguments that these other countries simply have to move towards the US or UK model.

The main difficulty that arises in this respect is that the corporation recognized in law is both a 'thing' and a 'person' at the same time. It is a kind of 'cyborg': analogous to both human and machine (though not in the form of a natural person or natural thing). Shareholders own 'shares' (and stockholders own 'stocks'), but not the assets or property of the company as such, which are invested in the company itself: in a legal sense the company 'owns' itself (Ireland 1999, 2010). Thus we could say that it is subject to a double ownership relation: once by the shareholder who 'own' shares, and once by the corporation itself which owns the company assets. Shares (pieces of paper) give shareholders certain rights (or perhaps better put, afford them certain 'claims', see below): they share in the surpluses generated by the company, they have voting rights in respect to the officers of the company and in terms of mergers and acquisitions, and they can sell (and buy) shares. But that is about all.

In this respect—within Anglo-American legal practice at least—the shareholder is in a very similar legal position to any other creditor vis-à-vis the company as legal subject (Dodd 1932): they are both its 'claimants' and have no direct proprietary entitlements in the company's assets or property as such. Their interests *jointly* represent potential liabilities from the point of view of the company (Hadden 1995). In fact 'ownership' was precisely a legal category developed to prise apart property from possession, originally developed in the context of legal moves in the early medieval period in Europe to regularize the status of women—until then women were considered as the property of men and part of their direct possessions (Thornhill 2012).

Similarly, although the managers may be (formally at least) elected or appointed by shareholders, they are legally constrained to work in the best interests of the company in the first instance, not the shareholder: they have obligatory fiduciary duties.[1] Their role is to supervise the continuing organizational, financial, and legal reproduction of the company—to maintain it as a 'going concern', to 'keep the capital intact', and so on. And as McSweeny (2009) has pointed out, when actionable endeavour has been sought in the courts over what or who has primacy in terms of fiduciary duties, judgment has invariably fallen to the management rather than to the shareholders (see especially Marens and Wicks 1999; Lan and Heracleaus 2010).[2] The judgments

[1] As Iwai comments:

> These duties specify the standards for judging the 'trustworthiness' and 'fairness' of the managers' decisions and transactions which may conflict with the best interests of the corporation. And these standards usually include the so-called 'duty of care', the restraint on 'excessive' managerial compensations, the strict rule on the disclosure of information, and the prohibition of self-dealing, trading corporate opportunity, trading on inside information, and outright theft (1999: 623)

When shareholders enter the Board they too must adopt these standards and constraints.
But this idea of fiduciary duties is controversial. Despite some ambiguities, Kraakman et al. (2004), and particularly Parkinson (1993) argue against this position. Indeed, these authors of well-established textbooks remain the main contemporary supporter of the direct shareholder ownership position.

[2] McSweeny quotes from *Aranson v Lewis* 473 A.2d 805 Supreme Court of Delaware, [1984] where Justice Moore argued 'A cardinal precept of the General Corporation Law of the State of Delaware is that directors, rather than shareholders, manage the business and affairs of the corporation' 8 Del.C. § 141(a). This is doubly important since Delaware is the state where most US businesses are incorporated, and is thought to have the most 'liberal' (read 'business friendly') corporate law regime. But these declarations have a longer history and apply to other jurisdiction in the USA. For instance, as pointed out by Moore and Rebérioux (2011) the idea that a company's

reviewed in footnote 2—which form the basis for the 'business judgment rule' in the US courts (which has been similarly embodied in the commercial law in other jurisdictions, particularly the UK) protects the directors in the conduct of their 'duty of care' for the corporation and its employees. If the directors act in good faith, in the best interests of the corporation, on an informed basis, in a non-wasteful manner and without personal interest (i.e. that they are 'duly diligent'), then the courts have protected their position. But this is the site of a real issue because, despite this, it is often thought that the 'default position' in respect to company operations is that they should operate to maximize profits. Is it the ultimate purpose of a firm in current business law to generate profit, any deviation from which makes the managers 'liable'? This is a complex issue which would ultimately have to do with legal interpretations of the articles of association, but it looks as though this requirement so far remains an untested default position.[3]

board of directors is subject to any sort of direct 'agency' relationship with that firm's shareholders, requiring ongoing subservience to the latter's expressed interests, was dispelled in a line of cases decided by the New York courts over a century ago. "In one of the earliest and also most clear refutations of the so-called 'principal-agent' model of corporate governance, Comstock, J. of the Court of Appeals of New York stressed the fundamental corporate law tenet that:

> [t]he board of directors of a corporation do not stand in the same relation to the corporate body which a private agent holds toward his principal. In the strict relation of principal and agent, all the authority of the latter is derived by legislation from the former... [b]ut in corporate bodies the powers of the board of directors are, in a very important sense, original and undelegated... in the sense of being received from the State in the act of incorporation.

Moreover, according to Comstock. J.:

> The recognition of this principle is absolutely necessary in the affairs of every corporation whose powers are vested in a board of directors. Without it the most ordinary business could not be carried on, and the corporate powers could not be executed. (*Hoyt v Thompson's Executor*, (1859) 19 N.Y. 207 (Court of Appeals of New York), p. 216)

Over fifty years later Chase, J. of the same Court reiterated this basic line of reasoning, expressing the principle that 'the individual directors making up the board are not mere employees, but a part of an elected body of officers constituting the executive agents of the corporation.' Setting out the parameters of what is today known in corporate law jurisprudence as the business judgement rule, Chase J explained that directors 'hold such office charged with the duty to act for the corporation according to their best judgment, and in so doing they cannot be controlled in the reasonable exercise and performance of such duty' (*People ex rel. Manice v Powell*, (1911) 201 N.Y. 194 (Court of Appeals of New York), p. 201) (Moore and Rebérioux 2011, pp. 96–7).

A similar legal position can be discerned in the case of UK company law, despite that fact that shareholders in the UK model are granted somewhat wider democratic powers. Moore and Rebérioux (2011, p.45) quote from Lord Justice Couzens Hardy to the effect that: 'it is a fallacy to say that the relation [between shareholders and the board] is that of simple principal and agent.... I do not think it is true to say that the directors are agents. I think it is more nearly true to say that they are in the position of managing partners appointed to fill that post by a mutual arrangement between all the shareholders.' (*Automatic Self-Cleansing Filter Syndicate Co. v Cunninghame*, [1906] 2 Ch 34 (Court of Appeal)).

[3] Drawing from Moore and Rebérioux (2011, p. 134) once again: '[i]f powers of management are vested in the directors, they and they alone can exercise those powers. The only way in which the general body of shareholders can control the exercise of the powers vested by the articles in the directors is by altering the articles, or, if the opportunity arises under the articles, by refusing to

Some would argue however, that it is continually tested by the range of measures associated with 'shareholder protection': involving not just 'hard-case' company law but also provisions found in securities law and in the 'soft law' of codes of corporate conduct and takeover regulation (Armour et al. 2008). This discussion arose out of the seminal contribution of La Porta et al. (1998) who put forward the proposition that there were two basic forms of 'legal origin' as far as shareholder protection is concerned: civil law societies and common law societies. They went on to claim a) that common law societies systematically provided more effective protection of the shareholder interests and, b) this stimulated more robust economic development and growth. Whilst, in their terms, there had been some subsequent convergence between these legal systems—and a growing recognition that there were other 'sub-systems' within (or around) each core grouping (like a distinctive Scandinavian grouping within the civil law tradition)—underlying differences between the two groups of countries have continued to provide the same differential consequences along the original lines (Djankov et al. 2008).[4]

This set of arguments has attracted a great deal of attention. Many criticisms have been made of—and suggestions for improvements to—the original La Porta formulation, particularly in respect of how to construct a 'correct' index of 'shareholder protection,' and allocate countries in respect to this (e.g. Siems 2007; Spamann 2010; Siems 2008; Armour et al. 2008—Thompson and Mortensen 2009 discuss the Danish literature on this issue). Broadly this challenges the idea of two clearly defined groupings as the differentiation and hybridization of each separate legal system is uncovered. Nevertheless the basic thrust of the attempt to link legal/regulatory systems to different degrees of shareholder protection continues in these critical studies. This remains contentious however.

In general, this literature and debate ignores the earlier case histories that established the 'business judgments rule' discussed above. It takes this as a given, so it is not so much concerned with the deeper questions of ownership raised earlier. But, of course, it is centrally concerned with control, though

re-elect the directors of whose actions they disapprove. They cannot themselves usurp the powers which by the articles are vested in the directors any more than the directors can usurp the powers vested by the articles in the general body of shareholders' (*John Shaw & Sons v Shaw & Shaw* [1935] 2 KB 113).

[4] Here it is recognized that the discussion of shareholder rights remains solely within the frame of differences between legal traditions: common law versus civil law jurisdictions, and does not consider alternative explanations of how shareholder rights are constructed, e.g. political explanations. The political literature in this respect is particularly instructive (see Roe 2003, Gourevitch 2003, Gourevitch and Shinn 2005, Coffi 2010 and Culpepper 2011), but a thorough discussion of these contributions would take us into a somewhat different territory. The analysis provided here concentrates on the legal literature for the good reason that a critical examination of this exposes the ambiguities and contradictions in one of the strongest justificatory discourses supporting shareholder supremacy .

here one might need to remain cautious. There is a considerable attention to the detail of control as demonstrated in the *ex ante* sense of what laws, rules, and conventions are in place to try to prevent managers/directors exercising their 'agency' at the expense of shareholders (see Armour 2008 in particular and the detail at: http://www.cbr.cam.ac.uk/pdf/Shareholder%20protection%20index%20references%2025%20countries.pdf; accessed 11 April 2011).

Broadly speaking this involves the collection of data on the ease of challenge over 'self dealing' on the part of directors, likelihood of success if action is taken, and some attention to important case judgments. So there is some consideration of the *ex-post* outcomes when challenges have been made in the courts or other arenas of regulation. But this is always difficult to judge and tends to vary on a case by case basis. It is all very well having *ex-ante* mechanisms is place, but success with proof of misdemeanours and malpractices on the occasion of litigation is another matter. In general, this still takes place under the shadow of the business judgment rule—which tends to protect the managers if they exercise due diligence. And—as recent events associated with various pre-crisis financial scandals and the financial crisis itself have surely demonstrated—these mechanisms proved hopelessly inadequate to prevent widespread abuse of shareholder interests and potential wrongdoing in common law countries in particular (though there have been few individual cases of managerial negligence perused in the courts).

The point, then, is not to continually lament the lack of shareholder control, or to seek some further robust ultimate rule that guarantees shareholder primacy, but to recognize that—in situations of 'normal business'—shareholders are of minor importance for the provision of capital. And despite there being enormous effort devoted to catering for shareholder interests and providing them with information about day-to-day operations and long-term strategy—all geared up to serving shareholder value considerations, shareholders are necessarily remote from actual decision-making. The emphasis, instead, needs to shift to better preparing the managers/directors for their role as the actual guardians of the company as an institution that owns itself, which is pursued below. Given that, the legal obligations under which managers work are by no means as unambiguous as the principal–agent model (and its offshoots in shareholder value) imply, and this opens up an arena for policy discussion and managerial discretion.

Obviously a different set of legal conditions hold if the company is in liquidation, creditors having a prior claim over shareholders in this instance (see Carruthers and Halliday 1998; Halliday and Carruthers 2009). But even under these circumstances, neither creditors nor shareholders can seize the company's assets at will, so nor do they 'own' it in this sense. Here both shareholders and creditors are similarly constituted as 'claimants', with only a contingent title in respect to the company's assets (Hohfeld 1919).

In addition, claimants must act in accordance with due legal process. What this means is that legal rights in respect to any company are always highly specific and contingent, and what they impart to different agents are differential capacities and capabilities to undertake actions or engage in litigation. Legal rights do not exclusively or unconditionally guarantee access to 'ownership' or anything else, but only arrange possibilities for undertaking litigation or initiating actionable endeavour in the courts.

This point is important in several respects, particularly in the debates about 'property rights' in economics (and by extension for the 'Law and Economics' school of analysis which informs many of the hard 'shareholder ownership' positions mentioned above). These do not impart an exclusive, unconstrained, or unconditional *possession* to a definite subject or agent. It is not the case, then, that any attenuation of those rights—involving a circumscription or restraint on their exercise, usually thought to be imposed by the political process or the State—necessarily represents an unwarranted challenge to those rights of possession. 'Property rights' attribute no more (or no less) than a capacity or capability to initiate something (like a claim on the assets of a firm). But that guarantees nothing in terms of outcomes. It only contingently and conditionally arranges a series of possibilities for legal disputation and action.

The more general importance of this formulation is to move away from a discourse of 'rights' to one about 'claims'. Rights imply a possession by a constituted subject, whereas claims only imply a contingent entitlement, one dependent upon particular circumstances (in the case here as specified by a legal framework). And this aspect of the law confirming claims rather than rights is well illustrated by bankruptcy law. Although Carruthers and Halliday's comprehensive analysis situates bankruptcy in the terminology of rights in the first instance, it is clear from the discussion that it imparts various parties with a range of claims that must be tested in law (Carruthers and Halliday 1998; Halliday and Carruthers 2009). For instance, their Table1.1 'Ranking of *Claims* in Bankruptcy' (my emphasis, 1998, pp. 39–40) sets out the hierarchy of claimants in the US and the UK, while 'The Legal Constitution of Markets' (Chapter 1, 2009) extends this approach about the potential for disputation and enforceability during bankruptcy proceedings to the Asian countries. What is clear from this extensive analysis is that there are no general 'rights fights', only contingent claims dependent upon the particularities of each jurisdiction, its characteristics and institutional limitations.

So with this conception there is no general public or private privileged possession of, or exclusion from, 'ownership'. In principle, the law could thus establish a set of 'claims' that impart capacities and capabilities to any number of stakeholders without this necessarily undermining a deeper or more fundamental 'ownership' relation because, as agued above, rights in law are never rendered with respect to an exclusive possession, but only in respect to a claim. Here we see the way a discussion of the nature of company law could establish the principles for the wider notion of stakeholder democracy without this necessarily compromising a 'deeper' set of fundamental truths about ownership (as pursed in detail in Thompson 2008).

Trends in the financing of companies

In this and the subsequent sections the chapter moves on to consider the policy implications of the analysis presented above. In the first instance this is designed to highlight empirical trends informing shareholder interests in the financing of corporate activity. The context for the subsequent discussion is illustrated by Figures 12.1 and 12.2 reproduced below.

Figure 12.1 shows that in the case of the USA's non-financial corporations there has been an almost continuous net consumption of equity since 1980, while for banks and insurance companies net consumption of their equity base

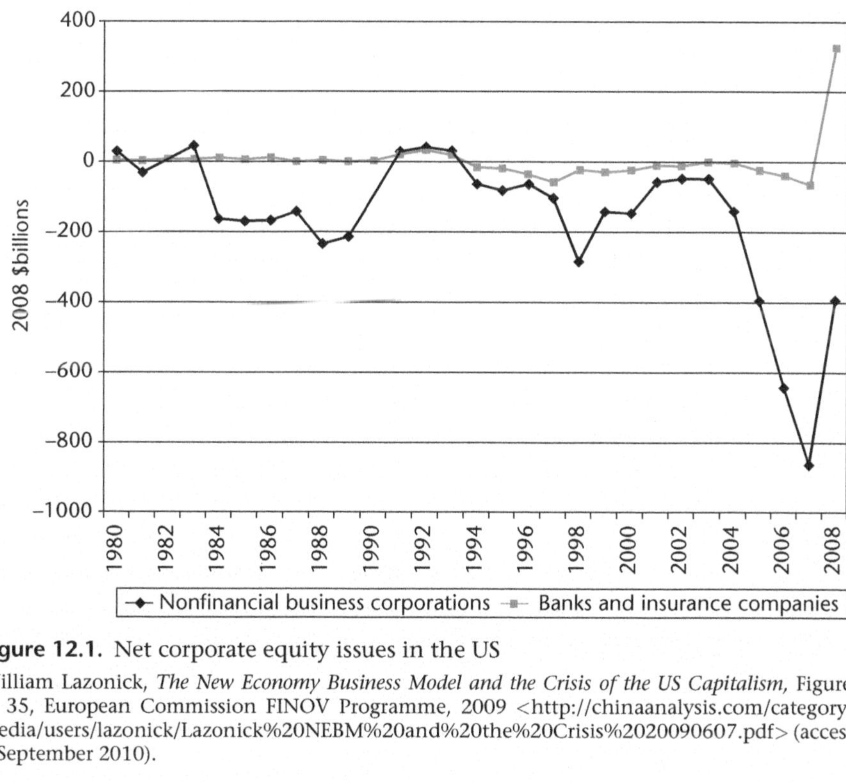

Figure 12.1. Net corporate equity issues in the US

William Lazonick, *The New Economy Business Model and the Crisis of the US Capitalism,* Figure 2, p. 35, European Commission FINOV Programme, 2009 <http://chinaanalysis.com/category_1/media/users/lazonick/Lazonick%20NEBM%20and%20the%20Crisis%2020090607.pdf> (accessed 6 September 2010).

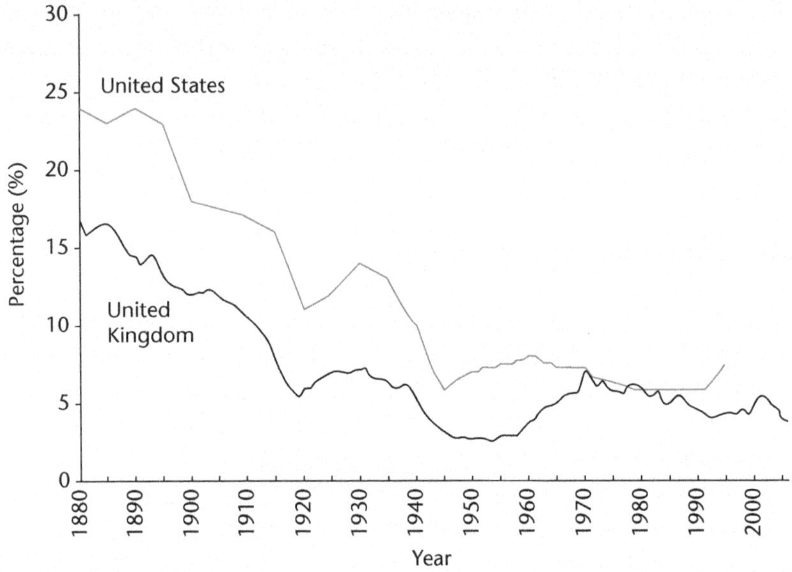

Figure 12.2. Capital ratios for UK and US Banks

Alessandri, P. and Haldane, A. G. (2009), 'Banking on the State', Bank of England, November, Chart 2. <http://www.bankofengland.co.uk/publications/speeches/2009/speech409.pdf> (accessed 9 April 2011)

began in the early 1990s (Lazonick 2008; Mitchell 2009). For both business sectors, however, post the 2007/08 crash there was an increase in equity issue (part of a re-active process of 'rebuilding balance sheets'). And a similar position was observable in the UK for the 1990–2005 period (Froud, et al. 2006, chapters 3 and 4) with net-equity issue hovering at just above zero.[5] In the case of US and UK banks, Figure 12.2 shows the decline in their capital (mainly equity) base since 1890, so that in the early 2000s it was down to well below 10 per cent in each case (Alessandri and Haldane 2009). The position of UK banks deteriorated (or escalated, perhaps) somewhat in the run-up to the crisis. According to Lapavitsas (2010, Figure 3) commercial banks equity as a percentage of their assets was only 2 per cent in 2007. The US remained steady at about 10 per cent, but German and Japanese banks were also low at 5 per cent.

Clearly, these trends have both long-term and shorter-term determinants (and consequences). But in the most recent period of the 'great moderation' (1995–2007) they were a consequence of complex relationships to 'shareholder value' and regulation. The two main ways investment resources have traditionally been generated by US and UK companies—through equity issue and retained earnings –collapsed under the onslaught of the 'originate and distribute'

[5] For an analysis of buy-backs in the UK between 1998–2000 see Hill and Taylor (2001). For a general account of possible consequences of these trends for the G7 countries see Bank of France (2006).

model for extracting and distributing 'shareholder value'. These have been replaced by debt financing on the one hand, and obscure 'off-balance sheet' items on the other—both of which, in a period of very low interest rates, proved a cheaper short-term option than financing via equity issue. This latter trend was a particular characteristic of the banks as they resorted to financing themselves in the credit markets with short-term collateralized debt obligations and other 'exotic' ('toxic' as it turned out) financial instruments. In the case of the commercial banks, international regulatory requirements put added pressure on banks to reduce their equity base as this attracted a 'financial penalty' in the form of the capital adequacy ratios attached to such capital kept on the balance sheet.

But it is important to note two things. First, non-financial companies have also heavily adopted this trend. Companies are literally 'eating themselves' in this respect. They had become net-lenders to the rest of the economy (Bank of France 2006). The hundreds of billions of dollars—trillions even—collectively spent on buybacks eliminated an equivalent value that could have been ploughed into innovation, R&D, job creation, or lower product prices. And second, in the case of the banks in particular and as Figure 12.2 shows clearly, the move away from equity capital was a long-term secular trend, so it cannot just be attributed to recent shareholder-value extraction pressures and Basel II regulatory requirements.

However, the paradoxical feature of these trends is that just as the equity base of all companies was shrinking rapidly in these respects, and shareholders became less and less important as providers of capital (indeed, quite unimportant) the ideology of shareholder control increased. More and more emphasis was placed upon the importance of shareholder control just as their actual contribution to financing companies was being rapidly eroded. Quite how and why this situation arose is a complex issue and one that has not been completely settled (Ireland 1999, 2010). This is associated with a central issue pursued in this contribution, which has to do with the precise legal constitution of companies: the nature of corporate personality and ownership as discussed above.

Debates about ownership and control of the modern corporation

Pursuing the consequences of this form of analysis of the precise relationship between ownership and control invites a return in the first instance to the debates in the 1930s and 1940s over the original 'divorce of ownership from control' thesis, which took place mainly around Berle and Means book *The Modern Corporation and Private Property* (1932). The thesis of this book is too well known to be rehearsed in detail so I concentrate upon the way this is being currently re-interpreted (Ireland 1999, 2010; Ireland and Pillay 2009; Strasser and Blumberg 2011; Biondi et al. 2007; Ho 2009). This has largely to do with the notion of 'enterprise entity' and 'enterprise analysis' that was widely discussed in the 1930s and 1940s (Berle 1932, 1947; Berle and Means 1932; Dodd 1932, 1935, 1941). As we will see in a moment the company considered as an entity is contrasted to it being viewed as a multi-layered company with many subsidiaries and holding structures. While these separate elements may have no necessary operational significance as a matter of business reality or social expectation, the standard legal practice is saturated with them, focusing on separate subsidiary corporations and imposing legal requirement of responsible behaviour only on them. The result is often poor legal decisions in respect to the requirements for corporate social responsibility.

Berle and Means posed the issue of the consequences for 'corporate governance' of the divorce of control from ownership, and the growth in importance of the managers (controllers) relative to the shareholders (owners). Originally, Berle in particular was concerned to re-establish the traditional conception of shareholders as owners, though later he modified his position and developed the idea of the firm as an 'entity' which needed to be considered as such in its own terms.[6] But the nature of this entity is the key issue (Bratton and Wachter 2007). Under pressure from Dodd's arguments, the idea of an entity not exclusively beholden to the owners/shareholders emerged. And this was the 'reality' of the way the modern company operated—so these authors adopted the corporate 'real person' conception of company personhood as outlined in Thompson (2009a). Berle recognized that the company was not just a 'bank account with rules about who had access to its resources'—a definition once offered to me of the nature of a company in law by a corporate lawyer: it was not just a collection of corporate papers, minute books, account books, and a bank account, but a *real organizational entity* with many functions and aspects. Increasingly this organized entity was being pressured to operate socially and recognizing the need to operate in a *socially responsible manner*, mainly at the behest of outside social influences, but also, crucially, by the insider managers and directors rather than the shareholder-owners—who were now remote from the company as an organizational entity. This was the concrete consequences of the divorce of ownership from control.

So, the firm needed to be both reconfigured conceptually *and in a legal sense*—to recognize this changed nature of its existence. It needed to be reconceptualized as a 'singular entity' and confirmed in law as such. Hence the ideas of the 'enterprise entity' and of 'enterprise analysis'. Berle and Means argued that the

[6] Many years ago I discussed the nature of the corporation as a 'dispersed social agency' (Thompson 1982). I insisted then, as I would reiterate now in the context of this debate, that considering the firm as an 'entity' does not necessarily involve considering it as a 'unity'.

established difference between limited liability and corporate personhood in respect to company law inhibited this 'unifying' conception: the distinction needed to be reformulated so that the cyborg nature of the firm could be overcome (it being both a 'person' and an 'entity' in law as discussed above).

Several political implications follow from this presentation. First it enables us to revisit the question of shareholder ownership. In effect the idea of an 'enterprise entity' undercuts this further. The company must be run 'for itself,' by managers, who become the 'trustees' of the institutional assets (Berle 1932; Dodd 1932), taking account of a diverse range of variable social *and* commercial objectives.[7] And the idea of an 'internalized' trusteeship of managers nicely complements the idea of the 'externalized' corporate persona being constructed by/for the company as outlined in Thompson (2009a, see also Thompson 2012 forthcoming).[8] Trusteeship would involve cultivating obligations to stockholders, to employees and to customers and the general public—safely, honestly, wisely, properly, and stressing the obligations of performing public duties as a good citizen (Dodd 1932: 1154: quoting a speech by the business executive Mr Owen D Young, 1928—this involved the first explicit reference to the idea of 'corporate citizenship' that I have been able to find in the English language literature).

Of course quite how this form of internal trusteeship might be formed and 'enforced' would be crucial. Here one might appeal to the idea of civic prudence and fortitude, originally proposed as a way of constructing an impartial integrity amongst public officials (Pufendorf [1668] 1991; Hunter 2001; Minson 2006). This is predicated on a system of impersonal and jurisdictionally delimited offices cultivated by the wise and worldly application of sociality and reason. It involves neither a reliance on the higher moral values of officials as enlightened human beings nor the blind trust in the virtues of their guardianship. Rather it involves a system of practical obligatory commitments and integrity built amongst officials who relate their activities to the capacities of the office to which they are attached, rather than to their own personal interests, values, or proclivities. Whilst this 'system of offices' was originally conceived to relate to public officials, the suggestion here is to extend its applicability to the directing personnel of a new 'quasi-civic milieu' within the private but citizenly corporation. This would be 'policed' in the first instance through social entanglements and peer pressures amongst the office bearers within the corporation, and beyond—a self-disciplining via mutual scrutiny of tasks, advice giving, and monitoring.

[7] This is what Clerc (2009) terms 'the corporate interest' model of corporate governance.

[8] The idea of a corporate persona is to focus attention on the way a particular 'self image' of the corporation is actively constructed via a range of cognitive and social mechanisms which, whilst including its legal designation, would not rely exclusively on this.

Given that—again as a matter of fact—shareholders do not contemporarily contribute much net investment resources in the aggregate for American (or British) corporations as pointed out above, any strong idea of legitimate shareholders rights in control is further undermined. What is more, enterprise analysis could in principle 'solve' the problem of 'hiding behind the veil' (Strasser and Blumberg 2011; Thompson 2009a). It would treat corporate holding companies in a group as a single 'enterprise entity' from the point of view of corporate law. Virtually all large contemporary businesses are organized into separate corporations—subsidiaries—which are owned in a hierarchical structure by a parent company which is in actual charge of the whole enterprise group. Standard corporate law treats each of these subsidiaries as a separate legal entity, with its own rights and responsibilities. What is more, the shareholders of the subsidiaries are not responsible for its obligations beyond the extent of their investments, even when the shareholder is the parent corporation which controls the whole enterprise. Thus limited liability means the parent may not be held responsible for the obligations of the whole enterprise. Strasser and Blumberg (2011) suggest six criteria for determining and assessing enterprise entity analysis: the extent of control between parts of company, the extent of economic integration between these parts, the extent of administrative interdependence, of financial interdependence, and of employee interdependence, and finally whether the company has a common public persona. These criteria would be used to determine whether a company and its parts comprised a single entity or not. Such an entity would then be treated as a single persona from the point of view of its legal incorporation.

Thus revisiting the idea of 'enterprise analysis' enables a reconsideration of the legal constitution of companies, and sets out an agenda for the reform of corporate law that provides a more effective way of reconciling the fact that the shareholder does not 'own' the company. It also provides an intellectual case for a wider consideration of 'stakeholder democracy' (Gerencser 2005—see also Davies 2009).

But what of the general trajectory for companies of the future? What can we expect from both the context of corporate development and the nature of corporate engagement itself with this evolving business environment? Here we first need to sketch out what might be the macro framework for economic reform in a post crisis world, and what role companies could play in this. Thus here we shift from an analysis of the legal constitution of companies to consider the consequences of the issues and problems it highlights for corporate reform in the context of how the modern corporation is influenced by the wider economic and political environment. In particular, this discussion focuses on the specifics of the post financial crisis world as providing the crucial context for the evolution of corporate activity. Of necessity this will be more speculative that the previous formulations since it looks ahead towards future prospects.

Post 2009 prospects for the political reform of the company

Whist the era of strict 'market fundamentalism' and market hegemony may be over as a consequence of the 2007–8 financial crisis, market discipline may not be so readily dispatched. We live in a period of resigned, resentful, and disaffected consent to market disciplining, and will continue to do so for a long time yet. So a resort to market regulation and the celebration of the market mechanisms, with all it entails, is unlikely to go away. Since the business world knows this ground well, it would probably welcome such a return to the normal routine of 'business as usual' as quickly as possible.

On the other hand what about the possibility of reconstructing a new framework for social democracy in the wake of the crisis? Can Keynesianism be revived for instance, in relation to which companies would have to adapt their operational trajectories? There is an important debate to be had here, some of the possible contours of which have already been sketched out (Clift and Tomlinson 2006a, 2006b; Hay 2006; Crouch 2008). But whatever happens politically it is unlikely that traditional Keynesian in its 'fine-tuning' form could be easily revived, though some form of 'coarse-tuning' Keynesianism might still prove attractive and possible across the political spectrum. Indeed, this is exactly the reaction as a direct consequence of the crisis—massive stimulus packages in the USA, the UK, and elsewhere (and in China in a different context) to prevent wholesale economic collapse. But whether this could be repeated again, and what its full long-term consequences will be, remain unclear.

Colin Crouch (2008) suggests that after a period of 'privatized Keynesianism'—the maintenance of aggregate demand via private credit provision to stimulate consumption, which he suggests was a characteristic feature of the 'long moderation' between 1995 and 2007 (something Clift and Tomlinson would challenge perhaps)[9]—the likely alternative is to see a new, if uneasy, political modus operandi develop between big business and the state, where companies either

[9] As a matter of fact, consumption as a percent of GDP did not rise between 2001 and 2007, indeed in the UK and Germany it fell slightly (Lapavitsas 2010, Figure 8). However, household debt as a percentage of GDP did increase significantly in the UK and the USA (but not in Japan or Germany), and was used mainly to finance housing. The general problem for the 'privatized Keynesianism' thesis is the way public expenditure also expanded in the period of the long moderation in many countries. Thus—at a minimum—the thesis would need to examine the differences between countries where it genuinely was private lending that drove the boom (e.g.Denmark, where private household debt as a percentage of GDP had escalated to the highest level amongst OECD countries in 2008, closely followed by the Netherlands) and those countries where it was of less significance (e.g. Japan and Germany—and even the UK).

make public policy themselves or do so alongside governments and in partnership with them. This is an interesting suggestion and one that could easily develop serious momentum in one form or another as either neo-liberal market fundamentalism or any new social democratic Keynesianism prove insufficient to the task. Further off-loading 'public' provision of infrastructures and operational services to the private corporate sector will look like a temptation that fiscally constrained governments find just too difficult to resist. The headlong rush toward fiscal austerity—enthusiastically in the UK, out of necessity in most of southern Europe, perhaps less enthusiastically in the USA though significantly there nevertheless—confirms that the private sector will in all likelihood step into the gap left by the state as it further abandons socially provided welfare services[10] and infrastructure developments.

And this would place 'corporate social responsibility' (CSR) back at the centre of business strategy. As mentioned above in the introductory remarks to this chapter, individually vulnerable companies are trying to bolster their position politically in various ways. One of these is to seek the protection offered by being seen as practising 'social responsibility.' CSR, along with corporate citizenship, represents a way companies are seeking to secure their position: offering responsibility in exchange for claiming protective rights in various ways, seeking consumer brand loyalty, securing public commitments via best practice recognition of environmental and ethical standards, etc. Companies are tentatively exploring this territory, gradually feeling their way into a new politicized arena, not necessarily by seeking direct support or overt protection but by presenting themselves as agents of a public purpose, being 'good citizens', performing civic duties and virtuous deeds, etc.

But as companies are invited to take more and more responsibility for providing what were traditionally considered to be publicly provided services—or as they quietly draw these into the operational orbit—the demands for transparency and accountability for that provision will significantly increase. This would present the need to examine the possible contours of this in some detail. In this context an important distinction needs to be drawn between classic 'corporate social responsibility' (addressing mainly firm externalities); 'corporate charity' (extending and performing 'good works' in a local context); and, finally, 'corporate philanthropy': that is, the provision of public and merit goods on a much wider scale in contexts unconnected to the direct business activity of the firms involved, which is already a significant

[10] Of course there is always an alternative variation waiting in the wings. In the case of the private provision of welfare services, this is not to provide theses directly via private firms, but to organize a market in welfare derivatives, one where individuals insure themselves against loss of income arising for various reasons, through the development of insurance futures and tradeable derivative contracts (Hacker 2006). This would represent a return to a kind of market fundamentalism.

current development. And corporate philanthropy—or 'Philanthro-capitalism' as it is more grandly titled (Bishop and Green 2008)—offers a tempting solution to the problem fiscally constrained governments have in maintaining the provision of 'public services'. The foundations and funds financed by billionaire philanthropists, for instance—of which there are many with billions of dollars to spend (Fleishman 2009)—are rapidly moving in to fill the gap, based upon their own assessments of 'public need' and armed with business expertise to increase efficiency as they see it. This is a major trend and one that is likely to grow. But is it legitimate to let billionaire business persons determine the agenda here, and will it improve matters (Edwards 2010)? This is a pressing issue and one that poses deep political questions about corporate objectives, their transparency and accountability—and more generally about democratic control of their activities under these circumstances. In addition to these forms of private-backed initiatives we could see a renewed emphasis from this quarter on 'social entrepreneurship' and 'social enterprise',[11] which would again stress social responsibility and civic virtue in the establishment and conduct of new business ventures.

Thus we have the conditions for a revival of considerations of corporate social responsibility: the fact that private companies look set, in one way or another, to increase their activity in respect to concerns of civic virtue, and therefore need to be held to account for that activity. This should put added pressure on reforming the model of the Anglo-American corporation. The idea that this is almost exclusively beholden to the interests of shareholders, and to shareholder value, was undermined by the detailed legal analysis of the company form conducted above. This opens up the case for the recognition of a wider set of social obligations, for treating the company as an enterprise entity in law, and of foregrounding a new sensibility to the centrality of 'managerial responsibility' in the conduct of its business.

On the other hand, there is the wider challenge posed by the changed macro-environment in which companies are going to have to operate. The implications of this further splinter the notion of who owns the firm and what its purposes are. As new tasks are laid at the door of the traditional company, and new forms of company incorporation emerge, the case for reform is further strengthened. The company as an operational entity, its

[11] Hansmann (2000) explores the ownership implications of these types of enterprise in an interesting, if rather neglected, way. In the UK there are a range of corporate forms that might be mobilized into this social enterprise agenda: traditional Industrial and Provident Societies; Company Limited by Guarantee; Company Limited by Shares and Community Interest Company. As yet these company forms do not challenge the ubiquity of the traditional limited liability company, either in terms of extent or size, but they provide a mechanism by which social objectives could be pursued and charitable objectives advanced, particularly in the context of the 'Big Society' idea currently being popularized by the Coalition Government in the UK.

existence in law, its characteristic public persona, and its renewed mandate to support civic virtue should become the proper object of public policy.

Conclusions

By way of conclusion let us return to the idea of a 'socially responsible company' (SRC) mentioned above in connection to enterprise entity analysis. As Ireland (1999) has stressed, this is not the same as traditionally understood by CSR just described: it is much more radical in it implications, moving beyond simple amelioratory activity to encompass radical reform and corporate democracy. Such an idea of the SRC would seem to fit better with the current political conjuncture as just sketched. All the developments discussed in the previous section, for instance, pose the need for a deeper examination of the purposes of corporate behaviour and its public scrutiny. So perhaps even SRC—let alone CSR—does not go quite far enough to embed wider notions of company social and commercial responsibility: to provide it with a set of incentives and penalties that will ensure proper trusteeship and citizenly persona.

Thus, instead of treating corporate citizenship cautiously, essentially thinking of the company as not a 'proper citizen' but as a kind of secondary citizen (in contrast to the primary citizenship of natural persons), a very bold step would be to declare companies as 'full citizens' with many of the rights and obligations and responsibilities of other citizens, and enforce these rigorously through the law if necessary.[12] Giving companies full citizenship rights—indeed forcing them to become proper citizens—with all the consequences that follow from this: not only to perform friendly good works and civic duties as outlined above but, for instance, also 'to come to the aid of the state when threatened' (a key responsibility of citizenship—Skinner 1993)—would itself pose a radical re-appraisal of company form and activity. But it is one worth seriously considering as companies threaten to become the new primary providers of public goods and services more generally.

References

Alessandri, P. and A. G. Haldane (2009) 'Banking on the State', Bank of England, November. <http://www.bankofengland.co.uk/publications/speeches/2009/speech409.pdf>
Armour, J., S. Deakin, P. Sarkar, M. Siems, and A. Singh (2008) 'Shareholder Protection and Stock Market Development: An empirical test of the legal origins hypothesis',

[12] One might want to draw the line at allowing companies to vote in elections however (though in some jurisdictions this still happens, e.g. in the City of London—see Thompson 2009a).

World Economy and Finance Research Programme Working Paper Series WEF0041, Birkbeck College, University of London.

Bank of France (2006) 'Is Corporate Investment Behaviour "Normal"?' *Banque de France Bulletin Digest No.152*, August.

Berle, A. A. (1932) 'For Whom Corporate Managers *Are* Trustees: A note', *Harvard Law Review*, XLV, 8: 1365–72.

—— (1947) 'The Theory of Enterprise Entity', *Columbia Law Review*, 47(3): 343–58.

—— and G. C. Means (1932) *The Modern Corporation and Private Property*, New York: Macmillan (revised 1967).

Biondi, Y. et al. (eds) (2007) *The Firm as an Entity: Implications for economics, accounting and law*, London: Routledge.

Bishop, M. and M. Green (2008) *Philanthro-Capitalism*, London: A&C Black.

Bratton, W.W. and M. L. Wachter (2007) 'Shareholder Primacy's Corporatist Origins: Adolf Berle and *The Modern Corporation*', *Institute for Law & Economics, University of Pennsylvania Law School Research Paper No. 07-24*.

Carruthers, B. G. and T. C. Halliday (1998) *Rescuing Business: The making of corporate bankruptcy law in England and the United States*, Oxford: Clarendon Press.

Cioffi, J. W. (2010) *Public Law and Private Power: Corporate governance reform in the age of finance capitalism*, Ithaca, NY: Cornell University Press.

Clerc, C. (2009) 'Questioning the Legitimacy of Shareholder Power', pp. 92–5 in Touffut, J-P (ed.) *Does Company Ownership Matter?* Cheltenham: Edward Elgar.

Clift, B. and J. Tomlinson (2006a) 'Credible Keynesianism? New Labour macroeconomic policy and the political economy of coarse tuning', *British Journal of Political Science*, 37: 47–69.

—— —— (2006b) 'Complexity, Constraint and New Labour's putative Neo-liberalism: A reply to Colin Hay', *British Journal of Political Science*, 37: 378–81.

Crouch, C. (2008) 'What Will Follow the Demise of Privatized Keynesianism?' *The Political Quarterly*, 79(4): 476–87.

Culpepper, P. D. (2011) *Quite Politics and Business Power: Corporate control in Europe and Japan*, Cambridge: Cambridge University Press.

Djankov, S., R. La Porta, F. Lopez-de-Silanes, and A. Shleifer (2008) 'The Law and Economics of Self Dealing', *The Journal of Financial Economics*, 88: 430–65.

Davies, W. (2009) *Reinventing the Firm*, London: Demos.

Dodd, E. M. (1932) 'For Whom Are Corporate Managers Trustees?' *Harvard Law Review*, XLV, 7: 1146–63.

—— (1935) 'Is Effective Enforcement of Fiduciary Duties of Corporate Managers Practicable?' *The University of Chicago Law Review*, 2.2: 194–207.

—— (1941) 'The Modern Corporation, Private Property, and Recent Federal Legislation', *Harvard Law Review*, LIV, 6: 917–48.

Edwards, M. (2010) *Small Change: Why business won't change the world*, London: Demos.

Fleishman, J. (2009) *The Foundation: A great American secret—How private wealth is changing the world*, New York: Public Affairs Books.

Froud, J., S. Johl, A. Leaver, and K. Williams (2006) *Financialization and Strategy: Narrative and numbers*, London: Routledge.

Gerencser, S. (2005) 'The Corporate Person and Democratic Politics', *Political Research Quarterly*, 58(4): 625–35.

Gourevitch, P. A. (2003) 'The Politics of Corporate Governance Regulation', *Yale Law Review*, 112(7): 1829–80.

—— and J. Shinn (2005) *Political Power and Corporate Control: The new global politics of corporate governance*, Princeton, NJ: Princeton University Press.

Hacker, J. (2006) *The Great Risk Shift*, Oxford: Oxford University Press.

Hadden, T. (1995) *Company Law and Capitalism*, London: Butterworths Law Publishing.

Halliday, T. C. and B. G. Carruthers (2009) *Bankrupt: Global lawmaking and systemic financial crisis*, Stanford, California: Stanford University Press.

Hansmann, H. (2000) *The Ownership of Enterprise*, Cambridge Mass.: Harvard University Press.

Hay, C. (2006) 'What's in a Name? New Labour's putative Keynesianism', *British Journal of Political Science*, 37: 187–92.

Hill, I. and Taylor, R. (2001) 'Recent Trends in Dividend Payments and Share But-Backs', *Economic Trend*, 567, February: 42–4.

Ho, K. (2009) *Liquidated: An ethnography of Wall Street*, Durham, NC.: Duke University Press.

Hohfeld, W. N. (1919) *Fundamental Legal Conceptions as Applied in Judicial Reasoning*, New Haven: Yale University Press.

Hunter, I. (2001) *Rival Enlightenments: Civil and metaphysical philosophy in early modern Germany*, Cambridge: Cambridge University Press.

Ireland, P. (1999) 'Company Law and the Myth of Shareholder Ownership', *The Modern Law Review*, 62(1): 32–57.

—— (2010) 'Limited Liability, Shareholder Rights and the Problem of Corporate Responsibility', *Cambridge Journal of Economics*, 34(5): 837–56.

—— and Pillay, R. (2009) 'Corporate Social Responsibility in a Neo-liberal Age', University of Kent Law School, Mimeographed.

Iwai, K. (1999) 'Persons, Things and Corporations: The corporate personality controversy and comparative corporate governance', *The American Journal of Comparative Law*, 47(4): 583–632.

Kraakman, R. R., P. Davies, H. Hansmann, G. Hertig, K. J. Hopt, K. Kanda, and E. B. Rock (2004) *The Anatomy of Corporate Law: A comparative and functional approach*, Oxford: Oxford University Press.

Lall, P. (2009) 'Why Basel II Failed and why Basel III is Doomed' *Global Economic Governance Working Paper 2009/52*, Global Economic Governance Programme, Oxford University. <http://www.globaleconomicgovernance.org/wp-content/uploads/GEG-Working-paper-Ranjit-Lall.pdf>

Lan, L. L. and L. Heracleaus (2010) 'Rethinking Agency Theory: The view from law', *Academy of Management Review*, 35(2): 294–314.

Lapavitsas, C. (2010) 'Financialisation and Capitalist Accumulation: Structural accounts of the crisis of 2007–9', *Research on Money and Finance Discussion Paper no.16, February*, SOAS, University of London.

La Porta, R., F. Lopes-de-Silanes, A. Shliefer, and R. Vishny (1998) 'Law and Finance', *Journal of Political Economy*, 106: 1113–55.

Lazonick, W. (2008) 'The Quest for Shareholder Value: Stock repurchases in the US economy', *Recherches Economiques de Louvain*, 74, 4 <http://www.cairn.info/revue-recherches-economiques-de-louvain-2008-4-p-479.htm>

McSweeny, B. (2009) 'The Roles of Financial Asset Market Failure Denial and the Economic Crisis: Reflections on accounting and financial theories and practices', *Accounting, Organizations and Society*, 37(6–7): 835–48.

Marens, R. and A. Wicks (1999) 'Stakeholder Theory, Managerial Practice, and the General Irrelevance of Fiduciary Duties Owed to Shareholders', *Business Ethics Quarterly*, 9(2): 273–93.

Minson, J. (2006) 'Civil Prudence, Sovereignty and Citizenship in the Justification of Civil Forfeiture', *University of New South Wales Law Journal*, 29(3): 61–89.

Mitchell, L. E. (2009) 'The Legitimate Rights of Public Shareholders', *George Washington Law School Public Law Research Paper No.416*, March, <http://papers.ssrn.com/sol3/papers.cfm?abstract_id%20=%201352025>

Moore, M. T. and A. Rebérioux (2011) 'Unearthing the Institutional Roots of Anglo-American Corporate Governance', *Economy and Society* 40(1): 84–111.

Parkinson, J. E. (1993) *Corporate Power and Responsibility: Issues in the theory of Company law*, Oxford: Clarendon Press.

Pufendorf, S. (1991) [1668] *Pufendorf: On the Duty of Man and Citizen According to Natural Law*, Cambridge: Cambridge University Press.

Roe, M. J. (2003) *Political Determinants of Corporate Governance: Political context, corporate impact*, New York & Oxford: Oxford University Press.

Siems, M. M. (2007) 'Legal Origins: Reconciling law and finance and comparative law', *McGill Law Journal*, 52: 56–81.

—— (2008) 'Shareholder Protection around the World (Leximetric II)', *Delaware Journal of Corporate Law*, 33: 111–47.

Skinner, Q. (1993) 'Two Concepts of Citizenship', *Tijdschrift voor Filosofie*, 55: 403–19.

Spamann, H. (2010) 'The "Antidirector Rights Index" revisited', *The Review of Financial Studies*, 23(2): 467–86.

Strasser, K. A. and P. I. Blumberg (2011) 'Legal Form and Economic Substance of Enterprise Groups: Implications for Legal Policy', *Accounting, Economics, and Law*: 1: 1, Article 4. (Available at: http://www.bepress.com/ael/vol1/iss1/4).

Thompson, G. F. (1982) 'The Firm as a "Dispersed" Social Agency', *Economy and Society*, 2(3): 233–50.

—— (2008) 'The Interrelationship Between Global and Corporate Governance: Towards a democratization of the business firm', pp. 476–98 in A. G. Scherer and G. Palazzo (eds) *Handbook of Research on Corporate Citizenship*, Cheltenham: Edward Elgar Publishing.

—— (2009a) 'Companies as "Cyborgs"? Reflections on Limited Liability, Legal Personality and Citizenship', Paper for Workshop on '*The Constitutionalization of the Global Corporate Sphere?*', CBS, September 17–18, 2009.

—— (2009b) 'What's in the Frame? How the financial crisis is being packaged for public consumption', *Economy & Society*, 38(3), 520–4.

—— (2012) *The Constitutionalization of the Global Corporate Sphere?* Oxford: Oxford University Press, Oxford (forthcoming).

Thompson, G. F. and J. Mortensen (2009) *Danish Legal Incorporation and Corporate Governance: Ownership, sector and branch analysis of top 1,000 companies and of a sample of 201,700 from all Danish incorporated entities* (July), Copenhagen Business School: CBP.

Thornhill, C. (2012) 'Guilt and the Origin of Early Modern Law', *Economy and Society*, 40 (forthcoming).

Touffut, J-P. (ed.) (2009) *Does Ownership Matter?* Cheltenham: Edward Elgar.

13

Corporate Governance in Emerging Markets

Ruth V. Aguilera, Luiz Ricardo Kabbach de Castro, Jun Ho Lee, and Jihae You

Introduction

An unresolved issue in the comparative corporate governance literature is to understand how institutional factors shape cross-national differences in corporate ownership patterns (i.e., concentration/dispersion and types of owners) (Morgan, Campbell, Crouch, Pedersen, and Whitley 2010; Aguilera and Jackson 2003). While Berle and Means (1932) assumed the prevalence of widely held firms, the empirical literature reveals that a separation of ownership and control is the exception worldwide rather than the norm, particularly in emerging markets (Demsetz and Lehn 1985; La Porta, López-de-Silanes, and Shleifer 1999; Pedersen and Thomsen 1999, 2000; Claessens, Djankov, and Lang 2000; Becht and Mayer 2001; Franks and Mayer 2001; Faccio and Lang 2002; Franks, Mayer, and Wagner 2006; Franks, Mayer, and Rossi 2009). In this chapter, we offer an empirical analysis of ownership patterns in six countries spread across three emerging market regions, Latin America, Asia, and Central and Eastern Europe (CEE).

Comparative corporate governance research has identified politics, law, and economics as the main factors triggering different ownership patterns across countries (Gourevitch and Shinn 2005; Gilson 2006; Goyer 2010; Aguilera and Jackson 2010). Theories of capitalism and transition to capitalism encompass a complex set of forces ranging from global governance pressures (Morgan and Kristensen in this volume) to firms highly embedded in local political environments (Krug in this volume). Firms behave differently not only between institutional environments but also on the public/private dimension. We focus here on publicly traded firms in emerging markets to control for some of the market heterogeneity of enterprises and to answer the basic question of *whether there have been significant changes in patterns of corporate ownership among publicly traded firms in emerging markets*. In order to address this, we have built a corporate ownership dataset by collecting data from five different sources: Amadeus for CEE, Economatica and Osiris for Latin America, and TS-2000 and Korean Exchange Statistics (KRX) for Korea. Our data was complemented and cross-checked with annual reports when necessary. We take all publicly listed firms, including both financial and non-financial, from each country stock exchange and dropped firms where the ownership information was missing or data was unreliable.[1] Our full sample consists of 19,969 (16,024 Korea; 2,596 Brazil and Chile; and 1,349 CEE) firm-year observations.

This unique and highly representative dataset allows us to contribute to the comparative corporate governance literature and to add to existing empirical research, particularly regarding the patterns of firm ownership in countries where capital markets are emerging, information asymmetry among shareholders is high, and minority shareholders' legal protection is weak. This chapter also illustrates that emerging markets are very much characterized by their idiosyncratic national models of capitalism, each with their particular financial system (Morgan and Goyer in this volume). In the next sections, we discuss the corporate ownership structures in countries from these three emerging regions.

Ownership structure in Brazil and Chile

Understanding the institutional environment and the interconnections among economic actors in Latin American countries helps explain high levels of owner control of corporations. Schneider (2004), in a study on collective action in Latin America, reports a wide variation in the organization of business in Latin America. Nevertheless, the high level of industry concentration is a common pattern across countries. As an example, in Mexico, by 1989, thirty-seven members of the 'Consejo Mexicano de Hombres de Negocio' (CMHN), controlled seventy major industrial conglomerates (*grupos*) that accounted for 22 per cent of total GDP. In Chile, eleven *grupos* had control or influence over 290 corporations that accounted for 70 per cent of corporate capital in the fifties. Schneider also reports that, in 1983, the multinational

[1] For the Czech Republic, 25 observations did not have ownership data, and for Hungary, 65 observations did not have ownership data, and for Poland, 495 observations did not have ownership data. In Korea, 689 out of 16,713 observations did not provide ownership information and were excluded from the sample. In Brazil and Chile we have 2,596 of 3,205 firm-year observations, which represent 81 per cent of the number of listed firms for the period between 2004 and 2008 and 93.46 per cent of the market capitalization.

corporations and state enterprises in Brazil, Argentina, and Mexico accounted for three-quarters or more of the total sales of fifty of the largest corporations.

State intervention and the high industry concentration were often the result of the import substitution model of development that Latin American countries followed between the 1930s and 1980s (Furtado 1982; Bullmer-Thomas 2001). Protected by a tariff wall and other entry barriers, many industries presented a high rate of return on capital, favouring an oligopoly model and incentivizing both foreign and domestic capital investments. Such models drove high levels of concentration into the hands of multinational subsidiaries and state firms.

In the 1980s and 1990s, pressured by the 'Washington Consensus,'[2] Latin American countries undertook orthodox macro-economy policy reforms, which reduced many areas of state intervention in the economy and subjected most firms to greater competition (Kuczynski and Williamson 2003). Among a variety of policies, the one that had the greatest impact on the business organizational environment was the privatization process. Over different time periods, almost all Latin American countries have experienced a period of privatization. The main aim was to reduce government debt levels as a way to signal good governance practices and to have access to financial support from Anglo-American financial institutions such as the IMF. Between 1988 and 1996, more than 900 companies were privatized in Latin America accounting for 55 per cent of total privatization revenues in the developing world in the 1990s (Serva 2003; Chong and López-de-Silanes 2005).[3] This process had a major effect on the reconfiguration of corporate ownership in Argentina, Brazil, Chile, and Mexico. Another important outcome of the market-oriented reforms was the emergence of a new set of institutions regulating privatized natural-monopolies sectors (i.e. water supply, oil, gas, telecommunications, and transportation industries) designed to improve market competition. Despite all these efforts to increase economic stability and to develop financial markets, the most important firms continue to be controlled by the business groups, *the Grupos*. Although there is very little comparative research on firm ownership in Latin America, Lefort (2005) using 1,010 firms from Argentina, Brazil, Chile, Colombia, Mexico, and Peru in 2002 and Santiago-Castro and Brown (2007) studying ninety-seven companies from

[2] Coined by John Williamson (1990) in the paper 'What Washington Means by Policy Reforms', where he identifies ten policy areas in which a fairly broad consensus might exist on what countries in Latin America and elsewhere should do: fiscal discipline, public expenditure priorities, tax reform, financial liberalization, exchange rates, trade liberalization, foreign direct investment, and privatization, deregulation, and property rights. The basic content of this agenda is summarized as macroeconomic prudence, outward orientation, and domestic liberalization towards a free market model.

[3] Refer to Chong and López-de-Silanes (2005) for a deep study of the privatization process in Latin America.

Chile, Brazil, and Mexico from 2000 through to 2002, show that family ownership and business group affiliation is a common pattern in these countries.

Brazil

Under the presidency of Itamar Franco, in 1994, the 'Plano Real' was established. This is a milestone in the economic and institutional reform in recent Brazilian history. The reduction of the annual inflation rate (2,708 per cent in 1993 to 15 per cent in 1995), macroeconomic uncertainty, and volatility, together with the monetary stability, trade liberalization, and privatization, allowed the country to experience relative economic stability. In the first-generation of reforms, the Brazilian government transferred its control of 119 firms to the private sector between the beginning of 1991 and July 2001 (Anuatti-Neto et al. 2005). The main sectors affected were electricity and telecommunications (which each accounted for 31 per cent of the total value of the transactions). The second-generation of reforms, which included the creation of mechanisms to boost competitiveness in the private sector, foster employment, and reduce the state intervention in the economy, were excluded from the Brazilian reform agenda (Fleury and Fleury 2009), but, reforms to increase investor confidence, and to expand domestic and foreign investments have been carried out, resulting in some increase in market competition and liberalization of the financial markets.

There are three illustrative examples. First, a new competition law was enacted in 1994 to introduce a merger and acquisitions control process and to reconfigure the Administrative Council for Economic Defence (CADE) into an independent agency. From 1994 to 1998, the pace of privatization process increased; the government agency responsible for general administration of prices was abolished, and new, independent regulatory agencies for telecommunications, petroleum, and natural gas, and electricity were created (OECD/IDB 2006). Second, regarding the capital markets, the Brazilian Securities Law (6.385/76) and Corporation Law (6.404/76) were amended in 2001 (10.303/2001) and, subsequently, in 2007 (11.638/2007) as a result of the Brazilian Corporation and Securities Laws reform. Among the main changes proposed by the new legislation, Lima Jr (2001) emphasizes those affecting: (1) separation between ownership and control, especially non-voting shares were capped at 50 per cent of the capital stock for new companies and IPOs of non-listed companies, (2) dispute resolutions, (3) calling of shareholders' meetings, (4) composition of the board of directors, (5) regulation on independent auditors, and (6) regulation on insiders' information and trading.

And third, the São Paulo Stock Exchange launched a self-regulation initiative in 2000, which defined different listing segments according to corporate governance practices. The more strict category called '*Novo Mercado*' established, among other things, that firms are allowed to issue only voting shares. Given all these efforts attempting to increase investor protection and confidence, and consequently, to increase the participation of households and small investors in the financial markets, have these reforms influenced the distribution of corporate control across publicly listed firms?

We have collected data from 2004 to 2008 and also relied on previous literature on Brazilian corporate ownership to illustrate that, although much has been done at the institutional and country level to promote the financial market development and liquidity, the high level of corporate ownership concentration across Brazilian listed firms persists as a common pattern. Leal and Carvalhal-da-Silva (2007), using a data set from the Brazilian Stock Exchange Commission (*Commisão de Valores Mobiliários*, CVM), report a median value of 69 per cent of direct voting shares concentrated in the largest shareholder (87 per cent for the three largest shareholders), and 66 per cent voting rights when measuring the indirect ownership of ultimate owner (87 per cent for the three largest shareholders) for 1998. In addition, they assess the ownership concentration over the period between 1998 and 2002, and report a uniform pattern towards high levels of concentration. In Table 13.1, we show the direct shareholding concentration for the largest shareholder (C1) and the three largest shareholders (C3) respectively: 49.1 per cent and 66.4 per cent, on average, for the period 2004–2008. Our data not only corroborates previous findings, which indicate that Brazilian firms have high levels of ownership concentration of control, but also shows that such a pattern has not changed over time.

Despite the initiatives to (1) boost the Brazilian capital markets into a more liquid market where households could have a role and the minority shareholders together could represent more than one single shareholder and (2) to foster major reductions on the levels of ownership concentration, the fact is that publicly listed firms continue to be highly concentrated in the hands of a small number of owners. This is in line with the argument that the average values of ownership concentration tend to be higher in countries with low institutional investor protection (La Porta et al. 1999; Bergström and Rydquist 1990).

We also studied the key characteristics of majority shareholders. Table 13.2 reports the mean values of ownership concentration according to distinctive types of shareholders and their origin. Among the largest shareholders of our sample, industrial firms are predominant, which, on average from 2004–2008, comprised 40.1 per cent of shareholdings. The next in importance are the banks (with an average of 29.95 per cent), followed by institutional investors (i.e. hedge and pension funds, insurance companies, etc., 12.75 per cent) and individuals and families (12.65 per cent). Government participation is, on

Table 13.1. Direct shareholdings concentration of Brazilian and Chilean firms, 2004–2008

Year	Brazil				Chile			
	Largest shareholder	Three largest shareholders	Foreign shareholders	Domestic Shareholders	Largest shareholder	Three largest shareholders	Foreign shareholders	Domestic shareholders
2004	50.3	66.1	18.0	82.0	51.1	69.5	18.7	81.3
2005	50.0	66.6	21.3	78.7	51.5	69.9	16.8	83.2
2006	49.3	67.0	25.8	74.2	50.9	69.4	16.7	83.3
2007	47.1	65.5	27.7	72.3	50.4	68.8	18.3	81.7
2008	49.2	66.9	28.2	71.8	49.1	68.1	16.5	83.5
Mean	49.1	66.4	25.0	75.0	50.6	69.2	17.4	82.6
SD	26.7	23.5	–	–	25.8	22.8	–	–
Min	4.5	5.7	–	–	0.4	0.7	–	–
Max	100.0	100.0	–	–	100.0	100.0	–	–
N	1,519	1,519	1,519	1,519	1,077	1,077	1,077	1,077

Source: Compiled by the authors. Mean value of ownership concentration by largest shareholder and three largest shareholders, between 2004 and 2008, of Brazilian companies listed on the São Paulo Stock Exchange and Chilean companies listed in the Santiago Stock Exchange.

Table 13.2. Direct shareholdings by type of shareholder of Brazilian and Chilean firms, 2004–2008

Country	Year	Type of shareholders					
		Individuals	Government	Bank	Institutional investors	Industrial firms	Others
Brazil	2004	12.6	5.3	25.1	10.2	45.9	0.9
	2005	12.8	6.2	27.1	7.7	46.0	0.4
	2006	12.4	4.7	29.3	13.4	38.6	1.7
	2007	13.1	4.0	31.6	12.9	37.6	0.7
	2008	12.3	5.0	32.3	15.4	34.0	0.9
	Mean	12.7	5.0	30.0	12.8	40.1	1.3
Chile	2004	3.3	1.6	2.8	20.1	71.4	0.9
	2005	3.0	1.6	3.2	17.9	73.5	0.9
	2006	3.0	1.5	3.8	18.7	72.2	0.9
	2007	2.9	1.5	3.4	20.9	70.4	0.9
	2008	3.0	1.0	2.7	21.8	70.6	1.0
	Mean	3.0	1.5	3.2	19.9	71.6	0.9

Source: Compiled by the authors. Mean value of ownership concentration by type of shareholders, between 2004 and 2008, of Brazilian companies listed on the São Paulo Stock Exchange and Chilean companies listed in the Santiago Stock Exchange.

average, only 4.96 per cent of our sample. Considering the sample period, we noticed a moderate decline in shares held by industrial firms (from 45.93 per cent in 2004 to 34.04 per cent in 2008, on average) where individuals and families, and government entities are the ultimate shareholders, while the relative share of banks and institutional investors rose from 35.32 per cent to 47.69 per cent. In addition, although foreign shareholders hold, on average 17.96 per cent in 2004 and increase their participation to 28.22 per cent in 2008 (see Table 13.1), the domestic shareholders are still the majority owners of direct shareholdings.

The bottom line is that industrial firms are the most important players in the direct ownership of Brazilian firms and hold, on average, 40 per cent of stocks. One explanation is that, in Brazil; the Securities Law allows companies to maintain and issue non-voting shares (i.e. preferred shares) and to have pyramidal schemes.[4] In fact, about 90 per cent of trading volume at the Sao Paulo's Stock Exchange involves non-voting shares (Leal and Carvalhal-da-Silva 2007). Thus, not surprisingly, direct shareholdings control is high and controlled by industrial groups who use preferred shares (e.g. nonvoting shares) to finance their projects. Also, previous studies (Aldrighi and Mazzer-Neto 2007; Aldrighi and Postali 2010) report that, on average, 54.4 per cent of firms under the Stock Exchange Commission regulation had pyramidal

[4] Pyramidal schemes mean that there is at least one firm between the firm and its ultimate shareholder (Aldrighi and Postali 2010).

arrangements in 2002 and, from those firms, 63.8 per cent had families as the largest ultimate shareholders. This situation is characterized as an implicit contract between the controlling and minority shareholders where the controlling shareholder obtains cheap equity on the understanding that he holds a large equity fraction, thereby making it credible that the value of the shares will be maximized (Bergström and Rydqvist 1990).

This ownership structure reflects to some extent the privatization strategy followed by the Brazilian Government in the mid 1990s. In order to maximize the bidding prices to the government's assets, they pushed for consortium coalitions where public entities, such as pension funds (Previ, Petros, Funcef), development and public banks (BNDES, Banco do Brasil, Caixa Econômica Federal) were the leading financiers of domestic private bidders.

Chile

In September 1973, Chile's annual inflation rate was 286 per cent, the nominal average tariff for imports was 105 per cent, and the fiscal deficit reached 20 per cent of GDP (Buc 2006). This situation led to a military dictatorship and to a new economic strategy. In 1974, Chile started a profound process of trade liberalization and institutional reforms. The first step was to reduce import tariffs for a flat 10 per cent in all products. Institutional reforms included changes in the Chilean Constitution that directly affected capital markets. First, private property rights were guaranteed by the Constitution as the baseline to a favourable environment to investments. Second, they established the autonomy of the Central Bank that could define monetary policies without political interventions. And third, the Constitution restricted government spending. Besides that, in 1981 the reform of the pension fund system took place, whereby an individual capitalization account programme was designed with specific contributions, administered by private institutions selected by the workers, the AFPs (i.e. *Administradoras de Fondo de Pension*).

The privatization of state-owned companies was also an important process intended to increase market competitiveness and reduce state intervention. In fact, Chile was the first Latin American country to implement a systematic privatization programme. In the first wave of privatization, in the early 1970s, 257 companies were transferred to the private sector, many of them previously nationalized by Allende (Serva 2003). In the 1980s, a second wave of privatization was undertaken, and in 1990s another thirty state enterprises had been fully privatized, including steel-producing companies, utilities, telecommunications, mining, and air carriers. During this period, pension funds had acquired about 25 per cent of the shares of privatized enterprises in open auctions (Baer 1994).

In 1990, Pinochet stepped down and a centre-left alliance, the *Concertación*, headed by Aylwin, became the first democratic government since Allende's. Despite the restoration of democracy and a decade of centre-left government, during the 1990s there was more continuity than change in economic and labour policies (Winn 2004: 51). The most significant initiative was the historic agreement between the major labour organizations, so-called 'Acuerdo Marco', where they explicitly recognized private enterprises as the principal and legitimate agent of economic growth (Frank 2004). The centre-left government legitimated and consolidated Pinochet's market-oriented policies, as it did with the opening of trade through multiple free-trade agreements, the enhancement of the private social security system, and the privatization of utilities services, highways, and other public services.

However, neither Pinochet's nor the *Concertación*'s initiatives were enough to change the Chilean corporate ownership patterns that, at a first look, were characterized by highly concentrated ownership in which industrial firms and institutional investors directly controlled most listed firms. Tables 13.1 and 13.2 illustrate this phenomenon where the largest shareholder controls, on average, 50.6 per cent of shares and the sum of the three largest shareholders, 69.2 per cent, which is significantly above the ownership concentration of developed countries' firms (Majluf, Abarca, Rodriguez, and Fuentes 1998; Lefort 2005, 2010; Lefort and Urzua 2008). Taking our sample period (2004–2008), we observe that this pattern does not change significantly over time and confirms prior empirical findings (Majluf et al. 1998; Lefort 2005).

Table 13.2 reports that industrial firms and institutional investors directly control firms, which together, account for 91.5 per cent of shares. The privatization process coupled with regulatory reforms has influenced this ownership composition. Unlike in Brazil, where the main motivation to the privatization was to restore public finance while keeping the influence of the state through public pension funds and development banks, in Chile the privatization process was implemented partly with the purpose of achieving dispersed firm ownership and of developing the capital market. However, Chilean business groups rapidly took over most newly privatized firms, sometimes in association with foreign companies (Lefort 2010). In fact, industrial firms held, on average, 71.6 per cent of listed firms between 2004 and 2008.

Chilean corporate law shaped the type of owners in at least two ways. First, the creation of AFP in 1981, established the ground for domestic and foreign institutional investors to own listed firms. And second, in 1982, following the debt crisis, the government restricted bank holdings of company shares. The latter explains the small presence of banking ownership in Chile (3.2 per cent on average). Foreign investors directly own 17.4 per cent of shares (see Table 13.1), with foreign multinational firms also making use of pyramidal structures (i.e. Grupo Agbar and Grupo Telefónica from Spain).

Additionally, international banks indirectly held shareholding through pension funds and insurance business (i.e. Grupo Santander).

Ownership structure in South Korea

Large business groups, often referred to as *chaebols*, characterize the ownership structure of corporations in Korea. *Chaebols* have significant economic influence in the Korean market. For example, in 2004, the *chaebols* accounted for 14 per cent of the total value added of the manufacturing sector and more than half of the total market value of all publicly listed firms (Almeida et al. 2007). *Chaebol* firms operate in many different sectors, maintain strong business and network ties with other affiliated firms, and are mostly family-controlled (Bae, Baek and Kang 2007). However, *chaebol* firms are not allowed to hold the shares of commercial banks and, as a consequence, diversify into non-banking financial institutions in order to expand the capacity and flexibility of their internal capital markets (Kim 2010).

Chaebols are also characterized by pyramidal structures and cross-shareholding, although pyramids in Korean *chaebols* are not 'complex' in the sense that the large majority of *chaebol* firms belong to pyramids with a total of two or three firms in the chain (Almeida, Park, Subrahmanyam, and Wolfenzon 2010). In addition, cross-shareholding enabled *chaebols* to develop a governance structure like the multidivisional organization, under which individual affiliates function as operating divisions that are controlled by group-level staff (Chang 2003). Cross-shareholding was significantly higher for *chaebols* and increased even just after the Asian financial crisis in 1997. For instance, in 1998, the cross-ownership for listed firms that belonged to *chaebols* averaged 27.7 per cent, compared to 17.8 per cent for non-*chaebol* firms (Bae and Jeong 2007). However, state intervention and efforts at corporate restructuring caused *chaebols* to gradually diminish cross-shareholding. From 1990 to 2009, except during the Korean financial crisis, internal ownership for the top ten business groups was less than 50 per cent (KFTC report 2009). Even though limited by law, the rate of cross-shareholding in Korea is above the average for the nine East Asian countries (Claessens et al. 2000). Also, as a result of pyramidal structures and cross-shareholdings, *chaebols'* shareholders have high control rights compared to cash flow rights, which becomes an incentive for tunnelling and propping up (Bae and Jeong 2007; Bae, Cheon, and Kang 2008; Almeida et al. 2010).

In 1997, during the Asian financial crisis, domestic and foreign economic institutions concluded that the high leverage, over-diversification, excess capacity and the resulting weak competitiveness of Korean firms, together with the poor corporate governance of the *chaebols* ownership structure, were the main determinants of the Korean economic collapse. As a way of controlling the 'Asian Contagion', the IMF stepped in and designed strict monetary and contractionary fiscal policy recommendations, which included fiscal policy discipline, tax reform, trade liberalization, inward foreign direct investment liberalization, privatization of state enterprises, deregulation, and legal security for property rights. Accepting much of this, Korea revised its financial regulation, the securities and exchange act, and the commercial codes to facilitate market-based governance and encourage diversified investors to invest in Korean firms. As an illustration, before the financial crisis, foreign investors were not allowed to hold more than 7 per cent of shares in Korean domestic firms. These barriers of entry were lifted, increasing foreign ownership in Korea from 13 per cent of publicly listed firms in 1997 to 42 per cent in 2006 in terms of market capitalism (Moon 2006).

As illustrated in Table 13.3, foreign shareholders exceeded more than 15 per cent of the stock market capitalization in 2003 and above 20 per cent in the following three years. More than 40 per cent of these foreign investments came from two Anglo-Saxon countries, the US and the UK, and two-thirds of investors were institutional investors as of the end of 2003 (Korea Stock Exchange 2004b). Foreign investors are more likely to hold the share of conglomerates or members of *chaebol* than middle-sized firms. Interestingly, during the 1997 Korean financial crisis, firms with larger equity ownership by foreign investors experienced a smaller drop in their share value. Firms with higher disclosure quality and those with access to alternative sources of external financing also suffered less from the exogenous shock. In contrast, *chaebol* with concentrated ownership by owner-managers, and those with concentrated ownership by affiliated firms experienced a larger drop in equity value (Baek, Kang, and Park 2004). Table 13.3 also reports the decrease in the

Table 13.3. Direct shareholdings by type of shareholders of South Korean firms, 2000–2009

Year	Type of shareholders				
	Individuals	Government	Institutional investors	Industrial firms	Foreigners
2000	37.7	12.7	15.8	20.0	13.8
2001	38.5	7.3	19.2	20.3	14.7
2002	35.4	7.4	24.6	21.0	11.5
2003	37.1	6.7	16.5	21.7	18.0
2004	33.8	6.4	18.9	19.0	22.0
2005	34.2	5.0	18.6	19.3	23.0
2006	35.5	4.8	17.0	20.4	22.3
2007	36.5	4.4	15.5	24.7	18.9
2008	45.8	4.6	7.1	26.4	16.1
2009	49.9	1.5	15.6	16.7	16.3

Source: Compiled by the authors from Korean Exchange (KRX) Statistics database.

governmental shareholding after the Asia financial crisis, which is an evidence of the privatization and divestitures of state-owned firms in Korea. Furthermore, and in line with previous research (Almeida et al. 2010), we report that individual investors, which include family-owned firms, hold more than 35 per cent of market shares.

After the financial crisis, the *chaebols* also had to undertake several structural reforms to improve financial transparency and strengthen their corporate governance structure (Bae et al. 2008). The Korean financial supervisory agency was concerned about the high level of ownership concentration of publicly listed firms and engaged in closer supervision on the amount of individual shareholdings. As a consequence, the Securities and Exchange Act defines 'largest shareholder' as a person or institution, domestic or foreign, who holds the largest number of outstanding shares (i.e. voting right shares) including common stocks or depositary receipts; 'significant shareholder' as a shareholder who owns more than 1/100 of total shares issued by a firm; and, 'minority shareholders' as stockholders who own stocks or certificates that represent less than 1/100 of the total amount of outstanding stocks. Thus, largest, significant, and minority shareholders are the categorization from which we can estimate the degree of ownership concentration in Korean firms.[5]

In this regard, Table 13.4 shows the ownership concentration of the largest, significant, and minority shareholders of the Korean Composite Stock Price Index (i.e. KOSPI) firms. It represents 80 per cent of listed firms for the period from 2004 to 2008.[6] Minority investors also have a large percentage of the total shares, which is almost the same as largest investors do. However, this does not necessarily mean that minority shareholders are well-protected by the Korean financial regulation.

In *chaebols*, lower levels of family and affiliate ownership does not imply that there is less monitoring, since affiliates function like business divisions in diversified corporations controlled by the *chaebols'* chairmen (Chang and Choi 1988). Any observed relationship between concentrated ownership and performance may be attributable to 'tunnelling', which Bertrand, Mehta, and Mullainathan (2002) defined as transferring resources from firms in which a controlling family has few cash flow rights to ones in which it has substantial cash flow rights. *Chaebols* families and affiliates may decrease their shares in

[5] Shareholders classified as 'others' include owners who have a special relationship with a largest shareholder, for example family members or managers. The Korean tax regulation, Article 20, Enforcement decree of basic act for national taxes, defines the scope of relatives and specially related persons.

[6] The number of listed companies in KOSPI is the following: 683 in 2004, 702 in 2005, 731 in 2006, 746 in 2007, 765 in 2008.

Table 13.4. Direct shareholdings concentration of South Korean firms, 2004–2008

Year	Largest shareholder	Significant shareholders	Minority shareholders	Others	Korea securities depository
2004	33.8	6.4	36.7	23.0	0.1
2005	34.3	5.4	36.7	23.7	0.1
2006	34.9	5.3	36.5	23.2	0.1
2007	38.4	4.6	35.8	21.1	0.1
2008	39.9	3.9	35.7	20.4	0.1

Source: Compiled by the authors from TS-2000, Korean Listed Companies Association database.

those affiliates that provide or receive such debt guarantees in order to reduce their own downside risk (Chang 2003).

Chaebol's controlling families have substantial incentives to maximize firm performance over time and to pass control of the firm to their descendants rather than consume the wealth during their lifetime (Anderson, Mansi, and Reeb 2003). In fact, these families are strongly identified with their business groups. These patterns have enabled family ownership and control to contribute to the rapid growth and long-term success of the *chaebol*. Joh (2003) finds that, between 1993 and 1997, a firm's profitability increases when the controlling family's ownership is high, controlling for firm, industry, and macro-economic effects. However, during the 1997 Korean financial crisis, family-controlled *chaebol* firms with concentrated ownership experienced a large depreciation in their market value. Firms in which the controlling shareholders' voting rights exceeded cash flow rights and those who borrowed more from the main banks also had lower returns (Baek et al. 2004).

Our sample reports that, from 2000 to 2008, family ownership among publicly listed firms gradually decreased from 7.5 per cent to 3 or 4 per cent, which implies that the traditional family-owned structure has weakened given the Korean government effort to dilute corporate ownership, especially the shareholdings of major shareholders, including the largest and significant shareholders.[7] However, this does not entail the collapse of the controlling power of families, particularly in business groups, as that would require not only that family control decreases but also that cross-shareholdings and pyramidal structures no longer exist. In fact, in 2009, the KFTC reports that internal ownership, which represents the sum of family direct shareholding and cross-shareholdings, of the top ten business groups is still more than 50 per cent. Despite criticism for their lack of transparency and patriarchal

[7] We measure the family shareholding (defined as the shareholding by the largest shareholder—individuals and their family members) as the sum of the direct equity ownership, not including the indirect shareholdings. We also sum up the outstanding stock shareholding.

management, *chaebols* are continuing to engage in the generation-to-generation transfer of ownership, with one-third of the top fifty family-owned businesses already having concluded the succession process.

In sum, although family owners have contributed to the rapid growth in the Korean economy, questions about their corporate governance efficacy, and their overall influence in South Korean society have long cast a shadow over their success. Family owners are expected to transform their corporate governance structures to demonstrate that they have turned a corner in terms of transparency, accountability, and integrity.

Ownership structure in Central and Eastern Europe

Since the collapse of the Communist system two decades ago throughout CEE, the region has undergone a remarkable economic and political transformation. Unlike Latin American countries, which undertook economic and political transitions at roughly the same time, the East European transition involved fundamental transformations of property regimes. And while the East Asia democratization started only after they established links to the globalized economy, Eastern European political transformations occurred simultaneously with economy liberalization, privatization, and a globalization process (Bandelj 2008).

At varied speeds and in different ways, Czech Republic, Hungary, and Poland transformed their former planned economies into market economies, implementing various political, economical, and institutional changes that characterized social change in CEE after 1989. Influenced by integration with the European Union and pressured by international financial institutions, the privatization and internationalization of CEE firms introduced new corporate ownership structures.

Czech Republic

After the 'velvet revolution' in 1989, Czech Republic was the third CEE country to start a privatization programme in the context of a transformation from a centrally planned economy to a market economy. There are three singular characteristics of Czech's approach (De la Dehesa 1991). First, the government used generous incentives to attract foreign investors into joint ventures. Second, a Restitution Law allowed the previous owners of state assets nationalized after 1948 to regain control. The restitution applied mainly to small and medium-sized service firms and to real estate (Havrda 2003). And third, the Czech Republic had the most state-ownership of any other CEE country due to the fact that the workers' councils had been dissolved in 1990 and the enterprises involved were re-nationalized.

The privatization process was divided into three schemes: the natural restitution, small-scale programme and large-scale privatization. The first two schemes were carried out in the early stage of the privatization process. Thus, small firms, stores, and real estate were returned to the original owners or their descendants based on the cut-off date set to the year 1948 (Havrda 2003). Also, small and medium-sized firms were privatized through auctions, sale in tender offers, or direct sales. By this scheme, foreigners could bid only if the first auctions failed to reach the minimum price, set at 50 per cent of book value (De la Dehesa 1991). The third scheme, defined by the 'Transformation Law', included the larger firms. The companies prepared privatization projects and presented them to the Ministry of Privatization, then potential owners competed and parliament made the final allocation decision. Light industries were privatized first, followed by heavy industry, including utilities and 'strategic' industries.

In these projects, the voucher privatization method was the main mechanism in redistributing companies' shares. Yet, only part of the firms' equity was available for auction using the vouchers, in many cases 40 per cent and, exceptionally, up to 80 per cent. For the remaining shares, a small percentage was distributed to employees, another amount was made available to foreign buyers, and finally, the states maintained ownership of the residual shares for future transactions (De la Dehesa 1991).

The voucher mechanism resulted in the creation of the Investment Privatization Funds (IPFs), mostly indirectly operated by banks, which control connected corporations (Khanna and Yafeh 2007). There were about 400 IPFs, which obtained over 70 per cent of all available vouchers and the seven largest funds obtained 46 per cent of all vouchers in the market (Havrda 2003). However, since the Czech government did not want the IPFs to be active monitors and influence the management of firms, it set strong legal limitations on the IPFs' actions. For example, an investment fund could not invest more than 10 per cent of its assets in the same company or could not own more than 20 per cent of the share of one company (Havrda 2003). As a result, in 1996, some IPFs began to transform themselves into holding companies to avoid such regulation and supervision, and consequently this led to ownership concentration, as existing regulation did not apply to the holding companies.

Due to the unintended consequences of the privatization process, ownership concentration reached high levels again by 2001. Klapper, Laeven, and Love (2006) report that in the Czech Republic 69 per cent of shares were concentrated in the largest shareholder and 89 per cent in the five largest shareholders. Also as a result of the privatization programme, which focused

Table 13.5. Ownership structure of CEE firms, 2001

	Number of firms	% of firms with ownership by: Foreigners	Government	Bank	Average % of firm shares held by: Foreigners	Largest shareholder	Five largest shareholder	% of firms with largest shareholder owning over 50%
Czech Republic	74	47	27	11	38	69	89	70
Hungary	56	70	7	18	43	52	96	52
Poland	56	32	11	4	19	39	64	25
All Sample[a]	224	46	17	11	31	56	83	54

Source: Adapted from Klapper, Laeven, and Love (2006). [a]The original data includes Slovak Republic.

on the participation of foreign investors as a way to develop an emerging capital market, and also due to foreign direct investments from other European countries, the foreign ownership in Czech publicly listed firms has a high presence as shown in Table 13.5. Almost half of the firms had a foreign investor in 2001 and, when present; they held, on average, 38 per cent of firms (Klapper et al. 2006).

Our 2004–2008 data shows another important trend. The Czech Republic has the highest remaining government ownership, while Hungary and Poland have very few state-owned firms among their publicly listed firms (see Table 13.5). Kočenda and Hanousek (2009) analyse the determinants of state ownership over privatized firms in Czech Republic during the post-privatization decade (1995–2005) and argue that there are three main institutions through which the state still keep the control of larger firms. The first institution, and the fundamental one, is the National Property Fund (NPF) that was set up to control the remaining shares after the privatization scheme was finalized. Also, Municipalities received various ownership stakes as free property transfers and became stakeholders in a diverse number of firms, mainly in utilities and transportation sectors. Finally, other state agencies were created to hold shareholdings in 'strategic' sectors to protect government interests. Kočenda and Hanousek (2009) suggest that the state remained as a major owner of privatized firms during the period between 1996 and 2005.

The data for the twenty-first century is consistent with prior findings regarding high ownership concentration. In Table 13.6, on average, the largest shareholder in Czech Republic holds 56.7 per cent and the three largest shareholders together hold more than 80 per cent, between 2004 and 2008. In 2004, the Czech Republic joined the European Union, and an immediate consequence of their membership was that foreign direct investment increased sharply, as investors positioned themselves to take advantage of the cheaper labour and the bigger and more stable internal market offered by the progressive unification of

Table 13.6. Direct shareholdings concentration of czech, hungarian and polish firms, 2004–2008

Years	Czech Republic				Hungary				Poland			
	Largest shareholder	Three largest shareholders	Foreign shareholders	Domestic shareholders	Largest shareholder	Three largest shareholders	Foreign shareholders	Domestic shareholders	Largest shareholder	Three largest shareholders	Foreign shareholders	Domestic shareholders
2003	53.9	84.9	29.4	70.6	42.6	64.1	52.5	47.5	39.7	53.6	26.5	73.5
2004	53.1	80.9	32.5	67.5	46.0	64.3	47.2	52.8	40.9	57.9	20.4	79.6
2005	52.4	80.4	31.5	68.5	43.8	64.6	53.4	46.6	41.0	57.6	22.3	77.7
2006	56.7	75.7	48.4	51.6	41.8	60.2	57.2	42.8	42.4	59.5	20.6	79.4
2007	63.4	82.6	57.7	42.4	49.6	65.4	62.2	37.8	40.4	59.3	19.7	80.3
2008	60.6	76.0	58.6	41.4	54.2	71.5	70.6	29.4	36.2	50.4	21.9	78.1
Mean	56.7	80.7	43.0	57.0	48.7	68.0	57.2	42.8	41.0	59.3	21.9	78.1
SD	20.4	20.0	–	–	25.1	27.6	–	–	24.0	28.4	–	–
Min	1.7	0.6	–	–	4.5	6.7	–	–	3.5	3.5	–	–
Max	100.0	100.0	–	–	100.0	100.0	–	–	100.0	100.0	–	–
N	71	71	71	71	96	96	96	96	1,228	1,228	1,228	1,228

Source: Compiled by the authors from Amadeus database.

Table 13.7. Average direct shareholdings of CEE firms by type of shareholder, %, 2004–2008

Country	Type of shareholders					
	Individuals	Governments	Banks	Institutional investors	Industrial firms	Others
Czech Republic	1.0	12.7	2.8	32.2	44.0	7.4
Hungary	4.3	2.4	2.7	12.2	62.8	15.6
Poland	37.6	4.8	2.9	14.1	40.1	0.4

Sources: Compiled by the authors from Amadeus database.

Europe. In fact, our data captures this trend and shows that foreign direct ownership has increased remarkably since 2004, from 32.5 to 58.6 per cent. Our data considers the 2004–2008 period (see Table 13.7) and confirms that the Czech Republic has the highest remaining government ownership, which is consistent with the late stage of the privatization process when compared to other CEE countries.

Hungary

Hungary was the first country in the CEE region to launch the privatization process, perhaps because unlike other CEE countries, in Hungary, the party-state did not collapse. Rather, its termination was negotiated in three months of intensive negotiations between representatives of both ruling and major opposition parties, who reached an agreement about the new rules of the political game, leaving aside the economic front. In spite of the economic policy 'vacuum', the Hungarian economy was not 'out of control', and two pieces of legislation formed the first mechanism of privatization. The first was the 1984 Law on Enterprise Councils, which transferred the ownership functions from ministries to enterprise directors. And the 1989 Law on Business Associations, contained a clause allowing state-owned firms to found shareholding corporations and limited liability firms. These two laws together enabled company managers to sell either assets or entire companies and get, in return, high salaries, guaranteed jobs, and excellent retirement terms (Stark 1990; De la Dehesa 1991).

A State Property Agency was established in 1990 with the responsibility to organize and supervise the privatization process. It is worth noting that to carry out its mandate and to mitigate the consequences of 'spontaneous privatization', the agency embarked on several privatization initiatives. First, the pre-privatization programme aimed at a rapid transfer of small and family-scale businesses into private hands through a simplified procedure. Second, the investor-initiated privatization was open to domestic and foreign parties alike. Third, the active privatization was a set of initiatives to solicit privatization of specifically designated state firms, typically the largest Hungarian firms. And finally, self-privatization was a mechanism whereby state-owned firms below a certain scale threshold but often still of reasonably size could select private consulting firms to assist them in the privatization process (O'Toole 1994; Stark and Bruszt 1998; Bandelj 2008).

Although the Law of Business Associations did not explicitly endorse concentrated ownership, establishing a minimum price of a share at one million forints made it accessible to institutional or corporate shareholders rather than to private individuals (Stark 1990). Indeed, previous research reports a highly concentrated ownership structure for Hungarian firms (see Table 13.5). Additionally, foreign investors were in the scene early in the transition as the privatization methods comprised insiders' buy-outs and direct sales to strategic investors, included foreign investors. Iwasaki (2005) suggests that few and strong owners were preferred to achieve a fast and effective privatization instead of widely dispersed owners. Our data for the early twenty-first century (2004–2008) confirms the continuation of this early concentration trends, as on average, the largest and three largest shareholders held 48.7 and 68 per cent of shares, respectively (see Table 13.6).

Among CEE countries, we can see that foreign ownership is most prominent in Hungary (see Table 13.6). This is because Hungary opened their economy to foreign direct investment earlier than other transition countries, and the Hungarian government and international pressures such as joining the EU made a considerable effort to attract foreign investors (Iwasaki 2005; Filatotchev, Isachenkova, and Mickiewicz 2007). Even sectors such as banking which have been typically left in domestic hands, were transferred to foreign hands—for example, 60 per cent of the capital in the banking sector was foreign by the end of 1997 (Iwasaki 2005).

Poland

In 1989, the Solidarity trade union established a new government in Poland and was a trigger to the political, economic, and institutional change. One of the first economic polices was to privatize state-owned firms. As in other countries, Polish firms were not all privatized at the same time. This was due to political constraints (Roland 2000) and practical reasons, such as the sheer logistic difficulty of privatizing an entire economy in one go (De Fraja and Roberts 2009).

The Polish government set up a three-stage privatization process whereby about 600 large and medium-sized firms were privatized. The first stage is defined by the commercialization of a state-owned firm, which can take one of three techniques, initial public offering, direct sales to investors, or a combination of both. The second stage is the establishment of twenty National Investment Funds (i.e. NIF) in the form of joint-stock companies. These funds were delegated to special consortia, which comprised commercial and investment banks, and consulting firms operated by Polish and Western partners which compete with one another according to the best offer to the government. The third, and final, stage comprised the distribution of certificates to Polish citizens who became indirect shareholders of the companies by receiving one share of each NIF.

In Poland, privatization played a significant role in improving firm incentive systems and restructuring corporations as it established corporate governance reforms to restructure firms. Grosfeld and Hashi (2007) argue that the Polish authorities focused on the proper development of the financial market and placed great emphasis on the creation of a well-established legal system and enforceable laws from the initial phase of transformation. However, the programme was also concerned with the potential danger of the private benefits of control, and therefore enforced the limit of 33 per cent on the lead fund's holdings in each firm.

As in Hungary, the Law on the Privatization of state-owned firms indirectly influenced the concentration of ownership on new publicly traded firms. In fact, Table 13.5 reports that the largest shareholder held, on average, 39 per cent of shares, while the five largest shareholders exceeded 64 per cent, in 2001. In addition, in our population of 1,228 Polish firm-year observations from 2004 to 2008, we show that such patterns have not changed and the largest shareholder continues to hold 41 per cent of shares, while the three largest shareholders account for 59 per cent.

However, Poland has relatively less concentrated ownership when compared to the Czech Republic and Hungary. Scholars suggest that ownership concentration is lower in Poland for the following three reasons (Grosfeld and Hashi 2007): investor access to greater amount of firm information (financial reports and governance practices); the financial market developed effective mechanisms to monitor firms; and the Warsaw Stock Exchange limited the level of ownership concentration.

Conclusion

Our basic argument in this chapter is that emerging countries carried out very different institutional and economic reforms to constructing market economies, becoming involved in the international markets and improving their domestic capital markets with the aim of ultimately increasing economic growth in an environment where there was high information asymmetry among owners (particularly majority and minority), and weak legal protection of minority shareholders.

Moreover, if we were to follow the globalization/convergence literature, we would expect that market-oriented legal and economic reforms in country-level governance would foster investor protection and, consequently, reduce highly concentrated ownership among publicly listed firms. Our data analysis for publicly listed firms in emerging markets in the first decade of the twenty-first century, as well as previous research covering ownership trends since the initial transformations to opened market-economies, demonstrates, however, that this was not the case.

Our unique dataset of 19,969 firm-year observations from 2004 to 2008 in six emerging markets shows that high levels of ownership concentration are still the common denominator in these countries, although the paths to this differ. In addition, in Latin America and South Korea, business groups represent the most important organizational form as the largest shareholder of publicly listed firms, not only through direct shareholdings but also using pyramids and cross-shareholdings. In Central and Eastern European countries, joining the European Union triggered the impulse for transfer of ownership from state to private hands, with the immediate consequence of large entry of foreign direct investments and its related foreign ownership of publicly traded firms. These patterns of corporate ownership illustrate that, although countries' corporate governance systems have been influenced by cross-border regulatory arrangements to facilitate and expand national capital markets, in emerging economies, business groups (Latin America), families (Korea) and the government (CEE) play an important role in defining the corporate governance agenda. As emerging countries become more important for inward investors from developed economies, these groups have significant authority and may influence the behaviour of foreign MNCs in emerging markets as argued by Whitley in this volume.

Our findings show that, together with ownership structure, legal systems and their related corporate law, the development and structure of capital, and the political and economic institutions help to constitute the myriad of varieties of capitalisms that characterize corporate governance systems in the emerging economies (Hall and Soskice 2001). And, more importantly, the similarities in ownership concentration level and legal systems only partially account for governance realities in these countries. This implies that to compare corporate governance practices across countries better, we need to take into account their economic history, formal and informal institutions, political processes, social actors, and the choices of firms themselves.

This chapter opens new avenues of future research in emerging markets. One is the role of business groups in shaping the corporate governance agenda in these countries, in particular, in East Asia and Latin America. Their internal governance practices, relationships between parents and subsidiaries, and between family members and other types of shareholders are still understudied. Our research has shown that ownership concentration continues to be a pattern in emerging markets, yet it is interesting to observe that there are shifts on who the owners are, and that Anglo-American investors are typically unwilling to invest in majority owned firms. Future research should also examine how different owners interact with each other in these path-dependent ownership concentration models as well as what is the role of new types of owners such as different institutional investors, family owners responding to international pressures for transparency and accountability, and sovereign wealth funds, just to mention a few.

When it comes to empirical research, it is worth noting that there has been a scarcity of systematic comparative research, particularly in emerging markets, usually due to the lack of reliable data. Therefore, there is an opportunity for those who can develop updated data sets to explore the characteristics of financial, ownership, governance, and business practices in emerging countries, and to study how structural firm characteristics interplay with broader industry and national institutional pressures.

References

Aguilera, R. V. and G. Jackson (2003) 'The Cross-National Diversity of Corporate Governance: Dimensions and determinants', *Academy of Management Review*, 28(3): 447–65.

—— —— (2010) 'Comparative and International Corporate Governance', *The Academy of Management Annals*, 4(1): 485–556.

Aldrighi, D. and R. Mazzer-Neto (2007) 'Evidências sobre as Estruturas de Propriedade de Capital e de Voto das Empresas de Capital Aberto no Brasil', *Revista Brasileira de Economia*, 61(2): 129–52.

—— and F. A. S. Postali (2010) 'Business Groups in Brazil', pp. 353–86 in A. Colpan, T. Hikino and J. Lincoln (eds) *The Oxford Handbook of Business Groups*, Oxford: Oxford University Press.

Almeida, H., S. Y. Park, M. Subrahmanyam, and D. Wolfenzon (2007) 'Beyond Cash Flow and Voting Rights: Valuation and performance of firms in complex ownership structures', Working Paper, University of Illinois at Urbana-Champaign.

—— —— —— —— (2010) 'The Structure and Formation of Business Groups: Evidence from Korean Chaebols', *Journal of Financial Economics*, 99: 447–75.

Anderson, R. C., S. A. Mansi, and D. M. Reeb (2003) 'Founding Family Ownership and the Agency Cost of Debt', *Journal of Financial Economics*, 68(2): 263–85.

Anuatti-Neto, F., M. Barossi-Filho, A. G. Caravalho, and R. Macedo (2005) 'Costs and Benefits of Privatization: Evidence from Brazil', pp. 145–96 in A. Chong and F. López-de-Silanes (eds) *Privatization in Latin America: Myths and realities*, Washington, DC: World Bank.

Bae, G. S., Y. S. Cheon, and J. J. Kang (2008) 'Intragroup Propping: Evidence from the stock-price effects of earnings announcements by Korean business groups', *Review of Financial Studies*, 21(5): 2015–60.

Bae, K. H. and S. W. Jeong (2007) 'The Value-Relevance of Earnings and Book Value, Ownership Structure, and Business Group Affiliation: Evidence from Korean business groups', *Journal of Business Finance and Accounting*, 34(5): 740–66.

—— J. S. Baek, and J. K. Kang (2007) 'Do Controlling Shareholders' Expropriation Incentives Imply a Link Between Corporate Governance and Firm Value? Evidence from the Aftermath of Korean Financial Crisis', SSRN eLibrary.

Baek, J. S., J. K. Kang, and K. S. Park (2004) 'Corporate Governance and Firm Value: Evidence from the Korean financial crisis', *Journal of Financial Economics*, 71: 265–313.

Baer, W. (1994) 'Privatization in Latin America', *The World Economy*, 7(4): 509–28.

Bandelj, N. (2008) *From Communists to Foreign Capitalists: The social foundations of foreign direct investment in post-Socialist Europe*, Princeton: Princeton University Press.

Becht, M. and C. Mayer, (2001) 'Introduction', in F. Barca and M. Becht (eds) *The Control of Corporate Europe*, Oxford: Oxford University Press.

Bergström, C. and K. Rydquist, (1990) 'Ownership of Equity in Dual-Class Firms', *Journal of Banking and Finance*, 14: 255–69.

Berle, A. A. and G. C. Means, (1932) *The Modern Corporation and Private Property*, New York: Commerce Clearing House.

Bertrand, M., P. Mehta, and S. Mullainathan (2002) 'Ferreting Out Tunneling: An application to Indian business groups', *Quarterly Journal of Economics*, 117(1): 121–48.

Buc, H. B. (2006) 'How Chile Successfully Transformed its Economy', *Backgrounder*, The Heritage Foundation, 1958: 1–10.

Bullmer-Thomas, V. (2001) *The Economic History of Latin America since Independence*, 2nd ed., Cambridge: Cambridge University Press.

Chang, S. J. (2003) *Financial Crisis and Transformation of Korean Business Groups: The rise and fall of chaebols*, Cambridge: Cambridge University Press.

—— and U. Choi (1988) 'Strategy, Structure and Performance of Korean Business Groups: A transactions cost approach', *Journal of Industrial Economics*, 37(2): 141–58.

Chong, A. and F. López-de-Silanes (eds) (2005) *Privatization in Latin America: Miths and realities*, Washington, DC: World Bank.

Claessens, S., S. Djankov, and L. H. P. Lang (2000) 'The Separation of Ownership and Control in East Asian Corporations', *Journal of Financial Economics*, 58(1–2): 81–112.

De Fraja, G. and B. M. Roberts (2009) 'Privatization in Poland: What was the government trying to Achieve?', *Economics of Transition*, 17(3): 531–57.

De la Dehesa, G. (1991) 'Privatization in Eastern and Central Europe', Occasion Paper, 34, Washington, DC: Group Thirty.

Demsetz, H. and K. Lehn (1985) 'The Structure of Corporate Ownership: Causes and vonsequences', *Journal of Political Economy*, 93(6): 1155–77.

Enforcement Decree of the Securities and Exchange Act, Article 9-2, 2000.

Faccio, M. and L. H. P. Lang (2002) 'The Ultimate Ownership of Western European Corporations', *Journal of Financial Economics*, 65(3): 365–95.

Filatotchev, I., N. Isachenkova, and T. Mickiewicz (2007) 'Ownership Structure and Investment Finance in Transition Economies: A survey of evidence from large firms in Hungary and Poland', *Economics of Transition*, 15(3): 433–60.

Fleury, A. and M. T. Fleury (2009) 'Brazilian Multinationals: Surfing the waves of internationalization', in R. Ramamurti and J. Singh (ed.) *Emerging Multinationals in Emerging Markets*, Cambridge: Cambridge University Press.

Frank, V. (2004) 'Politics without Policy: The failure of social concertation in democratic Chile, 1990–2000', pp. 71–124 in P Winn (ed.) *Victims of the Chilean Miracle: Workers and Neo-Liberalism in the Pinochet Era, 1973–2002*, London: Duke University Press.

Franks, J. and C. Mayer (2001) 'Ownership and Control of German Corporations', *The Review of Financial Studies*, 4(4): 943–77.

—— —— H. F. Wagner (2006) 'The Origins of the German Corporation: Finance, ownership and control', *Review of Finance*, 10(4): 537–58.

—— —— and S. Rossi (2009) 'Ownership: Evolution and regulation', *The Review of Financial Studies*, 22(10): 4009–956.

Furtado, C. (1982) *Economic Development in Latin America: Historical background and contemporary problems*, 2nd ed., Cambridge: Cambridge University Press.

Gilson, R. J. (2006) 'Controlling Shareholders, and Corporate Governance: Complicating the comparative taxonomy', *Harvard Law Review*, 119(6):1641–79.

Gourevitch, P. A. and J. Shinn (2005) *Political Power and Corporate Control: The new global politics of corporate governance*, Princeton: Princeton University Press.

Goyer, M. (2010) 'Corporate Governance', pp. 423–52 in G. Morgan, J. Campbell, C. Crouch, O. Pedersen, and R. Whitley (eds) *The Oxford Handbook of Comparative Institutional Analysis*, Oxford: Oxford University Press.

Grosfeld, I. and I. Hashi (2007) 'Changes in Ownership Concentration in Mass Privatized Firms: Evidence from Poland and the Czech Republic', *Corporate Governance: An international review*, 15(4): 520–34.

Hall, P. and D. Soskice (2001) 'An Introduction to Varieties of Capitalism', pp. 1–69 in Hall and Soskice (eds) *Varieties of Capitalism: The institutional foundations of comparative advantage*, Oxford: Oxford University Press.

Havrda, M. (2003) 'The Czech Republic: The case of delayed transformation', pp. 121–43 in M. Federowicz and R. Aguilera (eds) *Corporate Governance in a Changing Economic and Political Environment*, Hampshire: Macmillan Publishers Limited.

Iwasaki, I. (2005) *'Corporate Governance in Transition Economies: The case of Hungary'*, Discussion Paper no.31, Institute of Economic Research, Hitotsubashi University.

Joh, S.W. (2003) 'Corporate Governance and Firm Profitability: Evidence from Korea before the economic crisis', *Journal of Financial Economics*, 68: 287–322.

Khanna, T. and Y. Yafeh (2007) 'Business Groups in Emerging Markets: Paragons or parasites?' *Journal of Economic Literature,* 45(2): 331–72.

Kim, H. (2010) 'Business Groups in Korea,' pp. 157–79 in A. Colpan, T. Hikino, and J. Lincoln (eds) *The Oxford Handbook of Business Groups,* Oxford: Oxford University Press.

Klapper, L., L. Laeven, and I. Love (2006) 'Corporate Governance Provisions and Firm Ownership: Firm-level evidence from Eastern Europe', *Journal of International Money and Finance,* 25(3): 429–44.

Kočenda, E. and J. Hanousek (2009) 'State Ownership and Control in the Czech Republic', CESifo Working Paper No. 2801.

Korea Stock Exchange (2004a) 'Korea Stock Exchange 2004: An overview of Korean securities market'.

—— (2004b) 'Fact Book: 2003 facts and figure'.

Korean Fair Trade Commission Report (2009).

Krug, B. (2012) 'Political Embeddedness in China: Strengths and Limitations', in G. Morgan and R. Whitley (eds) *Capitalisms and Capitalism in the 21st Century,* Oxford: Oxford University Press.

Kuczynski, P. P. and J. Williamson (2003) *After the Washington Consensus: Restarting growth and reform in Latin America,* Washington, DC: Institute for International Economics.

La Porta, R., F. López-de-Silanes, and A. Shleifer (1999) 'Corporate Ownership Around the World', *The Journal of Finance,* 54(2): 471–517.

Leal, R. P. C. and A, L. Carvalhal-da-Silva (2007) 'Corporate Governance and Value in Brazil (and in Chile)', in A. Chong and F. López-de-Silanes (eds) *Investor Protection and Corporate Governance: Firm-level evidence across Latin America,* Washington, DC: World Bank.

Lefort, F. (2005) 'Ownership Structure and Corporate Governance in Latin America', *Revista Abante,* 8(1): 55–84.

—— (2010) 'Business Groups in Chile', pp. 387–423 in A. Colpan, T. Hikino, and J. Lincoln (eds) *The Oxford Handbook of Business Groups,* Oxford: Oxford University Press.

—— and Urzua, F. (2008) 'Board Independence, Firm Performance and Ownership Concentration: Evidence from Chile', *Journal of Business Research,* 61: 615–22.

Lima Jr, C. A. M. (2001) *Brazilian Corporation and Securities Commission Laws Reform,* São Paulo: Pinheiro Neto Advogados.

Majluf, N., N. Abarca, D. Rodriguez, and L. A. Fuentes (1998) 'Governance and Ownership Sructure in Chilean Economic Groups', *Revista Abante,* 1(1):111–39.

Moon, I. (2006) 'South Korea: An unruly guest from the West', *Business Week,* February 27.

Morgan, G., J. L. Campbell, C. Crouch, O. K. Pedersen, and R. Whitley (2010) *The Oxford Handbook of Comparative Institutional Analysis,* Oxford: Oxford University Press.

—— and M. Goyer (2012) 'Global Financial Architecture and National Capitalisms', in G. Morgan and R. Whitley (eds) *Capitalisms and Capitalism in the 21st Century,* Oxford: Oxford University Press.

Morgan, G. and P. H. Kristensen (2012) 'Theoretical Contexts and Conceptual Frames', in G. Morgan and R. Whitley (eds) *Capitalisms and Capitalism in the 21st Century*, Oxford: Oxford University Press.

Naím, M. (1994) 'Latin America: The Second Stage of Reform', *Journal of Democracy*, 5(4): 32–48.

OECD/IDB (2006) *Competition Law and Policy in Latin America: Peer reviews of Argentina, Brazil, Chile, Mexico and Peru*, Paris: OECD Publishing.

O'Toole, L. J. (1994) 'Economic Transition, Constitutional Choice, and Public Administration: Implementing Privatization in Hungary', *Journal of Public Administration Research and Theory*, 4(4): 493–519.

Pedersen, T. and S. Thomsen (1999) 'Economic and Systemic Explanation of Ownership Concentration among Europe's Largest Companies', *International Journal of the Economics of Business*, 6(3): 367–81.

—— —— (2000) 'Ownership Structure and Economic Performance in the Largest European Companies', *Strategic Management Journal*, 21(6): 689–705.

Roland, G. (2000) *Transition and Economics: Politics, firms, markets*, Cambridge MA: MIT Press.

Santiago-Castro, M. and C. J. Brown (2007) 'Ownership Structure and Minority Rights: A Latin American view', *Journal of Economics and Business*, 59: 430–42.

Schneider, B. R. (2004) *Business Politics and the State in Twentieth-Century Latin America*, New York: Cambridge University Press.

Serva, M. (2003) 'Análise de Empresas Privatizadas: O Desafio da Multidimensionalidade', *Civitas*, 3(2): 349–73.

Stark, D. (1990) 'Privatization in Hungary: From plan to market or from plan to clan?' *East European Politics and Societies*, 4(3): 351–92.

—— and Bruszt, L. (1998) *Post-Socialist Pathways: Transforming politics and property in East Central Europe*, Cambridge: Cambridge University Press.

—— and R. P. C. Leal (2000) 'Ownership and Control Structure of Brazilian Companies', *Abante-Studies in Business Management*, 3(1): 29–56.

Whitley, R. (2012) 'Internationalization and the Institutional Structuring of Economic Organisation: Changing Authority Relations in the 21st Century', in G. Morgan and R. Whitley (eds) *Capitalisms and Capitalism in the 21st Century*, Oxford: Oxford University Press.

Williamson, J. (ed.) (1990) *Latin American Adjustment: How much has happened?* Washington, DC: Institute for International Economics.

Winn, P. (2004) *Victims of the Chilean Miracle: Workers and neo-liberalism in the Pinochet era, 1973–2002*, London: Duke University Press.

14

Political Embeddedness in China

Strengths and Limitations

Barbara Krug

Introduction

The East Asian development model is characterized by having an authoritarian political system over a liberalizing economic system managed by neutral, technocratic bureaucracies. Singapore, South-Korea, and Taiwan are cases where economic development can be attributed to the credible commitment of political elites through, for example, efficient rules enforcement. In contrast, in China we observe an authoritarian regime committed to maintaining the notion of a socialist state yet embracing local experiments which since the beginning of the reforms in 1978 have questioned the ideological blueprint (Tsai 2007). Instead of a bureaucracy strictly implementing national guidelines, we observe a political elite flexibly 'reacting' to the wide-ranging policy changes at the local level. Thus, for example, firms enjoyed property rights protection long before private property rights were acknowledged in national legislation in 2004. The fact that reform initiatives are often situated at the local level is not the only feature which distinguishes 'Chinese capitalism' from other forms of capitalism. We also observe a variety of different forms of economic governance within China, as well as the co-existence of formal rules and informal procedures. Consequently, we face economic actors who apparently have no problem with switching between different forms of governance which had emerged within one institutional frame.

These aspects of China's emerging variant of capitalism are provocative. They question the dominant toolkit by which we analyse China's economy in a historical or comparative way (Walder 2003). They ask us to reconsider the role of the state in economic transformation and development. Moreover, they point to the influence of locality, informal norms, and institutional innovation in shaping a new capitalist economy, something which is rarely systematically analysed in 'macro' studies where the nation state is the focus of interest (Hall and Soskice 2001). On the other hand, the sociological perspective which identifies organizations or groups, offers valuable supplementary insights, such as political elite studies (Nee 1989; Walder 2003), villages (Jiang and Hall 1996), networks (Yang 2002; Hendrischke 2007) and, increasingly, firms (Peng 2003; Peng et al. 2009).

The contribution of this literature lies in

- clarifying the role of local government agencies in China's reform process. Concepts such as patron–client relations (Walder 1995), corporatism (Jiang and Hall 1996) or central-local relations (Wong and Chai 2000) identify conditions where the 'state' facilitates market transformation;
- moving the emphasis from the emergence of market-conforming institutions to the functioning of specific forms of governance or organizational capabilities (Whitley 2007) paves the way for further research which questions whether specific forms of governance are of a transitory nature only or will become entrenched (Yang 2002; Tsai 2004).

Our analysis starts from here. We agree with the sociological perspective that diversity across industries and localities in China has been caused by the fact that local government agencies via implementation particularize the general (national) institutional frame into binding local structures, incentives, and constraints. According to this view, differences in local business systems reflect differences in commitment to the reform course or differences in local state capacity to implement the general guidelines. In contrast however, we argue that this picture overemphasizes political factors, dismissing the influence of entrepreneurs and innovation as well as self-regulation based on shared interests between economic and political actors. We claim that a supplementary analysis is needed where specific forms of governance, such as patron–client relations are not a given, but rather the outcome of specific forms of interaction in different localities or sectors. In a more general sense, we ask which forms of interaction ensure the emergence of market-conforming organizations and coordination.

Local experimentation with different forms of firms and different governance structures does not mean that China is an *arm's length state.* The link between the 'spontaneous' emergence of markets and the state is political embeddedness at different levels of the state. As will be seen in what follows, political embeddedness (PE) in China appears in three forms: local autonomy, locally negotiated forms of firms and firm incentives, and locally centred business networks. PE in China is a mix of inherited business practices, such as the formal and informal incentive structures that require local government agencies (or, in the past, local magistrates) to contribute to the economic development of a locality, and consciously chosen strategic decisions by entrepreneurs and managers that do not primarily rely on central jurisdiction.

At first sight, it seems as if the unresolved questions concerning whether and how the state facilitates or hinders the emergence of a capitalist system are shifted to questions concerning whether and how PE facilitates or hinders the emergence and development of markets and a capitalist system. This turns an empirical into a conceptual problem. An analytical tool needs to be found which allows for the assessment of PE with respect to the development of 'markets', competition, and organizational capabilities. Here, the usual macro structures of (perfect) markets such as private property rights, the number of market participants, price competition or authority-sharing and the state's involvement) are appraised, and *variants in capitalism* are examined. However, these need to be 'supplemented' by an analysis of the interaction at the micro level. We offer Market Design as one way to supplement the concept of PE, and explain the emergence and development of sustainable or ill-functioning markets in China.

Political embeddedness

Establishing and maintaining good relationships with state agencies in China is crucial for the survival and operation of firms. Whether these relationships are seen as strategic alliances (Zhou and Peng 2010; Krug and Mehta 2004), culturally determined (Xin and Pearce 1996) or business activities (Hendrischke 2007), all empirical studies confirm the ubiquity of close relationships between firms and the state. Historical, path-dependency analysis stresses the fact that state involvement in business is taken for granted (Peerenboom 2005; Faure 2006), transaction cost economics analysis emphasizes the risk-mitigating role of 'public-private' joint ventures (Krug and Polos 2004), while the literature on transition economies draws attention to the roles and vested interests of state agents: managers of state firms only reluctantly accept competition; agencies in control of vital resources such as land, water, or electricity object to the splitting up of their monopolies; and agencies in charge of implementing laws and regulations fear they will lose power, income, and status if firms are able to bypass state agencies by interacting with each other (Nee 1989, 2000; Walder 2003).

The concept of 'political embeddedness', that is, *a specific form of social embeddedness characterized by a mix of formal and informal ties with political agents* (Granovetter 1985; Grabher and Stark 1997) allows the analysis to be taken one step further by asking: (1) how does political embeddedness function within the general set-up of China's institutional architecture, and (2) what are the consequences of PE for the emergence of functioning markets? To answer these questions, such an analysis needs to disaggregate 'the state'. To insist on analysing the general principles of conventional economics which stress the necessity of dismantling the state and introducing private property rights does not help in the case of transition economies where markets need to be *designed* by political agents, entrepreneurs, managers of state firms, or other groups in control of resources.

As empirical studies show, it is far from clear whether the state facilitates or hinders the emergence of functioning markets (Frye 2002; Frye and Shleifer 1997). This is best exemplified by the 'Grabbing Hand, Helping Hand' discourse, which shows the importance of focusing on specific government agencies and their contribution to the development of markets, instead of taking the state as a single unit of analysis. Firms are connected to, and controlled by, local governments, bureaus representing ministries, and branches of (state) banks and local tax offices. As the literature on state capture has further shown, firms are not merely recipients of law, regulation, and policy. They can force local government agencies to use their discretionary power to the advantage of firms. They can also persuade local government agencies to 'encode' rules which offer advantages to firms and sectors (Hellman et al. 2000).

The analytical challenge is therefore to identify under which circumstances PE leads to the emergence of sustainable markets. The question is of more than academic interest. After all, if political embeddedness results in functioning markets then we cannot expect political embeddedness to be only of a transitory nature. Rather, political embeddedness will become entrenched in the institutional architecture of the business system of China (Yang 2002).

The analytical tool 'imported' into the concept of PE is Market Design (MD), the findings of which allow us to specify criteria for, and take a dynamic view of, functioning markets (the best overviews are in Ockenfels 2009 and Roth 2007). In this chapter, I will present a short introduction to MD, followed by three cases of political embeddedness. The cases have been chosen for their illustrative rather than representative value. The first case is the well-known example of Townships and Village Enterprises (TVEs), in which the political embeddedness of TVEs resulted in the emergence of a competitive sustainable market. The second case takes the public utility sector as an example in which PE resulted in ill-functioning markets because private investment could not be mobilized. In this case, the state and non-state firms are embedded in a hierarchy of regulatory agencies coordinated via government contracts. The third case, which takes Enterprise Bankruptcy Law (EBL) as its example, deals with the question of whether attempting to embed firms within the law is actually a move away from PE (Peerenboom 1999; Potter 1999) or whether PE and the law supplement each other. Unlike the first two cases, in which PE is taken as given either locally or bureaucratically and is not disputed in the literature, in this example EBL is used to enquire whether a 'marketplace' for legal services such as court-mediated arbitration and litigation is emerging, and whether it can be expected to function. The findings will identify crucial configurations within PE which are decisive for its ability to contribute to the development of functioning markets.

Market design

Market Design (MD) provides the analytical tools to evaluate endogenous institution-building in local marketplaces irrespective of the institutional setting of the national economy. Implicit in this analysis of endogenous institution-building at the marketplace level is the recognition of institutional diversity, which in our case is linked to PE. MD originates from theoretical experiments based in computer simulations that are aimed at achieving market clearance in individual markets—that is, in achieving interactions between players that result in a functioning market capable of both attracting and retaining players. By focusing on market clearance, MD proceeds from a study of interactions and not from a study of defined players. It is for this reason that MD complements the PE perspective. While PE identifies the market players, MD focuses on their interaction and the consequences of that interaction for the development of markets. MD developed as a response to requests from companies and industry-specific regulatory agencies looking for a better way to organize 'auctions' or, as in the best-known example, a better way to allocate internships for medical students (overview in Kittsteiner and Ockenfels 2006; Roth 2007). MD, in its original form, was applied to game theory and computer simulations, and used to interpret empirical data, with a view to restructuring impeded private exchanges into functioning market places. Provided there is sufficient data, MD proceeds by testing, through repeated experiments, the systematic character of features identified through game theory iterations. Experiments using computer simulation first assume standard economic behaviour, that is, rationality. If this assumption does not offer satisfactory results, the simulation proceeds to search for 'effects', that is, non-standard economic behaviour provided by experimental economics or organizational psychology (Maskin 2008). Ultimately, MD analysis aims to improve interaction in marketplaces where 'market failure' is diagnosed. For MD, a functioning market is achieved when 'market clearance' occurs, in that each market player (such as a firm) has matching business partners and no incentive to search for better partners or opt for a different organizational/ coordination mechanism (Kittsteiner and Ockenfels 2006).

What matters for the present topic is that the MD approach is less concerned with a general notion of effective government than with the institutional capacity of political and administrative agencies in structuring specific markets. MD argues that, as elements of endogenous institutional change, firms come to terms with bureaucratic control, patronage, or an arm's length state, and they do so to different degrees across industries and localities, and even to differing degrees within one locality or industry. MD suggests that the political leadership or bureaucracies have to be seen not only as regulators but as active market players, whose influence is defined by their interaction in the market. Ultimately, the influence of the political leadership and bureaucracies is limited by the 'economic power' of firms, including the mobility of their assets in terms of their ability to move operations to other marketplaces (which could be other sectors or localities). From this perspective, both the private sector and government agencies are motivated to align the interests of all players in search of a suitable local market design and favourable local institutions. While the exit option granted by the mobility of the firm's assets may constrain the 'predatory' state at the micro-level, and compliance with the formal institutional frame may set benchmarks, the fact that firms derive their comparative advantage from negotiation with local government agencies or state bureaucracies contributes to a diversity of local marketplaces and local business environments. For MD, the observed iterative processes of bureaucratic coordination, patronage, and even the use of price controls and social mechanisms, are part of local institution-building among market players.

In its practical application MD prescribes institutional configurations which are able to sustain functioning marketplaces. Its reliance on empirical data and disregard for established market institutions does not mean that the MD perspective is not based in theory. By insisting that the strategic behaviour of firms and their performance in a marketplace depend on micro-level institutions that evolve from the interaction of firms with other market players, the MD perspective is well grounded in institutional economics and the institution-based view of the firm. By way of summarizing empirical studies and identifying systematic factors enabling discrimination between functioning and ill-functioning markets, MD has moved to a broader research agenda and more general results which can be fruitfully employed for analysing the functioning of PE. MD has formulated three requirements for functioning markets: institutional devices agreed upon in one marketplace such as PE must, at a minimum, be able to motivate a sufficient number of players ('thickness'); they must provide safe participation and interaction for these players; and they must achieve market clearance.

Taking PE as the starting point, the MD criteria for the emergence of well-functioning markets translate into three questions:

1) Can PE mobilize a sufficient number of economic players who are willing and able to interact in a marketplace?
2) Can PE generate sufficient trust among all market players to sustain their participation (the requirement of safe participation)?
3) Can PE match market participants to ensure market clearance at explicit or implicit relative prices, and what coordination mechanism is needed to let demand meet supply (the requirement of effective coordination)?

These three requirements serve as the yardstick for explaining the functioning of PE in China, in particular for explaining why PE at the local level succeeds in generating sustainable markets, why PE in the state bureaucracy cannot lead to the development of sustainable markets, and whether the promulgation of a new insolvency law will lead to institutional choice between legally embedded or politically embedded firms.

Township and Village Enterprises (TVEs) and the emergence of functioning markets

One of the most surprising features of China's economic development in the 1980s was the emergence of local firms under 'collective ownership' which were able to initiate and cope with market competition (Li 2005; Huang 1990; Kung 1993; Jiang and Hall 1996). The overall economic performance of these so-called Township and Village Enterprises (TVEs) and private entrepreneurship in the 1980s was so strong that they became the engine of growth in the 1990s and the major source of tax revenue and export earnings. This development seems to contradict the tenet of conventional institutional (North-based) theory that private property rights and the rule of law are prerequisites for market economies.

In contrast to other transition economies, the empowerment of China's firms was not dependent on private property rights. Instead, Chinese reforms started with a 'gift' in the form of a widespread transfer of decision-making rights (and control) to local government agencies, firms, and individuals; decentralization of administrative decision-making power within the state apparatus established a form of *fiscal federalism* if not *local autonomy* (Weingast 1995; Qian and Weingast 1997). The discretionary power of local government agencies with respect to control over assets, including land use, in combination with the right to levy local taxes and local fees led to variations in local business regimes and increased jurisdictional (tax) competition. From the perspective of firms, these variations presented choice over where to expand their business. Decentralization of managerial decision-making powers, including the right to allocate resources, where and when to invest, and the right to claim residual profit (Hansman 1996) turned managers and entrepreneurs into participants in a new business sector. From an MD perspective, we can argue that decentralization of decision-making rights and widespread transfer of control rights to individual firms and local government agencies ensured the 'thickness' of the new marketplace with concomitant opportunities for private exchange. Decentralization of decision-making rights to individual firms and local government agencies forms the first building block by which the three market requirements of MD are met.

In general, the transfer of decision-making power can be enough to unleash the search for self-help devices that harness the positive incentives in repeated games situations. For example, empirical studies from Vietnam have shown that the prospect of returns from future business relationships leads to the emergence of informally enforced trade in transition economies other than China (McMillan and Woodruff 1999).

However, the decision of economic agents to take an opportunity depends on safe participation. One aspect of safe market participation refers to legitimation which relies on (external) social and political acknowledgement (Cucco 2008; Goodman 2008) and acceptance of, if not legal protection for, private exchange, private investment, and entrepreneurship. So long as market participants refrain from revealing their true preferences, disclosing valuable information about business opportunities, or forego innovation, economic exchange gets stuck in short-term and arbitrage dealings. While trust attributed to (Chinese) culture or *guanxi* (Clegg and Redding 1990; best critique in Goodman 2007) does not survive empirical scrutiny, more generic approaches have shown that trust depends on repeated interaction (Axelrod 1984) and participation (Bohnet 2006). Further, trust evolves from, but also relies on, rational decision-making, when, for example, exchange partners agree on dispute settlement schemes (Güth and Ockenfels 2003). Trust, finally, will be provided by social groups or guilds (Coleman 1990; Greif 1989; Hendrischke 2007), and can be generated within a social frame (Greif 1997) or via institutions and organizations (Nooteboom 1996).

The Chinese answer to the need for trust, legitimatization and ultimately the safe market participation problem was to politically embed private exchange and investment, which forms the *second building block* for securing functioning marketplaces. TVEs are an example of this local and political, rather than resource or industry-specific, embeddedness. It is noteworthy that the TVEs were not local state firms, but included an increasing number of private firms or mixed-ownership firms with a solid base of private investment. The sharing of collective and later registered ownership rights was the most prominent feature of these Chinese firms. By initially allocating ownership shares to local government agencies, incentives were created to protect assets and contracts, share (political and market) knowledge, and secure a favourable mix of taxation and regulation. Moreover, while the conventional analysis quite rightly stresses the transaction cost advantage of this type of firm (Krug and Hendrischke 2008), the MD perspective draws attention to the dynamic and iterative interaction that this form of embeddedness generates. With an increasing number of firms and private exchanges successfully operating in the new business sector and an increasing number of 'honest' and credible interactions, market participation becomes attractive for more and more cautious economic actors (McMillan and Woodruff 1999).

Political embeddedness turns local government agencies into market players, as they are directly involved in market transactions instead of being the representatives and executors of formal institutions. The dominant coordination mechanism between the market players is negotiation, which forms the *third building block* for meeting market requirements. Negotiations can, but need not be, an effective device for coordinating interaction in a marketplace. Yet, as has been shown elsewhere, it is the combination of decentralization, political embeddedness, and the exit/voice (negotiation) option of the new business community which turns the coordination challenge into a restricted non-cooperative game (Zhu and Krug 2007). The structure of this appears as follows.

Both groups, the business community and local government agencies, that is, the dominant controllers of resources, share an interest in maintaining and increasing the value of local resources from which they both profit. Each party has an incentive to increase the individually appropriable share of overall outcome. This can be done by (re-)investing in the local resource base and/or by unilaterally increasing their individual share to the detriment of other players. In this game, local state agencies increase their share of overall returns by increasing taxes, while firms play a role depending on their ability and willingness to threaten to leave a locality (exit) or object to renewed negotiations (voice). Thus, both have an incentive to find a solution, that is, a sharing of local net returns, in which no partner can change strategy without hurting the total outcome (equilibrium solution, see Greif 1997; also in Zhu and Krug 2007). This game can be interpreted as an implicit contract which gives local 'firms' operational autonomy and profit in return for workplace generation, (tax) revenue, and a broadening of the tax base. There is also an implicit contract about joint investment (and cost sharing) into the local resource base that goes beyond mere road building or communication. It includes innovation when private investment in R&D is accompanied by access to state-controlled research, and perhaps also tax breaks and other subsidies.

All in all, PE at the local level is successful as it offers incentives for both firms and political agents to join the market. Moreover, ongoing negotiations and contractual security offered by political agents prove to be effective surrogates for missing private property rights. The outcome does not reflect a static equilibrium. In the 1980s the organizational form of TVEs was seen as the best-fitting organizational form, while in the 1990s a change of the institutional setting saw incorporated firms with registered capital and dividends take over. This organizational change within the marketplace points to a further advantage of PE, namely its ability to orchestrate ownership and organizational change in firms.

In summary, political embeddedness in combination with decentralization of decision-making power and ongoing negotiations were the building blocks for the emergence and development of functioning markets for TVEs as they ensured thickness, safe market participation, and effective coordination.

Public utilities and the failure to secure safe market participation

At first sight, state-run public utilities seem to exemplify the extreme form of PE, in that they are protected from competition and rarely need to turn a profit. Yet, unlike the TVE sector, in which decentralization activated PE for pursuing and aligning economic interests and led to functioning markets, the development of public utilities points to the opposite. Decentralization of decision-making, and in particular regulatory decision-making power, destroyed the ability of PE to generate 'trust', while frequent renegotiation points to opportunistic behaviour and rent-seeking rather than to a search for the best-fitting organizational response to changes in the environment.

As the literature on regulation (Laffont and Tirole 1991) and MD has stressed, and as no less than the present discussion around the Twelfth Five Year Plan illustrates, coordinating different interests within the administration of the state and the design of enforceable government contracts is crucial for the development of a public utility market with private-sector participation (see: several issues of *Caijing* July–August 2007; World Bank 2007). Empirical studies have shown that public utilities in developing and transition economies are not only hampered by insufficient political commitment to turn the public utility sector into a functioning market, a topic well researched in the theory of regulation, but also by enforcement problems (Guasch et al. 2008; Vives et al. 2008). Analysing the enforcement problem calls attention to the different political and administrative agents and their interaction with other (non-state) market players. Analysis from a market design perspective (for example: the studies by Laffont, see overview in Estache and Wren-Lewis 2009) identifies four factors which severely hamper any attempt to design a functioning market: lack of administrative capacity, limited accountability, limited commitment, and limited fiscal efficiency. In other words, if PE offers a means to mitigate these four factors then functioning markets will develop.

The decentralization of decision-making rights in public utilities started around 2002 with the decentralization of the single regulatory agency, namely the State Development and Planning Commission (SDPC). While the central SDPC remains in charge of setting prices, controlling market entry, and approving investment in 'large' projects, local branches of the SDPC do the same for small projects and are also in charge of price adjustment proposals (Laffont 2004). At the same time as decision-making rights were decentralized (around 2004), more and more regulatory powers, including the right to sign contracts with individual private producers or operators, were transferred from the local branches of the SDPC to local government agencies. While China's remarkable investment in infrastructure, sometimes as high as ten per cent of GDP, could rely on 'private' (that is, non-state or local state investment and operations) before 2003, the right to hand out government contracts to private investors after 2003 did not lead to a thicker market.

In general, it is assumed that government contracts are an effective coordination mechanism for aligning the interests of investors and producers with those of the state (Richter and Wellisch 1996). In other words, Market Design in the case of public utilities turns into Contract Design. This, however, implicitly assumes that contracts effectively allocate enforceable decision-making rights while coordination is secured by one coordination agency and (yardstick) competition (Johnson et al. 1999; Guasch et al. 2008).

As the literature on regulation and subsequent empirical studies have shown, the resulting conflicts (beyond technical issues such as contractual stipulations, auditing procedures, or scale and scope of regulation) concern the general enforceability of contracts, specifically their effectiveness to create actual and enforceable entitlements for producers, investors, and operators (March, Schultz, and Zhou 2000; Guthrie 2006; Le Lannier 2009). Under segmented administrative authority, conflicts about dispute settlement procedures arise when investors and local producers dismiss regulation agencies and dispute settlement regimes on the grounds that these have no formal authority over competition policy, or when local agencies or central ministries lack local authority but insist on hierarchical rules and regulations for dispute settlements. Furthermore, the central state regards infrastructure as part of the 'public order' notion in the Chinese constitution and insists on the prerogative to nullify agreements *ex post* (see analysis in Peerenboom 2005) through additional 'amendments' or new regulations.

Local government agencies and local branches of banks contest the legitimacy of other agencies to regulate and implement national laws and sign contracts (World Bank 2007). Depending on the local power play or interference from 'above' (usually from the ministries), contracts can be declared null and void, investors or operators can ask to renegotiate with another local government agency or regulatory body (Clarke 2008), while local regulatory agencies can renegotiate with superior bureaus or local government agencies. Unless more is known about the interactions between these different government agencies, the overall game-play will remain unclear (examples given in Estache and Wren-Lewis 2009). For the functioning of PE, this means that coordination failure can be described but not explained, and this will remain so long as decision-making mechanisms remain opaque.

This *ex post* interference from above means that political embeddedness offers neither an effective coordination mechanism nor the assurance of contractual security. On the contrary, strategic decision-making by firms further aggravates the problems of safe participation. This is because asymmetric information, the large sunk investment upfront, and the unpredictable behaviour of business partners offer strong incentives to private firms to strategically 'underbid' in order to ask for renegotiation later. Depending on the size and political leverage of firms, renegotiation reflects rent-seeking if not 'regulatory capture' (Laffont and Tirole 1991) when a coalition between regulatory bodies or local government agencies dismisses national or local regulation or fights off competition. On the other hand, settling on one contract partner exposes firms to the risk that their contracts lack legitimacy and cannot be enforced. The long-term nature and sunk costs of infrastructure investment compound the risk, as switching contract partners in order to correct initial misjudgements can be close to impossible (McNeil 1978). In other words, the inability to politically embed contracts in the public utility markets makes market participation an unsafe strategy, and leads to frequent renegotiation which acts as a further deterrent to private investment.

Comparing the development of the public utility sector with the development of TVEs and functioning markets highlights two aspects of PE. First is *the importance of informal rules or traditions*. Villages or townships were regarded as the 'natural' or quasi-owners of the land and industrial assets within their boundaries, with the effect that their right to re-allocate assets, sign (land deal) contracts or fully privatize village firms was never contested. This is, however, not the case in the public utilities sector, where the prevalence of contested decision-making has broad ranging consequences. As empirical studies have further shown, an effective regulatory agency can still generate local solutions in the form of trust, which in turn helps to mobilize private investment or private operators. This is because effective authority is regarded as a proxy for commitment and contract enforceability (Guasch et al. 2008). The co-existence of different kinds of regulatory agencies, whose interaction depends more on ad hoc coalitions than on a coordination mechanism, makes any attempt to establish effective regulatory regimes in one locality an unlikely affair. This points to the second aspect of PE, namely that its spatial dimension needs to be acknowledged. The interplay between formal and informal rules based on tradition or past experience is linked to localities. The analysis suggests that whenever the spatial dimension of an economic problem or operation exceeds the spatial dimension of PE, additional coordination mechanisms have to be sought.

All in all, Market Design in the case of public utilities turns into contract design. If decision-making rights in contracting are contested, then major coordination failures lead to opportunistic renegotiation *ex post* and ineffective local (and national) regulatory agencies. For non-state market players, this signals a lack of commitment or regulatory capacity to offer enforceable contracts. Ultimately, private sector participation shrinks.

Enterprise Bankruptcy Law (EBL) and the failure to secure market clearance

For conventional economics, the rule of law is the condition sine qua non for the emergence of a functioning market. However, more recent analysis questions this causality, arguing that the law emerges as a response to a failing self-enforcement mechanism (Dixit 2007; historical example in Greif 1997), state capture and rent-seeking (Laffont and Tirole 1991), or generally weak institutions (Aoki 2007).

China (and many other transition economies) offers a new view on the emergence of laws and the rule of law (for example McMillan and Woodruff 1999; Johnson et al. 1999; Hellman et al. 2000), and draws attention to the gap between a national (uniform) written law and variations in local enforcement (see Potter 1999; Peerenboom 2001). The usual accounts mention an unequal distribution of professional courts, law firms, and lawyers, and ignorance as factors that help to explain the poor performance of China's commercial laws (Peerenboom 2001). From the MD perspective, the market for legal services and court-mediated dispute settlement between market players remains 'thin'. Instead, economic actors rely on administrative solutions as coordinated by PE. Yet, PE does not facilitate the emergence of the rule of law (in business life) in the way PE facilitated the emergence of functioning markets, as described in the TVE example above. Why this is so will be explained with the example of the insolvency law, or EBL which, generally speaking, claims to offer a coordination mechanism for debtors, creditors, work forces, banks and firms.

The first Chinese insolvency law was stipulated in 1986 and was followed by numerous amendments and clarifications. Nevertheless, in the first eight years of its existence, not more than 1,153 firms filed for bankruptcy at a time when around fifteen million firms were registered and where it was known that many incurred losses. From 2006, the new 'state of the art' EBL harmonized the various insolvency processes in China and enacted a unified law that replaced the old patchwork of insolvency legislation (Kargman 2007). Yet, between 2006 and 2009, not more than 5,000 court cases have been reported. Moreover, it does not look as if the decreasing trend in the use of court-mediated arbitration has stopped (Clarke et al. 2006).

In other words, the law remains underused, offering a very 'thin' market for court-mediated litigation and arbitration. As with the case of a product market, which develops if a sufficient number of market players makes use of the market, court-based litigation and arbitration develops only if a sufficient number of players make use of the courts, and when enough (local) government agencies are committed to employing and enforcing court rulings. As will be shown presently, the under-use of the law can be explained by the coordination failure and unsafe participation engendered both by the written law and in the way local government agencies are included in the process.

The first problem is *ambiguity*. In particular, the creation of a bifurcated insolvency system for SOEs and non-SOEs between 1986 and 2006 generated massive confusion over the employment of the legal process: the state responded with clarifications and amendments which added to the confusion rather than improving content and process. As a result, knowledge about the law and insolvency processes remains low. This is compounded by the fact that there is no principle of free access to court documents in China. Thus, it is only through use of the courts that legal procedures get entrenched, general knowledge is disseminated, and problems of asymmetric information are mitigated.

The second problem is *verifiability*. The usage of courts depends crucially on the verifiability of claims. In China, verifiability takes two forms, both of which are problematic. The first is the correct identification of plaintiffs and defendants, creditors and debtors. For example in the late 1980s, local government agencies forced local banks to convert their (faulty) loans into shares. The effect was that banks were no longer the creditors but the owners of bankrupt firms. Similarly, cross share-holding and unrecorded bank loans by private investors makes the identification of the claimants in a bankruptcy case difficult and time-consuming. Likewise, it is also difficult to put a monetary value on the different claims, with the effect that the costs for calculating whether a firm is bankrupt at all can be prohibitively high. The murky situation of ownership, loopholes in corporate law, and poor auditing procedures do not allow easy calculation of the balance sheet. It is also worth stressing that litigation is often used simply as a mechanism to verify claims and, once this is done, the plaintiff retreats from the procedure (Clarke et al. 2006).

The problem of verifying claimants and the value of their claims (or the net debt position of a firm) is connected with the missing ranking scheme for claims stipulating which debts will be served first. One peculiarity of the EBL is that before the net debt position of a firm is calculated, all housing estates owned by the firm are set aside and transferred to the local government agency in charge of the 'resettlement' of the unemployed workforce. It is not hard to see that the allocation of decision-making rights over the distribution of returns from land sales or from the disposal of other industrial assets unleashes a 'race for assets' between competing courts and local government agencies rushing to execute confiscation orders, even before a court order is issued (Zhang and Booth 2002). This asset-scrapping often leads to a situation where firms which otherwise would have had a chance to restructure are left without the means to repay debts (Rona-Tas 1994; Roth 2007).

There is also evidence that the courts know that enforcement lacks credibility due to 'out of court' settlements. Both the confiscation of assets and the pressure to privately settle cases prior to any court order unleash a kind of unravelling effect. As has been shown in other markets, this contributes to the 'thinness' of the market, that is, there are an insufficient number of parties making full use of the EBL, which leaves those parties which insist on using the EBL with few courts and enforcement agencies at their disposal. In other words, there is no market clearing.

In short, courts cannot offer safe participation in the sense that there is a coordination failure in the proceedings forcing all parties concerned to wait for court orders and court-mediated ranking of debts and claims. Instead, which claimant gets served first is locally and inconsistently determined. Even if they are not immediate players in an insolvency case, local government agencies will use their discretionary power over local enforcement to manipulate procedures in favour of firms under their jurisdiction. Thus, resolving local issues caused by coordination failure and the allocation of rights depends on prestige, nomenclatural rank, short-term ad hoc coalitions, or normative appeals to superior courts (Peerenboom 2002).

All in all, PE does not, in this case, contribute to the developing of a functioning market. Ambiguity and unverifiability limit the use of courts, and contested ranking schemes for claims, and the need to rely on the discretion of local government agencies for enforcement set incentives for opportunistic behaviour. As in the case of the market for public utilities, decision-making rights remain contested within the state administration, and the problem of the spatial dimension of PE forestalls stable solutions while similarly undermining the 'the letter of the law'.

Findings

To sum up, political embeddedness, in combination with the decentralization of decision-making powers and ongoing negotiations, are the building blocks identified by Market Design Theory for the emergence and development of functioning markets. This was demonstrated in the example of TVEs as these three elements ensured thickness, safe market participation, and effective coordination. In contrast, in the public utility sector, PE has been shown to be of limited help in situations where decision-making rights, whether formal or informal, are contested (resulting in opportunistic renegotiations), and where the spatial dimension of 'marketplaces' exceeds the spatial dimension of PE. In the final example, PE fails in the market for court orders. Ambiguity and unverifiability limit the use of courts, and contested rating schemes for claims unleash an unravelling process wherein uncoordinated asset scrapping prior to court ordering forestalls the use of the EBL. The findings are summarized in Table 14.1.

All in all, it can be seen that PE contributes to the development of functioning markets only in conditions where the use of informal norms harnesses (weak) institutions and aligns the interests of all parties involved. As has been shown in the examples of the utilities sector and the EBL, PE rather adds to the hazards in a market, which suggests that uncontested decision-making rights and equivalence between the spatial dimension of the market and the spatial dimension of political embeddedness are necessary requirements for the functionality of political embeddedness.

Finally, what is the contribution of a PE analysis to the explanation of the different variants of capitalism? The analysis draws attention to the fact that there is choice within the general (nation state) frame. Formal institutions do not completely determine intended institutional changes. The case of China warns us not to assume that the difference between intended and actual institutional change indicates a lack of commitment to the reform course in the political elite. Instead, the PE analysis identifies specific state agencies which are no longer seen as neutral but need to be modelled as active market players. Likewise, firms are no longer seen as recipients of institutional constraints. Instead, in their interaction with government agencies, they unleash

Table 14.1. Political embeddedness: success and failure

	Case 1	Case 2	Case 3
Empirical domain	Township and village enterprises (TVEs) as initial stage of a private sector	Public utility sector	Enterprise Bankruptcy Law
Interaction	Negotiated participation	Opportunistic *ex post* renegotiation	Unverifiability of claims
	Political embeddedness	Contested decision-making rights	Unclear priorities of claims
	Renegotiated contracts	Contractual insecurity	'Unravelling effect'
Outcome	Development of functioning markets	Thinning out of private participation in public utility sector	Under-usage of law

further institutional change when they agree *ex post* on a form of governance that deviates from the general blueprint. The analysis also shows that PE turns into a strategic variable. Whether or not it politically embeds a firm depends on the marketplace the firm faces, and differs according to locality and sector. This suggests that large firms will choose to invest in the localities and sectors that ensure higher returns and organizational capabilities. PE offers a supplementary explanation for the observation that Chinese firms are characterized by weak boundaries, frequent organizational change and broad, often unconnected product lines. While usually these are attributed to weak institutions or high transaction cost, the PE analysis allows us to pinpoint specific agents, that is local government agencies and firms, and identify how they align their interests, and deal with institutional weakness.

That leaves the question of the explanatory value of the MD-approach in explaining the differences among capitalist states. Two findings are worth emphasizing. The MD approach is a step forward in explaining endogenous institutional change, by identifying the arena of change, namely the marketplace, and the underlying motivation, namely the interest of all market players to search for a form of governance by which the interests of all players can be aligned. The identification of the market players points to a factor seldom endogenized in the models, namely that the initial allocation of decision-making rights and the possibility to alter these rights ex post are as crucial as private property rights.

Finally, we must ask what is distinctive about Chinese capitalism? This is especially necessary since the political commitment of China's political leadership to a capitalist economic regime remains unclear, governance remains opaque, and economic developments are often driven by the private sector. The Chinese variant of a capitalist system has three significant features. First, *local autonomy* empowers local resource owners (such as firms or local government agencies) to find ways in which their economic interests can be aligned. This results in, second, horizontal *organisational and market diversity* across industries and regions. Third, informal institutions (locally embedded business practices, for instance) are in widespread use in the context of local autonomy and horizontal diversity. These three features are mutually reinforcing, and are deeply entrenched in the formal and informal architecture of China's new capitalism.

References

Aoki, M. (2007) 'Endogenizing Institutions and Institutional Changes', *Journal of Institutional Economics,* 3(1): 1–31.

Axelrod, R. (1984) *The Evolution of Cooperation*, New York, NY: Basic Books.

Bohnet, I. (2006) 'How Institutions Affect Behaviour: Insights from economics and psychology', pp. 213–37 in D. de Cremer, M. Zeelenberg, and J. K. Murnighan (eds) *Social Psychology and Economics*, Mahwah: Lawrence Erlbaum Associates.

Clarke, D., P. Murrell, and S. Whiting (2006) *The Role of Law in China's Economic Development: Public law and legal theory, Working paper No. 187*, George Washington University Law School.

Clarke, D. C. (2008) 'Legislating for a Market Economy in China', *The China Quarterly*, 191: 567–85.

Clegg, S. R. and S. G. Redding (eds) (1990) *Capitalism in Contrasting Cultures*, Berlin, New York: de Gruyter.

Coleman, J. S. (1990) *Foundations of Social Theory*, Cambridge, MA: Harvard University Press.

Cucco, I. (2008) 'The Professional Middle Classes: Management and politics', pp. 148–67 in D. S. G. Goodman (ed.) *The New Rich in China*, London: Routledge.

Dixit, A. (2007) *Lawlessness and Economics: Alternative modes of economic governance*, Princeton: Princeton University Press.

Estache, A. and L. Wren-Lewis (2009) 'Toward a Theory of Regulation for Developing Countries: Following Jean-Jacques Laffont's lead', *Journal of Economic Literature*, 47(3): 729–70.

Faure, D. (2006) *China and Capitalism: A history of business enterprise in modern China*, Hong Kong: Hong Kong University Press.

Frye, T. (2002) 'Capture or Exchange? Business lobbying in Russia', *Europe-Asia Studies*, 54(7): 1017–36.

——— and A. Shleifer (1997) 'The Invisible Hand and the Grabbing Hand', *American Economic Review*, 87: 354–8.

Goodman, D. S. G. (2007) 'Narratives of Change: Culture and local economic development', pp. 175–201 in B. Krug and H. Hendrischke (eds) *The Chinese Economy in the 21st century: Enterprise and business behavior*, Cheltenham: Edward Elgar.

——— (2008) 'Why China has no New Middle Class: Cadres, managers and entrepreneurs', pp. 23–37 in D. S. G. Goodman (ed.) *The New Rich in China*, London: Routledge.

Grabher, G. and D. Stark, (1997) 'Organizing Diversity: Evolutionary theory, network analysis and post socialism', *Regional Studies*, 31(5): 533–44.

Granovetter, M. (1985) 'Economic Action and Social Structure: The problem of embeddedness', *American Journal of Sociology*, 91: 481–93.

Greif, A. (1989) 'Reputation and Coalitions in Medieval Trade: Evidence on the Maghribi traders', *Journal of Economic History*, 49: 857–82.

——— (1997) *Self-Enforcing Political System and Economic Growth: Late medieval Genoa, Working paper no. 97-037*, Stanford, CA: Stanford University Department of Economics; CESifo (Center for Economic Studies and Ifo Institute for Economic Research).

Guasch, J. L., J-J. Laffont, and S. Straub (2008) 'Renegotiation of Concession Contracts in Latin America: Evidence from the water and transport sectors', *International Journal of Industrial Organization*, 26(2): 421–42.

Güth, W. and A. Ockenfels (2003) 'The Coevolution of Trust and Institutions in Anonymous and Non-Anonymous Communities', pp. 157–72 in M. J. Holler, H. Kliemt,

D. Schmidtchen, and M. E. Streit (eds) *The Political Economy of Institutional Evolution*, Tuebingen: J. C. B. Mohr.

Guthrie, G. (2006) 'Regulating Infrastructure: The impact of risk and investment', *Journal of Economic Literature*, 44(48): 925–72.

Hall, P. A. and D. Soskice (2001) *Varieties of Capitalism: The institutional foundations of comparative advantage*, New York: Oxford University Press.

Hansman, H. (1996) *The Ownership of Enterprise*, Cambridge: Belknap Press.

Hellman, J. S., G. Jones, and D. Kaufmann (2000) 'Seize the State, Seize the Day': State capture, corruption, and influence in transition, Policy Research Working Paper 2444, Washington DC: The World Bank.

Hendrischke, H. (2007) 'Networks as Business Networks,' pp. 202–22 in B. Krug and H. Hendrischke (eds) *The Chinese Economy in the 21st Century: Enterprise and business behaviour*, Cheltenham: Edward Elgar.

Huang, Y. (1990) 'Web of Interests and Patterns of Behaviour of Chinese Local Economic Bureaucracies and Enterprises during Reforms', *The China Quarterly*, 123: 431–58.

Jiang, S. and R. H. Hall, (1996) 'Local Corporatism and Rural Enterprises in China's Reform', *Organization Studies*, 17: 929–52.

Johnson, S., J. McMillan, and C. Woodruff (1999) *Contract Enforcement in Transition*, Working paper 211, CESifo, Munich.

Kargman, S. T. (2007) 'Solving the Insolvency Puzzle: China's new bankruptcy law improves the country's insolvency regime but faces significant implementation challenges', *China Business Review*, 34(5): 44–8.

Kittsteiner, T. and A. Ockenfels (2006) 'Market design: A selective review', *Zeitschrift für Betriebswirtschaft*, 5: 121–43.

Kung, J. K. (1993) 'Organizational Response to Monitoring and Sharing Problems: The choice of reformation system in Chinese collective agriculture', *Journal of Institutional and Theoretical Economics*, 149(3): 597–600.

Krug, B. and H. Hendrischke (2008) 'Framing China: Transformation and institutional change', *Management and Organization Review*, 4(1): 81–108.

—— and J. Mehta (2004) 'Entrepreneurship by alliance', pp. 50–71 in B. Krug (ed.) *China's Rational Entrepreneurs: The development of the new private business sector*, London: Routledge.

—— and L. Polos (2004) 'Emerging Markets, Entrepreneurship and Uncertainty: the Emergence of a Private Sector in China,' pp. 72–96 in B. Krug (ed.) *China's Rational Entrepreneurs: The development of the new private business sector*, London: Routledge.

Laffont, J.-J. (2004) 'Management of Public Utilities in China', *Annals of Economics and Finance*, 5: 185–210.

—— and J. Tirole (1991) 'The Politics of Government Decision-Making: A theory of regulatory capture', *The Quarterly Journal of Economics*, 106(4): 1089–127.

Le Lannier, A. (2009) 'The Enforcement of Incentive Regulatory Contracts: Individual versus yardstick competition,' viewed 10 December 2010, www.extranet.isnie.org/uploads/isnie2009/le-lannier.pdf

Li, P. P. (2005) 'The Puzzle of China's Township-Village Enterprises: The paradox of local corporatism in a dual track economic transition', *Management and Organization Review*, 1: 197–224.

McMillan, J. and C. Woodruff (1999) 'Interfirm Relationships and Informal Credit in Vietnam', *The Quarterly Journal of Economics*, 114(4): 1285–320.

McNeil, I. (1978) 'Adjustment of Long Term Economic Relations under Classical, Neoclassical, and Relational Contract Law', *Northwestern Law Review*, 72(6): 863–905.

March, J. G., M. Schultz, and X. Zhou (2000) *The Dynamics of Rules: Change in written organizational rules*, Stanford: Stanford University Press.

Maskin, E. S. (2008) 'Mechanism Design: How to implement social goals', *American Economic Review*, 98(3): 567–76.

Nee, V. (1989) 'A Theory of Market Transition: From redistribution to markets in state socialism', *American Sociological Review*, 54: 663–81.

——— (2000) 'The Role of the State in Making a Market Economy', *Journal of Institutional and Theoretical Economics*, 156: 64–88.

Nooteboom, B. (1996) 'Trust, Opportunism and Governance: A process and control model', *Organization Studies*, 17: 985–1010.

Ockenfels, A. (2009) 'Market design und experimentelle Wirtschaftsforschung', *Perspektiven der Wirtschaftspolitik*, 10: 31–53.

Peerenboom, R. (1999) 'Ruling the Country in Accordance with Law: Reflections on the rule and role of law in contemporary China', *Cultural Dynamics*, 11: 315–458.

——— (2001) 'Seek Truth from Facts: An empirical study of enforcement of arbitral awards in the PRC', *The American Journal of Comparative Law*, 49: 249–328.

——— (2002) 'Let One Hundred Flowers Bloom, One Hundred Schools Contend: Debating the rule of law in China', *Michigan Journal of International Law*, 23, viewed 10 December 2010, http://papers.ssrn.com/sol3/papers.cfm?abstract_id = 316962.

——— (2005) 'What Have we Learned about Law and Development? Describing, predicting and assessing legal reforms in China', *Michigan Journal of International Law*, 27: 823–62.

Peng, M. W. (2003) 'Institutional Transition and Strategic Choices', *Academy of Management Review*, 28: 275–96.

—— S. L. Sun, B. Pinkham, and H. Chen (2009) 'The Institution-Based View as a Third Leg for a Strategy Tripod', *Academy of Management Perspectives*, 23: 63–81.

Potter, P. B. (1999) 'The Chinese legal system: Continuing commitment to the primacy of state power', *The China Quarterly*, 159: 673–83.

Qian Y. and B. R. Weingast (1997) 'Federalism as a Commitment to Preserving Market Incentives', *Journal of Economic Perspectives*, 11: 83–92.

Richter, W. F. and D. Wellisch (1996) 'The Provision of Local Public Goods and Factors in the Presence of Firm and Household Mobility', *Journal of Public Economics*, 60: 73–93.

Rona-Tas, A. (1994) 'The First shall be the last? Entrepreneurship and Communist Cadres in the Transition from Socialism', *American Journal of Sociology*, 100(1): 40–69.

Roth, A. E. (2007) *What Have we Learned from Market Design?* Working paper no. w13530, NBER Working Paper Series, Washington, DC.

Tsai, K. S. (2004) *Back-Alley Banking*, Ithaca: Cornell University Press.

—— (2007) *Capitalism without Democracy*, Ithaca: Cornell University Press.

Vives, A., J. Benavides, and A. M. Paris (2008) *Financial Structuring of Infrastructure Projects in Public-Private Partnerships*, Inter-American Development Bank, Washington. http://idbdocs.iadb.org/wsdocs/getdocument.aspx?docnum=1481612.

Walder, A. G. (1995) 'Local Governments as Industrial Firms: An organizational analysis of China's transitional economy', *American Journal of Sociology,* 101: 263–301.

—— (2003) 'Elite Opportunity in Transitional Economies', *American Sociological Review,* 68: 899–916.

Weingast, B. R. (1995) 'The Economic Role of Political Institutions: Market-Preserving Federalism and Economic Development', *Journal of Law and Economic Organization,* 11: 1–31.

Whitley, R. (2007) *Business Systems and Organizational Capabilities,* Oxford: Oxford University Press.

Wong, C. P. W. and J. C. H. Chai (2000) 'Fiscal Reform and Local Industrialization', pp. 158–88 in J. C. H. Chai (ed.) *Reforms and Opening Up since 1979,* vol. 3, Cheltenham, UK: Edward Elgar.

World Bank (2007) *World Bank Development Report 2007: Development and the next generation,* New York, Oxford: Oxford University Press.

Xin, K. R. and J. L. Pearce (1996) '*Guanxi*: Connections as substitutes for formal institutional support', *Academy of Management Journal,* 39: 1641–58.

Yang, Mayfair M. (2002) 'The Resilience of *Guanxi* in its New Developments: A critique of some new *Guanxi* scholarship', *The China Quarterly,* 170: 459–76.

Zhang, X. and C. Booth (2002) 'Beijing's initiative on cross-border insolvency: Reflections on a recent visit of Hong Kong professionals to Beijing,' *American Bankruptcy Institute Law Review,* 29: 29–39.

Zhou, J. and M. Peng (2010) 'Relational exchanges versus arm's-length transactions during institutional transitions,' *Asia Pacific Journal of Management,* 27(3): 355–70.

Zhu, Z. and B. Krug (2007) 'China's emerging tax regime: Local tax farming and central tax bureaucracy,' in B. Krug and H. Hendrischke (eds) *The Chinese economy in the 21st century: Enterprise and business behaviour,* Cheltenham: Edward Elgar, pp. 145–74.

Index

The manufacturer's authorised representative in the EU for product safety is Oxford University Press España S.A. of El Parque Empresarial San Fernando de Henares, Avenida de Castilla, 2 - 28830 Madrid (www.oup.es/en or product.safety@oup.com). OUP España S.A. also acts as importer into Spain of products made by the manufacturer.
Printed and bound by CPI Group (UK) Ltd, Croydon, CR0 4YY
14/09/2026
02216293-0011